Administration of
Energy Shortages

Administration of Energy Shortages

Natural Gas and Petroleum

by
Mason Willrich,

with
Philip M. Marston,
David G. Norrell, and
Jane K. Wilcox

Ballinger Publishing Company ● **Cambridge, Massachusetts**
A Subsidiary of J.B. Lippincott Company

This book is printed on recycled paper.

International Standard Book Number: 0-88410-606-3

Library of Congress Catalog Card Number: 75-46542

Printed in the United States of America

Library of Congress Cataloging in Publication Data

Willrich, Mason.
  Government administration of energy shortages.

  Bibliography: p.
  Includes index.
  1. Gas, Natural—Law and legislation—United States. 2. Petroleum law and legislation—United States. 3. Energy policy—United States. I. Title.
KF1852.W5   353.008'232   75-46542
ISBN 0-88410-606-3

Contents

List of Figures   ix

List of Tables   xi

Acknowledgments   xiii

Introduction   xv

Chapter One
Overview: Energy Shortages in Context   1

A Working Definition   1
Causes   3
Effects   6
Energy Shortages and the Energy Crisis   6
Administrative Criteria   8
Notes to Chapter One   9

Chapter Two
The Natural Gas Industry   11

The Natural Gas Shortage   11
Production, Transmission, and Distribution   14
Demand   24
Mechanics of Curtailment   31
Institutional Overview of Curtailment   33

Notes to Chapter Two   35

Chapter Three
Natural Gas Curtailment: Jurisdiction and Procedures   41

History of the Natural Gas Act of 1938   42
Extent of FPC Jurisdiction under the Natural Gas Act   43
Choice of Statutory Procedures in Formulating Curtailment Policy   49
Effects of FPC Orders   56
Rulemaking Authority Under the Natural Gas Act   61
Pending Legislation   67
Notes to Chapter Three   70

Chapter Four
**Natural Gas Curtailment: Administrative Development
and Implementation**   77

Administrative Efforts to Increase Supply   77
Development of FPC Curtailment Policy   80
Procedural Alternatives   99
Conclusion   101
Notes to Chapter Four   102

Chapter Five
Petroleum Industry Description   109

U.S. Oil Supply Vulnerability   109
Production and Distribution   111
Demand for Refined Products   119
Notes to Chapter Five   128

Chapter Six
Petroleum Allocation: Statutory Authority and Regulation   139

Federal Energy Administration Act (FEAA)   141
Emergency Petroleum Allocation Act (EPAA)   141
Energy Supply and Environmental Coordination Act (ESECA)   158
Defense Production Act (DPA)   161
Energy Policy and Conservation Act   163
Notes to Chapter Six   167

Chapter Seven
**Petroleum Allocation: Administrative Development
and Implementation**   179

Development of Regulation Pursuant to the EPAA   179
FEA Administrative Procedures   183
Congressional Review   201
Conclusion   202
Notes to Chapter Seven   204

Chapter Eight
Administration of Energy Shortages: Generic Issues and Options   211

Initiation and Termination   212
Administrative Options   215
Administrative Organization   231
Notes to Chapter Eight   236

Chapter Nine
**Constitutional Authority for Government Administration of
Energy Shortages**   245

Power to Regulate   245
Limits on the Power to Regulate   250
Notes to Chapter Nine   263

Chapter Ten
Administration of Natural Gas and Petroleum Shortages   271

The Problem Summarized   272
Conclusions   275
Recommendations   280

Index   285

Biographical Notes   291

List of Figures

2-1 Profile of Gas Disposition for 30 Large Pipeline Companies, 1973   20
2-2 Regional Distribution of Natural Gas Consumption, 1974   25

List of Tables

2-1 Lower 48 State Net Reserve Additions, Interstate vs. Intrastate   12
2-2 Curtailment Trends   13
2-3 Economic Impact in 1975–76 in Most Affected States   14
2-4 Gas Utility Firm and Interruptible Gas Sales by State, 1973
     (Trillions of Btu)   15
5-1 U.S. Domestic Petroleum Demand by Use (MB/D)   119
5-2 Sectoral Demand for Petroleum Products in Millions of Barrels   121
5-3 U.S. Domestic Demand for Distillate Fuel Oils by End Use (MB/D)   122
5-4 National Total Heating Fuel Demand in Percents of 42-Year
     Average Demand   123
5-5 U.S. Domestic Demand for Residual Fuel Oil, by End Use (MB/D)   124

Acknowledgments

This book embodies my final report to the Administrative Conference of the United States on government administration of energy shortages. It contains the results of a research process that began in January and ended in December 1975.

The first step was a seminar on the problem of energy shortages which I conducted at the University of Virginia Law School during the 1975 spring semester. The students in the seminar wrote individual research papers covering selected topics, and the seminar offered opportunities to exchange views preliminarily with Federal Power Commission (FPC) and Federal Energy Agency (FEA) officials.

During the 1975 summer months, Philip M. Marston, David G. Norrell, and Jane K. Wilcox, working under my direction, gathered information, conducted interviews, and engaged in library research. Thereafter, the tasks of analysis and writing were very much our joint effort.

The report in draft form was submitted to the Administrative Conference in September 1975. It was circulated widely among interested federal agencies for review and comment. The report was also subjected to review and discussion by the Conference Committee on Ratemaking and Economic Regulation, chaired by Ira M. Millstein. In light of numerous comments received, some additional research in certain areas, and our own review of legislation enacted by or pending before the Congress in December, we undertook a revision which is the book published here.The views expressed herein are our own and do not necessarily reflect those of any agency of government or other institution.

We wish to acknowledge and express our appreciation for the valuable assistance we received from many persons too numerous to name here: the Virginia Law School seminar students, the staffs of the FPC, the FEA, the Senate Commerce and Interior Committees, and the Congressional Research Service of the Library of Congress.

We wish to thank the Administrative Conference of the United States for providing financial support for our research work. We are grateful to the Committee on Ratemaking and Economic Regulation for their comments and the benefit of participation in their discussions. A special note of appreciation is due to Robert A. Anthony, Chairman of the Conference, for his cooperation, understanding, and constant willingness to help move our project along.

Finally, I would like to express a personal and deeply felt thought about my three student research assistants on this project. Philip, David, and Jane were superb to work with professionally. Their research was outstanding in quality and quantity. We learned a lot from each other and we also had good times together. I am grateful for the experience.

Mason Willrich
December 1975

Introduction

An affluent, industrial society such as the United States would soon strangle if it were deprived of a large fraction of its energy supplies. Even a small reduction in energy supply for a short time could cause widespread economic disruption and dangerous social conflict if the shortage were managed ineffectively.

This study considers the role of the federal government in managing energy shortages within the United States. Its purpose is to contribute to the development of an administrative capacity within the government to manage fairly and effectively the kind of energy shortages that may occur in the United States in the late 1970s.

The study focuses on natural gas and petroleum. Together, these two primary fuels account for three-fourths of current U.S. energy consumption.

Chapter One defines what we mean by energy "shortage" and shows how the particular problem of shortages is related to the matrix of other problems constituting America's continuing energy crisis. Chapters Two through Four analyze the experience of the Federal Power Commission (FPC) with natural gas curtailments through 1975. Chapters Five through Seven contain a parallel analysis of the petroleum allocation experience of the Federal Energy Administration (FEA) and a discussion of the relevant provisions of the Energy Policy and Conservation Act, which became law in December 1975.

Drawing upon the previous discussion, Chapter Eight considers the generic issues and options involved in the development of an administrative capacity to manage the kind of energy shortages or threatened shortages that are reasonable contingencies for which to prepare in the near future. Chapter Nine contains an analysis of federal constitutional issues relevant to the administration of energy shortages. Finally, Chapter Ten sets forth our general conclusions and recommendations.

The study is limited to non-price methods for government administration of energy shortages. Of course, the administrative problems related to the use of non-price methods, such as curtailments and allocations, are considered mainly in a price-controlled environment, since this is the actual environment in which natural gas and petroleum shortages have been administered so far. The merits of price deregulation are not examined.

It should not be implied from this limitation on the scope of our study that we favor non-price methods of government administration of energy shortages and oppose actions that would increase prices either by lifting present government controls or imposing taxes. Three reasons prompted us to focus on non-price methods:

1. The recent experience of the FPC with natural gas curtailments and of the FEA with petroleum allocations has received very little critical analysis from a disinterested viewpoint, while the issue of deregulation of natural gas prices in particular has been studied recently and in depth (see references in note 1 of Chapter One.).

2. Regardless of what government action is taken affecting energy prices, non-price methods will be required in order to administer the energy shortages that are reasonable to anticipate in the late 1970s.

3. Inclusion of actions aimed directly at prices would have made unworkable an already extensive research project.

Furthermore, we do not consider in any detail coupon rationing of gasoline because there is no recent operational experience to analyze. However, from the study and collateral research, it appears clear that coupon rationing in some form would be necessary in order to manage the distribution of fuel for motor vehicles in a protracted petroleum shortage in excess of 10–15 percent of demand. Another device we have not considered is a government-administered auction of available supplies in time of shortage. This device is excluded not because it lacks merit in principle, but because it has never been tried and seems unlikely to be put into widespread use in the near future.

Before proceeding, a word of caution is in order. The subject matter is inherently complex. The study focuses on the interactions between pervasive government regulation and gigantic and dynamic industries, and on the effects of those interactions upon every important part of the nation's economy. From our detached vantage point, the best we can achieve and convey to others is a simplified understanding of the dimensions and characteristics of energy shortages and how to deal with them.

Moreover, the subject matter is new and developing rapidly. Energy shortages did not arise as a serious peacetime problem in the United States until the 1970s. The Energy Conservation and Policy Act, which now provides the government with comprehensive legal authority to administer potential petroleum shortages, was finally enacted into law after a painful gestation only in December 1975. As we shall see, a legal framework adequate to administer future natural gas shortages does not yet exist at the end of 1975. Therefore, our analysis and conclusions should be viewed as tentative. We hope our work will stimulate further research by others in administrative law and policy pertaining to shortages of essential raw materials.

Administration of
Energy Shortages

 *Chapter One*

Overview: Energy Shortages in Context

It is important at the outset to obtain an overview of the problem of energy shortages. We begin by explaining what we mean by energy shortage. Next we outline the possible causes and effects of shortages. Thereafter, we indicate the relationship between shortages and other problems that comprise America's energy crisis. Finally, we consider the basic criteria which may be applied in administering energy shortages.

A WORKING DEFINITION

For purposes of this study, we define an energy "shortage" as: *a situation of diminishing energy supply or increasing demand in which government action is deemed necessary in order to direct or control the distribution of available supplies by non-price methods.* (Our reasons for the limitation to non-price methods are set forth in the preface.) In order to be meaningful and useful, such a definition needs to be explained.

We have defined an energy shortage largely in terms of the appropriate response to a situation that itself remains undefined. Unless government action were deemed necessary, there would be no shortage. Thus, our definition assumes the existence of a mixed market economy in the United States.

In a normally functioning market economy, the price mechanism balances available supply against demand. Hence, the market response to excess demand at an established price is an increase in the price of the product concerned to a level that reduces demand or increases supply until equilibrium is restored. Indeed, according to an economist's view of the problem, a shortage exists when, at the prevailing price level, the quantity demanded exceeds the quantity supplied.

In the long run, a price increase may lead to an expansion in the supply of a particular energy form, the substitution of a different form of energy, the development of more efficient energy technology, or a reduction in energy demand. The market response will probably be a mixture of all these elements. The existence of an energy shortage, as we have defined it, indicates a situation where the distribution occurring or expected from the price mechanism is not deemed socially acceptable, and the determination of acceptability is an essentially political function.

The U.S. economy is "mixed" in that some parts are free of government price regulation while other parts are subject to such regulation. In many industries prices are set by individual firms within the limits established by competition among sellers. However, prices in some industries such as public utilities are subject to government approval. For example, prior to the 1970s, petroleum and coal prices were set by the market, while natural gas and electricity prices were fixed by government regulation. Regardless of whether prices are established competitively or by government regulation, when the mixed market economy is functioning properly, the price mechanism keeps supply and demand in balance. Our working definition of an energy shortage, therefore, recognizes the role of government as price regulator in certain sectors.[1]

Of course, government regulation of prices may itself cause an energy shortage eventually, but this is by no means an inevitable consequence. It should be noted, however, that any form of government regulation that establishes two or more prices for the same product unavoidably results in a shortage of the lower priced supplies. Thus, as long as government price controls are maintained on so-called old domestic crude oil, or if regulation of the price of natural gas produced from old wells or under old contracts is continued when the price of new gas is deregulated, some non-price method of distributing the more desirable cheaper supplies will be necessary.

Our definition of energy shortage excludes government programs aimed at promoting voluntary action by consumers to conserve energy in time of shortage. Voluntary programs have a role to play in easing through a small shortage or in the incipient stages of a potential large shortage. For obvious reasons, however, voluntary programs do not pose serious administrative problems, aside from their limited effectiveness.

Finally, it should be noted that our definition leaves open the possibility of debate as to whether government action "is deemed necessary" in a particular situation, and thus whether or not an energy shortage actually exists. At one extreme, it may be argued that an energy shortage, as we have defined it, should never arise because the appropriate response in every case is government inaction. Non-intervention ideally would permit prices to rise to whatever level is necessary to equalize supply and demand. At the other extreme, it may be argued that the energy situation in the United States requires government control over the distribution of supplies, not as a temporary expedient but as a permanent part of any long-term national energy policy. Between these two extremes lies a spectrum of possible situations and responses which would elicit more or less support within the government and from the American people. Our definition is thus framed to take account of the large political content of the threshold issue of whether or not an energy shortage exists. Indeed, because of the jobs, profits, lifestyles and votes at stake, it seems inevitable as well as proper under the American form of government that administration of a serious energy shortage will be a highly politicized process from beginning to end.

CAUSES

With our working definition in mind, we now outline some likely causes or credible threats of energy shortages in the near future in the United States. By near future, we mean roughly the period from 1976 to 1980. This limited time frame enables us to focus on the most important problems and to discuss them in concrete terms. Thus, we can quickly focus our attention on natural gas and pteroleum.[2] However, anticipated problems have deep historical roots.

Currently, natural gas accounts for about 30 percent and petroleum for 45 percent of the energy consumed in the United States. The federal government has already intervened massively in the energy market in order to control distribution of scarce supplies of these two fuels by non-price mechanisms. Shortages with respect to both fuels are, however, a very recent phenomenon, starting in 1970 with natural gas and in 1973 with petroleum products. Therefore, government experience in dealing with such shortages has so far been limited.

The causes of the natural gas shortage which emerged in the early 1970s are multiple, complex, and controversial. In retrospect, a substantial factor appears to have been the effect over the years of FPC regulation of well head prices of natural gas sold to the interstate pipelines.[3] At the prices authorized by the FPC, demand for natural gas ultimately outstripped supplies. The imbalance was aggravated by the FPC's limited jurisdiction over the natural gas industry, which led to a widening gap between natural gas prices in the FPC-regulated interstate market and prices in the various intrastate markets that developed in the producer states.

It is worthwhile recalling that the Supreme Court, by its expansive reading of the Natural Gas Act in the *Phillips Petroleum* decision in 1954,[4] pushed a reluctant FPC into regulating the price of sales by independent gas producers to interstate pipelines. Congress passed legislation in 1956 which would have deregulated natural gas prices. President Eisenhower vetoed the legislation because of improprieties by the natural gas industry in lobbying for the legislation. Thus, the lead independent agency, every branch of the federal government, and the industry itself contributed in various ways to the creation of the natural gas shortage that now confronts the nation.

In addition to FPC price regulation, there are numerous other possible causes of the natural gas shortage. Some producers may be withholding available supplies from the market in order to take advantage of an expected price rise or deregulation. Some interstate pipelines may have contracted for deliveries to new customers without having adequate coverage of gas reserves. Some industrial customers may have failed to maintain adequate alternate fuel capabilities. Environmental restrictions on the use of coal and oil as fuel in industrial boilers and electric power plants led to expanded use of natural gas for these purposes. Some gas distributors competing with electric utilities in the commercial and residential markets used aggressive promotional practices which, in hindsight, appear to have aggravated the current shortage. Of course, natural gas consumers responding to prices that were relatively cheap and declining in real terms adopted practices that now appear wasteful. Last but not least, natural gas resource exhaustion may be rapidly approaching.

The causes of the petroleum shortage which occurred in the winter of 1973–74 are also manifold, complicated, and highly debatable. Supplies of petroleum products were already tight in the 1973 summer and fall. The immediate cause of the crisis was, of course, the Arab oil embargo against "unfriendly" countries following the October 1973 Arab-Israeli war. Behind the Arab embargo lay perhaps the most intractable and explosive problem in international politics since World War II, and nearly three decades of U.S. government involvement in that problem. Behind the embargo also lay the fact that almost 60 percent of the world's known petroleum reserves are concentrated in the Middle East and 85 percent of world reserves are controlled by the 13 non-industrial countries which are members of the Organization of Petroleum Exporting Countries (OPEC). The Arabs had tried half-heartedly and unsuccessfully to use oil as a weapon in previous Middle East wars in 1956 and 1967. What made the difference in 1973 was that in the interim the United States had shifted from being largely self-sufficient in petroleum to become the world's largest oil importer. There are several causes of this dramatic shift in U.S. energy posture which, in effect, handed the oil weapon to the Arab countries. They may be summed up by the enormous consumer demands built up during the post-World War II decades of abundant supplies of cheap oil which was marketed worldwide by a few private multinational companies.

Before the Arab oil embargo, however, spot shortages of certain petroleum products were experienced in the U.S., beginning with heating oil in the 1972–73 winter and gasoline in the summer of 1973. There may have been an effort by some of the larger, integrated oil companies to squeeze their small independent competitors out of the market. A shortage of refinery capacity in the U.S. was also emerging.

The incipient refinery shortage was itself the consequence of multiple causes, including tax incentives for foreign refinery operations, quotas limiting crude oil imports, environmental constraints on refinery location, uncertainty concerning environmental standards for refined products, and the distorting effects of price controls after 1971 on the profitability of various refined products. However, the refinery shortage was at least temporarily postponed when the OPEC members successfully engineered the enormous jump in world oil prices in 1973–74, thereby reducing demand for petroleum products.

Fortunately, a number of factors made the natural gas and petroleum shortages in the early 1970s relatively easy to manage. Mild winters during most of this period reduced demands for natural gas for space heating and utilities. Voluntary energy conservation efforts were somewhat helpful, especially in response to government appeals immediately after the October War in 1973. U.S. diplomacy in the Middle East was successful in obtaining an early lifting of the Arab oil embargo, just as its impact was beginning to be fully felt. The OPEC oil price increases also dampened the expected growth in energy demand. However, perhaps the most important factor making natural gas and petroleum shortages more manageable was the reduction in energy consumption resulting from deep economic recession in 1974–75.

Looking ahead to the 1976–80 period, we can foresee a variety of factors which might cause energy shortages in the U.S. that would be substantially more severe in amount and duration than any experienced so far. U.S. natural gas production will continue to decline, whether or not government price regulation is lifted. A colder than normal winter would lead to large increases in demand for natural gas for space heating, reducing the already curtailed supplies available for other uses. A cold winter would increase demand for heating oil and at the same time increase demands for petroleum as a substitute fuel for curtailed natural gas supplies.

A future contingency for which the U.S. should be prepared is another Arab oil embargo. If it occurs, the next embargo might be more effectively managed by the Arab countries and longer in duration than the 1973–74 embargo. Despite the national security risk, the volume of U.S. oil imports from Eastern Hemisphere sources in general, and Arab countries especially, is likely to increase in the near future. Progress toward an overall Arab-Israeli political settlement would not substantially reduce the risk involved in the increasing U.S. energy vulnerability, but lack of progress toward such a settlement would greatly increase the risk.

There are a variety of actions that the U.S. might take to reverse the present trend and ultimately to reduce U.S. oil imports from the Middle East to a reasonably low level from the viewpoint of national security. However, most of these steps are still being debated, and those which are finally adopted will take several years, in some cases at least a decade, to become effective.

The U.S. position regarding oil imports in the 1976–80 period may be summarized as follows: if for some reason the U.S. is unable to increase its oil imports, it will surely face a serious petroleum shortage. But if the U.S. increases its imports, it will become increasingly vulnerable to an oil supply interruption. The bulk of U.S. oil import increases are likely to come from Middle

East sources. Finally, if the U.S. fails to make adequate preparations to manage a supply interruption, the likelihood of such an interruption will increase.

Yet another factor contributing to energy shortages may be the maintenance of price controls. The continuation of price controls may be deemed necessary for other purposes. However, such controls will inevitably result in some increase in the amount of shortfall that must be distributed by government non-price methods.[5]

Finally, a strong economic recovery would provide the basis for rapid increases in energy demand. It would be a tragedy if mismanagement of energy shortages were a major factor that caused the recovery to abort.

EFFECTS

The importance of energy in the economic and social life of the United States is difficult to overestimate. The role of energy is pervasive and vital; yet most Americans took for granted an abundance of energy at low prices until the Arab oil embargo. Since the embargo, few persons have modified their behavior significantly in order to prepare for future energy shortages.

The effects of an energy shortage will depend on its amount and duration, on the general political and social circumstances at the time it arises, and on how it is managed.

The 1973-74 Arab oil embargo is estimated to have cost the U.S. economy $10-20 billion in lost output, and 500,000 jobs;[6] fist fights at gas pumps and freeway entrances blocked by trucks were evidence of substantial indirect social costs. Natural gas shortages during the winter heating seasons in the years immediately ahead may affect tens of thousands of jobs in each of several states. The Middle Atlantic and Middle Western regions may be especially hard hit.

An energy shortage in the 1976-80 period might arise in an atmosphere of mistrust of private industry, rising and frustrated expectations of the poor, and lack of confidence in government. The absence of a wartime emergency would further increase the danger that lack of public support and cooperation might make a large energy shortage unmanageable.

ENERGY SHORTAGES AND THE ENERGY CRISIS

Energy shortages are an acute aspect of America's chronic energy crisis. Policies, procedures and structures for dealing with energy shortages should be integrated with broad national policies relating to the crisis as a whole. A logical way to proceed would be to formulate first a coherent national energy policy, and to develop thereafter ways of managing possible energy shortages which are consistent with that broad policy. Unfortunately, the President and the Congress remain far from agreement on a comprehensive energy policy, and Congress is itself divided into factions on almost every major issue involved. The development of the federal government's administrative capacity to manage serious energy shortages in the short run cannot, therefore, await the enactment of an overall energy policy. In the energy policy vacuum, however, it is important to bear in mind the key relationships between the set of underlying problems that constitute the energy crisis.

The U.S. energy problem may be viewed from three long-term perspectives: national security, the economy, and the natural environment. Viewed from each of these perspectives, an energy shortage is a disruptive and complicating occurrence. If the energy problem as a whole is managed effectively, existing shortages or undue risks of shortages will disappear, and new shortages or potential vulnerabilities in the U.S. energy posture will be anticipated and prevented.

The concept of national security in a decentralized political system embraces the contradictory demands for freedom of action and stable international relations.[7] Ths issue is to what extent dependence on foreign energy supplies— oil, primarily—is compatible with U.S. national security and commitments to other countries.

From an economic perspective, the U.S. energy system may be evaluated both in terms of the efficiency of each energy-related activity and in terms of the relationship between the energy system and the economy as a whole. The issue is how to assure the development, production, and consumption of energy resources in an economically efficient manner. Efficiency may be considered from a national or a global perspective with radically different conclusions as to the appropriate pattern and timing of resource development. In any event, economic efficiency equates with the least cost.

Many serious air and water pollution problems and land use impacts result from energy-related activities. From an environmental perspective, one issue is how energy-related activities can be conducted consistently with established environmental standards and values. Another issue is whether and when existing standards should be modified in response to changing values and policy priorities.

The possibility of an interruption in oil imports with ensuing sudden shortages of petroleum constitutes a serious risk to U.S. national security. The natural gas shortage is in part responsible for the growth in U.S. imports of foreign oil, thus compounding the security problem. Considerations of both economic efficiency and environmental quality combined in the late 1960s to override the national security criterion and led to rapid increases in low-priced foreign oil imports in the early 1970s.

At current high world oil prices, a wide range of options for the development of additional energy resources in the U.S. and elsewhere are economically feasible. Yet such domestic development would have major irreversible impacts on the natural environment in several regions in the U.S. More immediately, increased use of coal in order to reduce industrial uses of natural gas may cause increased air pollution. In the long term, an energy conservation strategy may be one way simultaneously to improve national security and to enhance environmental quality. However, such efforts may lead to an inefficient pattern of overall economic development unless they are cost-justified. In any event, energy conservation efforts will have only a small effect in dealing with immediate energy shortages.

Overall there hangs the question of research and development policy. What new technologies are to be developed in order to increase national security by reducing U.S. vulnerabilities to foreign energy supply interruptions, or to increase economic efficiency within the energy system, or to reduce environmental pollution caused by energy-related activities?[8] While the payoffs of energy research and development may be enormous, most of them lie in the distant and highly uncertain future.

The preceding discussion suggests that, while energy shortages may be viewed as temporary, they may also be viewed as recurring. Therefore, an administrative capacity to manage short-term energy shortages is an essential part of any long-term U.S. energy policy.

ADMINISTRATIVE CRITERIA

Specifying criteria to guide the design and to evaluate the effects of government programs is always a difficult and elusive task. Criteria enacted in statutes are often meaningless in their generality, or no more than statements in law of the problem to be solved. Criteria evolved in the course of administering a law are as likely to embrace competing interests as to establish priorities between them. The task of resolving many important conflicts thus tends to be delegated downward to operational levels with little concrete guidance as to how the most painful choices are to be made. Useful criteria evolve only gradually as operational experience modifies preconceptions up and down the line of administrative authority.

Developing criteria for non-price energy distribution schemes may be a more important and yet more elusive problem than for most other government programs.

In general, government programs involve the distribution or redistribution of certain benefits, costs, and risks within society. While some persons obtain larger benefits than others and some persons pay more than others, society gains on balance. This is an essential political premise.

A governmental scheme to deal with an energy shortage distributes a net loss or injury across society, and the program will be justified in terms of damage limitation. When it comes to distributing the loss, some persons will be hurt more than others, and a few may escape injury altogether. In a competitive economy, the strength of some may be enhanced relative to their competitors. However, society as a whole realizes a net loss due to the shortage.

Three general criteria appear to be both obvious and essential in administering energy shortages. The administrative program should be: (a) fair in every respect; (b) practical in both an administrative and technical sense; and (c) result in minimum interference with other important public policies. In administering an energy shortage, the criteria may be applied in three main areas: among energy consumers; within the energy industry; and between states or geographic regions of the country. These criteria are also applicable to the procedures used in both the development and implementation of programs.

A program to deal with a serious energy shortage will be the immediate cause of damage to large numbers of people, yet such a program is likely to fail without substantial cooperation from those who are affected adversely. Therefore, it is especially important for the administrative program to be flexible and capable of continuous adjustment in a dynamic and tense situation.

Criteria such as those specified above are, of course, highly abstract, and they are by no means unique to the management of energy shortages. Fairness, practicality, and consistency with other public policies are no more than useful points of departure for analysis and debate about the specific ends and means of particular programs. It is important to bear the criteria problem in mind throughout the analyses of natural gas curtailments and petroleum allocations. We will return to it specifically in Chapter Eight when we consider the generic issues and options involved in administering energy shortages.

NOTES TO CHAPTER ONE

1. For an excellent analysis of the FPC's role in natural gas price regulation and a justification for deregulation, see Breyer & MacAvoy, *The Natural Gas Shortage and Regulation of Natural Gas Producers,* 86 Harv. L. Rev. 941 at 952–957 (1973). See also P.W. MacAvoy & R.S. Pindyk, *Price Controls and the Natural Gas Shortage* (1975); R.B. Helms, *Natural Gas Regulation: An Evaluation of FPC Price Controls* (1974); and Hawkins, *Structure of the Natural Gas Producing Industry* and MacAvoy, *The Regulation-Induced Shortage of Natural Gas* in *Regulation of the Natural Gas Producing Industry* (K. Brown, ed. 1971).

2. Beyond 1980 a variety of other serious energy shortages might arise. Some experts warn of the possibility of serious electric power shortages as a result of slippage in nuclear power plant construction schedules and cancellation of a number of new plant orders (in order to ease the severe financial strains that many electric utilities were experiencing in 1974–75. Others warn that beyond 1985, domestic petroleum reserves and production are likely to decline at a faster rate than presently, despite the addition of reserves and production from the Alaskan North Slope, unless dramatic action is taken to expand secondary and tertiary recovery in existing fields and to accelerate exploration and development of the Outer Continental Shelf. The extent of domestic uranium reserves is also uncertain. Known reserves are only adequate to support expected nuclear power growth, based on existing light water reactor technology, through the

early 1990s. A nuclear fuel shortage might also develop in the late 1908s unless additional uranium enrichment capacity goes into operation in time.

3. *See* note 1 *supra.* For a comprehensive overview from a policy perspective, see *Staff of the Senate Comm. on Interior and Insular Affairs, 93d Cong., 1st Sess., Natural Gas Policy Issues and Options* (1973).

4. Phillips Petroleum Co. v. FPC, 347 U.S. 672 (1954).

5. Underlying the debate concerning the appropriate roles in solving the energy crisis for the price mechanism and the market economy on the one hand, and government intervention and public forms of enterprise on the other, is profound disagreement in political philosophy. At a technical level, however, there is wide disagreement among economists concerning the price elasticities of energy supply and demand. If demand for a particular form of energy were price elastic, then the removal of price controls would have a large dampening effect on demand. Similarly, if supply were price elastic, then deregulation would result in a large expansion of supply. Most economists concede that price elasticity studies, using currently available techniques, are highly imperfect tools for prediction. Analysis for energy products is particularly complicated by the effect of non-economic factors in determining supply and demand.

6. *Department of State, Bureau of Public Affairs, Encouraging Investment in Domestic Energy, Special Report No.* 16 (1975). For a recent assessment of the effects of the natural gas shortage, see Jimison, *Natural Gas Curtailments and Their Effects, 1975–76,* (Congressional Research Service Study TP880, 76–16E, December 1975).

7. I have dealt with the international dimensions of the energy crisis elsewhere. See M. Willrich, *Energy and World Politics* (1975).

8. *See generally, Energy Research and Development Administration, 1 A National Plan for Energy Research, Development & Demonstration: Creating Choices for the Future* (ERDA-48) (1975).

Chapter Two

The Natural Gas Industry

THE NATURAL GAS SHORTAGE

The current natural gas shortage did not develop suddenly and without warning, but has been becoming increasingly evident since 1968. Net additions to reserves decreased in that year and have continued to decrease for six subsequent years, while the reserves-to-production ratio for interstate reserves has declined from 16.8 to 9.3 over the same period.[1]

The reserve situation of interstate pipelines is deteriorating more rapidly than that of intrastate suppliers. During the five-year period of 1965–1969, net reserve additions dedicated to the interstate markets averaged over 71 percent of the nationwide total. For the following five years, the portion of new reserves dedicated to the interstate market fell to an average of less than 8 percent. In 1970, 1972, and 1974, there were *no* net reserve additions dedicated to the interstate market (see Table 2-1).

Presumably the major cause of this turnabout is the price differential which has opened between the interstate and intrastate markets. The present ceiling set by the FPC for sales to interstate pipelines is $0.51/Mcf (thousand cubic feet); intrastate sales bring much more, with some spot sales going for nearly $2.00/Mcf.

Total production of natural gas has also begun to decline. From the 1973 peak of 22.5 Tcf (trillion cubic feet), annual production dropped to 21.2 Tcf in 1974, a drop of nearly 6 percent.[2] Production dedicated to the interstate market fell from the 1972 peak of 14.2 Tcf to 13.7 Tcf in 1973 and 12.9 Tcf in 1974.[3]

Supply shortages first appeared in November 1970 on the United Gas Pipe Line system and have since become endemic for many pipelines and their cus-

Table 2-1.   Lower 48 State Net Reserve Additions Interstate vs. Intrastate

Year	Total Net AGA Reserve Additions Tcf	Net Interstate Reserve Additions (Form 15) Tcf	Percent	Inferred Intrastate Reserve Additions[a] Tcf	Percent
1965	21.2	13.3	63	7.9	37
1966	19.2	14.2	74	5.0	26
1967	21.1	14.8	70	6.3	30
1968	12.0	9.5	79	2.5	21
1969	8.3	6.1	73	2.2	27
1970	11.1	0.0	0	11.1	100
1971	9.4	2.0	21	7.4	79
1972	9.4	(0.2)	0	9.6	100
1973	6.5	1.1	17	5.4	83
1974	8.3	(1.0)	0	9.3	100

[a]Derived by assuming that intrastate reserve additions are equal to the difference between total AGA reserve additions and the reserve additions committed to the interstate market.
Source: FPC Bureau of Natural Gas Staff Report, "A Realistic View of U.S. Natural Gas Supply," Dec. 1974, p. 17.

tomers. The rapid deterioration of the supply situation is reflected in the dramatic increases in curtailments of firm service as shown in Table 2-2.

In August 1975, the FEA estimated that net curtailments of firm service for the 1975-76 winter heating season (November to March) would reach 1.3 Tcf, or over 18 percent of firm requirements.[4] The FPC expected curtailments of interruptible requirements to reach 139,833,000 Mcf during the same period, a supply deficiency of over 71 percent.[5]

The methodology and dire conclusions of the FEA and FPC were criticized, however, in reports to the Congress by the General Accounting Office and the Office of Technology Assessment in October and November 1975.[6] The FEA and FPC estimates were challenged as being based entirely on industry-supplied data, and as not reflecting inventories of gas in storage or the availability of alternate fuels. Moreover, the estimates showed only the difference between the amounts of gas expected to be delivered and the volumes of gas the interstate pipelines had contracted to deliver, not the difference between the amounts expected to be delivered and the projected requirements of natural gas end-users.

As of December 1975, other factors indicate that the magnitude and economic consequences of the natural gas shortage during the 1975-76 winter heating season are likely to be less than originally forecast. The weather during the first part of the winter was warmer than normal in those regions of the country where the most severe shortages were predicted. Economic activity responsible for commercial and industrial demand is now expected to be at a lower level than earlier assumed. Many industrial firms now have alternate fuel capabilities, and such fuels are available. In addition, utilization of existing FPC

Table 2-2. Curtailment Trends

Year (April–March)	Annual Firm[a] Curtailments (Tcf)	Heating Season (Nov.–Mar.) Curtailments (Tcf)
1970/71	0.1	0.1
1971/72	0.5	0.2
1972/73	1.1	0.5
1973/74	1.6	0.6
1974/75	2.0	1.0
1975/76 (expected)	2.9	1.3
1976/77 (forecast)	4.0	about 1.9

[a]Pipeline to pipeline curtailments not included in 1974–1976 data.

Source: FEA Report "The Natural Gas Shortage: A Preliminary Report" (August 1975).

authorities for 60-day emergency sales to interstate pipelines and for direct purchases by certain customers of interstate pipelines at unregulated prices has drawn substantial volumes of intrastate gas into the interstate market.

National curtailment figures conceal pronounced regional differences in the impact of the shortage. For example, the Transcontinental Gas Pipeline Corporation, projecting close to a 40 percent firm service deficiency for the 1975–76 winter season, is the sole gas supplier for much of North and South Carolina as well as parts of Virginia.[7] The Columbia Gas Transmission Corporation, the sole supplier of the Baltimore area, is projecting a 28 percent deficiency for this winter.[8] The extent to which employment depends upon a continued supply of gas also varies considerably in different parts of the country (see Table 2-3).

The impact of these regional differences is further compounded by the availability of alternate fuels, and by the relevant air quality standards. Many gas users in the Northeast could switch to fuel oil, but this would increase pressure for additional oil imports from insecure Middle East sources. Air pollution control difficulties created by the increased use of fuel oil are substantially greater in the Northeast than in the Southwest.

Even historical contracting patterns create important regional differences. In the South Atlantic region, industrial sales are typically interruptible, allowing the supplier to cut off service when necessary to meet firm contracts. In the East and West South Central regions, the pattern is reversed, with industrial users contracting principally for firm service (see Table 2-4).

Although stimulated exploration and production, particularly from the federal offshore domain and Alaska, may help somewhat in the future, the long-term prospect for eliminating the shortage through increased supply is not good. Even under optimistic assumptions, projected production through 1985 falls far short of current levels and will not cure the present shortage, much less allow for any growth.[9] Thus, even if alternative energy supplies can relieve the shortage over the long run, the need for a well-conceived, politically

Table 2-3.   Economic Impact in 1975-76 in Most Affected States

State	Projected Reduction As % of 1974/75 Deliveries	Reduction As % of 1973 Industrial Gas-Consumption	State Employment In Gas-Using Industry	
			As % of Total Employment	In Thousands
New Jersey	8%	41%	32%	717
Maryland	19	60	20	202
Virginia	20	50	9	116
North Carolina	29	41	33	552
South Carolina	12	20	29	227
Pennsylvania	8	17	23	854
Ohio	9	22	29	996
New York	(1)[a]	(3)	21	1,249
Kentucky	4	11	28	196
West Virginia	16	26	19	77
Delaware	16	33	7	11
Missouri	10	31	18	249
Iowa	5	11	14	101
California	4	10	18	972

[a]Parentheses indicate an increase.

Source: FEA Report, "The Natural Gas Shortage: A Preliminary Report" (August 1975).

acceptable means of allocating this premium fuel will become more and more pressing over the next decade. The government must be prepared to administer the natural gas shortage during a cold winter and high level of economic activity.

PRODUCTION, TRANSMISSION, AND DISTRIBUTION

The supply side of the industry is readily divisible into three distinct segments: production of the gas in the various producing areas; transmission by pipeline across country to the numerous gas utility distributors; and distribution by the local utilities to the ultimate gas consumers. Imports of natural gas either by pipeline (from Canada and Alaska) or as liquified natural gas (LNG), mainly from Algeria, are unlikely to alter this basic division substantially, especially over the short term.[10]

Production
Both petroleum and natural gas are hydrocarbons formed by closely related geological processes. They are frequently found together in the same geologic formations.[11] But in recent years, the industry has developed substantial "directional drilling" capability, enabling the producer to identify gas-prone or oil-prone formations, especially in previously explored areas. Thus, today, only about 25 percent of U.S. gas reserves are the result of a search for oil.[12] Never-

Table 2-4. Gas Utility Firm and Interruptible Gas Sales by State, 1973 (Trillions of Btu).

	Firm	*Interruptible*
South Atlantic (Delaware, District of Columbia, Florida, Georgia, Maryland, N.C., S.C., Virginia, W. Va.)	274.9	440.8
East South Central (Alabama, Kentucky, Mississippi, Tennessee)	377.4	174.5
West South Central (Arkansas, Louisiana, Oklahoma, Texas)	1,675.0	635.7

Source: American Gas Association, *1973 Gas Facts,* Table 72, p. 86.

theless, natural gas and petroleum remain largely joint products of a single exploratory effort. Naturally enough, the corporations that dominate the oil industry dominate natural gas production as well.[13]

This close relationship between oil and gas production makes it very difficult to obtain accurate cost information for the production of natural gas alone, particularly where the producer is also a petroleum refiner and marketer. Any attempt to monitor or affect natural gas production separately must take account of this joint aspect of gas production.[14]

Production of natural gas involves exploration, drilling, and lifting of the gas which is then processed in order to remove natural gas liquids, water, and impurities. The natural gas liquids, extracted by a process known as "shrinkage," consist of liquified petroleum gases (LPG) such as propane and butane, natural gasolines, and small amounts of other petroleum products. "Shrinkage" reduces the volume of the input gas by about 5 percent and lowers its Btu (British Thermal Units) content as well. The "dry" gas is then ready for sale to the pipelines.

The principal costs of gas production are in the exploratory and drilling phases. Once a producing well is completed, the cost of actually lifting the gas is quite small. Accordingly, the costs of production represent only a small part, perhaps 17 percent of the total cost of gas to the average residential user.[15] The bulk of the cost to the end consumer comes from transmission (and distribution) costs. For example, while prices paid to producers by interstate pipeline companies (under FPC rate-setting) averaged between 16 and 17 cents per Mcf throughout the 1960s, the price received by the pipelines from wholesalers at the city gate averaged between 36 and 38 cents.[16] The cost of natural gas to the residential user at the end of 1970 varied between $.70 per million Btu in San Francisco and $1.57 in Boston.[17]

Although a relatively small number of major integrated oil companies (i.e., also engaged in oil refining, transportation, or marketing) occupy a dominant place in natural gas production, there exists alongside these companies a very large number of relatively small independent gas producers, numbering in the thousands.[18] In addition, some of the large gas transmission companies are integrated upstream into gas production, as discussed further below.

There are a number of important differences between the major producers and the independents, which carry implications for regulation and curtailment. The 20 largest producers accounted for almost 70 percent of total sales to interstate pipelines in 1971,[19] and hold almost all of the offshore leases (mostly under joint arrangements between two or more producers).[20] The independents, however, appear to be reacting to higher natural gas prices more sharply than the major integrated firms. In 1974, the independents drilled 85.9 percent of all new natural gas wells, discovering 70 percent of the initial potential natural gas reserves.[21]

In the past, independents frequently operated as drilling contractors for the majors who actually owned the reserves. Under such a "farm-out" arrangement, the major retained part of the leasehold interest and assigned the remainder to the independent who developed and operated the property.[22] Evidence now indicates that the independents retain ownership of the gas they discover, reversing the earlier pattern.[23]

One explanation offered for the rapid response of the independents to the recent shortage is that they are more concerned with the production of natural gas by itself while the majors are basically concerned with their immense investment in oil refineries and retail marketing.[24] Further, some of the majors also control considerable amounts of alternate resources—oil, coal, and even uranium. A shortage of natural gas merely helps drive up the price of these alternate fuels, reducing the opportunity cost incurred by not producing more natural gas.

The producing segment of the industry is generally considered to be at least "workably competitive," due to a variety of factors.[25] One salient factor is an apparent absence of any substantial economies of scale associated with exploring for or producing natural gas, although a broader perspective might emphasize the advantages of drawing on a greater pool of experience in the larger firms.

A potential barrier to new entry in the producing business, affecting large and small concerns differently, is the ability to withstand risk. Since only 1 new-field wildcat well in about 10 is successful in finding economically recoverable reserves,[26] larger companies are better able to absorb the cost of a series of dry holes, waiting for their luck to turn.[27] It is not surprising that the high-risk, high-cost offshore areas are almost entirely in the hands of the large firms, as noted above.[28] In any event, potential effect on the competitive structure of the producing industry is an important factor in formulating natural gas policy.

At the present time vertical integration between the production and transmission segments of the industry is not too prevalent, although there appears to be a trend in that direction. Of the 20 largest gas producers, only 5 had an interstate pipeline subsidiary in 1971.[29] Many large pipelines, however, have become involved in the producing end of the business.[30]

Rather than integrate formally, many pipelines and producers cooperate closely through the use of advance payments. Under this arrangement, the pipeline advances funds to the producer to use in exploring or developing an area. In return, the pipeline receives the first opportunity to purchase any gas found. Under most agreements, if the pipeline does not exercise its right to buy, the producer must repay the advances. If the pipeline does decide to take the gas, the advance is repaid by granting the pipeline credits against the cost of the gas taken. The FPC has authorized these arrangements with interstate pipelines as a means of stimulating production.[31]

A trend toward vertical integration between producers and pipelines may pose substantial difficulties for the successful enforcement of an end-use curtailment plan. When producer and pipeline are separated, the producer is not particularly concerned with who purchases his limited supply of gas. He has little incentive not to provide relatively objective, accurate information as to his supply. Further, under an end-use plan, each pipeline which is competing for the producer's supply does have an incentive to verify the claims of other pipelines as to the consumption by each end-use served by that pipeline. This division of interest allows the regulatory scheme to harness private resources, tending to provide more accurate data and a more equitable allocation. But where the producer is integrated with a pipeline, he obviously would prefer to see competing pipelines curtailed before his affiliate.

The Natural Gas Act of 1938 specifically exempted the production or gathering of natural gas from federal regulation.[32] However, in the Phillips Petroleum case in 1954, the Supreme Court held that the sale of natural gas by an independent producer to an interstate pipeline was within the ambit of federal jurisdiction.[33] Since that time the FPC has regulated the wellhead price charged by producers to interstate pipeline companies.[34]

Transmission

The transmission network for natural gas includes more than 200,000 miles of pipeline costing nearly $16 billion and extending into all of the lower 48 states.[35] The interstate pipelines transport about two-thirds of all natural gas consumed, while intrastate lines account for the remainder.[36]

There are only about 107 interstate gas pipelines in the country, about a third of which are considered most important. Just 22 pipelines supply 71 percent of all natural gas shipped through interstate pipelines.[37]

Although natural gas has been transported by small pipelines for many years, the first modern lines were not constructed until the late 1920s and early 1930s. Even though gas had long been available on the East Coast from Appalachian fields, Southwestern gas did not reach that far until 1947.[38]

Nationwide average figures concerning the disposition of gas by the transmission companies can be very misleading, for there is great diversity in the various pipelines' sales profiles. For example, Algonquin Gas Transmission Company sells over 90 percent of its gas to distribution customers and makes no direct industrial sales, while direct industrial sales constitute nearly 70 percent of total sales by the Lone Star Gas Company (see Figure 2-1).

The present structure of the pipeline industry, the types of service offered, and the rates charged are all substantially influenced by technical demands of gas transmission. Both economic and safety considerations require that natural gas be transported by pipeline. Natural gas is very bulky at normal atmospheric pressure, occupying a large volume in relation to its heating content. It is also very difficult to contain and poses dangers of explosions if allowed to leak out. Transmission under pressure (of around 700–1000 pounds per square inch) in a continuous pipeline minimizes the safety hazard while at the same time compressing the gas and thus reducing its volume in relation to its heating value to an acceptable ratio. The pressurization also provides the impetus required to keep the gas moving along "downhill" toward the consumer.

Transmission by pipe implies that there is a fixed maximum capacity for any given pipeline which is determined by the diameter of the pipe itself and the maximum pressure which the compressor stations can build up in the line. The closer a pipeline comes to transporting its maximum capacity, the lower is the unit cost of each cubic foot of gas as fixed costs are spread over more and more units. In the gas transmission business, where fixed costs account for perhaps 90 percent of total costs, this load factor problem becomes extremely important. (A pipeline's annual sales load factor is the ratio, in percent, of *average* daily demand to *maximum* daily demand. For example, a pipeline with a 95 percent load factor is operating very close to its maximum capacity nearly all the time.)

Initial pipeline construction cannot proceed by bits and pieces, but must be undertaken in large increments. Thus, before a pipeline is laid to a new location, the pipeline company must be assured of a market for the large volumes which will be immediately available as soon as construction is completed. Industries and electrical generating utilities are contacted, and commitments for the initial large volumes are elicited. In most cases, the primary advantage these large users see in gas is its low cost, compared to other fuels. Once the pipeline is in place, interruptible contracts, which allow the supplier to cut off service to meet firm contract customers, may be signed. The purchasing industrial concern expects that service may be interrupted only several days a year, or in some cases not at all. The selling pipeline or distribution company thereby gains flexibility, enabling it to add under firm contract residential and commercial customers who are willing to pay a premium for clean, convenient gas.

In one sense, then, residential and commercial users are freeloaders: if the large-volume industrial and electrical generating concerns had not been willing and able to accept the large initial volumes of gas, the pipeline would not have been constructed. Yet once the line is in place the roles are changed. Residential, commercial, and other "firm" users pay higher rates for a preferred position, while the industrial user holding an interruptible contract pays lower rates and is subject to being cut off when service to firm users is threatened.

The problem is complicated by the seasonal nature of much natural gas demand. Heating requirements depend on the weather, so peak demand on the coldest days of the year must not exceed the pipeline's maximum capacity. During the rest of the year, demand for heating falls off, and the pipeline has substantial unused capacity.

A number of techniques can be used for load balancing. The interruptible contracts referred to above constitute one important means for increasing load factors. It should be noted that these contractual arrangements were developed in a period of abundant gas supplies when only occasional interruption of service on the 10 or 15 coldest days of the year was anticipated. Although one might suppose that any party with such a clause in his contract would have an alternative fuel capability, some interruptible customers do not. Industrial customers may merely have contemplated shutting down on those few days when supplies are expected to be cut off.

Most of the direct sales made by piplines to industrial users involve interruptible contracts.[39] All direct sales account for perhaps 10 percent of interstate pipeline sales although important variations are to be found both regionally and among different pipelines.[40]

Another load balancing practice is to store gas, either in suitable underground areas or in its liquified form (LNG). (Liquified natural gas takes up a much smaller volume than an equivalent quantity of natural gas in gaseous form and can be stored in suitable aboveground facilities. LNG storage costs $1.50 or more per Mcf and so is not widely used except for peak shaving on extremely cold days.) Storage helps a pipeline balance its load by using the main pipeline's excess summer capacity to bring additional gas from the producing area to a storage area not far from the ultimate consumers. From there, relatively short auxiliary lines bring the gas to distribution companies and direct sales customers during the period of peak winter demand. Many distribution companies maintain their own storage facilities or "buy" storage capacity from a pipeline.

Underground storage is problematical since it requires finding a suitable geologic formation sufficiently close to the ultimate consumers. In many of the Southeastern and Northern Plains states, for example, there are few if any underground storage sites.[41] Additionally, about one-third to one-half of the gas placed in storage must be kept there for the life of the facility in order to provide the pressure needed to make large deliveries on peak days.[42] Underground storage costs run about 16 to 18 cents per Mcf which is relatively expensive, but still cheap enough to allow large-scale storage facilities to operate successfully. In 1972, underground storage capacity amounted to almost 27 percent of total U.S. production.[43]

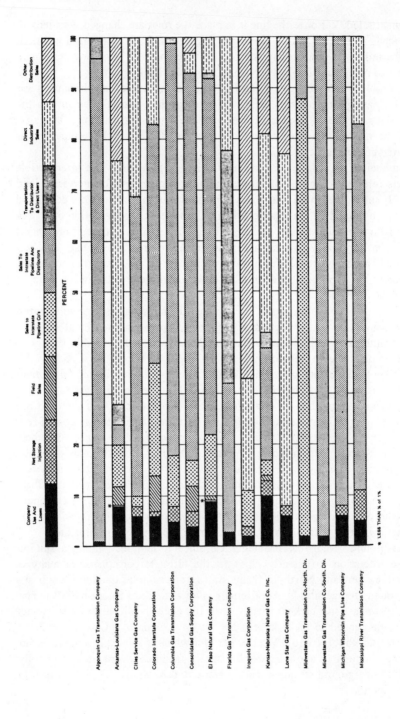

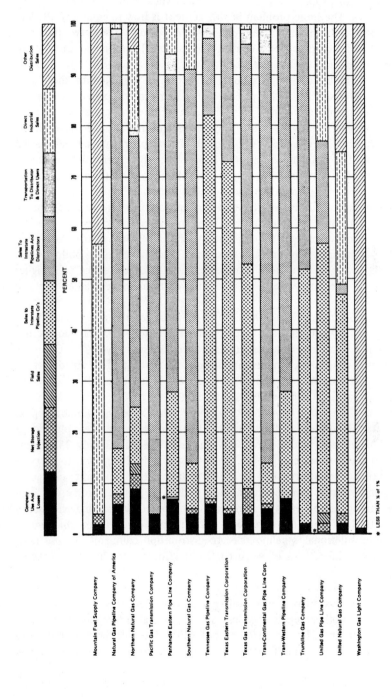

Figure 2–1. Profile of Gas Disposition for 30 Large Pipeline Companies, 1973. *Source: Hearings on FPC Oversight before the Senate Comm. on Commerce, 93d Cong., 2d Sess., pt. 2 (1974),* p. 656.

The load factor problem also affects the rate structure under which the pipelines make sales. The basic problem in this context is how to equitably allocate the fixed costs of the pipeline itself among the different users. A two-part rate structure is used, composed of a demand (or capacity) component and a commodity (or volumetric) component.[44]

Under a formula to fully distribute the costs of service into these two components, all fixed costs are placed in the demand component, while the commodity component includes only the cost of the gas actually delivered. Typically, customers receiving interruptible service do not pay a demand charge since that type of service does not require the supplier to incur additional capacity costs. The rationale is as noted above: since the interruptible customer takes gas only as it is available, the pipeline need not construct a larger diameter pipe or increase the pressure in the line.

One important advantage of this two-part approach to rate design is that it allows the promotion of interruptible sales in the off-peak season, thereby increasing the load factor of the pipeline. At the same time, distribution companies have an incentive to install peak shaving equipment and to build storage facilities. By lowering their peak requirements, and taking service at a higher load factor for the entire year, average unit costs of the gas taken are also lowered.

In *Atlantic Seaboard Corporation,* the FPC discussed the role of each component and emphasized the fact that "pipelines are built to supply service not only on a few peak days but on all days throughout the year."[45] Choosing a rough compromise, the Commission allocated 50 percent of the fixed costs to demand and 50 percent to commodity, establishing the so-called Atlantic Seaboard formula, which was generally used from 1952 to 1972.

In 1973 in *United Gas Pipe Line Company,*[46] the Commission embarked on a new course. It ordered a "reverse tilt" in the company's rates, placing 75 percent of fixed costs in the commodity charge, while leaving only 25 percent allocated to the demand component. The effect of this change was to increase the cost of service to interruptible users who paid only the commodity charge.

The Commission is considering a more radical step in its policy of "conservation through rate design." A notice of proposed rulemaking was issued February 20, 1975, inviting comments on a proposed regulation that would require all jurisdictional pipeline sales to distribution companies to use new, end-use rate schedules.[47] As of August 1975, the Commission had not yet acted on the proposal.

Although the pipeline network is of vast dimensions, each pipeline operates its own individual system. Unlike oil, gas in one pipeline system cannot be transferred to another pipeline unless some physical interconnection exists between the two lines. Under current law the FPC does not have the authority to order pipelines to establish such connections and transfer gas from one line to another.[48]

The feasibility of establishing such interconnections, given the authority, depends somewhat on the particular circumstances of each case. Although interconnection may not be feasible in all circumstances, there are pervasive interconnections in the producing areas which would permit the transfer of large volumes of gas. Pipelines already engage in voluntary exchanges of gas among themselves, subject to FPC approval.

The competitive structure of the pipeline industry is also heavily influenced by the necessity of transporting gas by pipeline. Like railroads, cross-country pipelines are highly capital intensive and tend to constitute a "natural monopoly" as viewed by their customers,[49] particulary in areas to which gas service has only recently been extended.

Most of the pipelines are independently owned, although a few are controlled by holding companies.[50] A third ownership pattern involves control by the pipeline's principal customer,[51] while a final pattern, control by a conglomerate, is found with increasing frequency.[52]

From the producer's viewpoint, the pipeline industry appears to be somewhat monopsonistic (i.e., the buyer has market power rather than the seller, as in monopoly). In 1971, the top eight pipelines accounted for over 58 percent of all interstate purchases and the top 20 companies for over 93 percent, considerably higher concentration ratios than on the producer side.[53]

The interstate pipelines are subject to extensive federal regulation under the Natural Gas Act of 1938. Their rates and conditions of service are regulated principally under Sections 4 and 5. Extensions of service and abandonment require certification under Section 7.

Distribution

The distribution segment of the natural gas industry is comprised of over 1,500 local gas utilities which purchase from the interstate pipelines and resell to the ultimate consumers.[54] The distribution companies vary in size from huge companies providing gas service in several states to small, municipally operated concerns.

The technology and economics of gas distribution are similar in many respects to the major cross-country pipelines. Like the transmission lines, distribution companies are very concerned with load balancing, more so, in fact, since it is more difficult for distributors to reach as high a load factor as the long distance pipelines. (The load factor for distribution companies is usually in the range of 35 to 50 percent, while transmission pipelines usually attain a factor in the 70 to 95 percent range.)

Distributors also use interruptible contracts. A principal difference, however, is that in many cases, institutional customers furnishing important, even essential, community services have contracted for interruptible service. These customers are prepared for a few days' interruption, but they are totally unprepared to be cut off entirely.[55] On the whole, though, interruptible contracts typically supply large-volume industrial or electrical generating uses.

Gas furnished on an interruptible basis accounts for approximately 22 percent of distribution company sales.[56] Here again, important regional differences exist. In the East North Central states (Illinois, Indiana, Michigan, Ohio, and Wisconsin), firm industrial volumes are four times interruptible volumes. Yet industrial users in the adjoining West North Central states (Iowa, Kansas, Minnesota, Missouri, Nebraska, North Dakota, and South Dakota) obtain nearly twice as much gas under interruptible contracts as they do under firm contracts.[57]

As an alternative to interruptible customers, a pipeline may seek seasonal summer customers to counterbalance the heavy winter peaks. The canning industry and irrigation pumping are two such possibilities; residential air conditioning is another. A pipeline may also try to build up a year-round industrial base (which shows little seasonal variation) while minimizing its residential load. As with most interruptible sales, these types of load balancing sales typically involve relatively large volumes of gas in uses where the form value of natural gas is minimal, and where the customer's choice depends primarily on the relatively lower cost of gas.

Many distribution companies also maintain peak shaving and storage facilities in order to even out their load. It should be noted that, from a conservation point of view, these last alternatives are preferable since they do not involve increased sales of gas for low-value uses where substitutes are readily available.

Even more than the transmission companies who supply them, distribution companies tend to be natural monopolies within their respective service areas. As customers of the interstate pipelines, the distributors are intended beneficiaries of federal regulation under the Natural Gas Act. As sole suppliers to the ultimate consumers, the gas companies are themselves regulated by state or local utilities commissions. In 1954 Congress enacted the "Hinshaw Amendment"[58] to the Act, thereby clarifying its intent that FPC jurisdiction not extend to distribution companies whose rates and service are subject to regulation by an appropriate state agency.

DEMAND

Natural gas is burned as fuel in an immensely diverse set of applications. It is also used as a nearly irreplaceable raw material (or feedstock) in the manufacture of a large number of petrochemical products. While it is possible to analyze demand for gas in terms of various generic uses (e.g., raising steam, industrial process or plant protection), in order to appreciate the impact of curtailment on the economy it is preferable first to break down gas demand into its various markets. We will then examine the generic uses within each market. In order of increasing consumption, the four basic markets are commercial, electric generation, residential, and industrial. As shown in Figure 2-2, there are pronounced regional differences in each of these markets.

American industry depends on natural gas for nearly half of its total energy

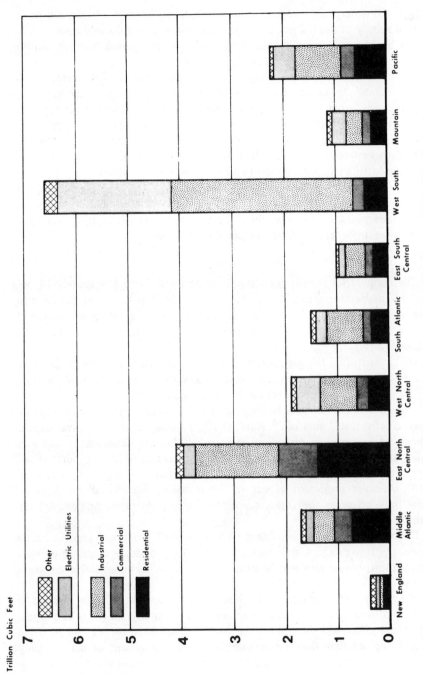

Figure 2-2. Regional Distribution of Natural Gas Consumption, 1974. *Source:* FEA, "The Natural Gas Shortage: A Preliminary Report" (August 1975).

input.[59] Obviously, thousands of enterprises and millions of jobs depend on an assured supply of natural gas. The regional differences in industrial consumption shown by Figure 2-2 imply that even an equally distributed shortfall will impact far more heavily on some areas than on others.[60]

Jobs lost due to plant closings would trigger more unemployment in the hard-hit areas. In many cases these closings would disrupt other industries "downstream" that rely on gas-fired factories for supplies of intermediate products. The petrochemical industry, for example, supplies a large number of such products. It has been estimated that a sustained reduction of 15 percent in feedstocks would trigger the loss of as many as 1.8 million jobs in downstream industries and perhaps $65 to $75 billion in lost production.[61]

Many industrial users do not buy gas from the distribution companies, preferring to engage in "direct sales" from a supplying pipeline. Although these direct sales account for only about 10 percent of all sales nationwide, their importance differs greatly from one pipeline to another.

Commercial

The commercial market for natural gas accounts for approximately 11 percent of total consumption,[62] and its share of total consumption has been increasing very gradually over the last 25 years. In 1973 the average annual use by the over three million commercial users was 685 million Btu or roughly 685 Mcf per customer.[63]

Well over half of the gas consumed by the commercial sector goes for space heating. Water heating accounts for perhaps a quarter of total use, while cooking and air conditioning account for most of the remainder.[64]

The price of gas for space heating has generally been below that of competing fuels, chiefly No. 2 fuel oil.[65] Additionally, natural gas presents advantages in cleanliness and ease of operation; storage facilities are unnecessary, and even boiler maintenance costs are reduced. (When gas is said to have a "form value" over and above its inherent Btu content, this refers to the type of advantages listed. Another important aspect of "form value," which will be discussed more fully below, is the ability to control flame temperature or flame characteristics with precision.)

Commercial gas users provide a wide variety of goods and services to the economy. This category includes most institutional customers such as universities, schools, private and governmental offices, as well as innumerable shops and stores.

Thus, although curtailment of commercial users might force closings or shortened hours for many establishments employing a great many employees, the actual effect will depend on the precise commercial users to be curtailed. It also appears that the "ripple effects" of unemployment or underemployment in this sector will be limited to the immediate communities and not have national significance.

There is no authoritative survey of the number of commercial users who maintain alternate fuel facilities.[66] Because commercial service is nearly always supplied under firm contracts, one may assume in the absence of solid information that most commercial users do not have alternate fuel facilities.[67]

The cost of converting commercial boilers for space heating to No. 2 fuel oil (computed on the basis of dollars per Mcf of gas saved) depends principally on the size of the boiler, with the unit costs decreasing as the boiler size increases. Since commercial use covers both one-room shops using residential-size equipment and huge universities using very large volume boilers, it is difficult to generalize as to size. However, it can be safely said that commercial boilers are generally much smaller than industrial boilers.[68]

Since we discuss the mechanics of curtailment in detail below, it suffices to observe here that trying to limit takes of, or totally cut off, this vast number of commercial units would require a great deal of time and effort, with a rather small yield per unit in terms of gas conserved.

Electricity Generation

Although fuel use for electric generation is often lumped in with industrial usage, it is helpful to deal with it separately in this context since nearly all gas in this market falls into the same end-use category: large-scale boiler use.

Consumption of gas by electric utilities accounted for 18 percent of total gas use in 1971.[69] The percentage share had been rising sharply since World War II, doubling since 1947.[70] In recent years, however, the trend has been reversed, and the utilities' share of consumption has begun to decline. In 1974 gas used in electric generation was down to about 16.5 percent of total consumption.[71]

The primary reason for the rapid rise in gas consumption by this sector has been the relative low cost of gas vis-a-vis other fuels. While natural gas prices to electric utilities in 1972 averaged 31 cents per million Btu, distillate oil averaged 82 cents, coal between 34 and 38 cents (3 percent to less than 1 percent sulfur), and No. 6 oil from 40 to 68 cents (3 percent to less than 1 perfur).[72] Secondary factors include the lessened air pollution control problems and geographic availability. Since gas is chosen primarily for its low relative costs, if fuel oil (or coal) is cheaper in a given locality, the cheaper fuel will tend to be preferred for these large-scale boilers. The form value of the gas is minimal, except in connection with air pollution problems.

The impact of curtailing gas supplies to this market depends on the availability of alternate fuels. Perhaps 60 percent of all utility boilers, accounting for nearly 1.5 Tcf of gas consumption per year, are already equipped to run on some other fuel—usually fuel oil.[73] Thus, if fuel oil is available, curtailing these boilers will have little economic impact in terms of lost jobs, although electric rates will be forced up substantially. Further, if a generating facility is shut down temporarily for conversion to an alternate fuel, the number of jobs directly affected is quite small compared to the amount of gas which will be made available for other uses.

If alternate fuels are not available (e.g., due to a new oil embargo or a refinery capacity shortage) the impact of cutting off gas service to steam-electric boilers would be very serious. Although the direct impact on employment by the utility itself would be minimal, the indirect effects of decreased electricity generation would affects homes, schools, businesses, and industry. The impact of a given cutback will likely depend in large part, however, on the particular local circumstances.

Pronounced regional discrimination could also result . As a result of historical availability, low pollution factor and particularly low-cost, gas-fired generating facilities are heavily concentrated in the producing areas. Three states, Texas, Oklahoma and Louisiana, burned over half the gas used for electrical generation in 1973.[74] With the addition of California, Kansas, and Florida the figure rises to nearly two-thirds.

The contracting patterns of electric utilities in different parts of the country are also worthy of note. Nationwide, electric utilities generally have contracted for gas on an interruptible basis.[75] To an extent, this was logical for many utilities because of their dual fuel capacity. The lower rates offered for interruptible service was a further inducement. Further, the actual frequency of interruption was very low in most areas. This preference for interruptible contracts has been especially strong in the South Atlantic and West North Central states, as well as in California. (California presents a special case since all large gas sales are required by state regulation to be made interruptible.) In Arkansas, Louisiana, and adjoining Mississippi, however, gas supply contracts with electric utilities generally call for firm deliveries.[76]

Adopting a longer term perspective, we find that there are no major technical problems involved in converting gas-fired boilers to alternate fuels. With very few exceptions, all large utility-type boilers can readily be converted.[77] Moreover, there are substantial economies of scale involved. For example, the conversion cost (per Mcf saved) for the largest utility boilers is in the range of 2-3 cents; for direct fired gas space heaters commonly used in foundries and machine shops, the figure is on the order of 50 cents to $1.00 per Mcf saved.[78] Two studies submitted to the FPC during hearings estimated conversion costs for utility type boilers at between 3 cents and 13.8 cents, far below the comparable figures for residences.[79]

Residential
Residential uses constitute the second largest market for natural gas, approximately 24 percent of all consumption.[80] The trend has been for residential uses to increase in comparison to other markets, although not as rapidly as the utilities' share was increasing prior to the recent reversal. Over 70 percent of residential consumption is used for space-heating. Another 20 percent is burned

to heat water, while the remaining 10 percent fuels gas ranges, clothes dryers, and air conditioners.[81] The average yearly consumption per customer is approximately 124 Mcf.[82]

The advantages of natural gas for residential use are several. Natural gas is generally the cheapest fuel for residential consumers.[83] More importantly, gas has a form value in residential uses which commands a premium on the market. Homeowners prefer the neatness and convenience of gas, as compared to the need to provide and maintain storage facilities for heating oil. This premium value is partly responsible for the increasing percentage of gas used for residential purposes (as compared, for example, to electric generation) as one moves away from the producing areas[84] (see Figure 2-2). Since the delivered cost of gas increases significantly with the distance it must be transported, an increase in the percentage devoted to a given market tends to indicate that buyers attach a premium to the fuel above and beyond its heating content (which could be supplied at lower cost by competing fuels).

The impact of curtailment on residential gas use goes to public health, safety, and comfort, and does not jeopardize jobs. Although this point is developed more below, it bears repeating that the residential market, like the commercial sector, consists of an immense number of very small volume users, posing important administrative difficulties for the successful implementation of a curtailment program.

Over the long term, residential users could convert their home heating facilities to fuel oil, but only at a considerable cost on both an absolute and a comparative basis. One estimate has placed the required initial investment in the range of $300 to $400, plus increased electrical and maintenance bills amounting to perhaps $30 to $65 per year.[85] The conversion cost per Mcf displaced has been estimated to run from $0.25 to $1.10, exclusive of the fuel price differential which was estimated to add 49-70 cents more per Mcf. (The fuel price differential was computed prior to the quintupling of oil prices by OPEC and the resulting increase in U.S. oil prices.)

Industrial (Other Than Electricity Generation)

Industrial uses of natural gas now constitute about 46 percent of total gas consumption,[86] the largest single market for gas. The number of industrial customers, fewer than 210,000, is quite small compared to the other markets, while the average consumption per customer is much greater.[87]

The principal gas-using industries are chemicals (and allied products) primary metals, petroleum and coal products, and the pipelines themselves (as compressor fuel). Other major gas-consuming industries are stone, clay and glass products, paper (and allied products), and food (and similar products).[88]

Within these diverse industries, however, one finds certain generic uses which cut across industry lines: boiler fuel, processing, and plant protection. Feedstock uses, where the gas is used as a raw material for its chemical properties rather than as a fuel, constitute a fourth category, but one which is confined to the petrochemical industry.

Boiler fuel use is the largest single use in the industrial market, accounting for perhaps 40 percent of all industrial use.[89] The gas is used either to generate steam for space heating, or as "process" steam which is then used in some further application.

Although industrial boilers are considerably smaller than those in the electricity generating industry, the mechanics of gas use are fundamentally the same. Gas is used primarily for its low cost, even though, as with the electric utilities, other factors may enter into the decision. The form value of gas for industrial boilers is minimal. Many industrial boilers may be equipped to take an alternate fuel when gas is not available, but most are not. Virtually all such boilers can be converted from gas, as with the larger utility boilers, but at a higher cost per Mcf of gas displaced.[90]

Process gas is used to provide the precise temperatures or flame characteristics necessary in many different types of manufacturing. Although no catalogue exists of all different process uses, it has been estimated that naural gas is used in over 25,000 different industrial applications.[91] Among the diverse processes utilizing gas are food preparation, automatic soldering and brazing,[92] ethylene synthesis and fabric finishing.[93]

In most of these applications, natural gas has a form value in addition to its Btu content. In many others, however, natural gas is used merely because it is the cheapest fuel available. But it is very difficult for an outsider to separate those process uses where gas carries a premium from those where gas is currently used for its low cost alone. An administrative agency in particular may find it extremely difficult to obtain the necessary information on this highly technical point, since each industrial user is inclined to feel that his process *really* requires natural gas. To the extent that the administrative decision is mistaken, competitive inequalities may be created among manufacturers.

The distinction between "true" process needs and situations where gas is preferred for its low cost is complicated by the fact that conversions to alternate fuels are *technically* feasible in most cases, but usually only at a cost in product quality or productivity. The *practical* feasibility of converting to an alternate fuel is a question of degree: at what cost in capital outlay and increased operating expense, and lost production during conversion will conversion be feasible? how much of a decline in output or deterioration in product quality would render it infeasible? Under a market allocation scheme, each user must decide for himself how much gas is worth for a given application. Where non-price allocation is used, these decisions must be made on a more generalized level by persons not thoroughly acquainted with each firm's particular situation.

The term "plant protection" gas is used to mean different things in different industries. Generally it designates gas volumes required only when a plant is to be shut down in whole or in part.[94] It usually includes gas for pilot lights, for sufficient steam generation to prevent freezing of lines, for water pumps to permit minimum flow to prevent the line freezing, and similar functions designed to prevent physical harm to plant facilities or personnel. Thus plant protection gas is in the nature of a minimum energy flow that is vital to maintain.

The technical and economic feasibility of converting to alternate fuels for plant protection depends substantially on the circumstances of each case. In any case, due to the relatively small volumes involved, administrative workability militates against forced conversions of this use.

The fourth main end use within the industrial market involves the use of gas as chemical feedstock in the production of petrochemicals. Although the petrochemical industry as a whole accounts for about 10 percent of total gas use, only about 40 percent of this gas is used as feedstock. The bulk is used for fuel and processing as in other industries.

The principal product of feedstock gas is ammonia, which is destined primarily for fertilizer production. Approximately two-thirds of natural gas feedstock falls into this category. About 13 percent of gas feedstock goes into methanol manufacture (used primarily for formaldehyde, films, and plastics), while 12 percent is used to make carbon black, a pure carbon product used in diverse products including tires and inks. (The natural gas liquids extracted during "shrinkage" in a gas processing plant are used as an indirect feedstock source for a great many other petrochemicals such as ethylene, propylene, and butudiene which are the basic building blocks of various synthetic fibers, synthetic rubber, plastics, and countless other products.)

Although natural gas is the strongly preferred raw material for such feedstock uses, substitutes are available. Light or heavy hydrocarbons can act as feedstock for ammonia and methanol manufacture, at conversion costs in the area of 30 cents per Mcf saved (not including the cost of the alternative feedstock itself). But after conversion, the plant would probably operate with a lower capacity than with natural gas.[95] Liquid hydrocarbons can also substitute for natural gas in the production of carbon black. In fact, the carbon black industry began turning away from natural gas as feedstock after 1950 as the wellhead price rose.[96]

MECHANICS OF CURTAILMENT

Although there are several different approaches to determining which natural gas users will be curtailed in a time of shortage, the actual operations required to cut off service are basically the same.

First, the end user must be notified of the planned curtailment. Notification is necessary so that the end user can cut off the gas supply to each pilot light before the main line is closed. Otherwise, the drop in pressure (following the cut off of the main line) would cause the pilot light to be extinguished. The gas, no longer safely consumed by the pilot light, would gradually seep out into the factory or home, creating serious danger of explosion or asphyxiation. And although many home appliances have a device which automatically closes off the gas line whenever there is a sharp drop in pressure in the line, not all appliances are so equipped. Nor are all appliances properly vented.

In the case of large industrial customers, this first step is relatively easy. The distribution company merely telephones its interruptible customers in some agreed-upon order of priority informing them of the need to curtail deliveries. If firm industrial service must be cut, notification becomes slightly more difficult, but remains manageable. If service to a residential area must be cut off, however, notification becomes a major problem. The distribution company may request the cooperation of the local news media and public authorities, in addition to trying to telephone as many customers as possible.

Once the gas company is certain that the gas supply has been cut off within the various homes or other buildings, it can then proceed to close off a distribution line serving the area. Again, this is much easier in the case of a few large industrial users (or schools or office buildings, etc.) than in the case of single-family homes.

When service is to be restored, the customers must again make certain that each gas outlet is closed prior to restoring pressure. Once a main valve is re-opened and pressure is again built up throughout the previously curtailed part of the system, trained personnel must be available to reopen the supply line to each appliance, boiler, or similar apparatus, carefully relighting the pilot light.

In the case of the large-volume industrial or commercial user, there will ordinarily be some employee who can perform this job safely. Where residential service is cut, however, gas company employees must go house-to-house if the procedure is to be performed safely. Obvious difficulties arise when families are away and cannot be contacted. It may take as much as one hour per house to cut and restore service.

Curtailment need not mean a complete cut off of all gas, but may imply only some upper limit on consumption. This is not accomplished by reducing the flow of gas in the pipeline. Instead the end user is ordered to consume less gas.

It is not technically feasible to cut consumption by decreasing the amount of gas in the pipeline. Although pressure could be reduced somewhat, thereby reducing the volume of gas moving through the line, this results in increasing costs to the consumer for each unit of gas by decreasing the pipeline's load factor. Moreover, this process would have no direct effect on the volume of gas ultimately taken by each customer: gas-fired equipment would merely have to run longer to liberate the equivalent heating value.

The proper way to apply partial curtailment is to maintain full pressure in the main system while requiring the ultimate consumer to limit his takes to a prescribed amount. The industrial customer, for example, may be required to shift to an alternate fuel. If none is available, running on a shorter work day or eliminating some production lines may be required. For the residential or commercial user, partial curtailment means cutting back the thermostat or installing storm windows and other insulation.

For both types of users, the program may be merely voluntary. Normally, however, the gas supply contracts of industrial users provide that, when partial curtailment is necessary, stiff penalty surcharges apply, at perhaps 10 times the regular tariff, to all gas taken in excess of the prescribed amount. This technique makes possible the pro rata sharing of a shortage among the industrial end users served by a single distribution company. As noted earlier, most industrial and large commercial contracts for firm service, if they make any provision for curtailment, call for pro rata cut backs for each customer.

Residential customers are not currently subject to such penalties. In the past the penalties have not been needed; today they appear politically unacceptable to many. Additionally, there are serious administrative difficulties involved in trying to implement such a program equitably.

Finally, penalties for overtakes by distribution companies may also be used to bring home to the local utility its role in helping its consumers cut down on their consumption. For example, Texas Eastern's interim pro rata plan for 1972-73 called for all customers (distribution companies as well as direct sales customers) to reduce gas takes subject to a $3/Mcf penalty for the excess.

Currently, the FPC does not have the statutory authority to impose overtake penalties on the ultimate gas consumers, although it does have this authority as to the jurisdictional pipelines' distribution company customers. The authority of the various state utility commissions to impose such penalties may vary from one state to another.

The safety risks involved with curtailment pose an interesting question of liability for accidents resulting from government ordered curtailment. Although there do not appear to be any examples of this as yet, it would seem that the distribution companies, which are most likely to be doing the actual curtailing, or the large institutional customers, using their own personnel, would only be liable for their negligence. They might, however, be able to assert that the supplying pipeline was negligent in allowing this shortage to develop, and that "but for" the pipeline's negligence, there would have been no curtailment and no injury.

INSTITUTIONAL OVERVIEW OF CURTAILMENT

It may be helpful at this point to provide a brief summary of how curtailment operates from an institutional perspective.

The initiative in determining whether curtailment is necessary is left to the individual pipelines. This assignment of institutional responsibility is logical since only the pipeline has access to the information necessary to make the threshold determination of necessity. The decision to begin implementing curtailment also belongs to the pipeline. With no incentive to begin curtailing until necessary, the pipeline seems well suited for this role as well.

The responsibility for assigning customers to the various classifications is presently divided among the pipeline, the distributors, and the ultimate end users, all subject to some review by the FPC staff. The pipelines have been given primary responsibility for developing the needed end-use data, but without any grant of legal authority to do so. Thus the pipelines have had to rely on the distributors' information to a great extent. The distributors in turn have depended in varying degrees on the voluntary data submissions of their customers. Although the figures are examined by data verification committees composed of representatives of the pipeline, distributors, some end users and the Commission staff, the system is largely one of self-assignment by each of the various users, and particularly by each of the distribution companies.

This approach tends to produce figures which upgrade end-users into higher priorities, and it may result in substantial inequalities depending on how well or how sharply a given party has played the numbers game. However, given the limited jurisdiction of the FPC and the limited resources it has available for this purpose, such a self-assigning procedure may be the only reasonably workable alternative.

The enforcement of required volumetric cutbacks at the pipeline-distribution level, as distinguished from enforcement of end-use priorities, does not appear to be a substantial difficulty. This is true at least at present levels of curtailment. Given the shortage situation, if a single distribution company exceeds its allocation, the extra gas can only come at the expense of another customer. The metering points are few enough so as not to present substantial difficulty in maintaining reasonable accuracy.

As a general rule, the Commission has no authority to determine how the gas will be allocated by the distributor. It is at that level that compliance problems might become more difficult if curtailment priorities were required to "flow through" to the burner tip. The Commission can however, determine gas allocation at this level in the case of extraordinary relief. Accompanying the grant of relief is the condition that it only be used for the use stated in the petition. The Commission staff apparently feels that "self-policing" will operate in these cases: if the recipient of the extra gas uses it for some other purpose, the Commission will be unlikely to grant any further petitions for relief to that party. The Commission may also expect competing end-users to assist enforcement by reporting companies which are using extraordinary relief for unauthorized purposes. Other companies have an incentive to report since all gas allowed under extraordinary relief comes directly from the allocations to other users of the same class.

As shortages deepen and the number of relief petitions rises, however, abuses may develop due to the difficulty of determining which gas is used for what purposes. Under these circumstances, enforcement problems may intensify. But without additional grants of jurisdiction, the FPC is powerless to change the present institutional roles.

NOTES TO CHAPTER TWO

1. Statement of John Nassikas, Chairman of the FPC, before the Subcommittee on Conservation, Energy and Natural Resources of the House Committee on Government Operations, June 12, 1975.

2. FEA, *The Natural Gas Shortage: A Preliminary Report,* at 1 (August 1975) [hereinafter cited as FEA, *Preliminary Report*].

3. FPC Press Release No. 21456 (June 6, 1975).

4. FEA, *Preliminary Report, supra* note 2, at 3. See also FPC Press Release No. 21454 (June 6, 1975).

5. FPC Press Release No. 21454 (June 6, 1975).

6. GAO, *The Economic and Environmental Impact of Natural Gas Curtailments During the Winter of 1975-76* (October 31, 1975); OTA, *An Analysis of the Impacts of the Projected Natural Gas Curtailments for the Winter 1975-76* (November 4, 1975).

7. FPC Press Release No. 21454 (June 6, 1975).

8. *Id.*

9. FPC Bureau of Natural Gas, *A Realistic View of U.S. Natural Gas Supply,* at 10-13 (December 1974). See also FEA, *Preliminary Report, supra* note 2, p. 4.

10. Statement of John Nassikas, Chairman of the FPC, before the Subcommittee on Conservation, Energy and Natural Resources of the House Committee on Government Operations, June 12, 1975. Difficulties have been experienced both at the producing end in finalizing contracts with Algeria, and at the receiving end where vocal environmental opposition has been expressed concerning the LNG-receiving terminals.

The policies followed by potential exporters will have an important influence on the import picture. For example, a number of Arab countries presently flare natural gas which is released as a byproduct of oil production. This gas could be used as cheap energy to help fuel industrial development, in which case the producing country would be unwilling to export substantial amounts. However, the natural gas liquids—primarily propane—could be extracted and shipped in large quantities as liquid fuel in tankers.

11. Perhaps 80 percent of U.S. gas production consists of "unassociated" gas (i.e., not dissolved with crude oil in the reservoir), while the remainder is "associated" with crude oil. *American Enterprise Institute for Public Policy Research, Natural Gas Deregulation Legislation,* at 15.

12. *Hearings on Federal Power Commission Oversight—Natural Gas Curtailment Priorities Before the Senate Comm. on Commerce,* 93d Cong., 2d Sess., pt. 2, at 346 (1974), [hereinafter cited as *Curtailment Hearings*].

13. See Table 3-3, 1 *Federal Power Commission, National Gas Survey,* at 57 (1975) [hereinafter cited as *Survey*]. The top 10 listed in 1971 were Humble

Oil and Refining Co., Shell, Amoco, Gulf, Phillips Petroleum, Mobil, Texaco, Union Oil, Atlantic Richfield, and Continental Oil.

14. For a discussion of the difficulties involved in trying to separate out the costs of each, see Stephen A. Breyer and Paul W. MacAvoy, *The Natural Gas Shortage and the Regulation of Natural Gas Producers,* 86 Harv. L. Rev. 941, 952–957 (1973). For a more abstract view of how the problem of common cost is approached by regulatory agencies, see Alfred E. Kahn, *The Economics of Regulation: Principles and Institutions,* vol. I, at 77–83 (1970).

15. *Staff of the Senate Comm. on Interior and Insular Affairs, 93d Cong., 1st Sess., Natural Gas Policy Issues and Options,* 14 (1973) [hereinafter cited as *Gas Policy Issues and Options*].

16. *Id.* at 220.

17. *Id.* at 224. One million Btu is approximately equivalent to 1,000 cubic feet of gas.

18. Statement of John Nassikas, Chairman of the FPC, before the Subcommittee on Antitrust and Monopoly of the Senate Committee on the Judiciary, 92d Cong., 2d Sess., June 26, 1973, at 26.

19. 1 *Survey, supra* note 13 at 60.

20. *Id.* at 59.

21. *S. Rep. No. 94-191,* 94th Cong., 1st Sess.

22. For a description of several types of farm-outs, see 1 *Survey, supra* note 13 at 60.

23. *Hearings on the Consumer Energy Act of 1974 Before the Senate Comm. on Commerce,* 93 Cong., 1st Sess., 885 (1973).

24. *S. Rep. No. 94-101,* 94th Cong., 1st Sess., at 12.

25. See E.J. Neuner, *The Natural Gas Industry* (1960); L. Cookenboo, *Competition in the Field Markets for Natural Gas* (The Rice Institute Pamphlet, Monograph in Economics, vol. 44, no. 4, 1958); C. Hawkins, *Structure of the Natural Gas Producing Industry,* in *Regulation of the Natural Gas Producing Industry* (Keith C. Brown ed. 1971); P. MacAvoy, *Price Formation in Natural Gas Fields: A Study of Monopoly, Monopsony and Regulation* (1962). For a more recent assessment of the competitive situation, see Statement of John Nassikas, Chairman of the FPC, before the Subcommittee on Antitrust and Monopoly of the Senate Comm. on the Judiciary, 92d Cong., 2d Sess., June 26, 1973.

26. *American Gas Association, Gas Facts 1973,* 40 [hereinafter cited as *Gas Facts*].

27. *Id.* at 45. In 1972, the average cost of drilling a dry hole was $94,899.

28. *Id.* at 46. Dry holes in the offshore areas averaged $565,169.

29. 1 *Survey, supra* note 13, at 69–70.

30. *Id.*

31. FPC Order 499, 50 F.P.C. 2111, 39 Fed, Reg. 1262. As of August 31, 1973, advance payments amounted to over $1.2 billion.

32. 15 U.S.C. §717(b)(1970).

33. Phillips Petroleum v. Wisconsin, 347 U.S. 672 (1954). The Supreme Court had earlier upheld FPC jurisdiction over natural gas sales by producing affiliates to interstate pipeline companies in Interstate Natural Gas Co. v. FPC, 331 U.S. 682 (1947).

34. FPC wellhead price regulation has gone through three stages. From 1954 to 1962, the Commission sought to regulate each producer individually through formal proceedings. From 1962 to 1974, areawide proceedings were used, the Commission setting an areawide ceiling (subject to modification under certain circumstances in individual cases). Since 1974, a uniform nationwide rate has been set. See Opinion 699, 51 F.P.C. 2212, 39 Fed. Reg. 23953.

35. 1 *Survey, supra* note 13, at 60.

36. No firm statistics are available on the percentage of gas sold interstate. The FPC estimates that the intrastate market moves one-third of all gas. Clark Hawkins has compared several techniques for estimating the size of the intrastate market and has concluded that between 33 percent and 40 percent of the total remains intrastate. See Hawkins, *supra* note 25, at 159.

37. *Gas Policy Issues and Options, supra* note 15, at 25.

38. 1 *Survey, supra* note 13, at 33.

39. J. Muys, *Federal Power Commission Allocation of Natural Gas Supply Shortages: Prorationing, Priorities and Perplexity,* 20 Rocky Mt. M.L. Inst. 301 (1975).

40. See Appendices C and D to letter from FPC Chairman Nassikas to Senator Magnuson, in *Curtailment Hearings, supra* note 12, at 656 et seq.

41. 1 *Survey, supra* note 13, at 45.

42. *Id.*

43. *Id. at 46.*

44. For a lucid discussion of the functioning of rates in shortage conditions, *see* Haskell P. Wald, "Pipeline Rate Design Under Conditions of Increasing Cost and Restricted Supply," paper presented at the 7th Annual Conference of the Institute of Public Utilities, Troy, Michigan, May 5, 1975.

45. Opinion 225, Atlantic Seaboard Corporation and Virginia Gas Transmission Corporation, 11 F.P.C. 43, 54 (1952).

46. Opinion 671, United Gas Pipe Line Company, 50 F.P.C. 1348, 3 P.U.R. 4th 491 (1973).

47. *See* FPD Dkt. No. RM75-19, 40 Fed. Reg. 8571. For a summary of the proposal, see Wald, *supra* note 44, at 16.

48. *See* statement by FPC Chairman Nassikas in *Curtailment Hearings, supra* note 12, at 328–330, and discussion of interconnection authority in Chapter Three.

49. 1 *Survey, supra* note 13, at 39.

50. Id. at 60.

51. For example, Carnegie Natural Gas Company is a wholly owned subsidiary of United States Steel.

52. Tenneco, Inc. entirely owns Tennessee Gas Transmission Co. and has full control over Midwestern Gas Transmission Co. and East Tennessee Natural Gas Co. See Table 3-10, 1 *Survey, supra* note 13, at 69.

53. 1 *Survey, supra* note 13, at 62. For a fuller discussion of the monopsony question, see Hawkins, *supra* note 25, at 146–151.

54. *Gas Policy Issues and Options, supra* note 15, at 25.

55. For example, in 1974, Piedmont Natural Gas Company was serving perhaps 20 hospitals under interruptible contracts. See *Curtailment Hearings, supra* note 12, at 285.

56. Derived from *Gas Facts 1973, supra* note 26, tables 64 and 72.

57. *Gas Facts 1973, supra* note 26, at 86.

58. 15 U.S.C. §717(c)(1970).

59. 1 *Survey, supra* note 13, at 148.

60. For example, at Transco's anticipated 40 percent curtailment level, 96 percent of all industrial use in North Carolina will be curtailed in the 1975–76 winter. Close to 190 gas customers employing over 70,000 workers are reportedly without any alternate fuel capability. See FEA, *Preliminary Report* (*supra* note 2).

61. *Hearings on Natural Gas Production and Conservation Act of 1975 Before the Senate Comm. on Commerce,* 94th Cong., 1st Sess., at 217 (1975).

62. FEA, *Preliminary Report, supra* note 2, at 2. See also 1 *Survey, supra* note 13, at 175 (table 6–15).

63. *Gas Facts 1973, supra* note 26, at 66, 69.

64. 1 *Survey, supra* note 13, at 175 (table 6–15).

65. *Gas Policy Issues and Options, supra* note 15, at 224. Although the figures given there are for residential use, commercial prices would be comparable.

66. The FEA is currently attempting to collect this information, however.

67. *Gas Facts 1973, supra* note 26, at 86.

68. For example, in 1973, the average consumption by industrial users was more than 15 times as great as the average for commercial users. See *Gas Facts 1973, supra* note 26, at 66.

69. 1 *Survey, supra* note 13, at 142.

70. *Id.*

71. FEA, *Preliminary Report, supra* note 2, at 2.

72. *Gas Policy Issues and Options, supra* note 15, at 31.

73. Arthur D. Little, Inc., *Report to the Office of the General Counsel, General Motors Corporation: Implications of Natural Gas Consumption Patterns for the Implementation of End-Use Priority Programs,* [hereinafter cited as *Arthur D. Little Report*].

74. *Gas Facts 1973, supra* note 26, at 82.

75. Id. at 83.

76. *Id.*

77. *Arthur D. Little Report, supra* note 73, at 54.

78. *Id.* at 196.

79. *Id.* at 59–63.

80. FEA, *Preliminary Report, supra* note 2, at 2.

81. 1 *Survey, supra* note 13, at 175.

82. *Gas Facts 1973, supra* note 26, at 66–67.

83. *Gas Policy Issues and Options, supra* note 15, at 224–234.

84. *Arthur D. Little Report, supra* note 73, at 42–43. Note also the relative prices of gas and No. 2 fuel oil in Boston, New York, Philadelphia, and Washington, D.C., in *Gas Policy Issues and Options, supra* note 15, at 224.

85. *Arthur D. Little Report, supra* note 73, at 193.

86. FEA, *Preliminary Report, supra* note 2, at 2.

87. *Gas Facts 1973, supra* note 26, at 67. The figures given here include electric utilities.

88. 1 *Survey, supra* note 13, at 175–76.

89. FEA, *Preliminary Report, supra* note 2, at 2.

90. *Arthur D. Little Report, supra* note 73, at 57.

91. 1 *Survey, supra* note 13, at 19.

92. 5 *Survey, supra* note 13, at 309.

93. *Curtailment Hearings, supra* note 12, at 302.

94. *Id.* at 304.

95. *Arthur D. Little Report, supra* note 73, at 95–105.

96. 1 *Survey, supra* note 13, at 197.

Chapter Three

Natural Gas Curtailment:
Jurisdiction and Procedures

The Federal Power Commission derives its curtailment authority from the Natural Gas Act of 1938.[1] In *FPC v. Hope Natural Gas Co.*, the Supreme Court interpreted the Act's purpose:[2]

The primary aim of this legislation was to protect consumers against exploitation at the hands of natural gas companies. Due to the hiatus in regulation which resulted from the *Kansas Gas Co.* case and related decisions state commissions found it difficult or impossible to discover what it cost interstate pipeline companies to deliver gas within the consuming states; and thus they were thwarted in local regulation. . . . Moreover, the investigations of the Federal Trade Commission had disclosed that the majority of the pipeline mileage in the country used to transport natural gas, together with an increased percentage of the natural gas for pipeline transportation, had been acquired by a handful of holding companies. State commissions, independent producers, and communities having or seeking the service were growing quite helpless against these combinations. . . . Congress addressed itself to those specific evils.

In 1938 Congress did not foresee the need to deal with a long-term shortage of natural gas like the one presently facing the United States. In its attempts to protect consumers, Congress addressed itself primarily to wholesale rate regulation. Consequently, the natural gas curtailments in recent years have required stretching the Natural Gas Act to cover situations for which it has no specific provisions. The Act has proved to be an unwieldy tool for fashioning a coherent curtailment policy.

HISTORY OF THE NATURAL GAS ACT OF 1938

Circumstances When Enacted

By the 1920s a small number of powerful holding companies had gained monopolistic control over the interstate gas pipeline systems. Neither state nor federal government possessed regulatory authority over these holding companies. In a 1906 amendment to the Interstate Commerce Act,[3] Congress had specifically excluded natural gas pipelines from the jurisdiction of the Interstate Commerce Commission.

Moreover, the states were powerless to effectively regulate the interstate pipelines because of several Supreme Court decisions based on the Commerce Clause of the U.S. Constitution. In *State of Missouri v. Kansas Natural Gas Co.,*[4] the Public Utilities Commission of Missouri had attempted to prevent Kansas Gas from increasing its rates in Missouri without the commission's consent. The issue was whether business of a natural gas supplier consisting of the transportation of gas from one state to another for sale, and the sale and delivery of that gas to distributors, was interstate commerce over which the states had no regulatory authority. In distinguishing between sale and delivery to distributors and the subsequent sale and delivery by distributors to consumers, the Supreme Court held that:[5]

> . . . the sale and delivery [to distributors] here is an inseparable part of a transaction in interstate commerce—not local but essentially national in character—and enforcement of a selling price in such a transaction places a direct burden upon such commerce. . . . It is as though the [state commission] stood at the state line and imposed its regulation upon the final step in the process at the moment the interstate commodity entered the State and before it had become part of the general mass of property therein.

Receivers of the gas transported interstate were therefore free to deliver the gas to local distributing companies without unreasonable interference by the state. State regulatory power was limited to sales occurring after the interstate pipeline had sold and transported gas to the distributor.[6]

A Federal Trade Commission report on public utility holding companies submitted to Congress on December 31, 1935, pointed out the need to fill the regulatory gap which had been created by Congress and the Supreme Court.[7] The FTC report stressed the ability of natural gas holding companies to set prices paid to independent producers, and thus to obtain the benefits of the market for themselves alone. Such price-setting ability arose from the fact that pipelines enjoyed a natural monopoly status with regard to producers;[8] that is, a pipeline purchaser was a monopsonist. The FTC emphasized the need to regulate natural gas production so that gas prices would be related to production costs rather than to the lack of competition in the gas fields.

Other factors warranting federal action were: (a) the large volumes of natural gas transported in interstate commerce; (b) state inability to deal with the problem; (c) abuses deriving from the absence of interstate pipeline regulation; and (d) the demands of consumers for adequate and reasonably-priced supplies of gas. The report also called Congressional attention to the widespread waste of natural gas and the need for its conservation.[9]

Legislative Intent

The Natural Gas Act, then, was aimed at obtaining an adequate supply of natural gas at reasonable consumer prices. This aim was to be achieved by filling with federal regulatory authority the areas in which state regulatory commissions could not act.[10]

It was "the intention of Congress that natural gas shall be sold in interstate commerce for resale for ultimate public consumption for domestic, commercial, industrial, or any other use at the lowest reasonable rate consistent with the maintenance of adequate service."[11] However, the Natural Gas Act "[did] not attempt to regulate the producers of natural gas or the distributors of natural gas; only those who sell it wholesale in interstate commerce."[12] The Act was not intended to usurp in any way traditional state authority over natural gas regulation. Having faced only acute shortages in the past, the 1938 Congress did not make specific provision for any chronic shortage in the future. This lack of foresight, though perhaps not surprising, has hindered the FPC in its attempt to allocate the natural gas shortage.

EXTENT OF FPC JURISDICTION UNDER THE NATURAL GAS ACT

Section 1(b) of the Natural Gas Act gives the FPC jurisdiction over three general areas: (a) the sale of natural gas in interstate commerce for resale; (b) the transportation of natural gas in interstate commerce; and (c) natural gas companies engaged in such transportation or sale.[13] Throughout the Act, transportation and sale are treated as separate jurisdictional heads.[14] The courts have upheld curtailment as a regulation of the quantities of gas transported in interstate commerce under the FPC's transportation jurisdiction.[15] There are also three general areas exempt from Commission jurisdiction under section 1(b): (a) any other sale or transportation of natural gas, i.e., intrastate sales or transportation; (b) local distribution of natural gas; and (c) the production and gathering of natural gas.

Sales Jurisdiction and the Phillips Decision

The FPC originally believed that it lacked jurisdiction over independent gas producers because of section 1(b)'s production and gathering exemption.[16] "The companies to be subjected to regulation were conceived of as 'pipe line' companies, and it was assumed that production and gathering would enter the field of regulation only to the extent that the 'pipe line' companies, either directly or through affiliates, controlled the production or gathering of the gas so transported."[17]

Had the FPC's concept of its own jurisdiction continued in force, the Commission would have had no authority to regulate the wellhead prices of natural gas produced by independent companies that were not affiliated with the pipeline companies. With an unregulated wellhead price in effect, the market might have served to allocate gas efficiently among consumers, while providing large incentives to expand supplies. The United States conceivably might not have been forced to deal with the sudden curtailment problem it faces today.[18]

Phillips Petroleum Co. v. Wisconsin[19] destroyed the unregulated market for independents, however. In extending FPC rate-setting authority to the wellhead, the Supreme Court found that the Commission has jurisdiction over gas sales by independent producers to interstate pipeline companies. Phillips was a producer making interstate sales, but it was not affiliated with a pipeline company. The Court held that "production and gathering" as defined in section 1(b) of the Natural Gas Act ended before sales to pipelines were made. Phillips was therefore a jurisdictional company under section 2(6).[20] Thus, "[Phillips'] sales in interstate commerce of natural gas for resale are subject to the jurisdiction of and regulation by the Federal Power Commission."[21]

Since *Phillips,* the production and gathering exemption has been very narrowly construed. Indeed, the meaning of production and gathering is confined to the physical activities, processes, and facilities used for extracting gas from the earth and preparing it for distribution; it does not encompass the "business" of production and gathering, with the sale of gas considered as an integral part of such business.[22] The FPC has jurisdiction over all post-production sales of natural gas which are intended for resale in interstate commerce.

Requiring the FPC to regulate wellhead prices for gas is probably in harmony with the original FTC recommendations, but its concord with Congressional intent behind the Natural Gas Act is questionable.[23] Moreover, the wisdom of the *Phillips* ruling is doubtful in light of the resulting low gas rates which have powerfully stimulated demand for natural gas in the interstate markets while simultaneously increasing incentives for intrastate sales of natural gas at prices in excess of the FPC-regulated price for interstate sales.[24]

Transportation Jurisdiction and Authority to Curtail

The limits on the FPC's transportation jurisdiction are found in section 1(c) of the Gas Act. Thus, neither transportation nor sales jurisdiction extends to:[25]

any person engaged in or legally authorized to engage in the transportation in interstate commerce or the sale in interstate commerce for resale, of natural gas received by such person from another person *within or at the boundary of a State if all the natural gas so received is ultimately consumed within such State;* or to any facilities used by such person for such transportation or sale, provided that the rates and service of such person and facilities be *subject to regulation by a State Commission* [emphasis added].

Nevertheless, the Commission's transportation jurisdiction has greater breadth than does its jurisdiction over sales. It is from the transportation jurisdictional heading that the Commission derives its curtailment authority.

The curtailment issue first arose in 1947 when the Panhandle Eastern system experienced a gas shortage which rendered impossible the fulfillment of all the pipeline's firm contracts. In this case the FPC, in taking emergency measures, found that it possessed authority to order curtailments in order to equitably allocate supplies in times of scarcity.[26] Further, in a 1947 dictum in *Panhandle,* the Supreme Court indicated that "the matter of interrupting service is one largely related . . . to transportation and thus within the jurisdiction of the Federal Power Commission to control, in accommodation of any conflicting interests among various states."[27]

In the 1947 cases the FPC made no clear distinction as to whether curtailment authority arose under the transportation or sales jurisdictions. The scarcity of gas was of very short duration, and the curtailment question did not come up again until the Commission promulgated Order 431 in 1971,[28] announcing its intention to approve curtailment plans submitted by pipeline companies under the tariff provisions of section 4 of the Gas Act.[29]

In *FPC v. Louisiana Power and Light,*[30] the Supreme Court upheld the Commission's authority to curtail deliveries, both to resale customers and to direct sales purchasers. Louisiana Power, a direct sales customer of United, brought an action against the pipeline to enjoin curtailment to Louisiana Power pursuant to FPC orders including Order 431.

Louisiana Power claimed that the Commission lacked jurisdiction over curtailments to direct sales customers because of the proviso in section 1(b) of the Natural Gas Act.[31] The Court held, however, that the FPC does have the authority to regulate curtailment of direct interstate sales of natural gas under its section 1(b) transportation jurisdiction. Citing *FPC v. East Ohio Gas Co.,*[32] the Court explained that sales and transportation constitute independent grants of jurisdiction in section 1(b). Although the Act's application to "sales" is limited to sales of interstate gas for resale, "transportation" interstate is jurisdictional even if the gas is sold directly to a consumer.

Justice Brennan, writing for the Court, relied on legislative history to support the holding. The original section 1(b) stated that:[33]

. . . nothing in this Act shall be construed to authorize the Commission *to fix rates or charges* for the sale of natural gas distributed locally in low-pressure mains or for the sale of natural gas for industrial use only.

> *(Hearings on H.R. 11662 before a Subcomm. of the House Comm. on Interstate & Foreign Commerce,* 74th Cong., 2d Sess. 1 (1936) [emphasis supplied by court].

This original purpose did not change upon final passage of the Natural Gas Act.[34] The Court found the proviso to be of limited scope:[35]

> . . . Congress' grant of sales jurisdiction as to sales for resale and the prohibition as to direct sales were meant to apply exclusively to *rate setting,* and in no wise limited the broad base of "transportation" jurisdiction granted the FPC. That head of jurisdiction plainly embraces regulation of the quantities of gas that pipelines may transport, for in that respect Congress created "a comprehensive and effective regulatory scheme" . . . . to "afford consumers a complete, permanent, and effective bond of protection . . ." [emphasis supplied by court].

This expanded interpretation of the Natural Gas Act enables the FPC to reach transactions in interstate commerce which would otherwise be outside the scope of its jurisdiction.

Further, the Court found that FPC authority to curtail direct sales is consistent with original legislative intent to complement state authority in the Natural Gas Act. If the FPC had no authority over direct sales on the ground that all such regulation was forbidden by section 1(b) as a matter of local concern, then comprehensive regulation of pipeline operations during curtailments would be impossible.

> Comprehensive and equitable curtailment plans for gas transported in interstate commerce, . . . are practically beyond the competence of state regulatory agencies.[36]

Since regulation was impossible for the states, federal regulation of this area did not usurp state regulatory functions and was therefore in harmony with the purposes of the Act.

Under the *Louisiana Power* decision, then, the Commission may curtail gas deliveries under its authority to regulate the quantities of gas transported in interstate commerce. This transportation jurisdiction extends to the movement of gas between pipeline and end-user where the end-user purchases directly from the jurisdictional pipeline, as well as between pipeline and distributor. The Commission lacks authority, however, to prescribe curtailment policy for indirect pipeline customers (end-users purchasing from the distributor). State authority takes over once the gas reaches the distributor.[37] Consequently, state commissions may modify or completely ignore FPC curtailment policy after the gas reaches the distributor. This state power is especially important in view of the fact that less than 10 percent of natural gas transported interstate is sold directly to end-users. State power has thus loomed large and its exercise in some states has frustrated the Commission's attempts to implement a national policy of curtailment according to an end-use priority scheme.

The Interconnection Question

The FPC has taken the position that it lacks the authority to order interconnections and/or transfers between relatively well-supplied interstate pipelines and those experiencing shortages. Chairman Nassikas has stated that the Commission "does not have authority to compel interconnection and deliveries between interstate pipeline companies."[38]

The Natural Gas Act makes no mention of interconnection authority. Conceivably, the power might be implied, just as the power to regulate curtailments has been implied. Section 4(b) of the Act provides:[39]

> No natural gas company shall, with respect to any transportation or sale of natural gas subject to the jurisdiction of the Commission, (1) make or grant any undue preference or advantage to any person or subject any person to any undue prejudice or disadvantage, or (2) maintain any unreasonable difference in rates, charges, service, facilities, or in any other respect; either as between localities or as between classes of service.

The arugument would be that, in a time of severe shortage on one system, a relatively well-supplied pipeline has "maintained an unreasonable difference in . . . service . . . between localities . . .," subjecting another pipeline or its customers to an "undue prejudice or disadvantage." This argument would be used to justify an order by the FPC to interconnect and transfer gas between the two pipelines.

On balance, however, the FPC's assertion that it lacks authority to order interconnection and transfer is probably well founded. The designation of "no natural gas company" implies an individual pipeline with responsibility to its own customers, not to another interstate pipeline or its customers. Therefore, a pipeline fulfilling the section 4(b) standard with regard to its own customers could hardly be accused of making an unreasonable difference in service between them and the customers of a wholly different pipeline system.

Moreover, an order by the FPC to transfer gas from one pipeline to another would probably violate section 7(a) of the Gas Act:[40]

> . . . the Commission shall have no authority to compel the enlargement of transportation facilities for such purposes, or to compel such natural-gas company to establish physical connection or sell natural gas when to do so would impair its ability to render adequate service to its customers.

FPC v. *Transcontinental Gas Pipe Line Corp.*[41] indicated that the FPC is not authorized to order a pipeline to sell gas to users favored by the Commission.

In *Granite City Steel Co.* v. *FPC*[42] the Commission had ordered the reallocation of Mississippi River Fuel Corp.'s pipeline gas so that 35,000 Mcf per day
that had been going to the pipeline's direct industrial customers on a firm
basis would go instead to its existing public utility customers. Such reallocation was likely to cause Mississippi's service to its industrial customers "to be
interrupted regularly, frequently, and far more extensively than anything previously experienced or anticipated."[43] In finding that the FPC orders violated
section 7(a), the D.C. Circuit said:[44]

> The theory and purpose of the statutory restriction appear to be that
> persons desiring gas for the first time, or *desiring more gas,* should not get
> it by taking it away from existing lawful customers. We think Mississippi's
> service to its industrial customers will not be "adequate" within the
> meaning of section 7(a) unless it meets their present and reasonable fore-
> seeable requirements approximately as well as the service Mississippi has
> been furnishing them [emphasis added].

Certainly the reallocation of gas supplied from one interstate pipeline to another
would entail "taking [gas] away from existing lawful customers" on the trans-
ferring pipeline. Unless the pipeline had supplies so extensive that it could
provide its own existing customers with an "adequate" supply of gas at the
same time it was required to transfer gas to another system, an FPC transfer
order would almost surely violate section 7(a).

American Smelting and Refining Co. v. *FPC*[45] distinguishes between curtailment and interconnection as methods of allocating natural gas:[46]

> The curtailment plan does not order the sale of additional gas to one
> customer to the detriment of another. Rather, it prescribes a formula for
> allocating insufficient supplies among existing customers. . . . Section 7(a)
> is plainly intended to regulate *expansions* of service [emphasis supplied
> by court].

Thus, although the effects of curtailment and interconnection and transfer
may be basically the same, the two modes of allocation operate from different
perspectives. Interconnection and transfer allocate the gas supply while curtailments allocate the shortage, or lack of supply.

Whether or not state regulatory commissions could legitimately authorize
interconnection and transfer between interstate pipelines within the boundaries
of individual states is open to question. The states probably possess the requisite
constitutional authority, but it is highly probable that the FPC has preempted
the field as to the interstate pipelines through its section 1(b) jurisdiction over
"natural gas companies engaged in" the transportation or sale of natural gas in
interstate commerce.[47]

CHOICE OF STATUTORY PROCEDURES IN
FORMULATING CURTAILMENT POLICY

There is no section of the Natural Gas Act which specifically provides procedures to be followed in implementing curtailments. Sections 4[48] and 5[49] were designed to deal primarily with rate-setting procedures; section 7[50] concerns abandonment and extension of facilities or service. Consequently the Commission has been compelled to shape a curtailment policy to fit procedures which were originally designed for entirely different purposes. The appropriateness of one of these sections to a particular set of circumstances has often proved ambiguous.

Section 5(a): Change in Tariff Upon
Motion or Complaint
Section 5(a) of the Natural Gas Act states:[51]

> Whenever the Commission, *after a hearing* had upon its own motion or upon complaint of any State, municipality, State Commission, or gas distributing company, shall find that any rate, charge, or classification demanded, observed, charged or collected by any natural-gas company in connection with any *transportation* or sale of natural gas, subject to the jurisdiction of the Commission, or that *any rule, regulation, practice, or contract* affecting such rate, charge, or classification is unjust, unreasonable, unduly discriminatory, or preferential, the *Commission shall determine* the just and reasonable rate, charge, classification, rule, regulation, practice, or contract to be thereafter observed and in force, and *shall fix the same by order* [emphasis added].

Section 5(a)'s language stresses the rate-making authority of the Commission, and is designed as the main avenue for bringing about rate reductions. Nevertheless, section 5(a) does refer to the transportation jurisdiction, and to rules, regulations, practices, and contracts. These references make the section a possible procedural route for implementing curtailment plans.

Section 5(a) has definite limitations with regard to curtailments, however. The Supreme Court has said that[52]

> The section 5(a) procedure has substantial disadvantages . . . rendering it unsuitable for the evaluation of curtailment plans. The FPC must afford interested parties a full hearing on the reasonableness of the tariff before taking any remedial action, and, as we have observed, "the delay incident to determination in section 5 proceedings through which initial certificated rates [as well as "practices" and "contracts"] are reviewable appears nigh interminable." . . . In addition a prescribed remedial order can have only prospective application.

The FPC must follow a two-step decision-making process under section 5(a), first determining that an existing plan is "unduly discriminatory," and secondly finding that its own remedial plan is "just and reasonable." The Commission must conduct formal adjudicatory hearings and its decisions are subject to a substantial evidence review by the courts. As the Supreme Court indicated, under section 5 there is no provision for allowing a new plan to go into effect pending the outcome of a hearing, should an emergency curtailment situation arise. Accordingly, the FPC cannot affirmatively order a pipeline to implement a particular curtailment plan until after a section 5 hearing has been held.

American Smelting and Refining Co. v. FPC[53] involved the review of an interim curtailment plan ordered into effect on the El Paso system. The court upheld the FPC's authority to consider end use in determining a just and reasonable interim plan under section 5(a). The FPC had issued orders establishing a temporary curtailment plan for use on the Southern Division System of El Paso Natural Gas Co. This system served two large California customers and numerous customers in the Southwestern states east of California. Prior to the FPC orders, the east-of-California customers had borne the entire burden of service curtailments, in accordance with El Paso's plan which provided basically for curtailments according to the respective contract rights involved. El Paso had requested that the FPC prescribe interim emergency curtailment procedures to be followed until issuance of a final order. Various parties challenged the Commission's authority to prescribe the end-use interim curtailment plan, the adequacy of the fact findings on which the plan was based, and the appropriateness of the remedy it adopted.

As to the procedures used, the D.C. Circuit found that the FPC possessed authority to promulgate an interim gas curtailment plan pending final approval of permanent tariff provisions. This authority was based on section 16 of the Gas Act, which authorizes the Commission to perform "any and all acts" it finds to be "necessary or appropriate" to carry out the objectives of the Natural Gas Act.[54] The court continued:[55]

> As we have stated before . . . section 16 does not of itself grant independent powers but merely provides for implementation of the core sections of the Natural Gas Act. . . . The "core section" underlying the orders now before us is section 5(a) which empowers the Commission, on its own motion after hearing, to correct discriminatory practices by natural gas companies. Like any order issued pursuant to section 5(a), an interim order can only issue after full hearing and must include a statement of reasons based upon findings of fact which are supported by substantial evidence in the record. No emergency can excuse these procedural requirements. (citations omitted).

Stressing the FPC's duty to follow a two-step decision-making process, the court stated:[56]

The Commission's exercise of its authority under this statute is a two-step adjudicatory process: first, the Commission must find that an existing condition is unjust or discriminatory; second, the Commission must prescribe the remedy for that condition. Each step requires the Commission to draw a legal conclusion, *viz.*: the illegality of an existing condition and the justness and reasonableness of the remedy.

At issue in *American Smelting* were the FPC's conclusions that El Paso's former curtailment procedures according to contract rights were discriminatory and that the FPC's interim plan was reasonable and in the public interest. The court had to determine whether or not the FPC's decision followed as a matter of law from facts found and whether the facts found were based upon substantial evidence in the record. The FPC's action was to be sustained if reasonable.

Since the Commission had found that El Paso's former plan would have required a total cut-off of its customers east of California before any curtailment took place in California, the court found that the FPC's decision that the tariff provisions governing curtailment were unduly discriminatory was a reasonable one. Moreover, it was reasonable for the Commission to issue an interim plan of its own which gave highest priority to human needs customers, despite the fact that there was a pre-existing gas shortage in California. Had the FPC's plan been a permanent one under such circumstances, the Commission's failure to consider the pre-existing California shortages would probably have invalidated the plan. However, the court here took into account the temporary nature of the curtailment plan, along with the exigencies which prompted the FPC to grant interim relief. The court decided that an interim plan is not arbitrary simply because it fails to resolve all issues raised in a proceeding.

Nevertheless, the FPC had failed to offer specific findings or reasoning in support of its decision to place boiler fuel uses in the lowest priority category of its plan. The court therefore refused to hold that boiler fuel uses of natural gas were by definition inferior to other uses for curtailment purposes, without a proper and definitive determination by the Commission that such was in fact the case. The boiler fuel matter was remanded to the FPC to make a finding and state reasons why boiler fuel uses should be placed in the lowest priority.

Thus, the D.C. Circuit has found that section 5(a) procedures are applicable to the implementation of the FPC's curtailment authority. The Commission has found the section awkward in meeting emergency curtailment situations, however. Indeed, section 5(a), like the Gas Act itself, was designed not to provide a speedy remedy for an emergency allocation situation, but primarily for the determination and enforcement of "just and reasonable rates" to be charged by jurisdictional pipelines. Despite section 5(a)'s advantage of authorizing Commission initiative in ordering a plan of its own into effect, the FPC has been forced to look elsewhere in the Act for procedures which lend themselves somewhat more readily to the promulgation of curtailment plans.

Section 4: Change in Tariff Filed by Pipeline

Like section 5(a), section 4 is designed primarily for implementation of the FPC's rate-setting authority. Also like section 5(a), section 4's language makes it possible to use the procedures in a broader context than rate-making. The substantive standard applicable to both section 5 and section 4 proceedings is found in section 4(b):[57]

> No natural-gas company shall, with respect to any transportation or sale of natural gas subject to the jurisdiction of the Commission, (1) make or grant any undue preference or advantage to any person or subject any person to any undue prejudice or disadvantage, or (2) maintain any unreasonable difference in rates, charges, service, facilities, or in any other respect, either as between localities or as between classes of service.

Section 4(c) establishes the principal procedure for pipelines to seek rate increases. It also requires individual pipelines to file tariff schedules showing the rates and charges for any jurisdictional transportation or sale, and also the "classifications, practices, and regulations affecting such rates and charges, together with all contracts which in any manner affect or relate to such rates, charges, classifications, and services."[58]

Since pipelines have traditionally filed their curtailment schedules along with their contracts as part of the tariff filing, the FPC has been able to use section 4 procedures in curtailment proceedings. In contrast to section 5 practice, section 4 does not enable the Commission to initiate proceedings or impose its own plan. The pipeline must voluntarily file its curtailment plan as a proposed tariff amendment before the FPC can take any action.

When a pipeline files its proposed curtailment plan, the FPC may simply allow the plan to go into effect 30 days after filing. Alternatively, the Commission may suspend the proposed plan for a period of anywhere from one day to five months, pending a hearing on the lawfulness of the plan. The Commission must hold a hearing "either upon complaint of any State, municipality, State commission or gas distributing company, or upon [the FPC's] own initiative."[59] If the commission itself does not choose to hold a hearing, some interested party is almost sure to enter a proper complaint and thus require a hearing on the proposed curtailment plan. States, distributors, or any other interested parties may intervene, and they, as well as the Commission's own staff, may present alternate curtailment plans for consideration. The Commission itself may not adopt its own plan under section 4 procedures. The burden of proof rests on the proponent of a particular plan.[60] Commission findings under section 4 are subject to substantial evidence review, just as they are under section 5 procedures.

If the hearing has not been concluded by the end of the FPC prescribed suspension period, whatever that period may be, the proposed plan becomes effective upon motion by the pipeline company making the filing. Thus a short suspension period can be very helpful in enabling the FPC to deal with an emergency situation. Should the plan ultimately be found unlawful, however, it is unclear exactly how the pipeline should reimburse wronged customers. Section 4(e) stipulates that[61]

> Where increased rates or charges are thus made effective, the Commission may, by order, require the natural-gas company to furnish a bond, to be approved by the Commission, to refund any amounts ordered by the Commission, . . . and, upon completion of the hearing and decision, to order such natural-gas company to refund, with interest, the portion of such increased rates or charges by its decision found not justified.

Since curtailments do not affect rates, there are no "increased rates" to be refunded in a curtailment situation. Whether or not section 4(e) would require monetary reimbursements for amounts of natural gas unreasonably curtailed after a suspension period is open to question. The FPC has never invoked this provision in a curtailment proceeding and monetary reimbursement would seem inadequate compensation for past loss of gas service which cannot be recovered in the present. Moreover, payback is virtually impossbile on a pipeline already experiencing curtailments. Any payback gas would have to be diverted from other customers' allotments.

The FPC has chosen section 4 procedures for use in establishing permanent curtailment plans because under section 4, the FPC has the option of allowing a proposed plan to go rapidly into effect when a drastic shortage threatens on a particular pipeline. Nevertheless, the FPC's power under section 4 is one of approval only. In *State of Louisiana v. FPC*,[62] the court followed the *American Smelting* decision in upholding the Commission's authority to base curtailment plans on end-use considerations. Approval of such a curtailment plan under section 4 was held to be proper. However, the FPC in Opinion 647 had itself attempted to modify United's interim plan under section 4; at the same time it had approved United's past curtailment practices.[63]

State of Louisiana held that the FPC had acted outside its statutory authority in ordering a modification in the interim plan without first establishing that United's plan failed to meet section 4(b) standards. According to the court,[64]

> . . . when FPC holds a hearing and orders a new curtailment plan, or revises an old one, it is exercising authority granted by section 5(a) of the Natural Gas Act.

Therefore, any time the FPC wishes to order an affirmative change in a curtailment plan, it must first determine that the plan is unjust and unreasonable under section 4(b). Once this determination has been made, the Commission must establish that its own proposal is a just and reasonable one, and then proceed to order the change under its section 5(a) authority.

The confusing overlap between section 4 and section 5 procedures in implementing curtailments is another result of the Gas Act's lack of specific provision for curtailment contingencies.

Section 7: Certification and Abandonment

Under section 7(c), a natural gas company must obtain a certificate of public convenience and necessity from the FPC before engaging in the transportation or sale of natural gas in interstate commerce. Although officials at the FPC are apparently reluctant to use the certification power as a tool to enforce prospectively the Commission's curtailment policies, section 7(c) could be useful for this purpose. The Supreme Court upheld the FPC's authority to consider end use in a section 7 certification proceeding in *FPC v. Transcontinental Gas Pipe Line Corp.*[65] In this case a public utility had contracted for the direct purchase of natural gas from producers in Texas, with arrangements for Transco to transport the gas to New York. The utility planned to use the gas for consumption in its own boilers. Transco applied to the FPC for a certificate of public convenience and necessity under section 7(e) of the National Gas Act, offering unchallenged proof that its application met all conventional tests. The FPC denied the certificate, partly because it considered boiler fuel an inferior use of natural gas and not in the interests of conservation of a wasting resource. Transco claimed that considering end use under section 7 was outside the Commission's statutory authority.

According to the Court, the Commission was not free to base its decision solely on end use criteria, nor to make a flat rule on the subject:[66]

> The Commission cannot order a natural gas company to sell gas to users that it favors; it can only exercise a veto power over proposed transportation and it can only do this when a balance of *all* the circumstances weighs against certification [emphasis supplied by court].

Nevertheless, the Supreme Court held that "the 'end use' factor was properly of concern to the Commission" in deciding whether or not to grant a particular certificate of public convenience and necessity.[67]

Thus it seems that the FPC would be able to refuse initial certification not only of sales directly to consumers who put their gas to "inferior" uses but also to distributors whose customers' uses are inferior. *FPC v. Transcontinental* does not concern such indirect customers, of course, but officials at the FPC have intimated that the Commission could consider end use in such an instance. Section 7(e) seems to give the FPC considerable discretionary leeway in certification proceedings:[68]

> The Commission shall have the power to attach to the issuance of the

certificate and to the exercise of the rights thereunder such reasonable terms and conditions as the public convenience and necessity may require.

Therefore, the Commission could also refuse to renew a certificate in case its preferred end-use policies were not carried out by a pipeline's direct or indirect customers, as long as end-use considerations are not the only basis of refusal to renew.[69]

Section 7(b) requires Commission approval for any pipeline's plan to abandon any or all of its facilities or services subject to FPC jurisdiction. The essential characteristic of abandonment under section 7(b) seems to be a lack of present intent to resume use or services in the future, or cessation of use for an indefinite period.[70] Asserting that curtailments are of a temporary nature in that they involve no intent to permanently cease services, the FPC has declined to use section 7 procedures for curtailment proceedings.[71] In *Michigan Power Co. v. FPC*,[72] Northern Natural Gas Company's curtailment plan permitted 15-30 percent reductions in deliveries to Michigan during certain periods of the year, and prohibited direct sale or resale of gas to customers requiring in excess of 25,000 Mcf per day. Michigan contended that the plan constituted a section 7 "abandonment of service" which could not be approved by the FPC without a full hearing under that section. The D.C. Circuit held that the Northern curtailment plan was not a section 7 abandonment and that proceeding under section 4 was proper.

The Commission probably elected to use section 4 rather than section 7 for the same reason it chose not to use section 5; that is, section 7 calls for a more lengthy hearing process. There is no provision for allowing abandonment to take place pending the outcome of a hearing:[73]

No natural gas company shall abandon all or any portion of its facilities subject to the jurisdiction of the Commission, or any service rendered by means of such facilities, without the permission and approval of the Commission first had and obtained, *after due hearing,* and a finding by the Commission that the available supply of natural gas is depleted to the extent that the continuance of service is unwarranted, or that the present or future public convenience or necessity permit such abandonment [emphasis added].

Should the national gas shortage become permanent, as some believe it will or already is, section 7(b) might have more direct applicability to the situation. That the courts would require the Commission to resort to its cumbersome procedures when even the more expeditious section 4(b) procedures often take years to complete, is highly unlikely, however. The certification authority will continue to be section 7's chief use in regard to the prospective allocation of gas supplies.

General Hearing Procedures

The hearings required under sections 4, 5, or 7 of the Natural Gas Act are full adversary hearings as provided in section 556 of the Administrative Procedure Act (APA). The proceeding is conducted before an Administrative Law Judge and any affected person, organization or governmental body may intervene. The parties to curtailment hearings generally include large industrial customers, distributors, city gate customers, and the Commission staff, as well as the pipeline. It should be noted that the staff is independent of the Commission at this level. It can and does take positions inconsistent with prior Commission decisions. In short, the staff is essentially like any other participant in the hearing and has the same right to appeal the decision of an Administrative Law Judge to the full Commission. The staff does not, however, have the right to take an appeal from the Commission to a circuit court of appeals. Only the Solicitor's attorneys, under Commission supervision, represent the FPC in the courts.

Following a decision by the Commission, applications for rehearing may be filed within 30 days, specifying the ground on which the request for rehearing is based. An application for rehearing must be made before any proceeding is appealed to a court.

Court review may be obtained by filing an appeal within 60 days after Commission action on the petition for rehearing. The Commission's findings of fact, if supported by substantial evidence in the record, are conclusive. Commission determinations of law are, of course, subject to *de novo* review.

EFFECTS OF FPC ORDERS

Effect on Pipeline Contract Liability

In *United Gas Pipe Line Co.* (Opinion 606), United had filed a proposed section 4 curtailment plan which included an exculpatory clause in its tariff:[74]

> . . . nor shall Seller be obligated to pay or credit such customers any sums with respect to substitute fuels burned by such customers during such a period of proration or interruption.

This provision proposed to absolve United of any liability for the excess cost of substitute fuels during a period of curtailment, whether such liability arose from substitute fuel clauses[75] or from general contractual commitments to supply its customers.

The Commission refused to add the exculpatory clause to the tariff, stating that it was simply unnecessary. Ignoring any distinction between general contractual commitments and substitute fuel clauses, the Commission said that[76]

> [i]mplementation of the curtailment plan itself, pursuant to our proce-

dures, would be an absolute defense for United against all claims for
specific performance, damages, or other requests for relief under these
contracts affected by curtailments that may be initiated in the courts.

Soon after the decision in Opinion 606, several of United's customers brought
actions seeking to enjoin further curtailments of their deliveries, to obtain a
declaratory judgment that United was improperly curtailing their service, and
for damages. The district court dismissed the actions on the grounds that the
FPC had primary jurisdiction in the matter, and that the customers had not
exhausted their administrative remedy. In *Monsanto Co. v. FPC*,[77] the court of
appeals reversed with directions to the district court to retain the cases on its
docket since the Supreme Court had not yet ruled on the FPC's curtailment
authority.

Monsanto emphasized that Commission approval of a curtailment plan
would probably not bar a damages recovery from a pipeline which had willfully or negligently created the need for curtailment.[78]

The contract liability issue arose more directly before the Fifth Circuit in
its 1973 review of Opinions 606 and 606-A. In *International Paper Co. v.
FPC*,[79] the court held that mere adoption of a curtailment plan, without more,
would not serve as an absolute defense to an action for damages for private
breach of contract. *International Paper* did not pass on the question of contract
liability; rather it found the Commission's broad statement in Opinion 606 to
be inadequate in resolving the question. The court concluded that the "absolute
defense" language was "mere dicta" having "no force other than to reflect a
position taken by the FPC which lacks support in the record before it."[80]

According to the court in *International Paper,* the most appropriate forum
to determine the relevance of a curtailment order to a defense against an action
for breach is the court before which the actual damage suit and final FPC action
are pending. Even if the FPC should abrogate a contractual provision.[81]

> . . . there still must be . . . a showing that the FPC has made a deter-
> mination that the contract terms to be abrogated are "not in the public
> interest" and that the FPC's abrogation is within the power it is granted
> by the Natural Gas Act.
> Opinions 606 and 606-A do not adequately identify the existence of
> the power exercised or the reasonableness of the attempted exercise.

In order to provide the court with an adequate basis for review, the FPC must
(a) give clear reasons why it has determined that these substitute fuel clauses
are indeed "undue preferences," and (b) make findings and set forth its reasons
for holding that abrogation of these clauses is "in the public interest." It must
show that the recognized public interests in freedom of contract and contract
stability are outweighed by the public interest it seeks to assert under the
Natural Gas Act.[82] In other words, "allocation by curtailment may be in the

public interest but it does not necessarily follow that insulation from damages is so justified."[83]

On remand to the Commission, the FPC held that the record showed no instances of deliberate preferential conduct on United's part. Consequently, there was no basis for the charge that United had brought on the necessity to curtail through improvident additions to service.[84] The FPC reaffirmed its Opinion 606 decision that United's compliance with the Commission-approved plan would constitute an absolute defense to an action for damages. It left to the courts the question of liability due to negligence in creating the need for rationing.

Upon review of this decision of the Commission, the court in *Louisiana v. FPC*[85] followed a 1955 case, *Michigan Consolidated Gas Co. v. Panhandle Eastern Pipe Line Co.,*[86] in holding that the FPC has the authority to set aside any gas supply contract provision if it finds that such provision creates an undue preference under sections 4(b) or 5(a) of the Gas Act. The Court re-iterated, however, that the Commission's authority to abrogate gas supply contracts does not necessarily create an absolute defense to breach of contract suits against individual pipelines. The FPC had simply assumed that United's possibility of liability was so remote that no exculpatory clause was necessary to its tariff; there had been no evaluation of the clause pursuant to the require-ments of *International Paper,* and the final curtailment plan had not yet been approved by the Commission. Therefore, the 5th Circuit declined to decide the ultimate issue of contract liability and remanded the question with instruc-tions to the FPC to reconsider the exculpatory clause in light of section 4(b) criteria.

The damage suits against United are still pending. In December 1975 the question of a pipeline's contractual liability under an FPC-approved curtailment plan remains unanswered.

Effect upon the States

One of the chief constraints on the FPC's curtailment power is the intrastate exemption. Section 1(b) of the Natural Gas Act excludes from FPC jurisdiction all transportation of natural gas in purely intrastate commerce, and any "local distribution of natural gas."[87] The Hinshaw Amendment, section 1(c), states: "the provisions of this chapter shall not apply to any person engaged in ... the transportation in interstate commerce ... of natural gas received by such person from another person within or at the boundary of a State if all the natural gas so received is ultimately consumed within such State...."[88] The matters so excluded "are declared to be matters primarily of local concern and subject to regulation by the several States."[89]

By excluding from the reach of FPC authority those areas which state com-missions were already authorized to regulate, Congress hoped to avoid un-necessary duplication of state and federal jurisdiction.[90] However, since the Hinshaw Amendment was enacted in 1954, before Congress had recognized any threat of a serious gas shortage, the jurisdictional split has hampered the FPC in its attempts to implement a national curtailment policy.

In the case of sales for resale, the FPC lacks authority to regulate the use of gas to the burner tip. Once the gas reaches the intrastate distributor, it enters state jurisdiction and the FPC no longer has any regulatory authority over it. Thus, FPC curtailment orders have no binding legal effect on state regulatory commissions. The FPC has solicited state cooperation in carrying out its curtailment priorities, but the states are free to carry out their own curtailment policies with regard to gas transportation from distributor to end user. Since 90 percent of all interstate pipeline sales are sales for resale, rather than to direct customers, the states theoretically have the ability to completely reverse FPC curtailment policies if they so choose. They are free to implement a pro rata or contract-based curtailment scheme despite an FPC end-use plan in effect for the interstate pipeline.

The commission has the authority to apportion volumes to jurisdictional pipelines and customers on the basis of how nonjurisdictional customers ultimately use the gas, but such apportionment gives no assurance that the pipelines can persuade distributors to so allocate among the end users. Moreover, while such apportionment may influence state commissions' regulatory schemes, there is no guarantee that they will follow the FPC lead.[91]

Because the Natural Gas Act fails to provide the Commisson with a direct means of regulating curtailments on distributor-to-end-user sales, the FPC may seek indirect modes of enforcing curtailment policies on the state level. A plan of enforcement which would eventually be effective might be based on the section 7 certification authority. Under such a plan the Commission would, in granting a new certificate or in authorizing abandonment of service, impose end-use conditions on jurisdictional pipeline companies which would preclude them from selling gas to distributors whose curtailment plans do not reflect the FPC allocation policy.

Although implementation of curtailment policy through section 7 might be effective, there is serious doubt as to whether the courts would uphold such an action by the FPC. The enforcement method would certainly stretch the Natural Gas Act even farther beyond the original Congressional intent to avoid any usurpation of state power. Moreover, the FPC has indicated that it believes that its jurisdictional authority does not extend to regulation of the terms and conditions of sales by pipelines to distributors.[92] Consequently, the FPC remains virtually powerless to impose its curtailment orders on customers within the jurisdiction of state regulatory commissions.

Status of FPC Curtailment Orders:
Rules or Policy Statements?

In the FPC's attempt to implement its policy of curtailment on an end-use basis, it has tended to be unspecific as to the extent to which jurisdictional pipelines are bound to follow its orders. All pipelines complied with the initial curtailment Order 431 as if it had been a rule because it was issued pursuant to notice and comment, even though the FPC termed the order a policy statement upon promulgation.

Similarly, several pipelines interpreted the subsequent curtailment Order 467, which established definite end-use priorities, as a rule. (For discussion of Order 467, see the first part of Chapter Four.) In *Pacific Gas and Electric Co. v. FPC,*[93] petitioner contended that Order 467 was substantively defective for failure to compile an adequate evidentiary record pursuant to APA rulemaking requirements in section 4,[94] and procedurally defective for failure to comply with the APA and the National Environmental Policy Act.[95]

The court in *Pacific Gas and Electric* began by finding the distinction between a substantive rule and a statement of general policy to lie in the different practical effects that the two types of pronouncements have in subsequent administrative proceedings. In administrative proceedings involving a previously adopted substantive rule, the issues are whether the adjudicated facts conform to the rule, and whether the rule should be applied in that particular instance. A substantive rule has the force of a law, and the underlying policy involved in that rule is not generally subject to challenge before the FPC or other agency.

The court discussed the distinction between policy statement and rule:[96]

> A general statement of policy, on the other hand, does not establish a "binding norm." It is not finally determinative of the issues or rights to which it is addressed. The agency cannot apply or rely upon a general statement of policy as law because a general statement of policy only announces what the agency seeks to establish as policy. A policy statement announces the agency's tentative intentions for the future. When the agency applies the policy in a particular situation, *it must be prepared to support the policy just as if the policy statement had never been issued* [Emphasis added].

Thus, the Commission cannot escape its responsibility to present evidence and reasoning in particular administrative proceedings simply by announcing a general policy statement as binding precedent.

Finally, the court held that Order 467 is a statement of general policy, not a binding rule:[97]

> Thus it is apparent from Order No. 467 itself that there is no final, inflexible impact upon the petitioners. And since the statement will be applied prospectively, the courts are in a position to police the Commission's application of the policy and to insure that the Commission gives no greater effect to Order No. 467 than the order is entitled to as a general statement of policy.

As such, Order 467 is unreviewable. Judicial review thus applies to the individual decisions in which Order 467's policy is applied, not to the policy statement itself.[98]

RULEMAKING AUTHORITY UNDER
THE NATURAL GAS ACT

In addition to difficulties in obtaining state cooperation with its curtailment policies, the FPC also has substantial problems in implementing those policies with regard to jurisdictional pipelines and their customers. Procedures currently in use under sections 4, 5, and 7 are not rulemaking proceedings, but individual adjudications on a pipeline-by-pipeline basis. By nature these adjudications are time-consuming, confusing, and limited in scope. A decision at the conclusion of one of these proceedings is binding solely on the parties to the hearing. Moreover, the FPC general curtailment orders are not binding as rules applicable to particular curtailment proceedings, but are mere statements of the Commission's policy as to which form of curtailment plan it considers best.

Lack of clarity of rulemaking authority is perhaps the reason why the FPC has made no binding rules regarding curtailment. Since the Natural Gas Act predates the Administrative Procedure Act,[99] the absence of references to rulemaking in its provisions is not surprising. Nevertheless, the Gas Act's lack of specificity in this realm makes it difficult to determine whether, when, and how the FPC may proceed by rulemaking.

Section 16 of the Natural Gas Act

Under section 16 of the Gas Act, "[t]he Commission shall have power to perform any and all acts, and to prescribe, issue, make, amend, and rescind such orders, rules, and regulations as it may find necessary or appropriate to carry out the provisions of this chapter."[100] The "necessary and appropriate" language of section 16 has led the FPC in the past to interpret this provision as analogous to the broad Necessary and Proper Clause of the U.S. Constitution. Section 16 provides no such far-reaching authority, however. At most, section 16 is "designed to assure that the Commission will be able to perform the functions granted under the substantive portions of the Act."[101] The courts have found justification for the FPC's assertion of rulemaking authority within the substantive portions of the Gas Act as applied to particular problems which have faced the Commision.

Setting Rates Through Rulemaking

In the *Permian Basin Area Rate Cases,*[102] the Supreme Court upheld the FPC's authority to adopt a system of area rate regulation. The decision did not involve rulemaking per se since the Commission had begun proceedings in 1960 under section 5(a) of the Gas Act, and after extended hearings had issued a decision prescribing rates and various ancillary requirements for the Permian Basin area in 1965.[103] The Supreme Court stated that[104]

Although we would expect that the Commission will hereafter indicate more precisely the formulae by which it intends to proceed, we see
no objection to its use of a variety of regulatory methods.

Recognizing the difficulties inherent in attempting to regulate wellhead prices
with a case-by-case approach, the Court said further that "administrative authorities must be permitted, consistently with the obligations of due process, to
adapt their rules and policies to the demands of changing circumstances."[105]
The FPC's discretion in this regard was limited only in that the rates set must
not be arbitrary, discriminatory, or irrelevant to the policy being pursued by the
Commission.

Later cases have relied on *Permian's* broad language to uphold the Commission's rulemaking authority in the area of ratesetting. *Phillips Petroleum Co. v.
FPC*[106] involved an order by the Commission formulating a procedure to be
used in setting rates under section 5(a) of the Gas Act. The proposed procedures consisted of "notice-and-comment" rulemaking pursuant to section 553
of the APA. Petitioners asserted that the APA requires a formal evidentiary
hearing whenever a hearing is called for in a particular type of proceeding, and
that there could be no valid judicial review without an evidentiary record. The
Tenth Circuit found *Permian* to be dispositive in upholding the notice-and-
comment procedure. Quoting *Permian,* the court stated that "'the breadth and
complexity of the Commission's responsibilities demand that it be given every
reasonable opportunity to formulate methods of regulation appropriate for
the solution of its intensely practical difficulties.'"[107]

The *Phillips* court also noted that the legislative history of the APA indicates
that Congress meant to give administrative agencies wide latitude in adopting
rulemaking procedures. Further, the court stated that where hearings such as
the instant ones involved quasi-legislative rather than quasi-judicial activities,
informal proceedings are usually sufficient. Finally, the court decided that
adequate judicial review of record findings does not depend on the presence
of a record resulting from a formal evidentiary hearing, as long as there is a
record which allows an orderly review of the FPC's findings and conclusions.
According to the court, written comments submitted by gas companies to the
FPC together with questionnaire data filed by producers and pipeline companies
composited by FPC staff, would satisfy the requirements of the APA and
Natural Gas Act.

In *Mobil Oil Corp. v. FPC,*[108] the D.C. Circuit questioned the wisdom of the
Tenth Circuit's *Phillips* decision. The *Mobil* court interpreted *Permian* more
narrowly, finding that "[f]lexibility is not synonymous with uncontrolled
discretion."[109] Thus,[110]

We conclude that the FPC need not employ the precise procedures
set forth in sections 556 and 557 of the APA. It does not follow, however,

that the Commission may proceed with only the guidance of the less rigorous standards of section 553.

The *Mobil* case was a review of FPC orders which had set minimum rates for transportation charges for liquifiable hydrocarbons through a "notice and comment" rulemaking process. In responding to petitioners' challenge to the orders, the Commission contended that section 16 of the Gas Act gave it the authority to use informal rulemaking if such were found to be "necessary or appropriate." The D.C. Circuit, in finding that section 16 conferred no such authority on the FPC, stated that[111]

> The substantive provisions of the Act contemplate certain procedures, as incident to the functions provided. The range of permissible procedures must be derived from these sections, sections like sections 4 and 5 of the Natural Gas Act, and the functions they describe. Section 16, which uses a broad generality of "necessary or appropriate" that is not rooted in a function, cannot enlarge the choice of permissible procedures beyond those that may fairly be implied from the substantive sections and the functions there defined.

The court held that the Gas Act's requirement of "substantial evidence on the whole record" necessitates some kind of adversary, adjudicative-type procedures for the promulgation by the FPC of a valid rule.[112]

Mobil's holding that the Gas Act does require some form of an adversarial process in rulemaking under its provisions, was borne out in *American Public Gas Assoc. v. FPC.*[113] This case involved the FPC's determination of rates in the Rocky Mountain area via a rulemaking proceeding which did not include a formal adjudicatory hearing. The Commission had issued notices of the proposed rulemaking which stated precisely what it proposed to do and the methodology it proposed to follow. Without limiting the scope of any submittals on the issues, the FPC had set out the specific areas of inquiry and requested relevant information from the parties to the proceeding. Finally, the Commission had conducted public hearings in eight major states, where it received comments and submittals and made them available to all interested parties.

In finding the rulemaking procedures adequate in this case, the D.C. Circuit distinguished *APGA* from *Mobil:*[114]

> In the *Mobil Oil* case there was no adequate notice, and much of the data relied upon by the Commission was provided in an informal and to some extent *ex parte* conference, as distinguished from an adversary setting.

In *APGA,* on the other hand, the Commission had given the parties "fair notice of exactly what the Commission propose[d] to do, together with an opportunity to comment, to object, and to make written submissions; and the final order of the Commission [was] based upon substantial evidence."[115]

Seeking to build on *Permian* and its descendants, the FPC issued notice of a proposed rulemaking to establish a national rate for all jurisdictional sales of natural gas on April 11, 1973.[116] The notice made all large producers respondents to the rulemaking proceeding, and provided for the submission of written comments from all interested parties and named respondents. Accompanying the notice was a Commission staff study on the estimated nationwide cost of finding and producing new non-associated gas supplies. The Commission did not propose any specific rates, terms or conditions in the notice, but stated that it would amend section 2.56 of its Rules of Practice and Procedure, General Policy Statements and Interpretations.[117] These amendments would be in accordance with the Commission's findings and determinations based on responses submitted by the various parties, and the staff study.

In Opinion 699,[118] the FPC established a single uniform national base rate for jurisdictional sales of natural gas.[119] The Commission stated that[120]

> ... we have determined that a single uniform national rate promulgated in this rulemaking proceeding will enable us to establish just and reasonable rates for natural gas sold in interstate commerce without the inherent delays and stale records which have accompanied the traditional adjudicatory method of regulating producer rates. The prescription of a uniform national rate for all areas will avoid essentially duplicative procedures and evidence to prescribe just and reasonable rates for the various natural gas producing areas of the nation, and will enable the commission to utilize its power and resources for more effective administration of the Natural Gas Act.

Responses to the notice included several challenges to the Commission's use of informal rulemaking. In general, these challenges asserted that the Fifth Amendment of the U.S. Constitution, the Natural Gas Act, and the APA require the FPC to proceed by formal adjudication in rulemaking procedures. In dismissing these objections, the Commission relied on the prior Supreme Court and Circuit Court opinions interpreting the breadth of its rulemaking power:[121]

> We believe that any question as to the adequacy of the procedures followed in this case that may have been raised by the Mobil Oil decision were laid to rest by the decision of the Supreme Court not to review the Phillips decision. Moreover, the court of appeals for the District of Columbia Circuit has distinguished its holding in the Mobil Oil case in its holding that the Commission has the authority to establish initial rates by the use of rulemaking procedures. American Public Gas Assoc. v. Federal Power Commission (1974).

The Commission found no need for trial-type proceedings, and likened the national rate case to *APGA*:[122]

> Likewise, in this proceeding, every party has been given an opportunity to submit two sets of responses and replies to the responses of all other parties. Thus, no party can be heard to complain that he lacked an adequate opportunity to develop his case before the Commission.

In Opinion 699-H[123] the Commission again met challenges to its use of notice-and-comment rulemaking. By referring to *Mobil*, it dismissed the contention that the Gas Act's "substantial evidence" requirement necessitates formal procedures in a rate-making proceeding.[124] Further, the Commission found that public policy compels the use of informal procedures in the current situation:[125]

> The present gas shortage and the need for vastly expanded exploration and development programs to meet further demand dictates that the establishment of rates for "wellhead sales" of natural gas in interstate commerce not be unduly delayed and that administrative procedures such as rulemaking be utilized to prevent the prescribed rates from becoming stale before they are effective. Moreover, the continually increasing competition from the unregulated intrastate market demands that the interstate market have the ability to respond as may be necessary to assure the maintenance of adequate natural gas service to the customers of the interstate pipelines.

Opinion 699-H increased the uniform national rate for interstate natural gas sales to 50 cents per Mcf, plus one-cent annual escalations.

Review was sought in the Fifth Circuit in *Shell Oil Co. v. FPC.* The court supported the Commission on all points and held that the procedures used satisfied even the requirements of the formal hearing process. The court's refusal to require full adjudicatory type hearings was perhaps grounded primarily in considerations of policy:[126]

> Were the Commission to have allowed all interested parties to submit oral testimony and conduct oral cross-examination on an undertaking so massive and novel . . . the proceeding would have taken years, and the Commission's power to effectively regulate the industry would have been destroyed.

Rulemaking and Curtailment

The FPC apparently has the authority to promulgate binding rules under the APA and Natural Gas Act when the regulatory situation it faces calls for such action, and if the substance of the relevant section of the Gas Act permits it. Whether the Commission can go so far as to use mere notice-and-comment rulemaking is unclear due to the conflict between *Phillips* and *Mobil*. The courts have so far upheld rulemaking by the FPC only in the context of rate-setting, however, and the approval of rulemaking authority in one area is far from a general grant of that power in all areas of FPC regulation.

In *Pacific Gas and Electric Co. v. FPC*,[128] the court indicated that the Commission "is free to initiate a rulemaking proceeding to establish a binding substantive rule" on curtailment. Nevertheless, the court was not actually reviewing an exercise of rulemaking authority in that case;[129] it therefore could not reach the question of whether the Commission may curtail on a basis other than pipeline-by-pipeline adjudication.

Furthermore, it is significant that the FPC's rulemaking authority originates in the function of sections 4, 5, or 7 rather than in section 16. If the relevant "function" in the rate-setting cases is rate-setting alone, then rulemaking authority for the function of curtailment is not so easily implied. A court reviewing a rule could find either more or less authority to promulgate rules under the FPC's curtailment power than has been found under the rate-setting function.

There are practical problems as well with the promulgation of rules to implement curtailment policies. Each pipeline system is different and its supplies and customers are diverse. The establishment of a binding norm for all systems would be very difficult. Indeed, the relevant substantive sections of the Natural Gas Act would seem to require a case-by-case determination of "just and reasonable" curtailment plans so that the different situation of each pipeline and its customers could be taken into account. Any attempt to tailor rules to different situations would probably amount to the equivalent of a case-by-case determination.

In order to establish a binding rule, the FPC would have to proceed under section 5(a)—no FPC-promulgated rule for curtailment could go into effect until after a hearing (or at least some sort of determination) on its merits. The expeditious possibilities under section 4 would not be available since a proposed plan could not go into effect pending the outcome of the proceeding. As the Commission has already realized in its choice to pursue its policies under section 4 rather than section 5, such delay could prove disastrous in the face of an emergency demanding fast action.[130]

Secondly, a rule would be subject to full court review as to its justness and reasonableness, based on record evidence.[131] At present the FPC's policy statements are not subject to such review except insofar as a 467-type plan must be justified in each situation where it is proposed.[132]

Thus it seems that while the FPC may have the authority to make binding rules concerning curtailment, the utilization of that authority might prove to be practically infeasible.

PENDING LEGISLATION

A large number of bills to deal with the natural gas problem have been introduced in the 94th Congress. Price deregulation has been the strategic issue in the legislative process.

Those favoring deregulation, including the Ford Administration, the natural gas industry, and the producer states, won a signal victory in the Senate with passage of S.2310 in October 1975. This bill would deregulate prices for interstate sales of new natural gas, except for new gas produced from offshore federal lands which would be gradually deregulated over a five-year period.

However, the forces for deregulation suffered a major last minute defeat in the House in February 1976.

S.2310 as passed by the Senate was referred to the House Committee on Interstate and Foreign Commerce which, instead of acting on it, reported out the Natural Gas Emergency Act of 1975 (H.R. 9464) in December 1975. As reported by the Committee, the bill's purpose would be to provide temporary emergency authorities for minimizing the detrimental effects of possible natural gas shortages through the 1976–77 winter heating season. This would enable the Congress to consider carefully long-term legislation to deal with the natural gas problem, including the pricing issue.

H.R. 9464 as reported by the House Commerce Committee was, however, shunted aside by a series of parliamentary maneuvers. In February 1976, a substitute amendment which would have provided for price deregulation along the lines of S.2310 was first taken up and narrowly rejected. Immediately thereafter, a substitute amendment which would provide for a radically different approach to federal regulation of natural gas was adopted, again by a relatively slim majority.

As passed by the House in February 1976, H.R. 9464 would provide for price deregulation of interstate sales of new natural gas by so-called "independent producers" which do not produce more than 100,000,000 Mcf per year. However, FPC price regulation would continue to apply to interstate sales of new natural gas produced by the major producers. Moreover, federal price regulation would also be extended to intrastate sales of new natural gas by the major producers.

As these paragraphs are written (February 1976), the Senate and House thus appear to be at loggerheads over the natural gas pricing issue, with the Ford Administration strongly backing the Senate bill. The two houses of the Congress may yet find common ground acceptable to the President. As the winter heating season wanes and the presidential election campaigns warm up, however, the possibilities for compromise in the 94th Congress appear to be more and more remote.

Regardless of the outcome of the natural gas pricing debate, there is still a need for legislation to strengthen the FPC's authority to administer natural gas shortages. Even with deregulation of new gas followed by successful exploration efforts, substantial additions to natural gas production capacity would not occur before the 1980s. And even then, additional reserves may do little more than slow or arrest the decline in U.S. natural gas production.

As passed by the Senate, S.2310 would have permitted interstate pipelines with insufficient gas supplies for their high priority customers to make 180-day emergency purchases from intrastate markets and would also have permitted curtailed priority customers to make direct purchases from the intrastate markets. This legislation, which would expand the FPC's existing emergency purchase authorities, would extend only through the 1975-76 heating season. As passed by the House, H.R. 9464 did not contain any specific emergency provisions, except a narrow prohibition on new contracts for natural gas for use in electric power plants and specific protection of natural gas supplies for agricultural and related uses.

The Natural Gas Emergency Act of 1975 (H.R. 9464 as reported by the Committee on Interstate and Foreign Commerce to the House on December 15, 1975) is the most comprehensive and thoughtful natural gas emergency bill developed by the Congress so far.[133] The ensuing discussion is limited to the main features of this bill, which could be a basis for the supply emergency provisions of comprehensive legislation that would also establish a new pricing policy for natural gas.

The proposed Natural Gas Emergency Act, which would expire on April 15, 1977, would provide the authority and procedures whereby "distressed interstate pipelines" may obtain access to "new natural gas." The quoted terms provide the keys to the Act.

Section 3 of the proposed Emergency Act would define "new natural gas" to exclude all gas produced from the Outer Continental Shelf, and all gas already committed to interstate commerce on September 9, 1975, the date when the bill was introduced. This definition is designed to limit the applicability of the bill to those supplies of natural gas which would otherwise not be sold in interstate commerce. All gas production from the OCS is required to be dedicated to the interstate market in any event. However, reserves from which FPC authorized emergency sales have previously been made would be classified as new natural gas.

The meaning of the key term "distressed interstate pipeline" would be administratively determined by the FPC. In designating an interstate pipeline as distressed, the Commission would apply the pipeline's existing curtailment plan to its projected natural gas supplies and determine whether the pipeline is likely to be unable to meet the requirements of "essential users" which it supplies directly or indirectly.

The term "essential user" would also be defined by the FPC through administration. In establishing specific criteria for determining essential users, the bill mandates the Commission to consider the availability and price of alternate fuels, the costs of conversion, and the impacts of natural gas curtailment on employment, food production and public health, safety and welfare.

Section 4(a)(1) of the proposed Emergency Act would require the FPC to designate, on its own initiative, distressed interstate pipelines within 15 days of enactment. Of course, the FPC might decide to designate none, but the Committee Report states that "at least one, and as many as six, pipelines might qualify for the designation."[134] Under section 4(a)(2), an interstate pipeline which was not initially designated as distressed could petition for such a designation and the FPC would be required to act on the petition within 21 days.

Designation of an interstate pipeline as distressed would have consequences for both the pipeline and its customers. A distressed pipeline would be authorized to purchase new natural gas for resale. The first sale price for new natural gas purchased by a distressed pipeline would be exempted from section 4(a) of the Natural Gas Act, which would otherwise require an FPC determination that the price was just and reasonable. In order to prevent abuse, however, the FPC's initial certification authority under section 7 of the Natural Gas Act would remain applicable. Through the certification requirement, the FPC would, according to the House Committee report, be in a position to determine whether sales prices to distressed pipelines were "in line" with prevailing intrastate prices.[135] The certification review could thus prevent abuses, such as a distressed, integrated interstate pipeline purchasing new gas from a producer affiliate at an exorbitant price.

Section 5 of the proposed Emergency Act would provide special rate treatment for new natural gas purchased by a distressed interstate pipeline. The excess above the FPC-established maximum national rate of the prices paid by distressed pipelines for new natural gas would be passed through selectively. The incremental prices could not be rolled in, as is normally permitted. Instead, residential and small commercial users would be exempt from any passthrough surcharge and the burden of increased costs would fall primarily on industrial users. The purpose of the selective passthrough would be to "focus the burdens of purchases of new natural gas on those consumers who would most directly benefit from receiving additional supplies of natural gas."[136]

In implementing the proposed Emergency Act, section 9 would authorize the FPC to order physical interconnections among pipelines and to order any pipeline to transport new natural gas purchased by a distressed interstate pipeline. The interconnection authority would apply to all pipelines, intrastate as well as interstate.

The proposed Emergency Act appears to dovetail rather neatly into the FPC's existing curtailment policy. It would provide an expanded framework and firm legal foundation for FPC administrative actions, aside from price deregulation, aimed at increasing natural gas supplies in the interstate market. If enacted, the proposed Natural Gas Emergency Act might provide the nation with a means to slither through the 1976-77 winter heating season. A cold winter and a strong economy would, however, severely test the adequacy of such a narrowly conceived approach to the natural gas shortage.

NOTES TO CHAPTER THREE

1. 15 U.S.C. §717 et seq. (1970).
2. 320 U.S. 591, 603 (1944).
3. 49 U.S.C. §1 et seq.
4. 265 U.S. 298 (1924).
5. *Id.* at 308.
6. *See also* Public Util. Comm'n. v. Attleboro Steam and Elec. Co., 273 U.S. 83 (1927) (state where a commodity originates could not regulate the price charged to a purchaser in another state); Pennsylvania Gas Co. v. Public Util. Comm'n., 252 U.S. 23 (1920); Public Util. Comm'n. v. Landon, 249 U.S. 236 (1919).
7. *S. Doc. No.* 92, 70th Cong., 1st Sess., pt. 84–A (1936).
8. A natural monopoly exists when only a single firm (here, a pipeline company) may be economically justified within a single given area.
9. 1 *Federal Power Commission, National Gas Survey* 80 (1975).
10. *See H.R. Rep. No.* 709, 75th Cong., 1st Sess. (1937).
11. Atlantic Refining Co. v. Public Serv. Comm'n., 360 U.S. 378, 388 (1959).
12. Statement of Sen. Wheeler, 81 *Cong. Rec.* 9312 (1937).
13. 15 U.S.C. §717(b) (1970).
14. *See* FPC v. East Ohio Gas Co., 338 U.S. 464 (1950); Panhandle Eastern Pipeline Co. v. Public Serv. Comm'n., 332 U.S. 507, 516 (1947).
15. FPC v. Louisiana Power & Light Co., 406 U.S. 621 (1972).
16. *See H.R. Rep. No.* 827, 73d Cong., 2d Sess. (1935).
17. Columbian Fuel Corp., 2 F.P.C. 200, 207 (1940).
18. Federal regulation has played a major role in inhibiting the ability of the industry to locate, develop, and deliver needed gas supplies. Past regulatory policies have established rates at minimum cost-based levels, and administered these rates within a framework fraught with uncertainty and delay. The area rate approach to producer rate-making required years to establish just and reasonable rates for all producing areas of the country. Additional years are required after final Commission action for judicial review and confirmation to be complete. The Commission's attempts to reduce the detriments of regulatory lag through utilization of rulemaking procedures have been somewhat successful, but even then rates thus established have not been immune to the delays of appellate review. The end result has been that procedures initiated under the Natural Gas Act have dampened the search for new supplies, reduced proven inventories to improvident levels resulting in chronic deliverability problems, increased gas demand with much of it directed toward less efficient uses, diverted gas away from the interstate market, and damaged the industry's ability to develop new capital to explore for and develop new domestic sources of gas. 1 *Survey, supra* note 9, at 3-4.

19. 347 U.S. 672 (1954).

20. 15 U.S.C. §717a(6) (1970).

21. 347 U.S. at 677. *See also* FPC v. Panhandle Eastern Pipe Line Co., 337 U.S. 498 (1949); Interstate Natural Gas Co. v. FPC, 331 U.S. 682 (1947); Saturn Oil & Gas Co. v. FPC, 250 F.2d 61 (10th Cir. 1957); Deep South Oil & Gas Co. v. FPC, 247 F.2d 882 (5th Cir. 1957); FPC v. J.M. Huber Corp., 133 F. Supp. 479 (D. N.J. 1955).

22. *See* United Gas Improvement Co. v. Continental Oil Col., 381 U.S. 392 (1965).

23. *See* Note, *The Legislative History of the Natural Gas Act,* 44 Geo. L.J. 695 (1956). *See also H.R. Rep. No.* 827 *supra* note 17.

24. States retain jurisdiction over intrastate sales. *Central States Elec. Co.* v. *Muscatine,* 324 U.S. 138 (1945), *mandate amended on other grounds,* 325 U.S. 836 (1945). State authority also encompasses retail sale and distribution to local consumers by local distributors purchasing gas from interstate pipelines. 15 U.S.C. §717c (1970). Gas sales to local industrial consumers by one engaged in interstate commerce are also included in state jurisdiction. *See* FPC v. Louisiana Power & Light Co., 406 U.S. 621 (1972); FPC v. Panhandle Eastern Pipe Line Co., 337 U.S. 498, 508 (1949); Panhandle Eastern Pipe Line Co. v. Public Serv. Comm'n., 332 U.S. 507 (1947).

25. 15 U.S.C. §717(c) (1970). Section 1(c) comprises the "Hinshaw Amendment," which was added to the Act in 1953 in response to the decision in FPC v. East Ohio Gas Co., 338 U.S. 464 (1950). In 1950 a dispute had arisen over the interpretation of the section 1(b) transportation authority provision. East Ohio was a gas distributor selling gas exclusively within Ohio. Interstate gas pipelines connected with East Ohio's main lines within the state boundary. From there, gas bought by East Ohio from the interstate system flowed continuously to East Ohio's distribution systems. The issue in this case was whether the company was therefore exempt from FPC jurisdiction on the ground that all its facilities came under the section 1(b) proviso making the Natural Gas Act inapplicable "to the local distribution of natural gas or to the facilities used for such distribution."

The Supreme Court concluded that "transportation" under the Natural Gas Act does not necessarily pertain only to those engaged in the business of transporting gas in interstate commerce for hire or for sales to be followed by resales, i.e., interstate pipelines. In holding that East Ohio was subject to FPC jurisdiction under the Gas Act, the Court stated:

> We find no language in the Act indicating that Congress meant to create an exception for every company transporting interstate gas in only one state.... There is nothing in the legislative history which authorized us to interpret away the plain congressional mandate [338 U.S. at 474].

Thus the Hinshaw Amendment sought "to clarify the Natural Gas Act by further defining the limits of the FPC's jurisdiction with respect to operations of companies engaged in the local distribution within a State of out-of-State natural gas which has been received by such a company at or within the State

borders." *S. Rep. No.* 817 83d Cong., 1st. Sess. 2102 (1953). The *East Ohio*
decision had resulted in some duplication of state and federal jurisdiction
which had caused overlapping requirements regarding the filing of reports and
information by natural gas companies. Since this result was inconsistent with
the original aim of complementing state authority, section 1(c) was to eliminate any duplication in this area by leaving jurisdiction over companies like
East Ohio exclusively to the states.

26. Panhandle Eastern Pipe Line Co., 6 F.P.C. 196, 203 (1947). *See generally*
Panhandle Eastern Pipe Line Co., 9 F.P.C. 443 (1950), 7 F.P.C. 48 (1948),
7 F.P.C. 89 (1948), 6 F.P.C. 111 (1947), 5 F.P.C. 983 (1946).

27. Panhandle Eastern Pipe Line Co. v. Public Serv. Comm'n., 332 U.S.
507, 523 (1947).

28. 45 F.P.C. 570, 36 Fed. Reg. 7505 (1971).

29. 15 U.S.C. §717c (1970).

30. 406 U.S. 621 (1972).

31. Section 1(b) provides that "[t]he provisions of this Chapter . . . shall
not apply to any other transportation . . . of natural gas. . . ." 15 U.S.C. §171(b)
(1970).

32. 338 U.S. 464 (1950).

33. 406 U.S. at 639.

34. *H.R. Rep. No.* 709, 75th Cong., 1st Sess. 4 (1937).

35. 406 U.S. at 640.

36. *Id.* at 641. Moreover, states would be free to thwart FPC curtailment
policy at the pipeline-to-consumer level just as they can turn that policy around
once gas has passed to the distributor-to-consumer level specifically left to
state regulation.

37. 15 U.S.C. §717(c) (1970).

38. Statement of John N. Nassikas, Chairman of the FPC, before the Subcomm. on Conservation, Energy and Natural Resources of the House Comm.
on Government Operations, 94th Cong., 1st Sess., June 12, 1975.

39. 15 U.S. C. §717c(b) (1970).

40. *Id.* §171f(a) (1970).

41. 365 U.S. 1, 17 (1961).

42. 320 F.2d 711 (D.C. Cir. 1963).

43. *Id.* at 713.

44. *Id.*

45. 494 F.2d 925 (D.C. Cir. 1974).

46. *Id.* at 936.

47. 15 U.S.C. §717(b) (1970).

48. 15 U.S.C. §717c (1970).

49. *Id.* §717d.

50. *Id.* §717f.

51. *Id.* §717d(a).

52. 406 U.S. at 643-44, *quoting* Atlantic Refining Co. v. Public Serv.
Comm'n., 360 U.S. 378, 389.

53. 494 F.2d 925 (D.C. Cir. 1974). "An interim plan is one entered into
during the course of proceedings which resolves some of the issues of curtailment, while leaving others to be determined at a later date." *Id.* at 932.

54. 15 U.S.C. §717o (1970).
55. 494 F.2d at 933.
56. *Id.* at 940-41.
57. 15 U.S.C. §717c(b) (1970).
58. *Id.* §717c(c).
59. *Id.* §717c(e).
60. 5 U.S.C. §556(d) (1970).
61. 15 U.S.C. §171c(e) (1970).
62. 503 F.2d 844 (5th Cir. 1974).
63. United Gas Pipe Line Co., 49 F.P.C. 179 (1973).
64. 503 F.2d at 861.
65. 365 U.S. 1 (1961).
66. *Id.* at 17.
67. *Id.* at 22.
68. 15 U.S.C. §171f(e) (1970).
69. In light of the deepening energy crisis, the courts might be willing to reduce this proviso to practical insignificance.
70. *See* Continental Oil Co., 31 F.P.C. 1079, 1080, 1083 (1964).
71. Opinion 606, United Gas Pipe Line Co., 46 F.P.C. 786, 91 P.U.R.3d 247 (1971).
72. 494 F.2d 1140 (D.C. Cir. 1974).
73. 15 U.S.C. §717f(b) (1970).
74. International Paper Co. v. FPC, 476 F.2d 121, 124 (5th Cir. 1973).
75. A substitute fuel clause is an agreement in a contract whereby a pipeline agrees to reimburse a customer for any premium which that customer must pay to obtain fuel during periods of interruption in gas supply. *Id.* at 123 n.1.
76. 91 P.U.R.3d at 262.
77. 463 F.2d 799 (D.C. Cir. 1972).
78. *Accord,* Atlanta Gas Light Co. v. FPC, 476 F.2d 142, 150-52 (5th Cir. 1973).
79. 476 F.2d 121 (5th Cir. 1973).
80. *Id.* at 125.
81. *Id.* at 127-28.
82. *Id.* at 128.
83. *Id.* at 128-29.
84. Opinion 647, United Gas Pipe Line Co., 49 F.P.C. 179, 184-88 (1973).
85. 503 F.2d 844 (5th Cir. 1974).
86. 283 F.2d 204 (D.C. Cir. 1960).
87. 15 U.S.C. §717(b) (1970).
88. *Id.* §717(c).
89. *S. Rep. No.* 817, 83d Cong., 2d Sess. (1954). 1954 *United States Code Congressional and Administrative News* 2102.
90. Order 467, 49 F.P.C. 85, 38 Fed. Reg. 1503 (1973).
91. FPC officials indicate that only three states have implemented 467-type schemes.
92. *See* Opinion 622, Columbia LNG Corp., 47 F.P.C. 1624, 95 P.U.R.3d 145 (1972). But *see also* Order 539, 54 F.P.C. __ 40 Fed. Reg. 49571.
93. 506 F.2d 33 (D.C. Cir. 1974).

94. 5 U.S.C. §553 (1970).
95. 42 U.S.C. §4321 et seq. (1973).
96. 506 F.2d at 38.
97. *Id.* at 41.
98. Since the court found Order 467 unreviewable, it was precluded from considering whether the FPC had violated NEPA in promulgating the order.
99. 5 U.S.C. §551 et seq. (1970).
100. 15 U.S.C. §717o (1970).
101. Mobil Oil Corp. v. FPC, 483 F.2d 1238, 1256 (D.C. Cir. 1973).
102. 390 U.S. 747 (1968).
103. Opinion 468-A, 34 F.P.C. 1068 (1965); Opinion 468, 34 F.P.C. 159 (1965).
104. 390 U.S. at 800.
105. *Id.* at 784.
106. 475 F.2d 842 (10th Cir. 1973), *cert. denied* 42 U.S.L.W. 3401 (U.S. Jan. 14, 1974).
107. *Id.* at 850.
108. 483 F.2d 1238 (D.C. Cir. 1973).
109. *Id.* at 1254.
110. *Id.* at 1251.
111. *Id.* at 1257.
112. The court elaborated:

Informal comments simply cannot create a record that satisfies the substantial evidence test. Even if controverting *information* is submitted in the form of comments by adverse parties, the procedure employed cannot be relied upon as adequate. A 'whole record,' as that phrase is used in this context, does not consist merely of the raw data introduced by the parties. It includes the process of testing and illumination ordinarily associated with adversary, adjudicative procedures.

. . . .

Compliance with this standard could conceivably be achieved in a number of ways. There must, however, be some mechanism whereby adverse parties can test, criticize and illuminate the flaws in the evidentiary basis being advanced regarding a particular point. The traditional method of doing this is cross-examination, but the Commission may find it appropriate to limit or even eliminate altogether oral cross-examination and rely upon written questions and responses. . . . It is also possible that the Commission could use evidence incorporated by reference from other proceedings [*Id.* at 1260-62].

113. 498 F.2d 718 (D.C. Cir. 1974).
114. *Id.* at 723.
115. *Id.* at 722.
116. 38 Fed. Reg. 10014 (1973). The new national rate would apply to all jurisdictional sales of natural gas produced from wells commenced on or after January 1, 1973, except for those sales certificated under Orders 431, 491, and 455, or sales made by small producers under Order 428. Opinion 699, National Rates for Natural Gas, 51 F.P.C. 2212, 4 P.U.R.4th 401, 405 (1973).

117. 18 C.F.R. §2.56 (1975).

118. National Rates for Natural Gas, 51 F.P.C. 2212, 4 P.U.R.4th 401 (1973).

119. 42.0 cents/Mcf.

120. 4 P.U.R.4th at 407.

121. *Id.* at 410–11.

122. *Id.* at 411.

123. National Rates for Natural Gas, 8 P.U.R.4th 209 (1975).

124. *See* Mobil Oil Corp. v. FPC, 483 F.2d 1238, 1262 (D.C. Cir. 1973).

125. 8 P.U.R.4th at 215–16.

126. 520 F.2d 1061, 1076 (5th Cir. 1975).

127. The Southern Louisiana rate proceeding commenced on May 10, 1961, and was finally settled by *Mobil* on June 10, 1974. The first *Permian Basin* proceeding lasted seven years. *Id.* at 213–14.

128. 506 F.2d 33, 41 (D.C. Cir. 1974).

129. *See* discussion in text at note 93 *supra.*

130. If the FPC could indeed utilize the informal notice-and-comment procedure, this delay would be less, but it could still be critical in an emergency situation.

131. 5 U.S.C. §706 (1970).

132. *See, e.g.,* 506 F.2d 33 (D.C. Cir. 1974).

133. *H. Rep. No.* 94-732, 94th Cong. 1st Sess. (1975). [hereinafter cited as *Emergency Act Committee Report*].

134. *Emergency Act Committee Report* at 16.

135. *Id.* at 17.

136. *Id.*

Chapter Four

Natural Gas Curtailment: Administrative Development and Implementation

This chapter focuses on the relationship between the substance of the FPC's natural gas curtailment policies and the procedures used in their development and implementation. To place what follows in context, we begin with a brief description of administrative efforts to increase supply. Next, we examine current FPC curtailment procedures, noting how they have been tailored to the FPC's approach to curtailment and assessing the extent to which the procedures adopted suit the Commission's substantive curtailment options. Finally, taking a broader perspective, we examine briefly the basic procedural alternatives available to the FPC and consider their implications for curtailment.

ADMINISTRATIVE EFFORTS TO INCREASE SUPPLY

Ever since the natural gas shortage emerged in 1970, the FPC has tried through its limited administrative means, to stimulate supply to the interstate market. In its vigorous attempts to devise responses to the shortage, the Commission has been continually hampered by its statutory and administrative limits. In several areas the Commission has been skirting the bounds of its lawful authority, and, in some cases, has been found going beyond.

Encouraging New Investment

Administrative efforts to encourage increased investment in new and existing wells have focused on increasing the wellhead price. Advance payments by pipelines to producers have also been allowed as part of the pipelines' operating expenses.[1]

77

Emergency Sales

By orders 402 and 402–A, issued in early 1970, the Commission announced a policy that allowed certain exempt distribution companies to make emergency sales of gas to jurisdictional companies without jeopardizing their exempt status. These sales were at unregulated prices, but for no more than 60 days.[2] This policy was reaffirmed and expanded by Order 418, issued in December 1970, which allowed independent producers and jurisdictional pipelines to engage in emergency sales for up to 60 days without having to obtain a certificate from the Commission. These sales, too, were at unregulated prices, and without danger of refund.[3]

Sales made under these procedures amounted to 1.2 Tcf from 1971 through May 1973.[4] In theory, of course, this was gas that would not otherwise have been available to interstate consumers.

Faced with a growing shortage, the Commission determined in September 1973 to expand the scope of these emergency programs by extending the 60-day period to 180 days.[5] Several petitioners contested the legality of the extension, but the Commission declined to modify its stand. Appeal was taken to the D.C. Circuit. While the appeal was pending, however, the 180 day extension was terminated by Order 491-D.[6]

In March 1975 the D.C. Circuit found that the Commission had "unduly stretched" its authority under the Natural Gas Act.[7] Accordingly, the Court held that the Commission's extension of its limited certification power under section 7 to 180 days was invalid, but left to the Commission the question whether refunds should be ordered. The opinion concludes with the observation that courts ought not acquiesce in a "rubber stamping of non-regulation in agency trappings."[8]

Direct Purchases from Producers: Order 533

Another administrative initiative was the adoption of Order 533 in August 1975, following public notice and receipt of nearly 150 comments from a wide variety of firms, individuals, and public agencies.[9] The Order adopted, as a statement of policy, the position that the Commission will allow high priority industrial and commercial end users to purchase gas directly from producers in the on-shore (federal and non-federal) and off-shore non-federal domains. Certificates are to be issued to cover the transportation of the gas by interstate pipeline. Significantly, the price paid to the producer by the end-use customer is not subject to FPC regulation.[10]

A number of restrictions apply to these sales. The gas must be sold only for Priority 2 uses, or for those Priority 3 uses that would have been Priority 2 uses if the gas had been contracted for on a "firm" basis. The policy applies only to existing consumers currently subject to, or imminently threatened with, curtailment.

Order 533 will certainly be challenged in the courts and the outcome is not clear. The analogy to the 180-day unregulated sales, which were previously overturned by a court, appears close. The effect of either plan is to allow emergency sales of gas in interstate commerce at unregulated prices. Regardless of the court decision, however, it is clear that the Commission is again straining at the limits of its authority in its efforts to increase supply.

Enforcement of Producers' Delivery Contracts

During the summer and fall of 1975, Congressional concern focused on the question whether the producers were meeting the minimum delivery schedules set out in their contracts with the interstate pipelines.[11] The staff of the House Commerce Committee's Subcommittee on Energy has asserted that the producers' failure to deliver under these contracts was "the major cause" of the natural gas shortage.[12]

The Commission has adopted an intriguing, if somewhat cryptic, policy concerning enforcement of these contracts. Order 539, a statement of policy issued October 14, 1975, affirms that it is Commission policy that affected "producers, pipelines or distribution companies shall take all appropriate actions" to enforce producer delivery contracts in administrative or judicial proceedings.[13] Moreover, the Commission asserted its authority:[14]

> to enforce the rendition of *inter alia*, natural gas services, sales or operations as certificated by the Commission, including as a part thereof, necessary deliverability or production of natural gas to meet, *inter alia*, certificated operations, services, developments, quantities, volumes or sales.

In other words, the Commission's position is that the primary source of the producer's obligation to deliver gas is the FPC certificate and the Natural Gas Act, rather than the producer's contract with its purchaser. Failure to comply constitutes not just breach of contract but violation of federal law, and subjects the offending producer to the penalty provisions of the Natural Gas Act.[15]

To assist it in enforcing its new policy, the Commission invited complaints, pursuant to section 1.6 of its rules of practice and procedure,[16] "seeking enforcement of certificate, rate schedule or contractual obligations of any natural gas company producer or natural gas company pipeline" concerning deliverability of minimum volumes.[17] The Commission also stated its intention to condition future certificates on the making of periodic reports as to reserves.

At bottom, the Commission appears to be asserting the authority to control, to some degree at least, the rates of production of natural gas producers. It is difficult to see how this assertion is to be reconciled with the production and gathering exemption in the Act. Attempts to enforce the policy will doubtless be challenged in the courts, and the likely outcome is far from clear.

As with other FPC steps to meet the shortage, the Commission has pushed here to the limits of its authority. At the same time it becomes increasingly clear that the Commission is in the position of the agency attempting to solve, with ineffective administrative tools, a problem for which it is not designed.

DEVELOPMENT OF FPC CURTAILMENT POLICY

As pointed out in Chapter Three, the Natural Gas Act of 1938 was not framed with gas shortages and curtailments in mind, nor was the Commission designed as a gas allocation board. From the beginning of the gas shortage in 1970, the FPC has thus been forced to adapt procedures that were originally developed for other purposes.

As noted above, the first phase of Commission policy with respect to the shortage was to act to increase supply rather than to curtail demand. The resulting increase in supply was insufficient, however, and the Commission was confronted with the need to deal with curtailment.

In October, 1970, United Gas Pipeline Company petitioned the Commission for a declaratory order to the effect that United's curtailment proposals for the 1970-1971 heating season were consistent with its obligations under tariffs on file with the FPC. Negotiations between the pipeline and its customers were initiated, however, and an interim settlement was reached.

The shortages began to spread during the 1970-71 winter, and more pipelines began asking the Commission to approve their curtailment practices. By the end of the winter heating season the FPC had begun to appreciate the full extent of the projected future supply deficits.

Order 431

On November 4, 1970, the Commission issued a "Policy Statement Notice of Investigation and Proposed Rulemaking With Respect to Developing Emergency Plans," Docket No. R-405, which stated that the Commission proposed, after investigation, to issue rules governing curtailment policies and procedures.[19] The notice included the staff's proposed regulation and invited comment.*

The outcome of the proceeding was Order 431,[20] issued April 15, 1971, which continued the previously announced policies regarding emergency sales and purchases. The Order also provided that jurisdictional pipelines should

---

*(a) Each pipeline company subject to the Commission's jurisdiction shall observe the priorities of service to the extent appropriate in accordance with the following guidelines: I. Highest service priority: consumption for essential services, national defense and domestic use, and gas storage therefor. II. Firm service commitments in addition to those embraced under I above. III. Interruptible service commitments. (1) With respect to III above, the service curtailments shall be in accordance with priorities established in existing tariffs and/or service agreements for both direct and resale customers. (2) with respect to II above, priorities established should be in accordance with the following order: (i) Commercial uses. (ii) Industrial uses. 35 Fed. Reg. at 17431.

take all steps necessary for the provision of as reliable and adequate gas service as possible. Specifically, Order 431 called for all jurisdictional pipelines which expected curtailment to be necessary to file an amendment to their tariffs pursuant to sections 4 and 5 of the Natural Gas Act. These amended tariffs were to indicate the curtailment policy they planned to implement when and if needed. Although Order 431 did not adopt the guideline priorities as originally proposed in the notice, it did enunciate as basic principles that consideration should be given to curtailing interruptible service and large boiler fuel usage, where alternate fuels were available, before other types of service or uses.[21]

The pipelines responded to Order 431 by filing a wide variety of curtailment plans. The majority of the plans adopted some form of pro rata curtailment, although a minority chose end-use programs and others chose some type of contract plan.[22] In addition, most included provisions releasing the pipeline from contract liability for cutbacks in service made pursuant to the curtailment plan.[23]

It was not immediately clear whether these filings should proceed under section 4 or section 5 of the Natural Gas Act. Section 4 had the advantage of relative speed, but the FPC itself could propose plans only under section 5.

As noted in Chapter Three, Commission action on curtailment plans is a two-step proceeding drawing on both sections 4(b) and 5(a) of the Act. But in either case, section 556(d) of the Administrative Procedure Act places the burden of establishing that an order meets the substantive tests of section 4(b) of the Natural Gas Act concerning nondiscrimination on the proponent of that order. The approval of any plan must be supported by substantial evidence in the record.

Because of the importance of expediting curtailment plans, the Commission chose to proceed under section 4. The propriety of this choice was subsequently upheld by the Supreme Court in *F.P.C. v. Louisiana Power and Light Co.*, discussed in Chapter Three. Use of section 4 procedures enabled the FPC to achieve its immediate goal of assuring that plans were in effect for the winter heating season while hearings were still in progress.

The Commission also adopted the technique of allowing the submission of interim plans in addition to permanent plans.[24] The only functional difference between an interim plan and a permanent plan is that an interim plan is valid only for a fixed period, usually about a year or 18 months. A permanent plan is valid indefinitely. However, interim plans present a number of practical and procedural advantages over permanent plans.

First, use of interim plans makes it easier to arrive at compromise settlements in negotiations between the pipeline and its customers. Naturally, customers are usually more willing to compromise and settle on an interim plan of limited duration than on a permanent plan.[25]

If an interim plan is reached by a unanimous settlement there is no need for formal hearings. If, as is more often the case, agreement is not universal, the interim plan must also be presented in a hearing and be supported by substantial evidence on the record. But, again, under section 4 the interim plan may be put in effect pending completion of the hearings.

Another procedural advantage of using interim plans has developed: permanent plans must be accompanied by an environmental impact statement, while interim plans need not be.[26] This means not only substantial savings in time and manpower needed to prepare the statement, but freedom from litigation as to the sufficiency of the statement.

A third advantage is that the quantum of evidence required to support a Commission adjudication of an interim plan may not be as great as that required for a permanent plan.[27]

Order 431 defined the Commission's basic approach to curtailment. Planning for the shortage would proceed on a pipeline-by-pipeline basis with each pipeline having primary responsibility for formulating an acceptable plan for its system. The Commission rejected the rulemaking approach suggested in the November 4 notice and elected to participate in planning curtailment only by formal adjudication after hearings on the pipelines' submissions. The only guidelines the Commission offered in Order 431 respecting the content of curtailment plans were to suggest curtailing interruptible and boiler fuel users before other customers.

Given the possibility of allowing a proposed plan to be effective pending hearing, section 4 procedures were well adapted to this approach. The formula tended to put the Commission in a relatively passive position concerning the content of the plans. The pipelines submitted proposals, often following extensive negotiations with their customers. Under the adjudication approach adopted by Order 431, the Commission was forced to react to these submissions rather than to play a leading, active role. Nonetheless, this was the path the Commission consciously chose by not following up its own rulemaking proposal.

The first Order 431 curtailment plan to reach the Commission was an interim plan submitted by United Gas Pipe Line, which adopted an end-use approach to curtailment. The plan placed domestic uses in the highest category, followed by process uses, electricity generation for domestic users, industrial uses, and certain large power plant and industrial customers paying special rates.[28] In Opinion 606, issued October 5, 1971, the Commission approved United's end-use approach, although the priorities were modified somewhat.

The second FPC decision on the merits of a proposed interim plan, Opinion 634, was handed down nearly a year later in the El Paso proceeding on October 31, 1972.[29] The plan based on curtailment according to contract rights, which was proposed by El Paso, would have required all customers east of California to be curtailed before any California customers were curtailed. This would have resulted in residential consumers east of California being cut off, while industrial users in California were still being served. The Commission found this result to be unduly discriminatory under section 4(b) of the Gas Act.

The opinion emphasized the importance of end use in deciding how curtailment should be managed:[30]

[W]e would be negligent in our duties if we allowed human needs customers on any portion of the system to be cut off while industrial customers were still receiving gas on another portion of the system.

The Commission created a new curtailment plan for El Paso, combining proposals from several different parties. The resulting priorities were:

Priority 1. (To be curtailed last.) Residential, small commercial (less than 50 Mcf on a peak day) and residential needs associated with industrial requirements served directly or indirectly.

Priority 2. Large commercial requirements and industrial requirements for plant protection, feedstock, and process needs.

Priority 3. All industrial requirements not specified in Priorities 2, 4, and 5.

Priority 4. Industrial requirements for boiler fuel use of less than 3,000 Mcf per day, but more than 1,500 Mcf per day, where existing alternate fuel capability is present.

Priority 5. Industrial requirements for large volume (in excess of 3,000 Mcf per day) boiler fuel use where existing alternate fuel capability is present.[31] The responsibility for obtaining the end-use data necessary to implement the plan was placed on El Paso.[32]

In the course of these proceedings the FPC became more familiar with the issues associated with formulating and implementing curtailment plans. At the same time, the Commission appeared to be rethinking its approach to curtailment. Instead of leaving the formulation of curtailment plans with the pipelines and customers, the Commisson began to assert its own beliefs as to curtailment policy: human needs consumers needed protection; boiler fuel use was to be disfavored; contractual distinctions must give way when necessary to public policy considerations; pro rata sharing of the shortage by all distributor and direct sales customers was not sufficient.

But once the Commission concluded it should provide leadership in developing a nationwide policy toward curtailment, the adjudication approach was no longer suitable. A different procedural approach became necessary.

Order 467

On January 8, 1973 the Commission issued Order 467,[33] a "Statement of Policy" concerning the utilization and conservation of natural gas resources under the Natural Gas Act. It was promulgated without prior notice or hearing under the exception in the Administrative Procedure Act for "general statements of policy."[34]

The FPC explained that the curtailment plans which the pipelines had submitted pursuant to Order 431 contained "sharp differences" in basic approach, some opting for end use, others for pro rata. Similarly, the Commission noted the lack of uniformity in the amount of evidence presented in the hearings as to consumer impact and end-use allocation patterns.[35] The FPC considered this diversity to be a constraint on the articulation of the uniform national curtailment policy which the Commission believed necessary. Moreover, the lack of standards rendered long-range planning by the pipelines difficult. Therefore, the Commission sought to provide guidelines to the pipelines:[36]

> Order 467 was issued in order to focus the attention of all parties concerned with the natural gas industry upon the general policy views of the Commission in advance of the filing of particular applications with the Commission and thereby to permit affected entities the opportunity to evolve a rational energy resource development program considering national energy goals and objectives as they may be stated from time-to-time, and to minimize the complexity and length of administrative proceedings before the Commission.

Order 467 established a set of eight priority-of-service categories based principally on end use. The Commission believed the categories were "generally applicable industry wide" and could be utilized for establishing curtailment priorities "on any jurisdictional pipeline's system."[37]

The priorities initially established placed residential and small commercial users in the top priority, followed by large commercial users and certain firm industrial service for process needs, feedstock, and plant protection. Boiler fuel use was next, while large volume interruptible use was at the bottom. Specifically, the eight priorities were as follows:

1. Residential, small commercial (less than 50 Mcf on a peak day).
2. Large commercial requirements (50 Mcf or more on a peak day), and firm industrial requirements for plant protection, feedstock and process needs.
3. All industrial requirements not specified in (2), (4), (5), (6), (7), or (8).
4. Firm industrial requirements for boiler fuel use at less than 3,000 Mcf per day, but more than 1,500 Mcf per day, where alternate fuel capabilities can meet such requirements.
5. Firm industrial requirements for large volume (3,000 Mcf or more per day) boiler fuel use where alternate fuel capabilities can meet such requirements.
6. Interruptible requirements of less than 1,500 Mcf per day.
7. Interruptible requirements of intermediate volumes (from 1,500 Mcf per day through 3,000 Mcf per day).
8. Interruptible requirements of more than 3,000 Mcf per day.

The Commission explained its preference for this type of end-use scheme in Opinion 643, *Arkansas-Louisiana Gas Co.,* issued concurrently with Order 467:[38]

> We are impelled to direct curtailment on the basis of end use rather than on the basis of contract simply because contracts do not necessarily serve the public interest requirement of efficient allocation of this wasting resource. In time of shortage, performance of a firm contract to deliver gas for an inferior use, at the expense of reduced deliveries for priority use, is not compatible with consumer protection.

The Commission reasoned further that preference should be given residential and small commercial users because: (a) boiler fuel use is inefficient; (b) large-volume users can convert to alternate fuels with greater ease and safety and at less cost than can small users; (c) pollution control is more easily implemented for large users who switch to alternate fuels; (d) curtailing boiler fuel use would minimize the unemployment and economic dislocations which would result from other plant closings.[39] Finally, the FPC contended that interruptible sales contracts were usually based on end-use considerations, and that human needs customers did not contract for gas on an interruptible basis. Interruptible customers, therefore, could reasonably be expected to have alternate fuel facilities.

Order 467 required full curtailment of lower categories before any curtailment could take place in the higher priorities. It also placed direct and indirect customers having the same end use in the same category.

The precise immediate effect of Order 467 was to amend the Commission's General Rules of Practice and Procedure by adding section 2.78(a) which stated that "the national interests in the development and utilization of natural gas resources throughout the United States will be served by recognition and implementation of [the eight priority of service categories listed above]."[40]

The statement of policy went further, however, and added a puzzling paragraph:[41]

> The priorities-of-deliveries set forth above will be applied to the deliveries of all jurisdictional pipeline companies during periods of curtailment on each company's system; except however, that, upon a finding of extraordinary circumstances after hearing initiated by a petition filed under Section 1.7(b) of the Commission's Rules of Practice and Procedure, exceptions to those priorities may be permitted.

As pointed out earlier, in an adjudication under the Administrative Procedure Act, the burden of proof is on the party proposing an order. In other words, a pipeline filing a curtailment plan must carry the burden of showing that the plan is not unduly preferential or unreasonably discriminatory in violation of section 4(b). If the Commission is to disapprove the proposed plan, replacing it with some other plan, the FPC must first find, on the basis of substantial evidence in the record, that the proposed plan fails to meet the section 4 standard. Then, the Commission may proceed under section 5(a) to impose a just and reasonable substitute plan, if supported with substantial evidence on the record.[42] However, in Order 467 the Commission appeared to be turning the tables, in effect placing the burden on the pipeline to show why the Commission's preferred plan should not be applied.

The effect of Order 467 was further clouded by the fact that the Commission issued a notice of proposed rulemaking on the same day in Docket No. R–467. The Commission proposed to amend section 2.78(b) of its General Policy and Interpretations to read as follows:[43]

Except when extraordinary circumstances are found to exist, the public interest requires jurisdictional pipeline companies to recognize and implement the following priorities-of-service in submitting proposals to this Commission requesting service to new and/or additional direct and resale customers during this period of short supply of natural gas . . . [there followed the eight categories set out in Order 467].

The proposed rule in Docket No. 467 would thus have required jurisdictional companies to use the specified end-use priorities in submitting applications for *new* or *additional* customers. The proposed rule was also designated a statement of policy. When the policy was applied in specific cases, opportunity would be afforded parties to challenge or support the policies through factual or legal presentations.[44] The Commission stated that the policies reflected "public policy guidance" which the Commission proposed for the benefit of all concerned.[45]

The proposal received a great deal of negative comment from the industry, however, and the matter was dropped. Apparently, the main thrust of the criticism was that a uniform national approach, identical for all pipelines was simply impossible. The industry comments favored a continuation of the case-by-case, pipeline-by-pipeline approach.

The concurrent decision in Opinion 643, *Arkansas-Louisiana Gas Co.,* and Opinion 647, *United Gas Pipeline Co.,* issued only four days later, did not clarify FPC intentions. These were the first two permanent plans to reach the Commission. In each case the Commion considered the evidence and ordered its Order 467 set of priorities applied in place of the proposed plan which had gone through extensive hearings. Priorities 6, 7, and 8 were not used for United, however, since United made no interruptible sales.

Since both Ark-La and United had originally submitted end-use plans and introduced much evidence in the preceding hearings to support the various end-use distinctions,* it was not immediately clear whether the Commission was relying on Order 467 or on the evidence gathered in the hearings.[46] Nevertheless, these actions, coupled with the assertive language in Order 467, indicated that the Commission felt strongly about its end-use priorities, and meant to apply them when possible.

Following this flurry of Commission activity, numerous petitions were sent to the FPC requesting rehearing, reconsideration, modification, or clarification. The Commission considered these petitions and articulated its position more fully in Order 467-B, issued March 2, 1973. (Order 467-A, issued January 15, 1973, dealt with provisions for emergency relief to be included in pipeline tariff filings. It is discussed below in conjunction with the provisions concerning extraordinary relief contained in Order 467-C.) The Commission emphasized that Order 467 was only a statement of policy and "not finally determinative of the rights and duties of a given pipeline, its customers or ultimate consumers; it expressly envisions further proceedings."[47]

> Accordingly, those pipelines which do not yet have a curtailment plan approved by final order of the Commission are still free to file tariff changes under Section 4 in whatever form they choose. Tariffs not in accord with the policies expressed [in the 467 series of Orders] will be subject to suspension and hearing, and any curtailments made under non-conforming tariff sheets which have not received Commission approval may be found to be unjust and unreasonable, or preferential or discriminatory, dependent upon the facts proved in an evidentiary hearing. Proposed tariff sheets which conform to the policies expressed [in the 467 series] will be accepted for filing, and permitted to become effective, subject to the rights of intervenors to hearing and adjudication of any claim of preference, discrimination, unjustness or unreasonableness . . . and subject to the further right of any one adversely affected to seek individualized special relief because of extraordinary circumstances.[48]

Although the Commission added that the Order 467 priorities were only a "guide" in curtailment proceedings, the Commission pointedly advised that:[49]

> [b]y these orders, the parties are on notice that we consider the type of curtailment plan set forth in [Order 467] to be just and reasonable, non-discriminatory and nonpreferential. This does not mean that the parties

---

*(Ark-La's categories were: interruptibles; boiler fuel; industrial process and feedstock; small industrials, commercial and plant protection ; human needs. United's proposal divided use among four categories: domestic; industrial process; gas consumed to generate electricity consumed by domestic consumers; industrial uses. A fifth end-use category was rejected by the Commission in Opinion 606.)

may not propose or the Commission may not adopt variations on the [Order 467 type] plan, but there must be evidence in the record to support any such variations.

By implication, the Commission did not seem to believe that evidence in the record was needed to support the Order 467-type plan itself.

Order 467-B also modified the priorities somewhat, adding a ninth category, taking alternate fuel capabilities into account, and specifically dealing with storage injection. The FPC's preferred curtailment plan now comprises the following nine categories:[50]

1. Residential, small commercial (less than 50 Mcf on a peak day).
2. Large commercial requirements (50 Mcf or more on a peak day), firm industrial requirements for plant protection, feedstock and process needs, and pipeline customer storage injection requirements.
3. All industrial requirements not specified in other categories.
4. Firm industrial requirements for boiler fuel use at less than 3,000 Mcf per day, but more than 1,500 Mcf per day, where alternate fuel capabilities can meet such requirements.
5. Firm industrial requirements for large volume (3,000 Mcf or more per day) boiler fuel use where alternate fuel capabilities can meet such requirements.
6. Interruptible requirements of more than 300 Mcf per day, but less than 1,500 Mcf per day, where alternate fuel capabilities can meet such requirements.
7. Interruptible requirements of intermediate volumes (from 1,500 Mcf per day through 3,000 Mcf per day), where alternate fuel capabilities can meet such requirements.
8. Interruptible requirements of more than 3,000 Mcf per day, but less than 10,000 Mcf per day, where alternate fuel capabilities can meet such requirements.
9. Interruptible requirements of more than 10,000 Mcf per day, where alternate fuel capabilities can meet such requirements.

The explanation contained in Order 467-B was by no means sufficient to clarify the situation. It remained to be seen how the FPC would apply its new Order in practice.

As noted above, the Commission itself formulated 467-type plans for the pipelines in the *Arkansas-Louisiana* and *United* cases, Opinions 643 and 647. Although in each case hearings were held, some parties contested the sufficiency of the evidence supporting the Commission's decision. In both cases, reviewing courts ultimately found the evidence insufficient in some respects and remanded the cases to the Commission for further hearings.[51] The Commission apparently had attempted to implement the 467 priorities even where not substantially supported by the evidence. In other words, the Commission sought to give Order 467 more influence than a mere statement of policy.

On January 29, 1973, the Commission issued an order in Docket No. RP71-130, et al., *Texas Eastern Transmission Corp.*, which required Algonquin to show cause why it should not file an amendment to its tariff "to conform with Order 467-A," thus "exemplifying" its use of Orders 467 and 467-A.[52]

In at least two other cases, in March and May of 1973, where pipelines were reluctant to file Order 467-type plans, the Commission issued written warnings of the possible consequences of failure to comply with the Order. These warnings referred to the language in the Order as to nonconforming tariffs quoted above.[53]

In proceedings on a permanent plan, Columbia Gas Transmission Corporation filed a 467-type plan, in addition to its own plan, pursuant to a letter order of the Commission. Columbia made clear in its brief to the Commission that it did not support the 467-type plan and had submitted no evidence to support it. Columbia's brief further argued that the FPC could not lawfully order the 467-type plan into effect since it was not supported by substantial evidence in the record.

Some distribution companies have argued that the effect of Order 467 is to shift the burden of proof in curtailment cases from the pipelines to their customers by establishing a kind of presumption that a conforming plan is consistent with the standards of the Natural Gas Act. Another argument is that Order 467 in effect constitutes a substantive rule which is void for noncompliance with the notice provisions of the APA.[54] Additionally, it has been contended that the 467-type plans filed by some pipelines are the result of "coercion" on the part of the FPC and consequently void.[55] These arguments have ultimately been rejected by the courts, however, as discussed below.

In summary, the FPC is embarked on what might be called an "adjudication plus" strategy. The Commission had experience from November 1970 to January 1973 in dealing with curtailment plans on the basis of adjudication. Through adjudicatory procedures, the Commission was unable to implement a uniform national approach to curtailment. As the Commissioners' ideas on curtailment crystallized, a rulemaking of limited scope was attempted, proposing to require the 467 set of priorities in applications for certificates of public convenience and necessity covering new or additional customers. Given the shortage situation, it seems unlikely that such plans would have covered any significant volumes of gas. It is almost as if the Commission wanted to get industry comment on its Order 467 priorities without committing itself to making a rule. In any event, the proceeding was dropped after receiving a great deal of criticism from the industry. The FPC rejected the rulemaking route.

There remained for the Commission to attempt to find a middle ground, basically following adjudication procedures, but adding an announced policy in favor of a certain type of plan. Presumably, the Commission thought that the pipeline companies would rather adhere to FPC policy than face lengthy curtailment proceedings and subsequent litigation.

The principal lever the Commission possesses to influence the pipelines to submit and support 467-type plans is the authority to protect the pipeline in large part from possible liability for breach of contract. As noted in Chapter Three, although Commission approval of a curtailment plan may not absolve the pipeline from liability for breach of contract in all cases, Commission approval of necessary curtailments is an effective barrier to liability where the pipeline was not in some way responsible for the shortage. Needless to say, this carrot dangled before the pipeline companies may be a powerful inducement to submitting plans that conform to Order 467.

Despite the pressure which can be applied with this lever, the pipeline companies do in fact have a choice, particularly if they are not in some part responsible for the shortage on their own system. The preferred alternative is to maintain good relations with their customers. This involves working out and obtaining FPC approval of a settlement plan that everyone can accept. Only if the settlement plan is not approved by the Commission, or if a settlement is not reached, will most pipelines acquiesce and file a 467-type plan.

The Commission implied in Order 467-B that it might have another lever over the pipelines. That is, the FPC sought to differentiate between plans in conformity with Order 467 end-use priorities and those not in conformity. Nonconforming plans would be subject to suspension and hearing, and curtailments made under them might be found unjust, depending on the facts proved in the hearing. Yet in spite of the threat implied in Order 467-B, conforming plans are equally subject to hearing, on appropriate request by intervenors, and the Commission's determination must be supported by substantial evidence in the record. The Commission is free to state its belief that it considers an Order 467-type plan to be just and reasonable, non-discriminatory and nonpreferential. However, it cannot declare a particular 467-type plan to be just and reasonable in the absence of record support sufficient to pass substantial evidence scrutiny by a reviewing court.

In other words, the *legal* effect of not submitting a plan conforming to Order 467 appears to be slight. Nevertheless, the Commission has acted as if the 467 Orders had a legal impact, sending letters to pipelines warning them of the risks of curtailing under alternative plans. Perhaps most importantly, the Commission has put the industry unequivocally on notice that an Order 467-type plan is a preferred plan. Thus, despite the substantial evidence test for judicial review, a nonconforming plan carries a heavier burden of persuasion in the minds of the Commissioners.

FPC use of section 4 rather than section 5 facilitates this "adjudication plus" approach. Ordinarily, section 5 procedures would be used where the Commission seeks to require some affirmative action on the part of a jurisdictional pipeline. Under section 5, the Commission "on its own motion" can initiate proceedings, but no order can issue until after formal hearings have been held. The burden on the Commission to support its order by substantial evidence is more clearly visible.

By having the pipeline initiate the proceeding under section 4, where the pipeline clearly carries the burden of supporting its own plan with substantial evidence, the Commission's burden is less clear. Moreover, where a pipeline is persuaded to file and support a 467 type plan, substantial private resources have effectively been directed toward the creation and rationalization of a uniform, nationwide policy on natural gas curtailments.

This "adjudication plus" approach enables the Commission to assume a more active, leading role in formulating curtailment policy than permitted by merely sitting back and adjudicating pipeline proposals.

The extent to which the Commission can continue this approach is not entirely clear. Two major areas present difficulties: the status of Order 467 and the pressure the Commission has applied to pipelines to encourage the filing of conforming plans. Recent indications in both areas favor the Commission.

A number of distribution companies have contended that Order 467 is in effect a binding, substantive rule, which is void for non-compliance with the notice and comment requirements of the APA. The D.C. Circuit considered and rejected this contention in *Pacific Gas and Electric Co. v. FPC,* decided in mid-1974.[56]

The Court pointed out that Order 467 did not purport to be a binding, substantive rule. The opinion emphasized that the Commission had treated the Order as a mere policy statement and had only approved or prescribed plans using the 467 priorities after formal hearings had been held. The question of the sufficiency of the evidence collected in those hearings was not before the court.[57]

The court in *Pacific Gas and Electric* warned the Commission that if it substituted a 467-type plan for a nonconforming pipeline proposal, it must first, under section 4(b), find the proposed plan to be unduly preferential or unreasonable and then, under section 5(a), carry the burden itself of supporting the substitute 467 plan on the basis of substantial evidence on the record.[58]

> When an agency applies [a general statement of policy] in a particular situation, it must be prepared to support the policy *just as if the policy statement had never been issued.* An agency cannot escape its responsibility to present evidence and reasoning supporting its substantive rules by announcing binding precedent in the form of a general statement of policy [emphasis added].

The court reassured the distributing companies that, since Order 467 would only be applied prospectively, the courts were in a position to police the Commission's application of the Order, insuring that it was given no greater effect than that to which it was entitled as a mere general statement of policy.[59]

The question of coercion has been examined by the D.C. Circuit in several recent cases. In a short, per curiam opinion in *Consolidated Edison of N.Y. v. FPC*[60] decided rapidly in November 1974, the court reinstated a proposed settlement plan which the Commission had rejected in favor of a 467-type plan. The pipeline (Transco) filed the 467-type plan, stating that "the Commission having rejected the proposed interim settlement, Transco has no choice other than to make this filing."[61] The petitioning distribution companies claimed that the 467-type filing was the result of Commission "coercion." The procedural posture of the case, on motions to modify and vacate an existing stay, did not allow the court to reach the merits. The opinion noted, however, that if the 467-type plan were indeed the result of "coercion,"[62]

> . . . the plans are invalid, as the Commission cannot impose a change in an existing tariff without compliance with the requirements of Section 5 of the Natural Gas Act, which the Commission admits were not met here.

When the court reached the merits on May 19, 1975, it concluded that although "the pressure was on" the pipelines to submit conforming curtailment plans, this pressure was not sufficiently coercive to invalidate the filing.[63] The court discussed the contract liability issue but concluded that the pipelines were not in fact coerced. The court referred to the FPC procedure as regulation through "raised eyebrow" techniques.[64]

The court's chief concern was apparently with the openness of the Commission's proceedings. The opinion pointed out that the interested parties had received an opportunity to participate, although not exactly in the time sequence provided by the Gas Act and the APA.[65]

> The Commission policy appears, in fact, to have evolved from individual curtailment proceedings, and although 467's adoption was not preceded by notice and comment, the agency responded publicly to numerous petitions for rehearing, reconsideration, modification and clarification [in Order 467-B]. Further, consistent with the Commission's statement that 467 "expressly envisions further proceedings," extensive hearings in each of the cases have been held. The effect of the Commission's choice of procedures was thus to favor rapid implementation over prior hearing, not to avoid public scrutiny entirely. Under the circumstances, we cannot say that the Commission's timing contravened the Natural Gas Act . . . .

On petition for rehearing, the court gave further advice. First, it advised the Commission that a settlement agreement submitted by a pipeline must be considered, and reasons given for a rejection. Second, the court tried to clarify the role of the Commission, noting that:[66]

> Absent interim or permanent action based on the hearing record, or a rulemaking replacing the present general policy statement in Order 467 with a rule of binding effect, the FPC's role is primarily one of review of pipeline submissions.

This line of cases leads to the conclusion that the Commission may retain Order 467 as a statement of policy while taking care to support the implementation of the policy with substantial evidence in each case. Where hearing records have not been compiled however, the Commission is without authority to order pipelines to submit 467-type plans.

Emergency and Extraordinary Relief

A necessary complement to the FPC's curtailment policy is provision for flexibility within the overall end-use scheme. Orders 467-A and 467-C are designed for this purpose.

Order 467-A, issued just two weeks after Order 467, added to the 467 statement of policy as follows:[67]

> The tariffs filed with this Commission should contain provisions that will reflect sufficient flexibility to permit pipeline companies to respond to emergency situations (including environmental emergencies) during periods of curtailment where supplemental deliveries are required to forestall irreparable injury to life or property.

Under Order 467-A emergency relief may be granted privately by the pipeline in accordance with the provisions on file with the Commission. The individual end user or distributor decides when to seek emergency relief, and the pipeline makes the decisions granting or withholding relief. A distribution company seeking such relief must ordinarily demonstrate that it has exhausted all reasonably available flexibility in its system, and that emergency relief cannot be granted by the distributor directly to the needy end user without impairing service to other customers of the same or higher priority. When a pipeline grants emergency relief, it must report its action to the FPC. Emergency relief procedures are designed to avoid bureaucratic delays by allowing the pipeline to respond immediately to emergency situations.

For relief which goes beyond the period of an immediate emergency, or where there is no imminent danger to life or property, the extraordinary relief procedures of Order 467-C are to be used.[68] Under Order 467-C, a pipeline company, distributor, or state regulatory commission may petition the FPC for extraordinary relief. Petitions must use 467-B priorities and the definitions contained in Order 493-A, as well as provide basic information on volumes needed, efforts to secure alternate fuel, and other items. The specifics of this order are as follows:

1. The specific amount of natural gas deliveries requested on peak day and monthly basis, and the type of contract under which the deliveries would be made.
2. The estimated duration of the relief requested.
3. A breakdown of all natural gas requirements on peak day and monthly bases at the plant site by specific end uses.
4. The specific end uses to which the natural gas requested will be utilized and should also reflect the scheduling within each particular end use with and without the relief requested.
5. The estimated peak day and monthly volumes of natural gas which would be available with and without the relief requested from all sources of supply for the period specified in the request.
6. A description of existing alternate fuel capabilities on peak day and monthly bases broken down by end uses as shown in [(3) above].
7. For the alternate fuels shown in [6 above] provide a description of the amount of present fuel inventory, names and addresses of existing alternate fuel suppliers, and anticipated delivery schedules for the period for which relief is sought.
8. The current price per million Btu for natural gas supplies and alternate fuel supplies.
9. A description of efforts to secure natural gas and alternate fuels, including documentation of contacts with the Federal Energy Office and any state or local fuel allocation agencies or public utility commission.
10. A description of all fuel conservation activities undertaken in the facility for which relief is sought.
11. If petitioner is a local natural gas distributor, a description of the currently effective curtailment program and details regarding any flexibility which may be available by effectuating additional curtailment to its existing industrial customers. The distributor should also provide a breakdown of the estimated disposition of its natural gas estimated to be available by end-use priorities established [in Order 467] for the period for which relief is sought. [38 Fed. Reg. 12984.]

A petitioner indisputably bears the burden of proving special circumstances which justify exemption from operation of the curtailment plan in effect. This comports with the APA's mandate that the proponent of an order bears the burden of supporting it.

A petitioning distributor must attempt to obtain emergency relief from its supplying pipeline before petitioning the Commission for extraordinary relief, and an indirect customer may petition the FPC only through a petition by its state utility commission, distributor, or supplying pipeline. This requirement seeks to insure coordination and knowledge on all levels of the overall gas distribution system as well as to maintain continuity of the control of deliveries.

A petitioner may request various forms of relief, including total exemption of the pipeline customer from the curtailment plan's operation, entitling petitioner to its full contractual amount,[69] imposition on the pipeline of a firm minimum delivery requirement of a monthly or yearly average delivery requirement,[70] or special increase of a pipeline customer's priority.[71]

Relief may be subject to termination if the customer does not take certain action before a specified date.[72] The FPC may rule on peittions before[73] or after[74] the adoption of a curtailment plan. A provision for extraordinary relief may also be included in the proposed plan itself.[75]

The extraordinary relief procedure may be bifurcated between permanent and interim proceedings as is Commission action on curtailment plans themselves. Although formal hearing procedures are required, the Commission has allowed the filing of requests for interim extraordinary relief which are decided on the basis of the pleadings. This expedited procedure may take only a week or two.

If interim relief is granted, the pipeline will readjust its allocation and provide relief to the customer. The Commission must then commence formal procedures, generally taking a minimum of several months to reach a formal decision. If the Commission finds that the initial grant was unwarranted, it may impose a payback[76] obligation on the beneficiary of the grant. If temporary relief is denied, the petition proceeds along the arduous path of formal procedures until the Commission issues a final order disposing of the matter one way or the other.

At a regular hearing on a request for extraordinary relief, the Administrative Law Judge examines the evidence much as he would in a curtailment hearing. This evidence usually consists of market data, plus information on the special set of circumstances which petitioner faces.[77]

The following factors seem to be important in a decision whether or not to grant extraordinary relief:

1. Extent of unemployment that would result if the petitioner were curtailed according to the plan.[78]
2. Type of end use for which relief is requested. (The lower the end use on the 467-B scale, the less likely relief will be granted.)[79]
3. Availability of alternate fuel and cost of conversion.[80]
4. End product of customer's gas use.[81]
5. Effect of relief on other customers.[82]

When the FPC examines the availability of alternate fuels pursuant to a petition for extraordinary relief, the customer must demonstrate that every available option has been explored to the fullest extent, "for in these times of severe shortage all forms of energy must be allocated in the most efficient manner so as to serve the overall public interest."[83]

To insure compliance with grants of relief for a specific purpose, the Commission has stated that it would attach a payback provision to each grant, to become effective if the relief gas is used in any manner other than specified in the grant.[84] "Payback" implies that the recipient customer must take less than its normal allocation over a period of time after the emergency until it has "paid back" the volumes received. Since any grant of extraordinary relief gas must come directly from all other customers of the same priority, payback applies a rough sense of equity in providing that those who sacrifice gas should later be compensated in kind. (It is not entirely clear whether it is the distribution company which has the ultimate obligation or the final end user who obtained the gas.) Payback thus differs from "refund" in that refund involves a monetary repayment of excessive rates charged to customers by a jurisdictional pipeline.

As noted above, the commission may also require payback from a gas customer who has received relief pending hearing, and the relief granted is later found to be unwarranted. In this case, the provision seeks to prevent abuse of the interim extraordinary relief procedures.

The FPC has been quite chary in its grants of permanent extraordinary relief, although interim extraordinary relief is much easier to obtain. Perhaps due to their greater flexibility, larger distributors have found it very difficult to qualify for extraordinary relief. The task becomes easier when the requested relief involves *de minimis* volumes which can be distributed easily among the pipeline's customers.

A major criticism of FPC curtailment policies has been that the Commission's 467-B plan does not take economic factors and local impact sufficiently into account. The Commission's response has been that the appropriate place for considering such factors is in a proceeding for extraordinary relief. The reasoning is that the basic end-use plan will govern most cases rather well. If an individual consumer believes he is unduly injured by his classification, he may present his case to the Commission. Under this procedure, the customer has the burden of showing that an exception is justified in his particular circumstances. What is at stake in the extraordinary relief proceedings is the degree to which a particular user fits into the overall curtailment scheme, rather than the propriety of the scheme itself.

The extraordinary relief procedures have worked reasonably well through the summer of 1975. The number of petitions has been increasing rapidly, however. From perhaps 20 during the 1973-74 winter, the figure went to over 100 for the 1974-75 winter season. As the shortage deepens and customers realize that the gas shortage is not a temporary problem, the number of petitions is likely to increase dramatically. Officials on the FPC staff have made informal estimates that an exceptionally cold winter in the near future could trigger an avalanche of thousands of petitions. It is difficult to see how this contingency could be handled under present procedures.

The Commission reacted to the problem of mounting numbers of petitions by convening conferences of the 14 pipelines which expect curtailments of more than 20 percent during the 1975-76 season. The conferences, which were completed by mid-August of 1975, were intended to determine the expected impact of the coming winter curtailment and to explore alternatives in order to mitigate the effects. One benefit which the FPC hopes will emerge from the proceedings is some method of consolidating extraordinary relief petitions so that the administrative process will not break down under the weight of those requests. As of December 1975, it is still too early to know what impact the conferences will have.

There is one other source of flexibility in administering a 467-type plan which was quite unintended. As pointed out in Chapter Two, inherent in an end-use approach are incentives for each end user to try to upgrade his use into the highest possible category, and for distributors to do the same with their entire load. Given the monumental data verification problems involved in the program as currently administered, this tendency is likely to be pronounced. Accordingly, one must look at curtailment figures with caution. For example, when projections indicate that a pipeline will be curtailing 100 percent of Priorities 3 through 9 and 70 percent of Priority 2, one can suspect that a proportion of the customers in Priority 2 are, in fact, users which should be classified in lower priorities. It is impossible to determine the extent to which this phenomenon changes the overall picture, but its practical effect is to provide greater flexibility than first appears.

Definitional Difficulties: Orders 493 and 493-A

The successful implementation of the FPC's curtailment policy requires all parties to use common terminology.

In order to standardize the end-use classifications, the Commission issued Order No. 493 on September 21, 1973, following prior notice and substantial comment from interested parties.[85] On receiving petitions for clarification and reconsideration, the Commission issued Order 493-A on October 29, 1973, setting out the following definitions:[86]

1. *Residential.* Service to customers which consists of direct natural gas usage in a residential dwelling for space heating, air conditioning, cooking, water heating, and other residential uses.
2. *Commercial.* Service to customers engaged primarily in the sale of goods or services including institutions and local, state, and federal government agencies for uses other than those involving manufacturing or electric power generation.
3. *Industrial.* Service to customers engaged primarily in a process which

creates or changes raw or unfinished materials into another form or product including the generation of electric power.

4. *Firm service.* Service from schedules or contracts under which seller is expressly obligated to deliver specific volumes within a given time period and which anticipates no interruptions, but which may permit unexpected interruption in case the supply to higher priority customers is threatened.

5. *Interruptible service.* Service from schedules or contracts under which seller is not expressly obligated to deliver specific volumes within a given time period, and which anticipates and permits interruption on short notice, or service under schedules or contracts which expressly or impliedly require installation of alternate fuel capability.

6. *Plant protection gas.* Is defined as minimum volumes required to prevent physical harm to the plant facilities or danger to plant personnel when such protection cannot be afforded through the use of an alternate fuel. This includes the protection of such material in process as would otherwise be destroyed, but shall not include deliveries required to maintain plant production. For the purposes of this definition propane and other gaseous fuels shall not be considered alternate fuels.

7. *Feedstock gas.* Is defined as natural gas used as raw material for its chemical properties in creating an end product.

8. *Process gas.* Is defined as gas use for which alternate fuels are not technically feasible such as in applications requiring precise temperature controls and precise flame characteristics. For the purpose of this definition propane and other gaseous fuels shall not be considered alternate fuels.

9. *Boiler fuel.* Is considered to be natural gas used as a fuel for the generation of steam or electricity, including the utilization of gas turbines for the generation of electricity.

10. *Alternate fuel capabilities.* Is defined as a situation where an alternate fuel could have been utilized whether or not the facilities for such use have actually been installed; *Provided however,* where the use of natural gas is for plant protection, feedstock, or process uses and the only alternate fuel is propane or other gaseous fuel then the consumer will be treated as if he had no alternate fuel capability.

Since the definitions were the result of a general rulemaking proceeding, they have no effect on specific persons without further proceedings.[87] The Commission recognized that all particular end uses would not necessarily fit neatly into the terms as defined. Application of the definitions to the markets of particular pipelines were left to individual curtailment proceedings.[88]

Two problem areas remain, however,. First, the definitions are somewhat ambiguous. For example, process gas has been defined as gas use for which alternate fuels are not *technically* feasible. Since alternate fuels are nearly always technically feasible if enough funds are available, the definition misses the practical, economic distinction between process and other uses. (See Chapter Eight for further discussion of the difficulties involved.)

Moreover, the distribution companies are not required to use the definitions in submitting end-use data to the pipelines. In the 1975 Columbia proceeding, for example, very difficult data problems remain despite the promulgation of Orders 493 and 493-A nearly two years earlier.

PROCEDURAL ALTERNATIVES

What alternatives to existing administrative procedures does the Commission have? Given the present middle course the FPC is following, the alternatives lie in the direction of rulemaking, on the one hand, and pure adjudication, on the other.

Rulemaking

The FPC might attempt to make the Order 467 scheme a binding rule. Apparently the Commission took one step down this path when it issued Docket No. R-467 outlining the Order 467 priorities of service for new customers and requesting comment. The resulting critical comments seem to have dissuaded the Commission from proceeding further with rulemaking. If that route were attempted in the future, numerous difficulties would be encountered.

The FPC's authority to promulgate a binding rule governing curtailment priorities is open to question. This issue is discussed in Chapter Three. Since the authority to promulgate such a rule is not clear, the Commission is probably wise in avoiding that path.

Even if the Commission clearly possessed general authority to promulgate a binding rule in this area, the rule would be subject to challenge and court review as to its content. The effective date of the rule might be postponed for many months, when what the Commission seeks is to insure that each winter curtailment proceeds under some rational formula. Further, by merely issuing a policy statement, the Commission is able to give the parties notice of its preferred policy without having to explain and defend that policy in the abstract. The Commission is then on more solid ground in applying the policy in a specific case, finding support for the policy in the particular hearing record.

Similarly, a binding rule as to curtailment is very likely to be "major federal action" requiring an environmental impact statement. At present, the Commission is required to prepare a National Environmental Protection Agency (NEPA) statement for permanent curtailment plans, but not for interim plans. A single uniform curtailment rule appears much closer to a permanent plan than a mere interim plan and would probably require the NEPA statement. If a national environmental impact statement were required and subjected to litigation, this too would frustrate the Commission's objectives.

Finally, and perhaps most importantly, the Commission may simply have heeded the industry comments that a single binding regulation covering all jurisdictional pipelines was unworkable. It is difficult to see how a single 467-type plan could accommodate the great diversity among pipelines and their customers.

On the other hand, if the Commission attempted to particularize the regulations in order to make them responsive to individual differences among the pipelines, the task would rapidly become extremely complex. For example, the hearing transcript for Columbia's permanent plan alone consumed over 13,000 pages. Given the present limitations on the FPC's curtailment authority and the inherent complexity of the task before it, the rulemaking approach seems impractical.

Pure Adjudication

The FPC might go back to the Order 431 approach, which involves adjudicatory procedures alone. Under these procedures, the pipelines would have the initial responsibility for formulating a curtailment plan subject to Commission review and approval. This approach would return the FPC to a strict pipeline-by-pipeline perspective, preventing the Commison from exercising end use policy leadership in the curtailment field.

An adjudicatory procedure would, however, work in harmony with a Commission policy of encouraging negotiated settlements. Under such a policy the responsibility for dealing with curtailment would be placed on the pipelines, their distributor customers, and the large end users. The negotiated settlement plan would be submitted to the Commission as a tariff amendment under section 4. The Commission might, indeed, issue a statement of policy indicating that it would look with favor on proposed settlements. The threat of protracted adjudication would provide a substantial incentive to settlement in particular cases.

Neither pure adjudication nor negotiated settlements appear well suited to achieving the Commission's present substantive end use goals. However, the main obstacle to implementation is not lack of procedural devices, but rather lack of sufficient statutory jurisdiction.

Thus, there are two basic alternatives to the present FPC approach of adjudication coupled with a strong preference for its own set of end use priorities. The Commission might give up its present goal of implementing a uniform nationwide approach to curtailments and merely approve or disapprove curtailment plans as they are presented. Alternatively, the Commission might ask for new legislation which would be better adapted to the realities of curtailment, and which would provide adequate jurisdictional authority and procedural paths tailored to the problem of managing the gas shortage.

CONCLUSION

The FPC has been wrestling with the natural gas shortage and the accompanying problem of curtailment since 1970. The first policy statement on curtailment, Order 431, gave the initiative for formulating curtailment plans to the interstate pipelines. The procedural mode was adjudication following formal hearings, as mandated by sections 4 and 5 of the Natural Gas Act and relevant portions of the Administrative Procedure Act.

Procedures designed primarily for rate-making proved to be ill-suited to the formulation of a national curtailment policy. The Commission was placed in a passive role, unable to implement its own ideas as to the proper way to proceed. As those ideas became firmer, the Commission changed course by issuing Order 467's set of end-use priorities. A general statement of policy, the Order was unreviewable in the courts. Yet, by establishing such "guidelines" and treating them as more than merely advisory, the Commission attempted to move toward a more uniform national approach to curtailment, based on the nine priorities established.

The FPC's curtailment procedure is a hybrid. It lies somewhere in the region between adjudication and rulemaking, though considerably closer to the former than the latter. The Commission did not exceed its powers, but rather adapted to its present needs procedures originally designed for other purposes.

As of December 1975, the Commission's procedures have passed muster in the courts. The D.C. Circuit has rejected a claim that Order 467 in fact constitutes a binding substantive rule, as well as the assertion that the pipelines were being coerced into filing 467-type plans. The court will allow the Commission to continue its policy of pressuring the pipelines to file plans conforming to Order 467, so long as that pressure does not rise to the level of "coercion."

Have the procedures ultimately adopted by the FPC been effective in helping the Commission to implement its end use policies for dealing with the shortage? In this respect, the FPC has faced three main difficulties.

First, the procedural paths established for the Commission by the Gas Act (and the APA) are simply inadequate to the task of allocating a scarce good such as natural gas. The adjudication proceedings are time-consuming and subject to lengthy court appeals. The situation existing at the time a curtailment plan is declared just and reasonable by the Commission may differ considerably from the circumstances at the time when the necessary data were gathered and the plan developed.

A number of persons with experience in curtailment hearings have expressed serious doubts as to whether the dynamic situation will ever permit most pipelines to implement permanent plans. This problem is inherent in the use of formal adjudicatory proceedings permitting written and oral presentations and cross-examination.

The problem is made more difficult, however, by the Commission's emphasis on end use. This approach requires extensive data-gathering and involves complex questions of data consistency and verification which are difficult to resolve in an adjudicatory hearing. Were the Commission's preferred policy basically one of favoring settlements, or even pro rata sharing of the shortfall, these data problems could be avoided, thus simplifying the hearing proceeding immensely. However, such a change in FPC policy might mean merely shifting this aspect of the hearings to another administrative proceeding at the state level.[89] The basic point, however, is that an end use approach to curtailment necessarily requires more lengthy hearings and more complex factual presentations than a pro rata plan.

Secondly, and from a broader perspective, the FPC's procedural problems are compounded by the limited jurisdiction the Commission exercises under the Natural Gas Act. On the one hand the Commission is unable to compel all gas users to submit the information necessary to determine end use profiles of the distribution companies. Yet even where the information is finally obtained and verified, the Commission is unable to compel the various distribution companies to apply the same priorities in servicing the final end-users. This tends to make the hearing procedures somewhat irrelevant.

The use of binding rulemaking, instead of adjudication, might help cut down on delay by narrowing the issues in dispute in a curtailment proceeding. Yet the FPC's authority to promulgate such a rule is debatable. Even if the authority to proceed in this way is found to exist, serious difficulties would remain in formulating a single rule with sufficient adaptability to particular curtailment situations.

Third, and at the most basic level, the FPC's procedures appear inadequate for what are essentially political reasons. In allocating a scarce good at a great deal less than the market-clearing price, any foundation of objectivity melts away. Particularly where the allocation is done on the basis of end use, the question becomes subjective: who should receive how much and under what circumstances? That question falls within the classic definition of politics—who gets what, when, and how? Formal adjudicatory procedures before an independent regulatory agency are not well suited to the resolution of such hard political questions.

NOTES TO CHAPTER FOUR

1. With respect to rate increases, see the discussion of Opinion 699 in Chapter Three. As to advance payments, see Order 499, 50 F.P.C. 2111, 39 Fed. Reg. 1262.

2. Order 402, 43 F.P.C. 707, 35 Fed. Reg. 7511, Order 402–A 43 F.P.C. 822, 35 Fed. Reg. 8927.

3. Order 418, 44 F.P.C. 1574, 35 Fed. Reg. 19173. The policy also covered emergency exchanges of gas between pipelines for the same period.

4. *See* Order 491, 50 F.P.C. 742, 38 Fed. Reg. 26603. About 385 Bcf came from the 60-day sales, while the remainder were made under limited term certificates. Prices ranged from 35 to 54 cents/Mcf. *See* Order 491–A, 50 F.P.C. 848, 38 Fed. Reg. 27606.

5. Order 491, 50 F.P.C. 742, 38 Fed. Reg. 26603. Such an extension had been suggested in several of the industry comments submitted prior to the issuance of Order 418. The Commission's attitude toward public notice of and participation in these decisions has been rather casual. Orders 402 and 402–A were issued without notice or any opportunity to comment. Order 418, how-ever, was the result of informal rulemaking procedures, allowing for public comment. Order 491 was issued as a statement of policy without prior notice, to be effective on issuance. On receipt of a number of petitions for rehearing, the Commission, while maintaining that notice and comment was not required, invited such comments. See Order 491–A, 50 F.P.C. 848, 38 Fed. Reg. 27606. The Commission responded to comments in Order 491–B, 50 F.P.C. 1463, 38 Fed. Reg. 31289, and denied motions for rehearing and a stay in Order 491–C, 50 F.P.C. 1634, 38 Fed. Reg. 32785.

6. Order 491–D, 51 F.P.C. 1139, 39 Fed. Reg. 8332. The termination date was 180 days after the initiation of the program by Order 491. Approximately 172 Bcf of gas was sold to interstate pipelines under the 180-day program. The average price was about 54¢ per Mcf.

7. Consumer Federation of America v. FPC, 515 F.2d 347 (D.C. Cir. (1975), *cert. denied,* 44 USLW 3225 (1975).

8. *Id.* at 360.

9. Order 533, 54 F.P.C. __ , 40 Fed. Reg. 41760. The Commission stated in footnote 8 that the Order was adopted under the Commission's "general power of rulemaking set forth in Section 553 of the APA and Section 16 of the Natural Gas Act," and accordingly did not require the notice and comment procedures which the Commission nonetheless chose to follow. As was pointed out in Chapter Three, the scope of the Commission's rulemaking authority has not yet been fully defined by the courts. While upholding the Commission's power to make binding rules in some circumstances, the courts have yet to hold that the Commission is endowed with "general" rulemaking authority.

10. On October 23, 1975, the Commission approved the first direct sale under Order 533 made to the Dan River Mills. The certificated sale price was $1.50/Mcf, nearly three times the current FPC national rate. As of October 24, 5 more applications were pending, and more were expected due to the Com-mission's favorable action in the Dan River Mills case. See "Mill Wins Right to Buy Natural Gas," *Washington Post* (October 24, 1975), p. A-1.

11. The delivery provisions are quite complex. Typically contract deliveries are computed by a formula based in part on a percentage of the producers' reserves.

12. *See* "FPC Aides Unsure on Natural Gas Delivery Data," *N.Y. Times,* Oct. 25, 1975, at 39. If the contention is that the shortage derives from the fact the producers have been unable to meet expected production schedules, it is a commonplace. If the accusation is rather that the producers have deliber-ately failed to meet the contracts in an attempt to artificially create a shortage, it appears only weakly supported by evidence.

13. Order 539, 54 F.P.C. __, 40 Fed. Reg. 49571.

14. Order 539, 40 Fed. Reg. 49571, 49572. The Commission explained in footnote 2 why it believed this assertion of authority was not blocked by the production and gathering exemption in section 1(b) of the Natural Gas Act.

15. Order 539, 40 Fed. Reg. 49571, 49572.

Natural gas pipeline companies and natural gas producers have obligations arising from the Natural Gas Act with respect to, *inter alia,* deliverability and receipt of certificated volumes of natural gas supplies, violation of which obligations will subject either to the sanction and/or penalty provisions of that Act. While this Commission is charged with responsibility for the administration of the Natural Gas Act, regulated pipelines and producers have affirmative obligations to enforce delivery of certificated volumes of natural gas supplies by reason of the requirements of that Act.

If in fact pipelines have an "affirmative obligation," then presumably a distribution company could sue the supplying pipeline for the pipeline's failure to meet its own obligation by suing the producer.

16. Section 1.6 reads

Any person, including any State or local commisson, complaining of anything done or omitted to be done by any . . . . natural gas company in contravention of an administrative rule, regulation or order administered or issued by the Commission, may file a complaint with the Commission [18 C.F.R. § 1.6 (1975)].

17. Order 539, 40 Fed. Reg. 49571, 49572.

18. United Gas Pipe Line Company, Opinion No. 647, 49 F.P.C. 179, 98 P.U.R. 3d 158, 162.

19. 35 Fed. Reg. 17428 (1970).

20. Order 431, 45 F.P.C. 570, 36 Fed. Reg. 7505.

21. *Id.* at 572.

22. For a summary of the pipelines' initial proposals under Order 431, see *Hearings on Federal Power Commission Oversight—Natural Gas Curtailment Priorities Before the Senate Comm. on Commerce* 93d Cong., 2d Sess., pt. 2, at 640-643 (1974).

23. Jerome C. Muys, *Federal Power Commission Allocation of Natural Gas Supply Shortages: Prorationing, Priorities and Perplexity,* 20 Rocky Mtn. M.L. Inst. 301 (1975).

24. Use of interim plans was upheld by the D.C. Circuit in *American Smelting and Refining Co. v. FPC,* 494 F.2d 925 (D.C. Cir. 1974).

25. *See, e.g.,* R.I. Consumers' Council v. FPC, 504 F.2d 203 (D.C. Cir. 1974).

26. State of Louisiana v. FPC, 503 F.2d 844 (5th Cir. 1974). This view may not be completely shared by the judges on the D.C. Circuit. *See* Consolidated

Edison Company of New York Inc. v. FPC, 511 F.2d 1332, 1346, *rehearing granted,* 518 F.2d 448 (D.C. Cir. 1975).

27. State of Louisiana v. FPC, 503 F.2d 844, 861. *See also* Consolidated Edison Company of New York Inc. v. FPC *order continuing stay,* 511 F.2d 372, 382 (D.C. Cir. 1974), 512 F.2d 1332, *rehearing granted,* 518 F.2d 448 (D.C. Cir. 1975).

28. United Gas Pipe Line Co. Opinion No. 606, 46 F.P.C. 786, 91 P.U.R. 3d 247.

29. El Paso Natural Gas Company, Opinion No. 634, 48 F.P.C. 931, 97 P.U.R. 3d 102.

30. *Id.* at 935.

31. *Id.* at 939.

32. *Id.* Opinion 634 was reviewed by the D.C. Circuit in American Smelting and Refining Co. v. FPC, 494 F.2d 925 (D.C. Cir. 1974). The Court upheld the Commission's reliance on end-use in general, but found the decision to place boiler fuel use in the lowest priorities was not supported by substantial evidence in the hearing record. The case was remanded on that issue.

33. 49 F.P.C. 85, 38 Fed. Reg. 1503.

34. 5 U.S.C. § 553(b) (1970).

35. Order No. 467-B (DKT No. R-469), 49 F.P.C. 583, 38 Fed. Reg. 6384.

36. 38 Fed. Reg. 1503.

37. *Id.*

38. Arkansas-Louisiana Gas Company, Opinion No. 643, 49 F.P.C. 53, 97 P.U.R. 3d 417, 428.

39. *Id.*

40. Order No. 467, *supra* note 33, at 1504.

41. *Id.*

42. State of Louisiana v. FPC, *supra* note 26, at 861.

43. 38 Fed. Reg. 1517, 1519 (1973).

44. *Id.*

45. *Id.*

46. On rehearing, however, the Commission made clear that it was not relying on Order 467 at all in prescribing the plan for Arkla. *See* 49 F.P.C., at 910.

47. Order 467-B, *supra* note 35, at 6385.

48. *Id.*

49. *Id.*

50. *Id.* The priorities are now codified in 18 C.F.R. § 2.78(a) (1975).

51. On review of Opinion 643, the D.C. Circuit found the firm-interruptible distinction unsupported by substantial evidence. Arkansas Power and Light Co. v. FPC, 517 F.2d 1223 (D.C. Cir. 1975). The Commission's assignment of high priority to gas for storage injection was also held without sufficient record support. A remand was ordered. A similar conclusion was reached by the Fifth Circuit on review of Opinion 647 in the *United* proceeding. See State of Louisiana v. FPC, 503 F.2d 844 (5th Cir. 1974). Again, the case was remanded to the Commission.

52. 38 Fed. Reg. 6384.

53. Consolidated Edison Co. of New York v. FPC, 512 F.2d 1332, 1340, (D.C. Cir. 1975).

54. See Pacific Gas and Electric Co. v. FPC, 506 F.2d 33 (D.C. Cir. 1974).

55. Consolidated Edison Company of New York, Inc. v. FPC, 511 F.2d 372, 377 (D.C. Cir. 1974).

56. 506 F.2d 33 (D.C. Cir. 1974).

57. For cases reviewing the sufficiency of the evidence in Opinions 643 and 647, see *supra* note 51.

58. Pacific Gas and Electric Co. v. FPC. *supra* note 54, at 38. This view has received the support of the Fifth Circuit Court of Appeals as well in State of Louisiana v. FPC, *supra* note 26, at 861.

59. *Id.*, at 41.

60. 511 F.2d 372 (D.C. Cir. 1974).

61. *Id.* at 377.

62. *Id.*

63. Consolidated Edison Company of New York Inc. v. FPC, 512 F.2d 1332, 1341.

64. *Id.*

65. *Id.* at 1342.

66. Consolidated Edison Co. v. FPC, 518 F.2d 448, 449 (D.C. Cir. 1975).

67. Order 467-A, 49 F.P.C. 217, 38 Fed. Reg. 2170.

68. Order 467-C 51 F.P.C. 1199, 39 Fed. Reg. 12984.

69. El Paso Natural Gas Co. Opinion 697, 51 F.P.C. 2053, 5 P.U.R. 4th 157, 177 (1974).

70. Texas Gulf Inc. v. FPC, 494 F.2d 789, 790 (5th Cir. 1974).

71. Panhandle Eastern Pipe Line Co., FPC News Release No. 21072, January 27, 1975.

72. *See* Texas Eastern Corp. FPC DKT # RP 74-39-8 Order Granting Extra-ordinary Relief, issued February 26, 1975.

73. *See* Texas Eastern Corp. Opinion 716 52 F.P.C. __, 8 P.U.R. 4th 195.

74. Texas Gulf, Inc. v. FPC, *supra* note 70, at 789.

75. El Paso Natural Gas Co., *supra* note 69.

76. A "payback" obligation requires the recipient of additional gas to cut back its consumption after the emergency, making available more gas to other customers, and thus paying them back. Payback is discussed in greater detail *infra*.

77. See, e.g., Texas Eastern Corp. FPC DKT # RP 74-39-8. Order granting extraordinary relief, mimeo at 2-7, issued February 26, 1975.

78. Texas Eastern Corp. Opinion 715, 52 FPC __, 3 Util. L. Rep ¶ 11,608.

79. Texas Eastern Corp., *supra* note 73.

80. Texas Eastern Corp., *supra* note 72.

81. Prior to February 26, 1975, the FPC disavowed any consideration of end product in ruling or requests for relief. See, for example, Texas Eastern Corp. *supra* note 73. Still, the pattern of approval indicated some reliance on end product. On February 26, 1975, however, FPC ruled in favor of a relief petitioner, and noted that it expressly considered the end product of the gas (in this case, amonia for fertilizer). Texas Eastern Corp., *supra* note 72.

82. Texas Eastern Corp., *supra* note 73.

83. Texas Eastern Corp., Opinion 716-A, 53 F.P.C. __, 3 Util L. Rep. ¶ 11,629, at p. 12,801.

84. Order 467-C, *supra* note 68.

85. Order 493, 50 F.P.C. 831, 38 Fed. Reg. 27351.

86. Order 493-A, 50 F.P.C. 1316, 38 Fed. Reg. 30432.

87. *Id.*

88. *Id.*

89. Even so, it may be that a proceeding at the state level, with fewer parties and less diverse issues might be more efficient. For example, while the FPC hearings alone on permanent plan for the Columbia system lasted over a year, the concurrent proceedings before the West Virginia Utilities Commission were completed in about six months.

✳ *Chapter Five*

Petroleum Industry Description

The United States petroleum industry involves complex interrelationships among many different firms. Depending on one's purposes, these firms may be categorized as: (a) suppliers and purchasers; (b) producers, refiners, and marketers; or (c) "majors" and "independents." This chapter describes the industry in order to provide insight into how government controls on distribution of petroleum products affect and are affected by the industry's structure and operations.[1]

U.S. OIL SUPPLY VULNERABILITY

Petroleum supplied the U.S. with 45 percent of its fuel needs in 1972. Total petroleum demand had been rising sharply until the Arab oil embargo, the quadrupling of the OPEC oil price, and deep economic recession checked the increase in 1973 and 1974. Domestic petroleum demand rose from 16.4 million barrels per day (MMB/D) in 1972 to 17.3 MMB/D in 1973. Demand declined in 1974 to 16.6 MMD/D.[2] By spring 1975, when seasonal demand is low, total demand was down to 15.6 MMB/D.[3]

In 1972 the Chase Manhattan Bank had predicted that oil demand would grow from 14.7 MMB/D in 1970 to 26.3 MMB/D in 1985, assuming there were no limits on the future supply of natural gas. However, the projected shortage of natural gas was expected to push oil demand to 30.2 MMB/D in 1985.[4] More recently, in 1975 the President's State of the Union message predicted that demand in 1975 would reach 18.0 MMB/D, 18.3 MMB/D in 1977, and 23.9 MMB/D in 1985, if no new actions are taken to restrain demand.[5]

The U.S. Geological Survey has estimated there are only 52 billion barrels of known recoverable domestic petroleum reserves. This figure represents less than a 10-year supply at 1972 levels of production.[6] In the spring of 1975, the Geological Survey revised its estimates downward to 34.25 billion barrels in known reserves, a possible 30 billion barrels in unexplored parts of known reserves, and 61 to 149 billion barrels yet undiscovered. At the same time, estimates of natural gas reserves were also adjusted downward.[7]

Total domestic production, which includes crude oil, lease condensate, and natural gas liquids, declined from 11.2 MMB/D in 1972 to 10.9 MMB/D in 1973 and 10.5 MMB/D in 1974.[8] In early 1975, domestic production continued to decline.[9] During the same period, imports of crude oil and refined products grew from 4.5 MMB/D in 1972, to 6.2 MMB/D in 1973, although falling slightly to 6.1 MMB/D in 1974. Imports in 1974 consisted of 3.5 MMB/D of crude and 2.6 MMB/D of refined petroleum products.[10]

During the first two months of 1975, crude oil imports hovered around 4.0 MMB/D, but fell shortly thereafter to 3.3 MMB/D in April. Similarly, refined product imports dropped to 1.8 MMB/D in April 1975. Nevertheless, total imports during the first four months of 1975 were 8 percent above the corresponding period in 1974, though they were 4 percent below 1973 levels.[11]

Crude oil imports equalled 32.2 percent of domestic refinery input in November 1974. This was up from 29.3 percent in October 1973, which was just before the Arab embargo, but the percentage fell in April 1975. Imports of refined products in November 1974 covered 17.6 percent of demand. Altogether imports were covering about 40.0 percent of total domestic demand for petroleum products in early 1975.[12]

The largest supplier of U.S. petroleum imports during 1974 was Canada (389 million barrels), followed by Venezuela and Nigeria (357 and 260 million barrels, respectively). Middle Eastern nations provided 378 million barrels. More recent data show that Arab countries supplied 21 percent of crude oil imports in April 1975, down from 27 percent during the fourth quarter of 1974. Major sources of crude oil imports in April 1975 were Nigeria (18 percent), Canada (14 percent), Venezuela (14 percent), Iran (9 percent), and Indonesia (9 percent).[13]

In the near future, U.S. dependence on supplies of crude oil imported directly from the Arab countries and on refined products derived from Arabian crude can only increase. The President's 1975 State of the Union message predicted that imports would average 6.5 MMB/D in 1975, and rise to 8.0 MMB/D in 1977. Absent any change in policy, imports were expected to rise to 12.7 MMB/D in 1985.[14] While total U.S. imports are likely to increase, Canada is cutting back on exports to the U.S. and currently plans to phase them out by 1981. Venezuela is not expected to increase, and may indeed reduce current export levels to the U.S. The only other major U.S. suppliers are Eastern Hemisphere nations, primarily Arab countries and Nigeria.

PRODUCTION AND DISTRIBUTION

There are five major steps from discovery to final sale in the petroleum industry. Although the dividing lines between the levels are often unclear, they include exploration and drilling, production, transportation, refining, and marketing.[15] There are two primary classes of petroleum firms. A "major" oil company is a firm which engages actively in most phases of the industry on a large scale at a near-national level. Some analysts divide majors into "integrated" and "semi-integrated" ("semi-major"), depending on the range of national distribution.[16] The major companies are more or less heavily involved in international operations. Worldwide, the seven largest integrated oil companies (Exxon, Gulf, Mobil, Texaco, Socal/Chevron, Shell, and BP) are generally referred to as the majors. Within the U.S. market, the 15 largest integrated companies are now generally considered as the majors. In addition to the above companies (minus BP), this includes Amoco, Atlantic Richfield, Cities Service, Continental, Getty/Skelly, Marathon, Phillips, Sun, and Union Oil of California.

An "independent" oil company participates in one or more, but not all, levels of the industry, leaving the other levels to majors or other independents. Originally, an independent was any company not affiliated with Standard Oil. Now independent has become something of a misnomer, since companies in this group are dependent on others for supplies or marketing outlets.

Exploration, Drilling, and Production

Almost all extensive pre-drilling exploration work is done by majors. However, independent producers drill 89 percent of wildcat wells and three-fourths of the exploratory wells in new fields.[17] A large amount of the drilling by independents is the result of lease acquisition from brokers, drilling deals, and farm-outs by majors. Most independent operators owning drilling rigs function primarily as drilling contractors for majors.[18]

The number of independent producers has declined from 20,000 to 10,000 during the last 15 years.[19] While the independents' share of discoveries is proportional to their share of drilling, most of the oil they discover remains the property of the 20 largest companies, which accounted for 68.3 percent of domestic production in 1971, up from 46.2 percent in 1955. Those same 20 companies own 93.5 percent of known domestic crude oil reserves.[20]

An oil well goes through several phases during its producing life—flush, settled, stripper, and secondary recovery.[21] The Emergency Petroleum Allocation Act (EPAA) creates four categories of domestic oil: old, new, released, and stripper. Old oil is subject to federal price controls, while new, released, and stripper oil are free of such controls.

1. "Old oil" is basically a residual category of all domestically produced oil that is not new, released or stripper.

2. "New oil" is oil produced from property first brought into production in 1973 or thereafter, and also oil produced from previously producing property in excess of the amount produced there in 1972.
3. "Released oil" is oil that would otherwise be classified as old oil, but it is released from price controls in an amount equal to new oil. Released oil provides an incentive for existing producers to develop new fields and increase production in old fields.
4. "Stripper oil" is oil produced from properties which produce less than 10 barrels per well per day. Of total current domestic production, 60 percent is old oil, 16 percent new oil, 11 percent released oil, and 13 percent stripper oil.[22]

Transportation

Large producing wells are often connected directly to transcontinental pipelines. Owners of smaller wells, or even large ones in areas without other wells, often sell to transportation companies which purchase the crude oil and then resell it to refiners. There are many independent pipeline companies gathering crude. However, 70.2 percent of the independent producers' sales were to the top 20 majors, who controlled 69.8 percent of the gathering lines used to collect oil from independents. In areas where the amount of oil production does not justify a gathering system, the oil is shipped by truck to the closest pipelines.[23]

Currently, pipelines transport 75 percent of all crude oil received by U.S. refineries from both domestic and foreign sources, including imports from Canada. Tankers and barges account for 24 percent and railroads and trucks for 1 percent. Of course, domestically produced oil is transported mainly by pipeline.

Some interstate crude oil pipelines are common carriers which are regulated by the Interstate Commerce Commission. These pipelines, which receive the oil from gathering systems, trucks, or tankers, charge a fee for transportation and never acquire title to the oil. Legally, they cannot discriminate among producers.[24]

Refining

Operating refineries require a constant flow of crude oil. They cannot stop production of one product and substitute another. As demand changes seasonally, however, adjustments are made in product yields and storage.[25]

Crude oils differ in their relative content of component fractions and types of hydrocarbons. Therefore, their yield of raw products also varies. Many refineries cannot process all types of crude, and older refineries begin to lose their capability to adjust product yields. If the yield is adjusted, other products made from that fraction must also be altered. For example, kerosene-based jet fuel and kerosene are made from similar fractions.

In U.S. refining operations as a whole, the product yield of gasoline from crude increased from 40.5 percent in 1945 to 46.2 percent in 1971. Distillate fuels rose from 19.1 percent to 29.4 percent, while residual fuel oil decreased from 27.2 percent to 6.7 percent.[26] The decline in residual fuel oil yield in U.S. refineries was largely due to the increase in imports of refined residual oil, making domestic production less desirable.

In the U.S., there are approximately 275 refineries,[27] owned by approximately 129 companies. Independent refiners do not control their own supply of crude (upstream integration), but some are integrated downstream, with their own marketing outlets. By one definition, there are 18 integrated refiners in the U.S., with an average refinery size of 100 thousand barrels/day (MB/D), and average total company capacity of 540 MB/D. The average size of an independently owned refinery is 20 MB/D and average independent company capacity is 29 MB/D. Integrated companies usually operate several refineries, while most independents have only one.[28]

The EPAA defines "small refiners" as those whose total company capacity does not exceed 175 MB/D. "Independent refiners" are defined as those controlling less than 70 percent of their crude oil supply and selling a substantial portion of their output to branded or nonbranded independent marketers.[29] In terms of total domestic refinery capacity, 5.9 percent is accounted for by companies with capacities less than 30 MB/D, 6.0 percent by companies in the 30-75 MB/D range, 7.6 percent in the 75-175 MB/D range, and 80.5 percent in the over 175 MB/D range.[30] The integrated companies processed 77.9 percent of crude oil refined in the U.S. during 1972.[31]

In building refineries in the past, cost-price projections were generally based on the expectation of operating a new refinery at 70 to 80 percent of capacity. Since refinery capacity is added in large increments, some excess capacity is inherent as the petroleum industry expands. Refining over the minimum 70-80 percent levels is profitable if the sales price for refined products only covers the marginal costs of production. This phenomenon has been a major factor contributing to the existence of the "spot" market, described below, and to the economic viability of independent marketers.[32] Other factors were the availability of crude oil and refined product imports at prices that were lower than domestic prices and the need for spare refining capacity within the industry in case of breakdowns.

Prior to the Arab oil embargo, U.S. refineries were operating at an average of 95 percent of capacity, due largely to the lack of new domestic refinery construction between 1969 and 1973. During the embargo, that percentage dropped substantially, but it climbed back to an average of 80 percent from March to June 1975.[33]

There are various types of refineries. Some are skimming (topping) plants that produce only one or two cuts of light distillate and residual fuel oil. Some are cracking plants, while others are complete refineries producing a full range of petroleum products. Because crude oils vary in their yields of raw products and their component fractions, each refinery must be equipped to refine its own supply in a manner which produces the greatest profit. It is cheaper to build a refinery that can only process certain types of crudes or can only refine some products than it is to build a refinery with maximum flexibility as to crude input and product output.[34] Studies indicate that roughly defined economies of scale for refinery size probably exist, but multiplant operations are probably not more efficient than single plants.[35]

Wholesale Marketing

After crude oil is refined, the resulting products are placed in storage tanks at the refinery. The major capacity of a company for storing supplies of finished products usually exists only at the refinery. Sometimes these refinery storage facilities are called terminals, but more often, the term "bulk terminal" (or "bulk plant") refers to the facilities receiving product from the refinery after shipment.

After leaving refinery storage, the product may be shipped by pipeline (45 percent), tanker (25 percent), barge, or tank truck and tank car (30 percent) to distribution terminals located in marketing areas. Terminals must be continually re-supplied, since they have storage sufficient only for their own working supplies.

There are approximately 30,000 companies operating bulk terminals or bulk plants. These are usually referred to as "wholesale distribution," intermediate distribution, or "bulk plant operations." Although the difference between bulk terminals and bulk plants is not always clearly defined, bulk plants are generally smaller facilities than terminals. This level of intermediate distribution is largely controlled by the integrated companies. Nevertheless, these terminals are not necessarily owned by the refiners.

Bulk terminals and plants sell their products in various ways, depending on the particular product.[36] Motor gasoline, middle distillate, non-utility residual oils, aviation fuel for private aviation, and propane each have large numbers of suppliers and purchasers. Butane, residual fuel oil for utilities and shipping, aviation fuel for civil air carriers, and petrochemical supplies have relatively few suppliers and purchasers.[37]

Before reaching the terminals, refined products are not differentiated by brand. The various products are, however, separately owned as they move in batches or slugs through the pipeline. Additives, which distinguish products between companies, are often added at the bulk terminal.

Bulk terminals make some direct sales to large consumers, but most of their products are sold for resale. Direct sales are made to large quantity purchasers such as commercial customers, government accounts, public utilities, transportation companies, and manufacturing plants and factories. Resellers who purchase from bulk terminals also make direct sales and sales for resale, largely depending on the particular refined product being sold.

Bulk terminals which are owned by refiners may sell their products to branded retail outlets without any further intermediaries. They may also make sales to distributors, known as wholesale dealers or jobbers. Distributors may operate under the brand name of the supplier, under their own brand name, or without a brand name. In general, branded distributors make sales to branded retail outlets, while unbranded distributors serve unbranded stations.[38]

Various transportation modes are used to carry refined products among these suppliers and from suppliers to consumers. Pipelines are ordinarily in use almost 100 percent of the time. A three- to six-month lead time is necessary for scheduling product shipments, although currently some excess capacity exists. Coordination among suppliers and their storage facilities is complex. Railroads are used where possible to extend pipeline systems to reach terminals. Truck transportation to terminals is limited to emergencies and short distances because trucks have limited speed and capacity. Water transport by barge or tanker is relatively cheap, but it is also the slowest means for moving refined products.[39]

These factors in combination mean that short-term reallocations of petroleum products in order to handle spot shortages is often difficult. Product exchanges may be the most practical alternative for getting products quickly to regions far from available suppliers. Such exchanges are accomplished by agreements between oil companies: one company may supply another with product in one region and a compensatory exchange may be made in another region. Exchanges are usually on a barter basis, sometimes with cash supplements.[40]

Terminals usually have storage capacity for at least 25,000 barrels or more than 1,000,000 gallons (42 gallons per barrel). Bulk plants, which are used by other wholesalers for storage, hold 10,000 gallons or more. From the storage facilities of the terminal bulk plant, or distributor, further distribution can be made by transport truck (6,000 gallons) or tank wagons (1,500 gallons).[41]

Aside from the wholesale distribution structure for petroleum products discussed above, there also exists a cargo wholesale market. This market is sometimes referred to as "Platt's cargo posting," but it is more generally known as the "spot market." The cargo market is supplied by independent refiners which do not have their own retail sales outlets and by majors and semi-majors with surplus refinery capacity. The market varies in size and price, depending largely on the extent of surplus refining capacity.[42] If the cargo market were to dry up permanently, the historical distribution pattern within the petroleum industry would be significantly altered.

Although some integrated companies purchase on the cargo market in order to cover for refinery closings and other emergencies, the majority of the products in this market eventually go to independent marketers. When an independent refiner sells his product on the cargo market or an integrated refiner sells his surplus, either a broker or independent distributor buys it and, thereafter, resells the product to service stations, commercial accounts, or other distributors. Sales can be made on a fixed "contractual" or indefinite "term" basis, usually covering an extended period of time with clauses providing for price escalation or renegotiation. A second type of transaction covers "spot" sales for a fixed number of cargoes over a very limited time span. This is the most volatile sector of the cargo market. In the past, the frequent availability of cheap products attracted many unbranded independent marketers.[43]

During the Arab oil embargo, the cargo market disappeared in the U.S. By 1975 it had not yet fully recovered. In the future, a substantially reduced rate of growth in demand may reduce surplus refinery capacity, thereby constricting the amount of petroleum products available on the cargo market. Thus far, basic changes in the distribution pattern since the embargo have been largely prevented by the supplier/purchaser freeze imposed by the FEA under the EPAA. (The freeze is discussed in Chapter Six.) Without the supplier/purchaser freeze and the existence of the cargo market, independent marketers would be unable to obtain supplies during even mild shortages, and perhaps at any time if the majors were able to continue their historical competitive practices.

Retail Marketing

Retail motor gasoline outlets may be categorized along several different lines. The EPAA creates three labels: (a) stations owned and operated by "branded majors" who also operate refineries; (b) "branded independent marketers" who contract with refiners to use their trademark or occupy their premises; and (c) "nonbranded independent marketers" who are not controlled by or affiliated with a refiner.[44] However, in describing the retail gasoline market structure, many of the older studies use terms such as integrated, semi-integrated, and unbranded independents.[45]

One study concludes there are 17 major vertically integrated marketers (e.g., Exxon), approximately 24 smaller integrated marketers (e.g., Fina), and an indefinite number of nonintegrated or partly-integrated independent marketers.[46] The Federal Trade Commission found that in 1973 major brand gasoline accounted for 69.9 percent of sales, semi-integrated brands for 12.1 percent and unbranded independents for 18.0 percent.[47]

Only about 7 percent of the retail gasoline stations in the U.S. are true nonbranded independents. Of the major branded stations, 90 percent are branded independents, who own or lease the station, and the remaining 10 percent are branded stations directly operated by the integrated companies. Unbranded independent stations are usually much larger volume gasoline sellers than branded stations.[48]

Historically, company-operated gasoline stations were relatively unprofitable for the majors. Accordingly, the majors were anxious to develop their retail distribution systems in ways whereby they would not be dependent on the station itself generating profits. It was profitable for a major to build and lease gasoline stations to branded independent operators because the rent was fixed, the capital investment was not risky, and the stations paid the major a fixed fee per gallon. Thus, sales volume largely determined the major's retail profits. Recently, however, the majors have been attempting to make greater profits per gallon sold at the retail level.[49]

Retail gasoline stations were relatively unprofitable for the majors for several reasons. Most often, majors selected expensive locations, such as corner property. They invested heavily in the station, building large and elaborate facilities. The operators of these stations planned to make most of their profits from repair and service work, rather than product sales. In the past, profits from the former subsidized losses on the latter. Finally, the companies owning these stations usually did not purchase on the spot market at lower prices, and consequently they had higher costs.

Many experts on the petroleum industry believe that non-branded independent gasoline stations offer most of the competition at the retail level. The non-branded independents are credited with lower prices and also more innovation (e.g., the creation of the self-service station in 1947). Independents operate as sole proprietorships or more frequently in chains, obtaining gasoline supplies on the spot market from independent refiners or semi-majors. While historically majors were often reluctant to deal directly with independent retailers, they were more willing to sell to semi-majors who could then sell more of their own gasoline to independents. While semi-majors sell only slightly cheaper retail gasoline than majors and offer the majors little competition of their own, they do enable independents to remain more competitive.[50]

To a degree the non-branded independents are really quite dependent on the major oil companies. In the past, the relationships between independents and majors were mutually beneficial. In the future, independents will be forced to rely more and more on majors to obtain supplies, while the majors will have little to gain from such sales. Prior to the embargo, Congress was constantly receiving testimony about efforts by majors to favor their own outlets to the detriment of independents. If the independents were forced out of the retail gasoline market, the reduction in competition would probably result in higher retail prices and profits, less significant marketing innovation, and perhaps a decline in overall industry efficiency.[51]

Aside from motor gasoline, other petroleum products with a large number of suppliers and purchasers have roughly similar distribution systems. However, the emphasis on particular levels may be different.

Liquified petroleum gas (LPG), which includes propane, butane, and a variety of other products, is produced by both oil refineries and natural gas processing plants. Approximately 32 percent of domestic propane is refined from crude oil, while the remainder is derived from natural gas.[52]

Middle distillates include kerosene, No. 1 and No. 2D diesel fuel, and No. 1 and No. 2 heating oil. Kerosene is refined somewhat differently from gasoline, since it must burn without smoke and is not used as a motor fuel. Because most kerosene is used for mixing with other refined products to decrease their viscosity, most sales are direct, large-volume transactions. However, kerosene used for home and space heating is sold in much the same manner as motor gasoline.[53]

A wide range of fuels may be classified as diesel. However, engine modifications designed to reduce exhaust emissions are likely to narrow the range of fuel specifications in the future.[54] This may be important for refinery yield regulation. More than 50 percent of all diesel fuel is sold directly to large end-users. The rest is sold through jobbers, distributors, and truck stops, much like motor gasoline.[55]

The designation for most domestic and commercial space heating oils is No. 2 fuel oil. These oils are subject to a variety of technical requirements in order to be suitable for particular uses in certain climates.[56] Major brands account for only 25 percent of market sales, primarily in large cities. The remainder is sold through bulk plants, distributors, and jobbers, many of whom operate fleets of home delivery trucks.[57] The difficulty of coordinating heating oil shipments with the weather also necessitates extensive use of spot market sales by refineries and bulk terminals.[58]

Residual fuel oils include Nos. 4, 5, and 6 fuel oils, Bunker C, and Navy Special Fuel Oil. Bunker C, which is the shipping industry fuel corresponding to No. 6 fuel oil, has a high viscosity. Grades 4 and 5 use middle distillate "cutter" stock to decrease viscosity and are more expensive than the heavier fraction, because middle distillate can be more readily converted into gasoline. Most residual fuel oil users can now use grade No. 6. This must be burned in equipment designed for steady operation and high firebox temperatures, due to its high flash point. Most residual fuel oil is sold directly to large purchasers, although some indirect sales are made.[59]

Historically, the oil industry has not been exceptionally profitable. In recent years, howerver, profits have picked up substantially. For the 20 largest U.S. petroleum companies from 1967 to 1972, average profits were 10.8 percent as a return on invested capital. This figure rose in 1973 to 13.7 percent. In comparison, profits for all manufacturing from 1967 to 1971 were approximately 10.8 percent. In 1967, the profits of the integrated companies were derived principally from production (63 percent), and refining and marketing (21 percent). Petrochemical operations contributed 10 percent of total profits, while transportation accounted for only 6 percent.[60]

The emphasis on taking profits at the production level within the U.S. may have been largely the result of the oil depletion allowance, on the one hand, and relatively more intensive price competition in refining and marketing, on the other. The decrease in the depletion allowance and growth in independent marketers forced the majors to begin adjusting their strategies. During the late 1960s and early 1970s, Congress received extensive testimony concerning allegations that majors were attempting to drive independents out of business through pipeline shipment harassment, price wars, and the use of secondary brands. Branded independent stations complained that the majors were attempting to shift to higher volume stations, without many of the traditional services.[61]

DEMAND FOR REFINED PRODUCTS

Total U.S. demand for petroleum products for selected years through 1972 is shown in Table 5-1.[62] Demand for many products is seasonal. Demand is greatest for motor gasoline during the summer, and for distillate and residual oils during the winter heating season (October 1 to March 31). Propane demand increases for wet autumns and cold winters. Total demand for all petroleum products is well above the yearly average during the winter heating season, and

Table 5-1.   U.S. Domestic Petroleum Demand by Use (MB/D)

	1946	1960	1970	1971	1972	Average Annual % Increase, 1960-1970
Total Gasoline	2,015	4,130	6,083	6,302	6,663	4.4
Automotive	1,920	3,845	5,785	6,015	6,377	4.7
Aviation	35	161	55	49	45	(14.6)
Special Naphthas[a]	60	124	243	238	246	3.9
Total Jet Fuels	–	371	967	1,010	1,045	9.9
Naph-type	–	280	249	259	242	(1.3)
Kero-type	–	91	718	751	803	16.6
Total Intermediates	909	2,143	2,775	2,910	3,148	3.0
Kerosene	244	271	263	249	235	(0.3)
Total Distillates	665	1,872	2,512	2,661	2,913	3.4
Heating	406	1,195	1,439	1,435	NA	2.0
Diesel[b]	148	563	534	586	NA	9.5
Other	111	114	538	640	NA	2.3
Total Residual	1,315	1,528	2,235	2,296	2,529	6.8
Heating	136	342	511	500	NA	3.6
Other	1,179	1,186	1,724	1,796	NA	7.9
Lubricants	96	117	136	136	144	1.1
Asphalt & Road Oil	135	302	446	457	468	5.4
Total LPG	109	621	1,224	1,251	1,420	7.7
Chemical Use	20	196	556	575	NA	10.1
Residential, Commercial	49	275	494	500	NA	9.6
Other	40	150	174	176	NA	1.3
Miscellaneous[c]	333	449	843	863	957	12.5
Total Demand	4,912	9,661	14,709	15,225	16,379	5.4
Net Imports	(42)	1,604	3,160	3,702	4,518	
% Imports	8.3%	16.6%	21.5%	24.3%	27.6%	

[a]1970 includes naphtha 400° for petrochemical use. Earlier years estimated at 3% of total gasoline demand.

[b]After 1970, includes only on and off highway use, excludes railroad, vessel, etc.

[c]Miscellaneous may include here some portions of total demand for the following products: Ethane, Petrochemical Feedstocks, Wax, Coke, and Still Gas.

is substantially below average during April and May.[63] Sectoral demand for petroleum products is shown in Table 5-2.[64]

Motor Gasoline

Gasoline is the largest quantity of refined product derived from available crude. Highway motor vehicles use about 90 percent of all gasoline, while airplanes, tractors, and non-highway vehicles and equipment use the remainder. Before the 1973-74 Arab embargo, gasoline demand was expected to increase by 5 percent each year, and the trend in refining was to increase the gasoline yield from each barrel of crude and improve the gasoline quality for use in modern engines.[65] In fact, average yearly gasoline production rose from 6,279 MB/D in 1972 to 6,475 MB/D in 1973, but demand dropped about 2 percent in 1974. During 1975, however, demand began to climb again, so that in early May it totalled 6,710 MB/D and during June surpassed 7,000 MB/D. This is somewhat higher than what the FEA had projected.[66]

At the same time, motor gasoline imports increased 94.1 percent in 1973 (over 1972) and about 35 percent in 1974 (over 1973). As with other refined products, imports declined during the first four months in 1975. Preliminary FEA data show that motor gasoline imports in April 1975 were only about 100 MB/D, compared to total demand of 6,649 MB/D, meaning that as far as refined products are concerned, motor gasoline has relatively low import levels.[67]

Many in the FEA believe that the fact that motor gasoline demand did not rise an expected 9-11 percent from 1972 to 1974 indicates that demand is price-elastic at current prices. Executive Branch policy is currently based on that assumption, and the spurt in demand during the summer of 1975 does not seem to have changed FEA assumptions. Nevertheless, the increase in demand in 1975 focuses attention on long-term elasticity and the need to change consumption patterns permanently.[68] In contrast, congressional staff members, relying on studies conducted separately by the FEA and the Rand Corporation, believe that demand for motor gasoline will not be affected significantly by anything less than a 30 to 60 cent per gallon increase above 1975 price levels.

Middle Distillates

Demand for distillate fuel oils, by end use, is shown in Table 5-3, not including sectoral demand for kerosene.[69] Small amounts of raw kerosene may be processed into gasoline. In warmer states, particularly the Southwest, kerosene is also used for home and space-heating. Otherwise it is used for blending to make diesel fuel, jet fuels, and No. 1 fuel oil. Of total diesel fuel supplies, 45 percent is used by trucks and buses, 25 percent by railroads, 5 percent for marine uses and the remainder by industrial plants, utilities, and the military. Electric utilities are installing gas turbines in metropolitan areas which burn jet or diesel fuel. This has been done at a low capital cost and with reasonably

Table 5-2. Sectoral Demand for Petroleum Products in Millions of Barrels

Year	Household and Commercial			Industrial				Transportation	Electric Generation	Misc.	Total Non-Fuel	Total Fuel
	Fuel	*Non-Fuel*	*Total*	*Fuel*	*Non-Fuel*	*Total*						
1970	965.3	163.1	1,128.4	546.5	414.9	961.4	2,902.8	333.8	38.1	578.0	4,786.5
1971	982.4	167.2	1,149.6	537.5	412.6	950.1	2,004.9	386.9	31.9	579.8	4,943.6

Table 5-3.   U.S. Domestic Demand for Distillate Fuel Oils by End Use (MB/D)

Year	Heating	Industrial	Electric Utilities	Highway Diesel	Other	Total
1967	1373	123	8	NA	NA	2,272
1970	1428	120	68	408	516	2,540
1971	1435	136	97	449	544	2,661
1972[a]	1535	155	150	506	571	2,917

[a]Estimated.

low pollutant emissions. As the electric utilities column in Table 5-3 demonstrates, such use has increased enormously since 1967.[70]

By far the most important use of middle distillates is in domestic and commercial heating. Grade No. 2 is the most common heating oil, and 60 percent of consumption of this product occurs in the nine Northeastern states. In fact, 75 percent of New England homes are oil-heated, and, significantly, 82 percent of those homes are supplied by independent oil retailers. Fuel oil distributors, utilities, and large industrial consumers build up large stocks in October and November for the winter heating season.[71] Demand for distillate fuel oils usually runs more than 1,500 MB/D higher during the winter heating season than during the summer.[72]

Demand for middle distillates increased an average of 3 percent annually from 1960 to 1970, but jumped 9.6 percent in 1972 over 1971, due largely to the cold winter and the shortage of natural gas. Due to the effects of price increases, conservation measures and the economic recession, demand during the 1973-74 winter was substantially below the corresponding period in the previous winter heating season. During the first two months of the 1974-75 winter heating season, the pattern continued. In the December–March period, however, demand began to climb again, although it remained below 1972-73 levels.[73]

Like demand, imports of distillate fuels are highest during the winter. Imports reached an all time high in February 1973 at 731 MB/D. During the 1973-74 heating season, peak imports fell to 492 MB/D. In 1974-75 peak imports rose somewhat, to 517 MB/D. FEA data show a lower level of distillate imports and a steady decline in imports during the first four months of 1975.[74]

The FPC estimated that 130 MB/D of the distillate demand during the 1973-74 winter was the direct result of natural gas curtailments. Cold weather can put further pressure on demand: on average of once every five years, the winter is cold enough to increase heating oil demand by 3.9 percent (120 MB/D). Table 5-4 shows the effect of cold winters on demand for natural gas, oil, electricity, and LPG.[75] Unless coal or nuclear power is used, the increased demand for each of these fuels will result in greater direct and indirect use of petroleum for heating. Many persons within the FEA and industry now con-

Table 5-4. National Total Heating Fuel Demand in Percents of 42-Year
Average Demand

		Gas	*Oil*	*Electricity*	*LPG*
Coldest year in	100	109.7	110.6	109.6	111.4
	10	105.4	105.9	105.3	106.3
	5	103.5	103.9	103.4	104.1
Warmest year in	5	96.5	96.1	96.6	95.9
	10	94.6	94.1	94.7	93.8
	100	90.3	89.4	90.4	88.6

sider demand for middle distillate heating oils to be more price-elastic than demand for most other petroleum products.[76]

Residual Fuel Oil

Residual fuel oil demand follows the same seasonal pattern as middle distillates, but end-use requirements are substantially different. Table 5-5 shows that in 1973, electric utilities were the largest users, followed by heating oil uses, industrial uses, shipping, oil companies, military, and railroads.[77] These fuels are used in installations larger than domestic and small commercial buildings, usually to provide steam and heat for industry and large buildings, and, of course, for the generation of electricity. Environmental considerations have disturbed the supply/demand balance for residual fuel oils, as consumers have switched from coal to low-sulfur residual fuel. In addition, forced conversion of industrial and electric utility boilers from natural gas has increased demand for residual fuel oil.[78]

Demand for residual fuel oil during 1974 dropped about 10 percent below the 1973 level, which was approximately the same as in 1972. In the first four months of 1975, demand dropped slightly below that for the same period in 1974. During the 1974-75 winter heating season, demand surpassed 3,000 MB/D in only one month, compared to four months in 1972-73 and three in 1973-74. Typically, demand in the coldest months remains around 600 to 900 MB/D above levels for the warmer months. Imports of residual fuel oil increased in 1973, but decreased in 1974 about 20 percent below 1973 levels. In the past, residual fuel oil imports often supplied two-thirds of the demand. However, in the 1974-75 winter, domestic production and imports were roughly the same, due to increased domestic production and reduced consumption.[79]

LPG

Data on demand for LPG, primarily propane, range from poor to non-existent. This is partly due to confusion over what the label really includes. There are four major types of users of LPG: homes, gas manufacturers and utilities, chemical manufacturers, and agricultural users.[80] In homes, LPG may be used for

Table 5-5.   U.S. Domestic Demand for Residual Fuel Oil, by End Use (MB/D)

Year	Heating Oils	Industrial Uses	Oil Co. Use	Electric Utilities	Railroads	Vessels	Military	Misc.	Total
1967	482	358	104	434	15	224	111	58	1,786
1970	509	383	105	856	6	246	79	20	2,204
1971	500	371	89	1,019	4	216	80	17	2,295
1972	511	400	121	1,190	3	213	67	24	2,529
1973[a]	487	474	125	1,430	2	220	60	12	2,810

[a]Estimated.

stoves, refrigerators, water heaters, space heaters, furnaces, air-conditioning, and infra-red cooking. Many home users are unable to obtain connections for natural gas, and conversion costs to electricity from LPG may be very high.[81]

Gas manufacturers and utilities use LPG for peak shaving and the enrichment of manufactured gas. When they need extra fuel to supplement their natural gas, LPG is injected into the system with the basic fuel. Propane is less expensive for these users to purchase than spot purchases of natural gas, and is now far easier to obtain, even though there is also an LPG shortage. Since these purchasers may need substantial quantities only during one week of the year, the timing of their demand is difficult to predict. This situation makes allocation more complicated.

Chemical manufacturers use LPG as a feedstock or raw material to produce intermediate materials. Their demand and uses will be described more fully below in the petrochemical section.[82]

LPG is used in many aspects of agriculture. As fuel for heating, it is used for incubators, brooders, and watering tanks. It is useful also for sterilizing milk utensils and equipment, dehydrating vegetables and fruits, preventing frost damage, and ripening fruits. Poultry farmers may also use LPG for scalding and waxing. Additional uses are for smoking meats, curing tobacco, and controlling weeds by flame weeding.[83]

Some FEA reports use the label "Natural Gas Liquids," which encompasses most LPG but includes a few additional products.[84] Domestic demand for this category is seasonal. Peaking demands occur in the first and fourth quarters of the year, particularly between November and February. Peak months usually require at least 600 MB/D more than June and July, which are the minimum demand months. During 1974, average daily production and domestic demand fell about 3 percent below 1973 levels, while imports fell about 8 percent. Imports typically range between 150 and 300 MB/D, while peak demand is between 1,700 and 1,900 MB/D. Data for the first quarter of 1975 show that demand is still declining slightly, but domestic production is also falling.

Wet falls and cold winters greatly increase LPG demand because of its utility for drying crops and heating purposes.[85] Along with middle distillates and residual fuel oil, propane is a major substitute for natural gas and propane demand is substantially affected by natural gas curtailments. Propane is the only petroleum product for which the FEA expects a shortage during the 1975-76 winter.

Aviation Fuel

There are two major types of aviation fuel: aviation gasoline (AVGAS) and jet fuel. Both are primarily dedicated to use in aircraft, although some small amounts of jet fuel are used for generating electricity in gas turbines. AVGAS must be used for spark ignition engines, while jet fuel is burned in turbine engines. Demand for AVGAS has fallen steadily from about 110 MB/D in 1965 to 46 MB/D in 1972. The decline is due largely to decreased military use of AVGAS and civil air carrier conversions in the late 1960s from piston engine planes to jets. By the end of 1971, 98 percent of fixed-wing planes in scheduled domestic service used jet fuel, so demand should continue to drop, although the growing number of private light aircraft might compensate somewhat for the conversion.[86]

Jet fuel may be subdivided into naphtha-types, used primarily by the military, and kerosene-types, used by both military aircraft and commercial carriers.[87]

Total jet fuel demand in 1972 was 1,045 MB/D, of which about 80 percent was kerosene-type. During the first half of 1974, demand fell substantially because of the Arab embargo and allocation, but in the latter half of the year, 1973 demand levels were resumed. Demand for all jet fuels in the first four months of 1975 is about what it was during the same period in 1972.

Imports of jet fuel usually supply about 100 to 220 MB/D, although imports were above that range before the embargo. In the first four months of 1975, jet fuel imports ranged from 135 to 166 MB/D. Imports of naphtha-type (military) fuels increased relative to kerosene-type during 1974.[88]

Petrochemicals

Petrochemicals are chemical compounds with a petroleum hydrocarbon as one basic component. Demand for petrochemical feedstocks averaged 338 MB/D in 1972.[89] Altogether, petrochemicals comprise about 5 percent of national oil demand, but demand in this sector is increasing faster than for other petroleum products. The most basic intermediate petrochemical products from petroleum oils are olefins and aromatics. Olefin derivatives are the source of 55 percent of all petrochemical products, while aromatics are responsible for 40 percent.[90]

Three-fourths of olefin-type intermediates are made from LPG stock (ethane, propane, and butane), while the remainder is made from crude oil derivatives such as naphthas and gas oils. Most of the LPG stock comes to the petrochemical manufacturers directly by pipeline from the natural gas field separation plants, but some comes from petroleum-based LPG. Petrochemical manufacturers which do not own refineries produce about 60 percent of all olefins. The remainder is produced by companies with their own operations in both industry sectors. Patterns in olefin production are expected to change as natural gas supplies tighten; more olefins will be produced from petroleum products.

Aromatic production is quite different from production of olefins: 90 percent is derived from petroleum and 10 percent from coal tars. Aromatics are most logically and economically processed by catalytic reforming of naphtha, a process which is also used for upgrading naphtha into gasoline. As a result, 85 percent of aromatics made from petroleum is produced by oil company refineries. However, over half of aromatic intermediates are purchased by chemical companies not associated with oil refineries.[91]

Olefins and aromatics are sold usually by the tank car or truck to chemical manufacturers which use them to make petrochemical derivatives. Some of these derivatives are synthetic rubber, carbon black, polyethylene and toluene. Polyethylene is used for such diverse products as electrical insulation, liners for bags and containers, and as packaging for foods, cosmetics, and pharmaceuticals. Toluene is used directly as a solvent, as a component of AVGAS, and as a principal ingredient in TNT. Petrochemicals are increasingly used for manufacturing many final products which have become a part of the American lifestyle. For many such products the petrochemicals used in their manufacture have no substitutes.[92]

Although petrochemical manufacturers sometimes produce their own consumer goods, they usually sell the petrochemicals to other companies engaged in the business of manufacturing and distributing consumer goods. Oil companies are now acquiring marketing outlets for their petrochemical derivatives, sometimes by forming a joint subsidiary with an established chemical marketing or manufacturing company. Much like other petroleum products, therefore, petrochemicals may be transferred through levels of a vertically integrated firm or sold to independent companies before reaching the ultimate consumer.[93]

Miscellaneous Refined Products

Lubricants may be divided into three general categories: automotive lubricating oils, industrial lubricating oils, and greases. Total demand for lubricants in 1972 was 145 MB/D.[94]

There are three major products within the automotive oil category: engine oils, gear oils, and automatic transmission fluids. Each product must meet specifications established by government agencies, equipment manufacturers and end-users. Engine oils are likely to change drastically in the future in response to anti-pollution standards. In the period from 1960 to 1969, total demand for automotive oils increased by only 11 percent.[95]

Industrial oils are divided into two broad groups: "industrial lubricating oils" for lubrication purposes; and "industrial other oils," a catch-all category. Included in these groups are hydraulic fluids and metal working fluids. From 1960 to 1969, industrial oil sales rose by 56 percent.[96]

Greases are composed of lubricating oil in a jelling agent. While greases are increasingly used in industrial activity, potential growth in demand has been counterbalanced by improvements in grease quality, allowing increased lubrication intervals.[97]

Special naphthas include "[a] 11 finished products, within the gasoline range, refined to specified flashpoint and boiling range, for use as paint thinners, cleaners, solvents, etc., but not to be marketed as motor gasoline, aviation gasoline, or used as petrochemical feedstocks."[98] Average demand in 1972 was 87 MB/D.

Aside from these more noticeable uses of petroleum, there are several less commonly known derivatives, which represent a significant portion of petroleum demand. Asphalt required an average of 447 MB/D of petroleum in 1972 and is mainly used for paving. Asphalt, however, is not considered to be a refined petroleum product subject to FEA regulation.[99]

Road oil includes any heavy petroleum oil used as a dust palliative and for surface treatment of roads. There are also three marketable grades of wax, which is composed of wax extracted from certain petroleum residues.[100] Together, these products comprise a very minor part of petroleum demand.

Petroleum coke, a solid residue, accounted for 241 MB/D in 1972. Coke is the final product of the condensation process in cracking petroleum. When calcinated, it can yield almost pure carbon or artificial graphite suitable for the production of carbon or graphite electrodes, structural graphite, motor brushes, and dry cells.[101]

NOTES TO CHAPTER FIVE

1. Portions of this chapter where sources are not indicated are based on interviews with FEA personnel, congressional and Library of Congress staff, and industry employees.

Officials in the Regulatory Programs Office of the FEA readily acknowledge that they lack information and accurate descriptions of some basic elements of industry. Historically, the oil companies have been very secretive, zealously guarding their "trade secrets." Lack of agreement on terminology has not caused serious problems for the FEA in developing regulations, since the agency merely chooses new functional labels and avoids troublesome areas. The regulations leave most of the terminology problems in the hands of the industry.

The definitions of kerosene provide a ready example of the confusion: aside from use for space-heating, some say that kerosene is blended with No. 2 fuel oil to make No. 1, while others contend that No. 1 is kerosene. American Society of Testing Materials (ASTM) and American Petroleum Institute (API) definitions alleviate most of this type of confusion. A greater problem arises in defining members of the distribution system, e.g., jobbers, distributors, and consignee agents.

2. FEA, *Quarterly Report, Energy Information Reported to Congress as Required by Public Law 93–319,* at 85 (Fourth Quarter 1974) [hereinafter cited as *Quarterly Report*].

3. *Monthly Energy Review,* June 1975, at 47.

4. Energy Economics Division (Chase Manhattan Bank), *Outlook for Energy in the United States to 1985,* at 44 (June 1972) [hereinafter cited as *Energy Economics Division*]. According to the *Monthly Energy Review,* June 1975, petroleum continues to supply 45 percent of U.S. fuel needs.

5. The President's 1975 State of the Union Message Including the Economy and Energy at 45 [hereinafter cited as 1975 State of the Union Message]. Needless to say, there are numerous such forecasts. The Chase Manhattan study could not have considered the OPEC price increases, but the President's analysts probably did not expect the spurts in demand during the summer of 1975.

6. *Energy Economics Division, supra* note 4.

7. *Energy Management Reporter,* May 12, 1975, at 1.

8. *Quarterly Report, supra* note 2, at 85. Note that we use both thousands and millions of barrels a day, depending upon the specificity required for the description.

9. *Monthly Energy Review,* June 1975, at 16.

10. *Quarterly Report, supra* note 2, at 85.

11. *Monthly Energy Review,* June 1975, at 12-18.

12. *Monthly Energy Review,* January 1975 at 6-8; *Monthly Energy Review,* June 1975, at 16-18.

13. *Monthly Energy Review,* June 1975, at 12. About 90 percent of refined product imports in April 1975 came from Venezuela and the Caribbean Islands.

14. 1975 State of the Union Message, *supra* note 5, at 45.

15. *Hearings on Market Performance and Competition in the Petroleum Industry Before the Senate Committee on Interior and Insular Affairs,* 93d Cong., 1st Sess., pt. 1, at 108 (1973) (testimony of Stephen A. Wakefield) [hereinafter cited as Wakefield].

16. The Lundgren data in particular use those classifications. These data have been heavily used by Congress and by the FTC in *Federal Trade Commission, An Evaluation of Mandatory Petroleum Allocation Program* (1974) [hereinafter cited as *FTC Evaluation*].

17. Wakefield, *supra* note 15, at 96; *Hearings on Market Performance and Competition in the Petroleum Industry Before the Senate Committee on Interior and Insular Affairs,* 93d Cong., 1st Sess., pt. 1, at 91 (1973) (testimony of Senator Bartlett) [hereinafter cited as Bartlett]. A "wildcat" well generally refers to any well drilled by an independent without participation by a large producer. Most wildcat wells are low-cost, fairly shallow, on land.

18. Wakefield, *supra* note 15, at 108. The independents tend to have lower drilling costs than individual majors. This is because they can work for several majors in the same area, reducing moving costs. They also tend to have lower overhead costs.

19. See Bartlett, *supra* note 17, at 91. The explanation for the decline varies; some contend that majors have forced independents out, while others suggest that the high-risk nature of the field naturally weeds out the least competitive firms. Also, as exploration and drilling continues there are fewer places to search and drill for shallow oil.

20. Wakefield, *supra* note 15, at 96, 120; T. Duchesneau, *Competition in the U.S. Energy Industry* 36-37 (1975) [hereinafter cited as Duchesneau]. In descending order, the 20 largest domestic crude oil producers in 1970 were: Exxon, Texaco, Gulf, Shell, Standard Oil of Calif., Standard Oil of Indiana, Atlantic Richfield, Getty, Mobil, Union Oil of California, Sun Oil, Marathon, Continental Oil, Phillips, Cities Service, Amerada Hess, Tenneco, Louisiana Land & Exploration, Superior Oil, and Standard Oil of Ohio. Many of these are considered major, integrated companies. The original data come from Annual Reports and Moody's *Industrial Manual.*

21. *FEO Industry Background* 20 (1974). Flush wells flow freely due to natural gas or water pressure. Settled wells must be pumped, but may still produce significant quantities. Stripper wells, of which there are over 30,000, produce little oil even with pumping (average 2.8 barrels/day). They are econom-

ically marginal. Artificial methods are used to recover oil in secondary recovery wells. Not all wells go through all phases.

22. 15 U.S.C. §753(e) (Supp. III, 1973); 10 C.F.R. §212.72 (1975); Note, *National Energy Goals and FEA's Mandatory Crude Oil Allocation Program,* 61 Va. L. Rev. 903; 909 n. 36 (1975).

23. See Wakefield, *supra* note 15, at 109; Duchesneau, *supra* note 20, at 38.

24. Much of the description of transportation relies upon Wakefield, *supra* note 15, at 109; *FEO Industry Background* at 12 (1974).

25. To some extent, elements of a refinery can be closed without stopping all operations. Certain elements may also be operated at lower levels. Reformers, which are used for making heavier ends into lighter ones for gasoline can be shut down. During the winter when gasoline demand is at a seasonal low, gasoline-making elements are easily closed for maintenance.

26. *FEO Industry Background* at 7, 11 (1974).

27. *FEO Industry Background* 5 (1974). Only 259 refineries have distillation units, while the remainder are blending plants or cracking units that change naphthas or unfinished oils directly, rather than distilling crude.

28. J. Lichtblau, *The Outlook for Independent Domestic Refiners to the Early 1980's,* in Duchesneau at 295–296 [hereinafter cited as *Lichtblau*]. The data are from Company Annual Reports, U.S. Bureau of Mines Mineral Industry Surveys, *Petroleum Statement, 1972* and lists those firms in descending order: Standard Oil of Indiana, Exxon, Texaco, Shell, Mobil, Standard Oil of California, Gulf, Atlantic Richfield, Phillips, Sun Oil, Union Oil of California, Continental Oil, Cities Service, Marathon, Getty, Amerada Hess, Kerr-McGee, and Pennzoil.

29. 15 U.S.C. §752 (Supp. III, 1973).

30. *FTC Evaluation, supra* note 16, at S–15.

31. Lichtblau, *supra* note 28, at 297.

32. Wakefield, *supra* note 15, at 112. See notes 42–43 and accompanying text.

33. *See Energy Management Reporter,* July 22, 1975, at 4. The FEA expected refineries to run at 97 percent of capacity during July–September 1975, and then to drop to 94 percent in October when refinery yields are changed to emphasize heating oils.

34. *See generally, FEO Industry Background* at 7, 19 (1974). By the most widely accepted system, crude petroleum may be divided into paraffin-base, mixed-base, and asphalt-base, depending on the relative amounts of paraffin and asphalt in the oil.

35. T. Moore, *Economies of Scale of Firms Engaged in Oil and Coal Production,* in Duchesneau, *supra* note 20, at 230–232.

36. For a preliminary discussion of this material, see *FEO Industry Background,* at 3, 13 (1974).

37. *FTC Evaluation, supra* note 16, at I–13.

38. *See FEO Industry Background,* 13–17 (1974); Wakefield, *supra* note 15, at 113–115.

39. *FEO Industry Background,* 58 (1974). State load limits may require

smaller cargos in trucks than ordinary capacity would allow, and gallon capacity will vary with the density of the product. As a general rule, trucks are not allowed to carry a completely full load.

40. *Id.* Since the FEA allocation program has been in effect and the embargo ended, spot shortages have been minimized even though inventories have been maintained at relatively low levels. Some congressional staff members contend this is attributable to better coordination, enforced by the FEA.

41. *Id.* A branded retail service station generally purchases motor gasoline from a branded dealer at the dealer's tank wagon price delivered to the station. An independent service station purchases gasoline from a branded dealer at a refinery gate price that is discounted from the tank wagon price to reflect the absence of company credit card costs, the costs of brand name promotional advertising, and the fact that the independent usually arranges for his own deliveries.

42. Wakefield, *supra* note 15, at 112. Many FEA officials know this market *only* as the spot market, which is in fact the major component.

43. For a general discussion, see Wakefield, *supra* note 15, at 112.

44. 15 U.S.C. §752 (Supp. III, 1973).

45. *E.g.,* F. Allvine & J. Patterson, *Highway Robbery* 21 (1974). The lack of consensus on descriptive terms has been the source of considerable difficulty in analyzing trends in the industry. This confusion in the meager data available can only hinder effective determination of the impact of petroleum allocation, particularly since data from different sources sometimes indicate different conclusions.

46. *Id.*

47. *FTC Evaluation, supra* note 16, at S-19. These shares should have remained relatively constant since that time. The beginning of 1972 found the non-branded independents with only 17 percent of the market, the lowest quarterly share of all 1972 and 1973. Congressional selection of 1972 as a base period, and slowness of the FEA to grant adjustments for growth, may have caused slight reductions. *Id.* at S-20. Even minor percentage changes can be important to the industry since most changes in this area can only be made gradually; the important issue is often the discernment of trends. The required FEA *Progress Report on the Retailing of Gasoline,* p. iii, (August 6, 1974), concluded that "[t]horough review of available industry and FEA data show considerably different proportions and trends in market shares for the classes of gasoline marketers and distributors identified in the Emergency Petroleum Allocation Act of 1973 (for the time period January 1972 through August 1974)."

The FEA has only recently gathered data itself on market shares, but uses different definitions than those in the *FTC Evaluation.*

The sales by semi-integrated companies complicate the existing data on sales substantially, and the sales by discount brand stations owned by majors but made to appear to be independents further cloud the picture. F. Allvine & J. Patterson, *Highway Robbery,* 34 (1974), Duchesneau, *supra* note 20, at 45 shows that sales by the 20 largest marketers amounted to 75.91 percent of the total gasoline sales in 1972 and 75.08 percent in 1973. In 1973 in descending order,

Percent of Total U.S. Gasoline Gallonage Sales Through Service Stations

	U.S. Total	Ref./ Mrktrs.	Non-branded Indepen.	Branded Independent			
				Total	Lessee Dealers	Open Dealers	Jobber Direct
1974							
October	100.0	13.3	7.4	79.3	52.9	20.2	6.2
November	100.0	13.5	8.3	78.2	52.3	20.4	5.5
December	100.0	14.0	9.0	76.9	53.1	18.8	5.0
1975							
January	100.0	15.3	9.1	75.6	52.9	18.1	4.5
February	100.0	14.5	9.6	75.9	53.7	17.5	4.7
March	100.0	15.1	9.6	75.3	53.2	17.5	4.6
April	100.0	14.6	10.2	75.2	53.6	16.8	4.8
May	100.0	14.3	9.9	75.8	53.6	17.0	5.2
June		14.8	9.7	75.5	54.3	16.6	4.6
July		14.5	9.6	75.9	54.8	16.7	4.4

those are Texaco, Exxon, Shell, Amoco (Standard Oil of Indiana), Gulf, Mobil, Standard Oil of California, Atlantic Richfield, Phillips, Sun Oil, Union Oil of California, Continental Oil Cities Service, Marathon, Ashland, Clark, Standard Oil of Ohio, Hess, BP Oil, and Tenneco. The data were taken from *National Petroleum News,* mid-May 1973 issue.

48. *Hearings on the Impact of Gasoline Marketing Practices on the Consumer Before the Consumer Subcommittee of the Senate Committee on Commerce,* 93d Cong., 1st Sess., at 1 (1973) (testimony of Senator Moss) [hereinafter cited as *Gasoline Marketing Practices*]; *FTC Evaluation, supra* note 16, at II–6.

49. *Gasoline Marketing Practices, supra* note 48, at 27 (testimony of Daniel Berman).

50. F. Allvine & J. Patterson, *Competition Ltd.,* at 76 (1972); F. Allvine & J. Patterson, *Highway Robbery* 34. These authors suggest that competition in the petroleum industry takes two forms—intratype and intertype. Intratype competition is major against major (e.g., Exxon against Texaco). Intertype is competition between majors and independents, etc. Intratype competition ensures that those in the same class do things identically, relying only on advertising to differentiate brands. There is no intratype price competition, since everyone acts the same, leading to less efficient marketing. Intertype competition is mainly along price lines.

Semi-majors are smaller integrated firms than the majors and cannot afford the advertising investment of the majors. Consequently, they tend to price products only slightly lower (e.g., 1 cent per gallon of gasoline). As majors' prices rise, the semi-majors tend to raise their prices also. The largest supplier of independent marketers are independent refiners, but the semi-majors are also large suppliers. Because majors can safely coexist with semi-majors, product sales and exchanges are possible, which facilitates sales by semi-majors to independents.

51. *See Gasoline Marketing Practices, supra* note 48. It is estimated that majors forced several thousand independent marketers out of business during 1973.

52. *FEO Industry Background,* 24 (1974); Statement of Frank G. Zarb, Administrator of the FEA Before the Senate Committee on Interior and Insular Affairs, May 19, 1975. Basically, LPG includes the products covered by 10 C.F.R. §§211.81-.87, 211.91-.97 (Subparts D and E) (1975). There is an unresolved dispute as to whether LPG includes ethane, but all agree that Natural Gas Liquids do encompass the product.

Generally, the LPG producer ships it in bulk to bulk plant operators, which may be owned by either the producers or independents. LPG is shipped by pipeline, tanker, barge, and pressure tank cars and trucks, and must always be stored under pressure. The bulk plants may supply consumers directly or sell to distributor-dealers, who later make final sales and deliveries. Bulk plant operators may ship LPG either in bulk or in cylinders. *FEO Industry Background,* at 24 (1974).

53. *FEO Industry Background,* 27 (1974). Middle distillate regulations are included in 10 C.F.R. §§211.121-.127 (Subpart G) (1975).

54. *FEO Industry Background,* 27 (1974).

55. *FTC Evaluation, supra* note 16, at II-8.

56. Specifically, they should not form sediment in storage, leave a deposit of ash upon burning, or emit high levels of smoke or sulfur dioxide. Further, they should be fluid under outdoor winter storage conditions. *Id.* at II-9.

57. *Id.*

58. Wakefield, *supra* note 15, at 114.

59. *FEO Industry Background,* 34 (1974). Residual fuel oil regulations are contained in 10 C.F.R. §§211.161-.167 (Subpart I) (1975) and add to this list crude oil burned directly. Some data and FEA price regulations include No. 4 as a middle distillate since it is a blend of Nos. 2 and 6.

60. Duchesneau, *supra* note 20, at 35, 157. The profit levels data were taken from *Fortune,* May issues; the breakdown of profits from *Oil and Gas Journal,* September 30, 1968, at 36. American Petroleum Institute, *Petroleum Facts and Figures* 513 (1971 edition) shows that average profits from 1925-1968, for the entire petroleum industry were 10.1 percent; for all manufacturing, 10.8 percent; and for all industry, 8.8 percent.

61. *E.g., Gasoline Marketing Practices, supra* note 48.

62. Table 5-1 is taken from *FEO Industry Background,* 53 (1974); the data were compiled from U.S. Bureau of Mines, *Mineral Industry Surveys* (Monthly and Annual Petroleum Statements; Annual Sales of Fuel Oil & Kerosene; Annual Sales of Liquified Petroleum Gases). The groupings of products often differ. Data from U.S. Bureau of Mines, Division of Fossil Fuels, *Crude Petroleum, Petroleum Products, and Natural Gas Liquids* (1973) show that in 1972, demand for ethane was 290 MB/D; liquified gases, 1,118 MB/D; petrochemical feed-

stocks, 338 MB/D; wax, 15 MB/D; coke, 241 MB/D; and still gas, 467 MB/D. Portions of this are probably included in the Miscellaneous category of Table 5-1.

63. *Monthly Energy Review,* June 1975, at 18.

64. Congressional Research Service, *Energy Facts, Prepared for the Subcommittee on Energy of the House Committee on Science and Astronautics,* 93d Cong., 1st Sess., at 346 (1973) [hereinafter cited as *Energy Facts Hearings*]. Data from U.S. Bureau of Mines, Division of Fossil Fuels, *Crude Petroleum, Petroleum Products, and Natural Gas Liquids* (1973).

65. *FEO Industry Background,* 26 (1974). Regulations for motor gasoline are contained in 10 C.F.R. §§211.101–.109 (Subpart F) (1975) and for aviation gasoline in 10 C.F.R. §§211.141–.147 (Subpart H) (1975). Finished gasoline is a blend of straight-run gasoline obtained from distilling crude oil, natural gasoline stripped from natural gas, cracked gasoline, reformed gasoline, polymerized gasoline, alkylate, and additives such as tetraethyl lead which improve anti-knock capability.

66. *Monthly Energy Review,* January 1975, at 10–11; *Monthly Energy Review,* June 1975, at 20, 47.

67. *Monthly Energy Review,* January 1975, at 10–11; *Monthly Energy Review,* June 1975, at 20.

68. FEA officials acknowledge that demand for motor gasoline may be more elastic in the short term than in the long term, meaning that as consumers become accustomed to a higher price after a recent increase, they return to old consumption patterns. This would necessitate continual price increases if demand is to be significantly curtailed through the price mechanism.

69. *Hearings on Conflicting Information on Fuel Shortages, Current Energy Shortages Oversight Series Before the Permanent Subcommittee on Investigations of the Senate Committee on Government Operations,* 93d Cong., 1st Sess., pt. 1 at 61 (1973) [hereinafter cited as *Conflicting Information Hearings*].

70. *FEO Industry Background,* at 27–28 (1974).

71. *H.R. Rep. No. 531,* 93d Cong., 1st Sess. 9–10 (1973), *reprinted at U.S. Code Cong. & Adm. News* 2582 (1973).

72. *Monthly Energy Review,* June 1975, at 24.

73. Table 5-1; *H.R. Rep. No. 531,* 93d Cong., 1st Sess. 30 (1973); *Monthly Energy Review,* June 1975, at 24.

74. *Monthly Energy Review,* June 1975, at 24.

75. *H.R. Rep. No. 531,* 93d Cong., 1st Sess. at 9, 30, 48 (1973). Mildly colder than normal weather occurs 4 out of 10 winters, and significantly colder weather in an additional three winters. *Id.* at 9. The data for Table V were supplied by the National Oceanic and Atmospheric Administration. *Id.* at 48. The coldness of a winter is measured in terms of heating degree days. Data show that total demand for petroleum products during the peak of the winter usually is several million barrels a day higher than during low points in the summer.

76. FEA, Office of Policy and Analysis, Quantitative Methods, *National Petroleum Product Supply and Demand: 1975,* at 15 [hereinafter cited as *National Petroleum Product*], concludes that price elasticity for distillates over

a three-month period is –.09; for six months, –.12; and for nine months, –.12. Only residual fuel oils and petrochemicals have higher price elasticities.

Currently, demand for distillates increases at the time of change-over from gasoline production in the refineries. If the use of distillates in the winter should decrease, while year-round utility usage increases, the pattern of higher distillate demand in the first and fourth quarters may change significantly. This would require adjustments in industry practices. The shift in sectoral demand would mean that gasoline yields could not be as easily emphasized during the summer at the expense of middle distillates.

77. Table 5–3 is taken from *Conflicting Information Hearings, supra* note 69, at 58.

78. *FEO Industry Background*, 34 (1974).

79. *Monthly Energy Review*, June 1975, at 28; *Monthly Energy Review*, January 1975, at 18-19.

80. This particular division of end uses is taken from the *FEO Industry Background* at 24–25 (1974). FEO, *Emergency Advisory Committee for Natural Gas, Subcommittee on LP-Gas Supply and Demand, Report on LP-Gas* (1974), uses different breakdowns. It divides the LP-Gas supply (in MB/D) as follows:

	Ethane	Propane	Butane	Total
1972	300	905	454	1,659
1973	321	933	473	1,727
1974	341	970	478	1,789
1975	358	994	487	1,839
1976	376	1,034	508	1,918

Only the 1972 figures are actual; the others are estimates. These totals include LP-Gas made from natural gas. Propane sources are divided as follows:

	Gas Plants	Refiners	Imports
1972	66.2%	29.1%	4.7%
1973	62.7	29.6	7.7
1974	62.4	28.7	8.9
1975	60.0	29.3	10.7
1976	57.1	30.9	12.0

The source projects this breakdown by end use in 1975 (millions of gallons): chemical (including synthetic rubber) 10,554.8; residential and commercial, 8876.8; industrial, 7652.2; internal combustion, 1704.4; utility, 836.3; and other, 427.9.

Agricultural uses were included in several categories above, but are separately divided for 1975 (in millions of gallons), as follows: farm residential, 3224.1; irrigation, 652.3; farm vehicle fuel, 330.7; miscellaneous, 287.6; grain drying, 118.9; for a total of 4613.6 million gallons.

81. *FEO Industry Background*, 24–25 (1974).

82. *Id.* See notes 89–93 *infra* and accompanying text.

83. *Id.*

84. The *Monthly Energy Review* data, from which this is taken, include

ethane, LPG (propane, butane, propane-butane mixtures), natural gasoline, plant condensate, and minor quantities of some finished products. They include production by refineries and natural gas processing plants, but exclude amounts used at refineries for blending purposes, which range between 700 and 850 MB/D. They include some consumption of natural gas liquids at refineries for fuel and petrochemical uses. The data may exclude what is often called still gas or refinery gas, the production of which averaged 467 MB/D in 1972. This gas may be defined as any "form or mixture of gas produced in refineries by cracking, reforming, and other processes, the principal constituents of which are methane, ethane, ethylene, butane, butylene, propane, propylene, etc." *National Petroleum Product, supra* note 76, at 142. Still gas is frequently used as refinery fuel.

85. *Monthly Energy Review,* January 1975, at 20-21; *Monthly Energy Review,* June 1975, at 30.

86. *FEO Industry Background,* at 30-33 (1974). Since specifications were issued for AVGAS, there have been six basic grades used, differentiated on the basis of anti-knock performance. Of those, two have all but completely disappeared, and another is being phased out. Soon there may be only one grade of AVGAS: low-lead Grade 100-130.

87. *Id.* at 31-32. All commercial jet fuel is kero-based, but the military also uses some. Naphtha-base jet fuel burns hotter and is better suited for most military uses. Commercial airline jet fuels in the U.S. fall into three grades: Jet A, Jet A-1, and Jet B. The first two are kerosene-type, and the latter corresponds to military JP-4 fuel. Demand for commercial jet fuel grew from 300 MB/D in 1965 to 700 MB/D in 1971, largely because of the conversion to jets. Now first generation jets are being replaced by jets which burn more fuel but have greater passenger capacity. Thus, the growth in demand should be more gradual in the future. Most of the demand is for Jet A and A-1, while Jet B is not used extensively.

88. *Monthly Energy Review,* January 1975, at 12; *Monthly Energy Review,* June 1975, at 22.

89. *Energy Facts Hearings, supra* note 64, at 348. This excludes demand for ethane and liquified gases.

90. Wakefield, *supra* note 15, at 113.

91. *Id.*

92. *FEO Industry Background,* 35 (1974).

93. *Id.*

94. *Energy Facts Hearings, supra* note 64, at 348.

95. *FEO Industry Background* at 36-41 (1974).

96. *Id.* The division is made by the U.S. Department of Commerce, Bureau of Census. "Industrial Lubricating Oils" includes "industrial, marine, and railroad oils intended primarily for lubrication purposes and including oils sold for cutting purposes." The second group, "Industrial Other Oils," includes all others except solvents, asphalts, and petroleum chemicals. Industrial oils in general are intended for lubrication, friction modification, heat transfer, and rust prevention.

97. *Id.* at 42-44. Components for greases are selected to maximize resistance

to heat and oxidation, and to provide anti-rust and extreme pressure lubricating properties. Grease improvements have been similar to those in lubricating oils, and are responsible for many industrial changes, such as in electrical motors.

98. *National Petroleum Product, supra* note 76, at 142.

99. *Energy Facts Hearings, supra* note 64, at 348; see Table 5-1.

100. *National Petroleum Product, supra* note 76, at 142.

101. *Id.; Energy Facts Hearings, supra* note 64, at 348.

✳ *Chapter Six*

Petroleum Allocation: Statutory Authority and Regulation

The authority of the Federal Energy Administration (FEA) to allocate petroleum and refined petroleum products is very broad, but there are limits on what types of regulation may be developed. This chapter discusses the basic features of FEA's statutory authorities and regulations and provides a basis for comparison with other options for allocation.

Five major statutes relate to FEA allocation authority: the Emergency Petroleum Allocation Act (EPAA),[1] the Energy Supply and Environmental Coordination Act (ESECA),[2] the Federal Energy Administration Act (FEAA),[3] the Defense Production Act (DPA),[4] and, finally, the Energy Policy and Conservation Act (Energy Policy Act) enacted in December 1975.[5]

The relevant history of federal petroleum regulation began with the mandatory oil import quotas program established by President Eisenhower in 1959.[6] The system of quotas represented an attempt to protect the domestic oil industry from lower priced foreign crude oil. In August 1971, President Nixon froze the prices of oil and refined products as part of his plan to fight inflation. Pursuant to the Economic Stabilization Act of 1970, the Cost of Living Council promulgated extensive regulatory procedures for enforcement, appeals, and adjustments. In April 1973, the President terminated the mandatory oil import quota program and substituted a fee system. A voluntary allocation program for crude oil was initiated in May 1973. A new price freeze was implemented in June, and the Cost of Living Council adopted more permanent petroleum price rules during August 1973. Because stocks were already low, a mandatory propane allocation program became effective on October 3, 1973, and middle distillates (heating oils) followed on November 1. The "Yom Kippur" war broke out in early October, and the Arab oil embargo created the possibility of drastic petroleum shortages in the U.S.

Congress passed the Emergency Petroleum Allocation Act during the crisis atmosphere of November 1973 in order to meet a particular supply emergency: the Arab oil embargo. At the time of passage, the President already had discretionary price control and allocation authority over petroleum under the Economic Stabilization Act, and the Energy Policy Office already existed for advising the President and the Cost of Living Council on energy matters. Immediately after enactment of the EPAA, the President established the Federal Energy Office (FEO) in the Executive Office of the President. Under Executive Order No. 11748, the FEO was delegated all of the President's authority under the EPAA, section 203 of the Economic Stabilization Act, and parts of the Defense Production Act that relate to control of energy. The petroleum allocation and pricing regulations which were mandatory under the EPAA were made effective on December 27, 1973, and fully implemented on January 15, 1974. The authority to control petroleum under the Economic Stabilization Act expired on April 30, 1974.

The Energy Policy Act has modified and extended the EPAA's mandatory petroleum allocation and pricing authorities for a 40 month period. Thereafter, the authorities become discretionary until the EPAA expires on September 30, 1981.

The Federal Energy Administration Act was passed by Congress on May 7, 1974. This Act created the FEA as an agency of the Executive Branch outside the Executive Office of the President. By Executive Order No. 11790 on June 27, 1974, the President transferred the functions of the FEO to the FEA. The Federal Energy Administration Act expires on June 30, 1976, and has not yet been extended. At least a two-year extension seems likely, however, in view of the FEA's many important tasks in the energy situation.

The Energy Supply and Environmental Coordination Act (ESECA) was passed in June 1974 to provide for conversion to coal of certain powerplants and other major fuel burning installations and to authorize the collection of certain energy information. Congress specifically assigned the Act to the FEA for administration. Authority to make new conversion orders under ESECA expires on June 30, 1977, and authority to enforce orders continues through December 31, 1984.

Meanwhile broad general authority to allocate scarce materials in a national emergency already existed under the Defense Production Act (DPA) of 1950. The Energy Policy Act has now amended the DPA to provide authority to allocate supplies of materials and equipment in an emergency in order to maximize domestic energy supplies, and this specific authority extends through 1984.

Finally, the Energy Policy and Conservation Act was enacted in December 1975 after a controversial compromise on the oil pricing issue was reached between President Ford and the Democratic-controlled Congress. In addition to amending the EPAA, ESECA and DPA, the Energy Policy Act contains new authorities which substantially enhance the government's capacity to administer energy shortages. Among the new powers, which expire on June 30, 1985, are standby authorities to implement energy conservation and motor fuel rationing plans in a supply interruption, authority to participate in international sharing of oil supplies with other cooperating industrial countries, establishment of a strategic petroleum reserve, emergency authority to order production of oil or gas at certain rates, and development of an energy information base within the government.

Each of the five principal sources of statutory authority for petroleum allocation and the main features of regulatory programs developed under them are discussed in the separate sections which follow.

FEDERAL ENERGY ADMINISTRATION ACT (FEAA)

The Federal Energy Administration Act (FEAA) created the FEA, but it gave the agency no new substantive authority for the allocation of petroleum. Section 5(b) sets out the various functions and purposes of the FEA.[7] This section, which established only 12 general requirements of the FEA, was subject to some controversy. Representatives Moss and Abzug added comments to the House Report, complaining that the vague language might give vast unspecified powers to the FEA.[8] The Conference Report replied to this charge by pointing out that section 5(a) limited the FEA so that no new program authority was granted to the agency.[9] Section 5(a) provides that the FEA shall have only three sources of authority: (a) that *specifically* transferred to or vested in it by the FEAA; (b) that delegated by the President pursuant to *specific* authority vested in him; and (c) powers *specifically* vested in the agency by Congress.[10]

The FEAA itself has provisions for rulemaking, administrative procedures, reports, collection of data, judicial review, and a comprehensive plan.[11] Section 6 provides for transfers of authority from the Department of Interior's former offices of Petroleum Allocation, Energy Conservation, Energy Data and Analysis, and Oil and Gas, as well as from the Cost of Living Council.[12] None of these reflects new allocation authority. Congress specifically vested the powers granted by ESECA in the FEA. By Executive Order No. 11790, the President delegated authority as described above to the FEA. Administrative and procedural requirements of the FEAA will be discussed in Chapter Seven.

EMERGENCY PETROLEUM ALLOCATION ACT (EPAA)

In the fall of 1973, when the EPAA was enacted, a shortage of petroleum and refined products clearly existed. Congress stated in section 2(a) that the purpose of the EPAA was to cope with these shortages.[13] Under current market conditions these shortages are over, with the exception of propane. No court has held that FEA regulation must end because the shortage is over, but it has been questioned whether a statute should be used when its language indicates that its express purpose has ceased to exist.[14]

Actually, the legislative history of the EPAA reveals three basic objectives for regulation: (a) distribution of scarce supplies to protect the public and economy; (b) protection of the public from price gouging; and (c) preservation of the market share of the independent sector and the competition the independents create.

Statutory Objectives and Requirements

Section 4(a) of the EPAA provides for mandatory allocation and price regulation:[15]

> Not later than fifteen days after the date of enactment of this Act, the President shall promulgate a regulation providing for the mandatory allocation of crude oil, residual fuel oil, and each refined petroleum product, in amounts specified in (or determined in a manner prescribed by) and at prices specified in (or determined in a manner prescribed by) such regulation. . . . Such regulation shall apply to all crude oil, residual fuel oil, and refined petroleum products produced in or imported into the United States.

Congress specified nine objectives in section 4(b)(1) which must be met to the maximum extent practicable in any allocation and pricing program established under section 4(a).[16] "(A) protection of public health (including the production of pharmaceuticals), safety, and welfare (including maintenance of residential heating . . .), . . . and the national defense; (B) maintenance of all public services . . .; (C) maintenance of agricultural operations . . .; (D) preservation of an economically sound and competitive petroleum industry; including the priority needs to restore and foster competition in the producing, refining, distribution, marketing, and petrochemical sectors of such industry, and to preserve the competitive viability of independent refiners, small refiners, nonbranded independent marketers, and branded independent marketers; (E) the allocation of suitable types . . . of crude oil to refineries in the United States to permit such refineries to operate at full capacity; (F) equitable distribution of crude oil . . . and refined petroleum products at equitable prices among all regions and areas of the United States and sectors of the petroleum industry . . . and among all users; (G) allocation of residual fuel oil and refined oil petroleum products . . . as may be necessary for the maintenance of exploration for, and production or extraction of . . . fuels, . . . and minerals essential to the requirements of the United States. . . .; (H) economic efficiency; and (I) minimization of economic distortion, inflexibility, and unnecessary interference with market mechanisms." Courts have repeatedly held that a particular regulation does not have to attain all of these objectives, and that the FEA must be given flexibility in maximizing benefits.[17] It is unlikely that an FEA regulation would be held invalid for failure to achieve some of these objectives.

While subsequent sections of the EPAA place limits on regulation, Congress intended that the FEA should have considerable flexibility. The Conference Report stated that it "may be necessary in selective cases to compel the allocation of product to particular end-uses," and there exists "full authority under this Act to identify permissible uses of covered fuels and to restrict the amounts which may be made available to such uses." Moreover, allocation levels need not be based on historical patterns, but may consider the relative benefits of end uses.[18] While these options were open to the FEA, Congress did not intend to require any one in particular.

Similarly, with regard to the oil pricing policy added to the EPAA by the Energy Policy Act, the Conference Report states:[19]

[T]he President is to have a substantial measure of administrative flexibility to craft the price regulatory mechanism in a manner designed to optimize production from domestic properties subject to a statutory parameter requiring the regulatory pattern to prevent prices from exceeding a maximum weighted average.

The details of the new statutory pricing policy will be considered in conjunction with the earlier FEA price regulations.

In support of the general allocation and pricing authority contained in section 4(a), the Energy Policy Act has added a number of specific provisions to the EPAA. Some were added in order to clarify areas where the FEA's authority was in some doubt, while others have considerably expanded the FEA's previous scope of authority under the EPAA.

Section 14 of the EPAA, as amended, provides the FEA with authority to "require adjustments" in the operation of refineries, thereby permitting the government to control directly, within the technical limits of the refinery involved, the yield of various petroleum products.[20] Section 15 provides authority to control petroleum inventories at all levels of the distribution system, subject to two limitations: the amount required to be held in inventory may not exceed 90 days of peak usage; and no person may be compelled to add new storage facilities in order to meet an inventory requirement.[21] On the other hand, section 16 prohibits, during a severe energy supply interruption, hoarding of any petroleum product in excess of a person's "reasonable needs." Each of these Energy Policy Act amendments to the EPAA provides clear statutory sanction for regulatory actions which might have been questioned under the general allocation authority of the EPAA as originally enacted.

In addition, the Energy Policy Act has amended the EPAA to clarify the scope of petroleum products covered. The term "petroleum product" is defined to mean "crude oil, residual fuel oil, or any refined petroleum product," and expressly including "any natural liquid and any natural gas liquid product."[22] This amendment removes any ambiguity concerning the FEA's authority to regulate propane, butane and natural gasoline that is derived from natural gas, as well as crude oil, making moot pending litigation on the issue.

Finally, the Energy Policy Act adds to the EPAA authority under section 13 whereby the U.S. government may exercise "the exclusive right" to import petroleum products of foreign origin for resale in the United States.[23] This expansive new option is not to be used for the purpose of providing a subsidy or preference, or to realize a profit or loss. Sales on a competitive bid basis would, however, be permitted if such sales would tend to lower the world market price for oil. Prior to exercise of the purchase authority, the plan would be subject to congressional review as discussed in Chapter Seven. In any event, it seems likely that the President will resist strongly the use of this statutory authority to move the U.S. government directly into the world oil market.

Statutory Limits on Regulation

The EPAA has several provisions which may limit regulation, or at least provide the basis for a judicial gloss not desired by the FEA.

Section 4(b)(2) requires that price regulations allow for "a dollar-for-dollar passthrough of net increases in the cost of crude oil, residual fuel oil, and refined petroleum products at all levels of distribution from the producer through the retail level."[24] This requirement is responsible for the "banking" regulations described later. Another requirement of section 4(b)(2) is that a single date must be used in computing the base prices of crude oil, residual fuel oil, and refined petroleum products at all levels of marketing and distribution.[25] This latter limit speaks to maintaining the same base period at all *levels,* not for all *products,* however. It has not really hampered agency initiative.

To the extent that it is practicable and consistent with other sections of the EPAA, section 4(b)(3) requires the FEA to give consideration to allocating supplies to those whose supply of natural gas has been eliminated. Similarly, according to section 4(c)(5), LPG should not be denied any industrial user who does not have a "substitute" fuel. Both provisions are designed to protect natural gas users who are subject to FPC curtailment.[26]

Section 4(c)(1) is designed to protect small independent refiners and marketers. It provides that refiners and marketers must be given an amount not less than that received during the corresponding period in 1972 unless the total of domestic production and imports falls below the 1972 levels.[27] This means that the FEA cannot use the EPAA to reduce available supplies below 1972 levels, whether to obtain long-term goals, conserve scarce resources, or change consumption patterns. The language of the section makes this limit applicable for crude oil and *each* refined petroleum product.

The consistent use of "each" emphasizes congressional intent to maintain constant market shares during administration of a shortage, through pro rata reductions in supply.[28] The extent to which this provision has been or can be a limit will be seen when the current regulations and alternatives are discussed below. The preference for pro rata reductions to suppliers does not reflect any congressional predisposition to favor pro rata over priority reductions for *consumers,* but rather concern about the survival of independent companies in various parts of the petroleum distribution system.

The EPAA's requirement of pro rata reductions for marketers and refiners may, nevertheless, be a barrier to an allocation scheme oriented more toward end use or efficiency. The allocation regulations are now designed so that supply levels determined by end use are applicable only to wholesale purchaser consumers and end users. Supply levels for resellers are set by base period volume. If for some reason petroleum demand could be most effectively curtailed by supplying resellers on the basis of their customers' uses, such a plan would likely be barred by the EPAA. Similarly, if large refineries are more efficient, perhaps consumers would be best served in a shortage by closing small refineries and allowing large ones to operate nearer to full capacity. Here again the Act would seem to prevent such an allocation scheme.

It is fair to say that the orientation of the nine objectives of the EPAA is toward increasing supplies, rather than toward permanently decreasing demand. In contrast to other rationales for allocation, a plan to force conservation when supplies are adequate might be challenged as contrary to congressional intent. The Conference Report on the EPAA stated that allocation should not be designed to have the "net effect of occasioning a substantial reduction in the total *supply* of crude oil, residual fuel oil or refined petroleum products."[29] "Supply" in that sense probably means the total amount available to the public. Moreover, the Energy Policy Act has added to the EPAA an express denial of authority to prescribe minimum prices for crude oil or petroleum products.[30] The FEA is thus prohibited from constricting the supply of a particular product by establishing an artificially high price for it.

FEA officials contend that practical and desirable options for allocation have never been stymied by the constraints of the EPAA. Nevertheless, the statutory language and legislative history of the EPAA have played an important part in shaping existing regulations, and could be a barrier to some plans for allocation. For example, the idea of class of trade allocation has been discussed briefly within FEA, but has never been seriously considered.[31] Such a plan would require suppliers to sell a certain percentage of total product to a particular class of marketers, such as nonbranded independents. There would be no allocation right for specific marketers, however. Some think the plan would be superior to and less complex than the allocation programs adopted. However, the EPAA seems to preclude adoption, since section 4(c) calls for allocation to "each" purchaser for resale. The extent to which class of trade allocation has been discounted because of these legal barriers is unclear, but the scheme itself has been mentioned as a possibility by FEA officials in Senate testimony.[32] It is, of course, difficult to ascertain what, if any, other ideas for regulation have been rejected because of the language of the EPAA.

In summary of what the EPAA anticipates, petroleum supplies may be allocated to protect independent companies, prevent price gouging, and/or cope with a shortage. Companies at all levels of the industry may be ordered to comply, although what is ordered could encounter constitutional or statutory limits.[33] What may not be ordered directly can often be achieved by pressure, e.g., a rule change in entitlements if supplies are not allocated properly by refineries. The extent of what may be ordered is illustrated below in the description of certain FEA regulations.

Allocation Regulations

FEA allocation regulations categorize oil companies as suppliers or purchasers, with respect to each product, so for different purposes a company may be both. Purchasers are classified as "wholesale purchaser-resellers" (WPRs), "wholesale purchaser-consumers" (WPCs), or "end users." A WPR is any "firm which purchases, receives through transfer, or otherwise obtains (as by consignment) an allocated product and resells, or otherwise transfers it to other purchasers without substantially changing its form."[34]

A WPC is an ultimate consumer of a large volume of a refined product. It is a firm that normally

> purchases or obtains an allocated product from a supplier and receives delivery of that product into a storage tank substantially under the control of that firm at a fixed location, and which either (a) purchased or obtained more than 20,000 gallons of that allocated product for its own use in agricultural production in any completed calendar year subsequent to 1971; (b) purchased or obtained more than 50,000 gallons of that allocated product in any completed calendar year subsequent to 1971 for use in one or more multifamily residences; or (c) purchased or obtained more than 84,000 gallons of that allocated product in any completed calendar year subsequent to 1971.[35]

An end user is any ultimate consumer other than a WPC.[36]

Although there is overlap, allocation regulations may be categorized in terms of their purpose: those to preserve competition (directed toward supplier-purchaser relationships) and those designed to allocate scarce supplies for particular end uses. The allocation regulations begin to apply at the refinery level for crude oil supplies, although some import control remains. The labelling of purchasers as WPR, WPC, or end user, and the distinction between suppliers and purchasers, are largely functional. Traditional terminology in the oil industry can be inconsistent and confusing. The FEA's labels enable a firm to know how to categorize itself with respect to any regulation.

Crude oil allocation. For crude oil allocation, the FEA has developed three major programs under the EPAA.

The first program is the freeze on domestic crude oil supply relationships in effect under contract on December 1, 1973.[37] The purposes of this freeze were to ensure a source of supply for small and independent refineries and to provide a basis from which to begin spreading supplies without constant industry changes.

The second program, called "buy/sell," provides a basis for allocating crude oil to certain small and independent refiners, at approximately 1972 levels, from certain large sellers.[38] It uses the supplier/purchaser freeze relationships as a data base. Very generally, the buy/sell program allows refiners with supplies below the national average to purchase from refiners with supplies in excess of the national average. For the most part, "refiner-sellers" were major integrated oil companies, and "refiner-buyers" were small and independent refiners.[39] Pricing rules protect the refiner-seller in that he may charge the weighted average price of all crude delivered to him in that area of the country, plus a handling fee of 30 cents per barrel. Adjustments for quality differences are possible, and increased prices for replacement crude may be passed through to refined products.[40]

Some type of crude oil supply allocation program for equalizing supplies is mandated by the EPAA. The FEA attempted to create a program that protected small and independent refiners and still maintained incentives for refiners generally to increase supplies. In the allocation quarter beginning March 1, 1975, only 60 to 70 percent of the total purchase opportunity was bought by refiner-buyers. Previously, the percentage ran from 85 to 90 percent. With present adequate supplies, the program is not very attractive. Many industry officials complained that the buy/sell program created disincentives to increasing imports. Although FEA officials did not believe this to be true, the program did contribute to price increases.[41]

The third crude oil allocation program, the entitlements program, is more recent.[42] The entitlements program is supposed to compensate for the widely divergent feedstock costs of various refiners resulting from the two-tier price system. Each month, a national average ratio of old oil supplies to crude runs is computed by the FEA. Refiners are then issued entitlements equal to the ratio. Refineries processing above-average amounts of cheaper, old oil are required to purchase entitlements from those processing below-average amounts.

Small refiners are given favorable treatment in the computation. They are issued more entitlements as their total refinery capacity decreases. Thus a small refiner is entitled to purchase a disproportionately large share of old oil entitlements. The preference is designed to protect the market viability of small refiners who are believed to be less competitive than large refiners. The Energy Policy Act has widened the protection afforded small refiners by exempting from any requirement to purchase entitlements up to 50,000 barrels per day of refinery input of a refiner whose total capacity does not exceed 100,000 barrels per day.[43] The result of FEA regulation plus subsequent congressional legislation is that small refiners without access to supplies of cheap, old oil are granted more than their proportionate share of entitlements, while small refiners with ample supplies of old oil are not required to purchase their proportionate share of entitlements in order to refine it.

The entitlements program is not a direct allocation program whereby oil is exchanged. All transfers are monetary. The sole rationale for the program is to protect the refiners who would otherwise have uncompetitive product costs because of heavy dependence on imports, or on uncontrolled "new," "released," or "stripper well" oil. Entitlement purchasers can pass the costs through to consumers, and sellers can use the proceeds to offset the costs of uncontrolled oil. These proceeds must also be passed through to consumers.[44] The cost per entitlement has increased substantially during the course of the program and reached $8.00 per barrel in October 1975.

Refined product allocation. FEA regulations covering the allocation of refined products are more oriented toward end-use priorities and distribution of scarce supplies than are crude oil allocation regulations, although the goal of preserving existing companies is reflected in the design of both programs. Again, there is a supplier/purchaser freeze[45] applicable to all purchasers and suppliers of refined products. The base period varies with the product, depending on historical market practices. The base period is a month or quarter of 1972 or 1973 corresponding to the same month or quarter in the current year.

Supplier/purchaser relationships are established for the duration of the allocation program, but they are somewhat flexible for purchasers who are consumers, as distinguished from resellers. WPCs and suppliers may terminate a supply obligation by mutual consent. However, new relationships between WPCs and suppliers must be assigned by the FEA. Small end users and their suppliers may terminate or form new relationships without FEA approval. On the other hand, relationships between WPRs and suppliers may not be terminated or initiated without FEA approval.

In all cases, a base period purchaser is not required to purchase his entitlement. In fact, with the current surplus, many purchasers attempt to find lower prices than those offered by their base period suppliers. The freeze interrelates with the "surplus product rule" described below. Basically however, surplus refined products can be sold without regard to freeze relationships. Consequently, purchasers who shop around help to create a surplus market filled by those sellers from whom they have failed to purchase their entitlements. The freeze thus results in supplier/purchaser relationships for purchasers to fall back on if supplies become short again, but it serves little or no useful purpose in a surplus market.[46]

The amount of product to be allocated to a purchaser depends on whether he markets the product, as a WPR, or consumes it, as a WPC or end user. A WPR is entitled to 100 percent of base period use, except in times of shortage, when his supply is subject to the allocation fraction described below.[47] This means that a WPR's allocation cannot be reduced because of his purchaser's use of the product. However, the allocation fraction may work to increase an allocation for a particular WPR, and this can in turn reduce supplies available to others through the operation of the fraction.

A WPC or end user is supplied on the basis of an allocation level which is determined on the priority of use for the product. For all refined products, agricultural and defense users are allowed 100 percent of current requirements, and are not subject to the allocation fraction. Petrochemicals receive that high priority for naphthas and gas oils, and nursing and medical facilities receive that priority for residual fuel oil and middle distillates for heating uses. Below that priority, other uses are classified, varying somewhat with each particular product. Some other classifications are: 100 percent of current requirements subject to fraction, 100 percent of base period use subject to fraction, 95 percent of base period use subject to fraction, etc.[48]

Not all consumers are given an allocation level. For example, allocation levels for motor gasoline apply only to WPCs and end users who purchase in bulk.[49] The reduction of gasoline supplies to each individual motorist requires coupon-rationing, rather than an allocation scheme, because many motorists will go from station to station and reduce purchases little, if at all. Purchasers without allocation levels, except for those (such as individual motorists) that are not readily identifiable with a particular supplier, are entitled to purchase only surplus products.

The difference between methods for computing allocation levels for consumers and resellers is a result of the EPAA requirement that marketers be subject to pro rata reductions.[50] The FEA determined early to develop some type of end-use control, but the agency could only apply the control to consumers that could be reached directly as a practical matter.

The allocation fraction is a device for pro rata reductions in product supplies, to be used when a shortage exists. Each supplier is responsible for computing his own fraction, and thus it may vary among suppliers.[51] A supplier's allocation fraction is the quotient of his total supply, minus supplies for uses not subject to fraction and for the state set-aside, divided by his supply obligation. The numerator is called "allocable supply." The supply obligation consists of the requirements of all purchasers subject to fraction, based upon their allocation levels. The allocation fraction is the percentage of an allocation level that can be purchased. Therefore, the final allotment to a purchaser is determined by multiplying the purchaser's allocation level times his allocation fraction. The allocation fraction seems to press the legal limits of the EPAA since it operates to increase supplies to marketers selling relatively large amounts of products to purchasers allowed 100 percent of requirements.

Each WPR must certify to his supplier the amount he sells to purchasers not subject to fraction. When that WPR is supplied, he is given the amounts required by those certified users, and then the base period volume subjected to fraction (less the certified amount).[52] Therefore a distributor who sells 10,000 barrels of gasoline to agricultural users and 10,000 to retail service stations will receive 10,000 barrels plus a fraction of the 10,000 barrels for the service stations. Of course, the distributor is required to make his sales along those lines, ensuring that agriculture really does receive first priority.[53]

If, as is often the case now, the allocation fraction for a supplier exceeds 1.0, the supplier first distributes the product as though the fraction were 1.0. Thereafter, the surplus is subject to the "surplus product rule."[54] This rule requires large suppliers, "prime suppliers," to report surpluses to the FEA, which may order the surplus either distributed to certain purchasers, or placed in inventory, or diverted to another supplier with a lower allocation fraction. If the FEA does not direct the dispostion of the surplus, as is always the case with small suppliers, the supplier must offer the surplus to branded and non-branded independent customers in the same proportion as he regularly supplies his product to them. If these customers do not purchase the surplus, the supplier may use his discretion in making further sales. Currently, many independents decline to purchase from their base period supplier, and, instead, use the surplus product rule to obtain cheaper supplies in a manner comparable to "spot" purchases in the past from refiners.[55]

State set-aside.   A state set-aside program exists for motor gasoline, propane, middle distillates, and residual fuel oil.[56] All refiners, importers, and other suppliers making their first sale of a product in a state for consumption there must report to the FEA and the state energy office the amount they expect to sell in the state during the next month. A portion fixed by the FEA, either 3 or 4 percent, is set aside. The state may then direct the sale of that fuel as it pleases (e.g., to cover emergency shortages). The state set-aside cannot be accumulated from one allocation period to the next. Therefore, the unused portions are usually released for distribution before the end of the period.[57]

Refinery yield control.   A refinery yield control program exists on a stand-by basis. Under this program, the FEA can order a refinery to increase its yield of any particular product.[58] The program has been used only once, and the FEA did not investigate whether or not refineries complied.[59] Generally, the FEA more subtly controls refinery yield by adjusting price regulations to make some products more profitable than others. One reason for this program's infrequent use is that the FEA lacks data concerning the degree to which refineries can *technically* shift their yield toward some products. Also, yields will vary depending on the type of crude which is refined. The FEA has been unable thus far to tackle such problems. As discussed above, the Energy Policy Act

has added to the EPAA specific statutory authority for direct control of refinery operations.

Price Regulations and Statutory Pricing Policy

While our main interest is in options for allocation, there is an important
and complex relationship between price and allocation regulations. Price regulations create a shortage of price-controlled products, thereby creating a need
for allocation regulations. Moreover, allocation in time of shortage requires
price regulation in order to prevent price gouging. Finally, price and allocation
regulation may both be necessary to protect the status of independent refiners
and marketers. The following is a brief description of the FEA price regulations
in effect up to December 1975, and the new statutory oil pricing policy of the
Energy Policy Act. At this writing, the FEA is in the process of developing a
new regulation under section 4(a) of the EPAA in conformity with the Energy
Policy Act amendments. It remains important to understand both the pre-
existing regulatory structure and the new statutory policy because Congress,
in enacting the Energy Policy Act, intended to modify and build upon the
existing price regulation.

Crude oil price controls. Under the EPAA, prior to the Energy Policy Act
amendments, the FEA established different sets of price regulations for producers, refiners and resellers and retailers.[60] The predominant feature of the
producer regulations was the two-tier price scheme, which was a remnant from
the old Cost of Living Council regulations.[61] Historically, foreign oil prices
had been cheaper than domestic. However, since the OPEC price increases in
1973, foreign prices have been well above domestic.

To minimize the inflationary impact of post-1973 OPEC prices on domestic
crude, a ceiling price was imposed on "old" oil, i.e., the amount of crude oil
produced from domestic property in 1972. The ceiling price consisted of the
May 15, 1973, average posted price in the field of $3.90 per barrel, plus $1.35,
for a national average of $5.25 per barrel for old oil.

There were a number of incentives for new production:

1. Any oil produced in excess of the 1972 production level from the same
   property was not subject to the price ceiling, and was called "new" oil.
2. For every barrel of new oil produced, the FEA released one barrel of that
   producer's "old" oil from price constraints, and this was called "released"
   oil.
3. The EPAA, as originally enacted, precluded price regulation of oil from
   stripper wells.[62] Furthermore, the first sale of imported oil into the United
   States is excluded from price controls since coverage would be likely to
   eliminate the imports as a source of supply.[63]

The new statutory crude oil pricing policy is contained in section 8 of the EPAA, added by the Energy Policy Act. Section 8(a) requires the President to promulgate by regulation "ceiling prices (or the manner of determining ceiling prices) applicable to any first sale of crude oil produced in the United States. . . ."[64] The ceiling prices must result in a "maximum weighted average first sale price" of $7.66 per barrel for domestic crude oil. The effect is a rollback of $1.09 from the December 1975 domestic average price estimated by FEA at $8.75 per barrel.[65]

The composite ceiling price system is mandatory for a period of 40 months from the effective date of the new pricing regulation. Thereafter, price controls become discretionary until the EPAA expires on September 30, 1981.[66]

Under section 8(d), the new pricing regulation may itself provide for upward adjustments in the initial $7.66 per barrel composite ceiling price to take account of inflation and to provide an adequate production incentive.[67] However, the production incentive adjustment must not increase the composite ceiling price more than three percent per year, and the combined effect of the inflation and production incentive adjustments must not increase the composite ceiling price more than 10 percent per year. A production incentive adjustment must be based on a finding that it is likely to provide a positive incentive for discovery or development of high cost and high risk properties, the application of enhanced recovery techniques to producing properties, or sustaining production from marginal wells, including stripper wells.

In addition, under section 8(e) if the President finds that a production incentive adjustment in excess of the three percent per year limit or a combined adjustment in excess of the 10 percent limit is necessary to provide an adequate incentive to increase production, he may propose an amendment to the oil pricing regulation providing for a larger adjustment.[68] The amendment is, however, subject to review by the Congress and may be disapproved by either House. The President may submit proposals under section 8(e) for adjustments in excess of the statutory limits at 90 day intervals.

Finally, section 8(g) requires the President to report to the Congress on April 15, 1977 on the impact of the ceiling prices then in effect on incentives to develop and produce oil from the North Slope in Alaska and to sustain or enhance production in the lower 48 states.[69] If he determines that a price sufficient to provide positive incentives for production of Alaskan oil would, because of the composite ceiling price requirement, unduly reduce incentives to produce oil in the lower 48 states and offshore, the President may then propose that up to two million barrels per day of Alaskan oil be exempt from the computation of the composite ceiling price. However, the special ceiling price prescribed for the North Slope oil cannot exceed the highest average price for another classification of domestic crude oil. A proposal to exempt Alaskan oil is also subject to review by the Congress and disapproval by either House.

Within the framework of the maximum weighted average first sale price and the various adjustment mechanisms, the President is given broad discretion-ary authority to develop oil pricing regulations. This includes authority to establish different classifications of crude oil and to prescribe different ceiling prices for the various classifications. According to the Conference Report, the President has authority to establish a ceiling price for a particular type of crude oil that is above the then current market clearing price as long as the composite ceiling price is within the allowable limit.[70] The number of tiers within the pricing system and the types of classifications are within the President's discretion to determine, subject of course to the limits and findings required by the EPAA, as amended. However, it seems likely that an increase in the number of tiers in the pricing system may increase geometrically the administrative complexity of the system.

In enacting the oil pricing policy embodied in section 8 of the EPAA, Congress contemplated considerable regulatory continuity and intended that differentiations between new and old oil in effect in December 1975 would be maintained at least initially. According to the Conference Report:[71]

It is the conferee's understanding that should the President structure the price regulatory system in this manner, an initial ceiling price of approximately $11.28 per barrel could be applied to new oil and production from stripper well leases so as to preserve significant price incentives for optimizing production from these sources.

Under section 8(b) the prices and classifications must be "administratively feasible" and "consistent with obtaining optimum production of crude oil in the United States."[72] However, no amendment to a crude oil pricing regulation may permit an increase in the price of old oil unless the President finds: (a) that the amendment will give positive incentives for enhanced recovery or deep horizon development or is necessary to take account of declining production; and (b) that the amendment is likely to result in a level of production greater than would otherwise be achieved. These findings are required because, working within the constraint of a composite ceiling price, any price increase for old oil would require a corresponding reduction in the amount of price incentives available for upper-tier oil production.

It may be noted in passing here that the Energy Policy Act also has added section 12 to the EPAA whereby the President may, subject to prior congressional review, exempt from the allocation and pricing regulations a class of persons or class of transactions. This mechanism for accelerated conversion of mandatory regulation under the EPAA to standby authority will be discussed further in Chapter Seven.

Refined product price controls. Price regulation for refineries is complex and has five major features.

The first feature is the dollar-for-dollar passthrough of cost increases which is required by section 4(b)(2) of the EPAA, as amended by the Energy Policy Act. This requirement, as we will see in the discussion of judicial interpretation, has helped the FEA to avoid the constitutional issue of taking for public use without compensation. The regulations limit refiners to charging the lawful May 15, 1973, selling price to a class of purchasers, plus product cost increases above May 1973 levels, plus some of the increased costs of doing business under certain circumstances. The latter are "non-product costs," and the sum of the former two is the "base" price.[73]

Increases in *non-product* costs may be passed through only if the refiner does not exceed his base period profit margin in the fiscal year of the pass-through. A firm's "profit margin" consists of its profits, expressed as a percentage of the firm's sales.[74] This leverage results from the wording of the EPAA, which requires only "a dollar-for-dollar passthrough of net increases in the *cost of crude oil, residual fuel oil, and refined petroleum products* at all levels of distribution from the producer to the retail level."[75]

The second feature of refiner price regulations concerns "banks," which in general permit carrying forward unrecouped increased product costs. Refiners incur costs unevenly. Requiring immediate price increases is considered administratively infeasible because it would necessitate constant price adjustments up and down. More important and relevant to market conditions prevailing in 1975, competitive pressures may limit the amount of cost increases that a refiner can pass through and maintain his market share. Under the FEA regulations, therefore, product cost increases which are not recovered in one month may be carried forward and, within limits, used in calculating prices in subsequent months. However, recoverable non-product cost increases may not be "banked," and must be passed through immediately or never at all.[76] As of November 1975, refiners' banks of unrecouped crude oil cost increases totalled about $1.4 billion.[77]

The Energy Policy Act amends section 4(b)(2) of the EPAA to place statutory restrictions on the ability of refiners to bank any crude oil cost increases they are unable to recoup immediately.[78] In general, a refiner must pass through a crude oil cost increase within the 60 day period which follows the month in which the increase is incurred. Later passthroughs may be permitted only if the President finds, and reports to Congress, that such delayed passthroughs are necessary to alleviate the impact on the petroleum industry of significant increases in costs, to provide for equitable cost recovery or to avoid competitive disadvantage. Any cost increase passthroughs later than the 60 day period are, however, limited to 10 percent per month of the total amount of unrecouped previously banked costs.

Regulations providing for the equal distribution of increased costs among *classes of purchasers* are the third major feature. They are closely tied to "banking" provisions. If refiners could pass through cost increases unequally to their purchasers, the base price computations for the various classes of purchasers would be meaningless.[79] The class-of-purchaser concept is intended to preserve historical price differentials. A single lawful price is set for each class (rather than for individual customers), and the recoupment of increased product costs since August 30, 1974, is calculated on the assumption that the largest amount passed through to one class of purchaser was equally applied to all classes.[80]

The fourth feature of refinery price regulations is the special treatment of certain products, sometimes called the "special products" rule.[81] This rule has generally been used to alter the amounts of increased costs which can be passed through to particular products. For some products, cost increases may be passed through only in direct proportion to total costs. For other products, the pass-through may include some cost increases attributable to other products. Non-product costs must always be allocated in the same proportions as product costs.

The net effect of the special products rule is to make some products more profitable for refiners, while keeping prices lower on others. An example of the rule's application is the early treatment of propane as a general product. This allowed larger than proportionate price increases to stimulate greater propane production. After prices rose substantially, propane was changed to "special product" status. Most recently, the FEA has attempted to use this technique to increase motor gasoline prices, which are well below world prices. Home heating fuels have been accorded special product status in the past in order to keep prices down for consumer protection.[82]

The Energy Policy Act modifies this regulatory scheme and elevates it to statutory status. Section 4(b)(2)(D) of the EPAA, as amended, provides that no more than direct proportionate (by volume) cost increases may be passed through to home heating oil, diesel fuel, aviation fuel and propane.[83] The provision would, however, permit less than proportionate cost increases to be passed through to these products, thereby requiring other products, such as motor gasoline or residual fuel oil, to bear the brunt of future increases in crude oil costs. However, the President may deviate from the required proportionate distribution of costs if the departure is justified by refinery operations and if it does not result in inequitable prices for any class of users of the product involved.

The fifth feature of refiner level price regulation is the statutory requirement for a dollar-for-dollar passthrough in prices at all levels of distribution of *decreases* in costs of crude oil and petroleum products, specifically including decreases resulting from the crude oil price rollback mandated by the Energy Policy Act.[84] The amount, if any, of price decreases that will ultimately trickle down to the retail level is conjectural. It will depend on the size of the banks of unrecouped cost increases of those refining and marketing various products as well as market conditions for particular products in the near future. In early December 1975 the FEA estimated that the maximum decrease in domestic product prices would be about 2.5 cents per gallon, and the more likely decrease would be much less. Of course, any reduction would be a prelude to an expected prolonged, gradual increase in crude oil and petroleum product prices.

Reseller and retailer price controls. Price regulations for resellers and retailers are similar to those for refiners. The first feature of cost passthroughs has a few differences. Increased product costs may not be reallocated among products at this level. Rather than on an individual basis, non-product cost increases are allowed on a specified industrywide per-gallon basis which varies with the type of product, level of distribution, and volume sold. The large number of businesses involved also makes the profit margin limitation impracticable, because the FEA cannot maintain records and audit to detect violations.[85] The "banking" provisions for resellers are essentially the same as for refiners, and in general the carry-over provisions require equal application among classes of purchasers.

A unique feature is a freeze on the rent charged on real property used for gasoline retailing. Rent is limited to the level charged on May 15, 1973. However, the rule is applicable only to leases where all parties are refiners, resellers, or retailers.[86]

Court Challenges

Even though they have been in effect for a relatively short time, most major features of FEA price and allocation regulations have been challenged in court. In *Union Oil Co. v. FEA,*[87] the EPAA was held to authorize continued allocation even though the shortage was over. The court's holding was based on the congressional intent to protect independents.[88]

The supplier/purchaser freeze for crude oil was considered in *OKC Corp. v. Oskey Gasoline & Oil Co.*[89] OKC intended to stop supplying Oskey because of Oskey's credit problems, but the FEO had determined in a hearing that its regulations did not allow termination. OKC then claimed the FEO had not determined that termination was not a "normal business practice," and that the order was contrary to the intent of the EPAA. The court faulted the FEO for its procedures but found that the order, and presumably the rule, had a rational basis. However, the court also stipulated that if Oskey failed to pay within a certain time limit, OKC could terminate the relationship.[90]

The buy/sell program was similarly upheld against statutory challenges. This regulation and the freeze are fairly easy for a court to uphold against an "arbitrary and capricious" attack, simply because it is clear that, in enacting the EPAA, Congress intended such administrative actions to be taken. In both *Exxon v. FEO*[91] and *Gulf Oil Corp. v. Simon,*[92] the plaintiffs objected to the requirement that they sell part of their crude oil. Along with other arguments, the court in each case rejected the suggestion that the regulation was arbitrary and capricious.

The entitlements program, a very indirect system of allocation, was upheld repeatedly in challenges by refiners. While Congress intended to give the FEA considerable flexibility in administration, the Conference Report on the EPAA reflects thinking in terms of physically moving products around and not of purchasing entitlements to refine products which were already owned.[93] Nevertheless, *Marathon Oil Co. v. FEA*[94] rejected a claim by an entitlement purchaser that the entitlements program exceeded the scope of FEA's authority because it did not actually allocate oil or establish prices as Congress had intended.

Congress probably failed to consider the likelihood that small refiners would have to relinquish supplies to other larger refiners. Yet a court upheld a requirement that a small refiner purchase entitlements in *Mohawk Petroleum Corp. v. FEA.*[95] As discussed above, the result in this case has been overturned by the Energy Policy Act's exemption of small refiners from the requirement to purchase entitlements. All courts which have considered the entitlements program have also rejected claims that the program is arbitrary and capricious.[96]

Mandel v. Simon[97] involved an attempt by the Governor of Maryland to obtain a supplementary delivery of 16 million gallons of motor gasoline. The district court found that FEO use of incorrect data to calculate Maryland's share of gasoline made the allocation levels arbitrary and without rational basis. The Temporary Emergency Court of Appeals reversed, noting tersely that maladjustments alone will not destroy the rational basis of a program.

Even FEA regulation of the business practices of retailers was upheld in *Reeves v. Simon.*[98] Reeves, a branded independent motor gasoline retailer, had decided to sell to old customers on a preferential basis in order to stop customers from "topping off," and to allow him more time for repair and service work . The regulations prohibited such preferential treatment and the FEA had ordered Reeves to stop his plan. Again overruling a district court, the Temporary Emergency Court of Appeals found that the regulation and orders were not arbitrary, discriminatory, or without a rational basis.

Early court decisions on FEA regulations were influenced to a large extent by the emergency which existed at the time. Now that the serious shortage is over, courts are not as deferential to the FEA. Consequently, although the courts will probably not reverse precedent, the FEA may expect to lose cases it would previously have won.[99]

Several aspects of price regulation related to allocation have also been challenged. The two-tier price system for crude oil was finally upheld by a 4–3 vote of the Temporary Emergency Court of Appeals, after a three-judge panel had previously invalidated the regulation.[100] The appellate court decided that regulation of old oil prices kept the average price of all petroleum sufficiently regulated to satisfy section 4(a) of the EPAA as originally enacted.

The "banking" program was upheld in *Trans World Airlines v. FEO.*[101] While 75 percent of the fuel purchased by all airlines was by long-term contracts, only 44 percent of TWA's requirements were met this way, and the remainder was by short-term purchases. When increased product costs were passed through, the FEA would not allow suppliers to increase prices for *contract* purchasers above the bargained prices. Short-term purchase prices had no such limit and absorbed almost all of the increases. Hence, TWA was paying a disproportionate share of the cost increases. Given the banking provisions, what could not be passed on immediately to TWA could be banked and passed through later. Moreover, the difference in the contract price and the legal ceiling became an unrecouped cost which could be charged to TWA.

TWA claimed that sections 4(b)(1) (requiring "equitable prices") and 6(c) (allowing breach of contract defenses) implied that the FEA should have allowed contract prices to increase as much as non-contract. The court relied on the legislative history, where Congress reflected an intent to avoid breaching contracts whenever possible,[102] and decided that the FEA regulations were not arbitrary or in excess of EPAA authorization.

Finally, the "special products rule" was upheld in *Air Transport Association v. FEO.*[103] The Air Transport Association objected to the classification of aviation fuel as a "general product" which could absorb greater than proportional cost increases under the special products rule. This classification meant that cost increases which were attributed to other fuels were allocated to aviation fuel prices. The "banking" provisions compounded the increases, as in the TWA situation. Consequently, some airlines' operating costs soared. Yet the court found that the "banking" provisions were justified by section 4(b)(2)(A) on cost increase passthroughs and section 4(b)(1)(F) on "equitable prices," which also applied to suppliers. The regulations were not an "unnecessary interference with the market mechanism," as per section 4(b)(1)(I).

It is noteworthy that the airlines apparently have obtained a legislative remedy for their plight. As discussed previously, the Energy Policy Act amended the EPAA to provide expressly for no more than proportionate cost increase passthroughs to certain refined products, including specifically aviation fuel.

The FEA had been a party to 85 lawsuits as of June 1975. We have found no areas of major importance under the EPAA where litigation is still pending.[104]

ENERGY SUPPLY AND ENVIRONMENTAL COORDINATION ACT (ESECA)

The Energy Supply and Environmental Coordination Act (ESECA) gives the FEA three broad powers which bear directly on petroleum allocation: (a) to issue orders prohibiting some power plants and major fuel-burning installations from burning natural gas or petroleum products as the primary energy sources; (b) to require that "any powerplant or other major fuel-burning installation in the early planning process . . . be designed and constructed so as to be capable of using coal as its primary energy source;" and (c) in some cases, to allocate coal supplies among users.[105] These powers are subject to substantial qualifications which have tended to make FEA officials reluctant to use ESECA to its full potential. In our analysis we will treat the application of the Act, its qualifications, and the regulations promulgated thereunder as a whole.

Section 2(a) provides that the FEA *shall* prohibit any powerplant, and *may* prohibit any major fuel burning installation other than a powerplant from burning natural gas or petroleum products.[106] The first qualification is that the FEA must determine that, as of June 22, 1974, the powerplant or installation "had, or thereafter acquires or is designed with, plant equipment to burn coal." The FEA has defined the relevant equipment by regulation. The relevant regulations do not require every piece of this equipment to be installed before the FEA orders conversion (or prohibition).[107]

Second, section 2(b) requires that the burning of coal must be "practicable" and consistent with the purposes of ESECA. Under the FEA regulations, the agency's determination of practicability shall include "an analysis of the reasonableness of additional costs associated with burning coal, including its cost, costs of equipment for coal burning, and costs of complying with the requirements of section 119 of the Clean Air Act."[108] The requirement of consistency with the Act means merely that a prohibition should discourage use of petroleum and natural gas, while encouraging the use of coal.

A third requirement is that "coal transportation facilities" must be available during the period the order is in effect.[109] In the past, significant problems arose with railroad cars, labor troubles, capital shortages, and environmental restrictions, so that the clause was essential to protect against coal supply problems. Fourth, the "reliability of service in the area served by the plant" should not be impaired by the conversion. This provision is directed at powerplants, and is not applicable to other major fuel-burning installations.[110]

Finally, there are several environmental restrictions.[111] No Prohibition Order can become effective before the date certified by the Environmental Protection Agency (EPA) as the earliest date by which a plant will be able to comply with applicable air pollution requirements. For long-term conversion orders, the EPA may grant compliance date extensions, as long as certain conditions are met. Basically these conditions guarantee that the national primary ambient air quality standards, which are required to protect public health, and the regional limits will not be violated; only secondary air quality standards will be relaxed if necessary.[112]

For other major fuel-burning installations, there are additional requirements. "Major" is defined to include only facilities burning 100 million BTU's per hour or more on June 22, 1974. In selecting candidates for conversion, the FEA will also consider the location and output of the installation, the purpose for burning coal, the quantity of natural gas or petroleum presently burned, "the practicability of burning coal given the short-term variation of demand for output by the installation," and the burden that conversion would place on coal supplies.[113]

Section 2(f) of ESECA originally provided that authority to issue orders or rules under subsections (a) through (d) expired on June 30, 1975. The Energy Policy Act has extended this authority to June 30, 1977. Under ESECA, as amended, rules and orders issued prior to the expiration may become effective any time before January 1, 1985, and the authority to "amend, repeal, rescind, modify, or enforce" orders and rules continues until December 31, 1984.[114]

The procedure for ordering conversion is lengthy and complex. It begins when the FEA issues a Notice of Intent that it is considering ordering a facility to convert. After investigation, the FEA may issue Prohibition Orders to some or all who received notices. The FEA issued 32 Prohibition Orders to 25 utilities covering 42 powerplant units before its authority to issue further orders temporarily expired in June 1975. After the issuance of a Prohibition Order, the FEA must obtain certification from the EPA that all environmental requirements will be satisfied. When the EPA concludes its investigation, the FEA issues a Notice of Effectiveness to those plants which the EPA has determined can meet applicable environmental standards.[115]

The second major power granted by ESECA, to issue Construction Orders for powerplants and other major fuel burning installations in the "early planning process," is less restricted than in the case of Prohibition Orders. Although the FEA issued Notices of Intent to 74 facilities prior to temporary expiration of authority in June 1975, it had ordered only 41 to construct facilities capable of using coal as a primary energy source.[116] ESECA does not define "early planning process," but the FEA has defined it to exclude facilities on which boiler steel has already been erected.[117]

Section 2(c) of ESECA imposes restrictions on Construction Orders. In the case of a powerplant the FEA must determine that a Construction Order is not likely to impair the reliability or adequacy of service. There must also be a reasonable expectation of an adequate and reliable supply of coal. The FEA must consider the "existence and effects of any contractual commitment for the construction of such facilities and the capability of the owner to recover any capital investment made as a result" of the Construction Order.[118] And, finally, the plant or installation must be built in accordance with requirements imposed by environmental legislation.

The third power authorized by ESECA is in section 2(d):[119]

> The Federal Energy Administrator may, by rule or order, allocate coal (1) to any powerplant or major fuel burning installation to which an order under subsection (a) of this section has been issued, or (2) to any other person to the extent necessary to carry out the purposes of this chapter.

Coal is defined in section 2(e)(2) to include coal derivatives.[120]

The FEA promulgated regulations for coal allocation during the summer of 1975. The regulations have not yet been used because the only need for them currently is to ensure that converted plants get the fuel they need.

In addition to the environmental constraints described above, ESECA contains provisions restricting the applicability to FEA orders of the National Environmental Policy Act of 1969 (NEPA). No action taken by EPA under the Clean Air Act requires an environmental impact statement. Actions taken by the FEA pursuant to the three powers granted by ESECA do not require a NEPA environmental impact statement for a period of one year after the action is initiated, meaning about June 30, 1976. However, any such action which will be in effect for more than that one-year period is subject to the full requirements of NEPA.

Where NEPA is not applicable, there are substitute requirements. Within, at most, 60 days after significant action is taken, an environmental evaluation as close as possible to a NEPA-type impact statement must be circulated to government agencies and the public for 30 days. After this circulation, a public hearing must be held if requested.[121] Thus, the FEA is still obligated under ESECA to subject its actions to intense public scrutiny on environmental grounds.

FEA regulations impose stricter environmental requirements than ESECA demands. Prior to issuance of a Notice of Intent (to make a Prohibition or Construction Order), a "final programmatic Environmental Impact Statement" will be issued. Any Prohibition Order made effective after June 30, 1975, will follow regular NEPA procedures. This necessitates either a finding by the FEA that an environmental impact statement is not required, or the preparation of an impact statement prior to any Notice of Effectiveness.

Since the FEA orders issued under ESECA have not yet been evaluated by the EPA, officials are still uncertain what form environmental impact statements and subsequent hearings will take. This is because the EPA itself will hold public hearings on all compliance date extensions.[122]

Through December 1975 there were no published court decisions interpreting ESECA.

DEFENSE PRODUCTION ACT (DPA)

The Defense Production Act of 1950 (DPA) has repeatedly been extended.[123] The Act contains very broad general authority for allocating scarce materials, which obviously could include petroleum, natural gas, and other fuel material:[124]

> The President is authorized (1) to require that performance under contracts or orders (other than contracts of employment) which he deems necessary or appropriate to promote the national defense shall take priority over performance under any other contract or order, and, for the purpose of assuring such priority, to require acceptance and performance

of such contracts or orders in preference to other contracts or orders by any person he finds to be capable of their performance, and (2) to allocate materials and facilities in such manner, upon such conditions, and to such extent as he shall deem necessary or appropriate to promote the national defense.

There are two basic statutory limits on the exercise of the President's power, neither of which has ever caused the invalidation of any order issued under the DPA. Materials in the civilian market are not to be controlled unless: (a) they are scarce and critical to national defense, and (b) no better solution exists which does not create market distortions.[125] Additionally, the DPA may not be used to restrict the use of natural gas in any state which has a public regulatory commission willing to certify that it is regulating gas in a manner that achieves the objectives of the DPA.[126] Presumably, the President could invoke the DPA and override the FPC's natural gas curtailment policy.

The Energy Policy Act has amended the DPA, adding to its broad general authorities the specific authority to allocate "supplies of materials and equipment in order to maximize domestic energy supplies."[127] As a prerequisite to the exercise of this far-reaching authority, the President must find that the allocated supplies are "scarce, critical and essential" to maintain or further the domestic energy supply system and that the desired objective cannot reasonably be accomplished in some other way. This specific energy authority under the DPA expires on December 31, 1984, but it continues until that date, even though the DPA itself may expire earlier.

Currently, there are only two specific regulatory programs based upon the DPA which affect energy. The FEA has invoked the DPA to grant priority to contractors for the Trans-Alaska Pipeline in obtaining some materials.[128] The FEA has also promulgated, but never used, rules under the DPA which provide for the allocation of coal.[129]

As discussed in Chapter Nine, orders authorized under the DPA have withstood all constitutional attacks. Given a court's probable reluctance to examine substantively whether a particular Presidential action is actually necessary for national security, the FEA has enormous latent legal authority under the DPA. Only the simplest findings would be necessary, and public hearings would not be required prior to rulemaking or other administrative action.

The DPA gives the FEA, potentially, its widest authority for allocating energy supplies. The government has been able to justify numerous regulatory programs on the basis of national defense. Preservation of a sound domestic economy is frequently regarded as synonomous with national defense. Suppliers and purchasers at all levels could be required to produce and conserve energy with only constitutional limits applicable to the program. Some difficulties would arise with natural gas use restrictions, but the FEA could require state regulatory commissions to allocate or curtail in accordance with federal priorities.

Nevertheless, Presidents have been understandably reluctant to use the DPA. Probably no President would want to invoke such expansive authority unless a critical need were deemed to exist. To do so would risk congressional restriction or elimination of standby statutory authority which could prove invaluable in a real national defense emergency. Moreover, unilateral action by the Executive Branch under the DPA would locate in the President full responsibility for the consequences of government intervention, rather than distributing that responsibility between the President and the Congress.

ENERGY POLICY AND CONSERVATION ACT

As mentioned at the beginning of this chapter, in addition to amending the EPAA, ESECA and DPA, the Energy Policy Act contains substantial additional authorities which are relevant to the administration of possible future petroleum shortages and energy shortages in general. The Act mandates the development of contingency plans to meet future energy supply emergencies and also provides necessary legal authority for the U.S. to participate in the Agreement on an International Energy Program (IEP). The Act provides the President with authority to order oil and natural gas to be produced from some domestic fields at temporary emergency production rates during a severe energy supply interruption. The Act also mandates the creation of a strategic petroleum reserve. Finally, it provides sweeping authority for the government to gather energy information in order to provide the data base necessary not only for effective administration of possible future energy shortages, but also for the development and administration of national energy policy in general.

These provisions of the Energy Policy Act relevant to administration of energy shortages are considered briefly below.[130] It is, of course, much too early for evaluation.

In order to deal with a possible severe energy supply interruption or to fulfill U.S. international obligations under the IEP, the President is directed to prepare contingency plans. A "severe supply emergency" is defined as a national energy shortage which the President determines is "significant" and an "emergency," and which may result in a major adverse impact on the national safety or economy. The specified causes of a severe energy supply interruption include an interruption in the supply of imported petroleum products, sabotage, or an act of God.[131] Thus, the Energy Policy Act does not specify the severity of any threat with which the contingency plans are to cope. Performance criteria for designing plans are missing.

Two types of contingency plans are required: one or more energy conservation plans and a rationing plan.

An energy conservation plan is one which "imposes reasonable restrictions on the public or private use of energy."[132] Thus, the conservation plan must focus primarily on end-use controls, as distinguished from allocation regulation which focuses on the distribution system. An energy conservation contingency plan will apply nationwide, except that a state or political subdivision with a comparable program may be exempted. Therefore, the federal plan might serve as a model for states, and conformity with the federal guidelines could result in a delegation to conforming states of administrative responsibility with respect to energy conservation plans.

An energy conservation plan may *not:* (a) impose rationing or any tax, tariff or user fee; (b) provide for a tax subsidy; (c) regulate the price of petroleum products; or (d) deal with "more than one logically consistent subject matter," a phrase that is unexplained. Presumably, however, various plans could be developed to control the use of all forms of energy. A plan must take account of the "mobility needs of the handicapped." In other respects, the executive has a relatively free hand in designing such conservation plans.

A rationing contingency plan applies to "end-users of gasoline and diesel fuel used in motor vehicles."[133] Such a plan must establish priorities among classes of end-users and provide for the assignment of rights to obtain gasoline and diesel fuel to end-users in accordance with the priority of their respective classes. Clearly, some form of coupon rationing is contemplated. Once again, handicapped persons are to receive special consideration. The establishment and use of local boards by states or political subdivisions for administration is required "to the extent practicable." In other respects, the design of the rationing plan is left largely within executive discretion.

The substance of energy conservation and rationing plans is thus remarkably open-ended. As discussed in Chapter Seven, the administrative procedures required for development of contingency plans and the procedures for congressional review prior to their becoming effective assure ample opportunities for public in-put and legislative second-guessing.

Energy contingency plans are a form of advance planning to cope with energy supply interruptions like the 1973–74 Arab oil embargo. The plans may not only enhance U.S. preparedness, but also provide part of the foundation for full U.S. participation in the international oil sharing arrangements being developed as part of the IEP.[134] The Agreement establishing the IEP entered provisionally into force on November 18, 1974. It was the outgrowth of a major U.S. government initiative in response to the 1973–74 Arab oil embargo. The participating countries now include most of the OECD industrial countries, except France and Australia.

The Agreement provides a general framework for industrial country cooperation in the energy field and a specific series of common measures to meet oil supply emergencies. Each participating country undertakes to have ready, on a standby basis, a contingency plan enabling it to reduce its oil consumption by 7 percent initially and 10 percent subsequently. These figures may provide useful interim targets for the energy conservation contingency plans to be developed under the Energy Policy Act. Under the Agreement, the participating countries are obligated to begin sharing their available oil supplies if any participating country or the group as a whole sustains an oil supply interruption which exceeds 7 percent.

Although the specific formulas for international oil allocation are complex, the principles underlying the Agreement are straightforward. If oil imports of the group as a whole are embargoed, each participant must reduce its consumption pro rata and the remaining supplies are allocated pro rata within the group as a whole according to pre-embargo consumption rates. If oil imports of selected participants are embargoed, the countries targeted must first retrain their demands and then they will become entitled to pro rata allocations from the other members of the group. The principles are relatively easy to state, but they may prove to be very difficult to implement in an actual supply emergency. The Agreement contains intricate weighted-voting procedures for decision making and also very complicated machinery for involving the multinational oil industry in the development and actual operation of the sharing arrangements.

Section 251 of the Energy Policy Act provides the basic legal authority for the United States to participate in the international oil-sharing arrangements which are developed under the IEP.[135] The main requirement imposed by the Act is that the administrative rule governing U.S. participation in international oil-sharing must be consistent, to the maximum extent practicable, with the EPAA. The Energy Policy Act also provides detailed procedures governing oil company participation in the IEP and antitrust immunity for the companies in this regard.[136]

It is impossible to predict the effectiveness of international sharing arrangements in deterring and dealing with future interruptions in foreign oil supplies flowing into the OECD industrial countries. It is, however, clear that the Energy Policy Act has endowed the U.S. government with broad authority to participate in a collective response to a future embargo.

Section 106 of the Energy Policy Act authorizes the President to require crude oil and/or natural gas to be produced from certain domestic fields at the maximum efficient rate (MER) and, in case of a severe energy supply interruption, at the temporary emergency production rate (TEPR).[137] The fields covered are fields on federal lands, and fields on non-federal lands only if the state government in which they are located has established MERs and TEPRs.

In normal circumstances, the President has discretionary authority to order crude oil and natural gas to be produced from fields on federal lands at established MERs. He has no authority to control the production rate from fields on non-federal lands. During a severe energy supply interruption, the President may order production at TEPR from fields on federal lands, and he may also order production from fields with state-established MERs or TEPRs at the established rates. If a state government has not established relevant production rates for fields within its jurisdiction, the President may not order production at any particular rate, even in an emergency. Finally, if a TEPR order results in loss of ultimate recovery of crude oil or natural gas, the damaged property owner's remedy is a law suit to recover "just compensation," which shall be awarded if the court finds the loss "constitutes a taking of property compensable under the Constitution." (See Chapter Nine for further discussion of this issue.)

Section 151 of the Energy Policy Act declares it to be U.S. policy to provide for the creation of a strategic petroleum reserve of up to one billion barrels of petroleum products, including the buildup of an early storage reserve of not less than 150 million barrels within three years. Sections 152 through 166 provide detailed requirements for implementing this policy.[138]

The FEA is required to develop successively two plans: an early storage reserve plan and a strategic petroleum reserve plan. The early reserve plan must be drawn up and transmitted to Congress within 90 days of enactment of the Energy Policy Act. It is not subject to congressional review and implementation may begin immediately. The strategic reserve plan must be drawn up and transmitted to Congress by December 15, 1976. It is subject to congressional review and may be disapproved by either House.

The early storage reserve must contain not less than 150 million barrels of petroleum products within three years. These products will be stored, to the maximum extent practicable, in existing storage capacity. To implement the plan, the FEA may require each importer and each refiner to acquire and store in readily available inventories petroleum products in an amount up to 3 percent of the amount imported or refined during the previous year. "Readily available inventories" are defined as stocks which can be distributed "without affecting the ability of the importer or refiner to operate at normal capacity," and do not include minimum working inventories or other unavailable stocks.[139]

Even if U.S. oil import levels were reduced to six million barrels per day, the 150 million barrel early reserve would replace only 25 days of imports. The early storage reserve will thus afford thin protection against a possible embargo. This is especially true if, as is likely, petroleum import levels continue to rise in the future.

The strategic petroleum reserve will incorporate the early reserve and expand upon it. The strategic reserve plan must provide for a crude oil reserve equivalent to three months of crude oil imports. However, the base period specified for computing the amount is the three consecutive months within the *past* two years during which average monthly import levels were the highest.[140] If crude oil imports continue to increase as expected, three months' protection may turn out to be less than two by the early 1980s.[141]

The strategic reserve plan is required to include a distribution plan. No drawdown and distribution may be made from either the early or the strategic reserve unless the President finds that distribution is required by a severe energy supply interruption or by U.S. obligations under the IEP.[142]

It remains to be seen whether the petroleum reserves mandated by the Energy Policy Act will turn out to be effective insulation for the U.S. against future embargoes or little more than bookkeeping. It is clear, however, that whatever insulation the reserves may provide could be eroded away by continued increases in U.S. oil import levels.

Adequate, accurate information is essential for rational policy making and effective administration. For decades prior to the 1973-74 Arab oil embargo and ensuing energy crisis, the petroleum industry had concealed the internals of its worldwide operations behind a veil of secrecy. Moreover, since the petroleum industry was largely unregulated by government, policy makers could assert as a matter of high principle: "we don't know, and we don't want to know." With the onslaught of the energy crisis, the petroleum industry has not only been subject almost overnight to massive government regulation, but the veil of secrecy has been shredded and the industry has been forced to expose its most private parts to the government administrator's eye, and often to public view.

Section 11 of ESECA provides sweeping discretionary authority for the FEA to request and collect "energy information," which is defined to include: all information on fuel reserves, exploration, extraction and energy resources; production, distribution and consumption of energy and fuels; and energy matters such as corporate structure and proprietary relationships, costs, prices, capital investment and assets.[143] The Energy Policy Act extends this authority to December 31, 1979.[144] In addition, the Act requires the Securities and Exchange Commission to develop and implement within two years accounting practices to be followed by persons engaged in crude oil or natural gas production.[145] Finally, the Act empowers the General Accounting Office, on request of a committee of the Congress, to conduct "verification examinations" to assess the accuracy and adequacy of energy information.[146] (Verification examinations are considered further in Chapter Seven.) If an energy shortage is ineptly managed in the future, it will not be for any lack of legal authority for government to acquire the necessary information.

In summary, with enactment of the Energy Policy and Conservation Act, Congress has substantially strengthened the federal government's capacity to administer future petroleum shortages. The basic legal authority now appears adequate, but much remains to be developed administratively. The administrative process will be complex. Political principles and rhetoric to the contrary notwithstanding, pervasive government regulation of the petroleum industry in the United States is an accomplished fact that will be irreversible during the remainder of the 1970s.

NOTES TO CHAPTER SIX

1. 15 U.S.C. § §751 *et seq.* (Supp. III, 1973).
2. 15 U.S.C.A. § §791 *et seq.* (Supp. 1975).
3. 15 U.S.C.A. § §761 *et seq.* (Supp. 1975).

4. 50 U.S.C. App. §§2061 *et seq.* (1970).

5. Pub. L. No. 94-163 (1975).

6. For a brief history of federal petroleum regulation, see Statement of Frank G. Zarb, Administrator of the FEA, Before the Senate Committee on Interior and Insular Affairs, at 8-24 (May 19, 1975) [hereinafter cited as Zarb]. The best historical record of Cost of Living Council and its petroleum regulation is C. Owens, *History of Petroleum Price Controls* (1974), reprinted from *The Historical Working Papers on the Economic Stabilization Program Part II* (Supt. Doc. No. 4800-00261, 00262, 00263).

7. 15 U.S.C.A. §764(b) (Supp. 1975) provides:

(b) To the extent authorized by subsection (a) of this section, the Administrator shall—

(1) advise the President and the Congress with respect to the establishment of a comprehensive national energy policy in relation to the energy matters for which the Administration has responsibility, and, in coordination with the Secretary of State, the integration of domestic and foreign policies relating to energy resource management;

(2) assess the adequacy of energy resources to meet demands in the immediate and longer range future for all sectors of the economy and for the general public;

(3) develop effective arrangements for the participation of State and local governments in the resolution of energy problems;

(4) develop plans and programs for dealing with energy production shortages;

(5) promote stability in energy prices to the consumer, promote free and open competition in all aspects of the energy field, prevent unreasonable profits within the various segments of the energy industry, and promote free enterprise;

(6) assure that energy programs are designed and implemented in a fair and efficient manner so as to minimize hardship and inequity while assuring that the priority needs of the Nation are met;

(7) develop and oversee the implementation of equitable voluntary and mandatory energy conservation programs and promote efficiencies in the use of energy resources;

(8) develop and recommend policies on the import and export of energy resources;

(9) collect, evaluate, assemble, and analyze energy information on reserves, production, demand, and related economic data;

(10) work with business, labor, consumer and other interests and obtain their cooperation;

(11) in administering any pricing authority, provide by rule, for equitable allocation of all component costs of producing propane gas. Such rules may require that (a) only those costs directly related to the production of propane may be allocated by any producer to such gas for purposes of establishing any price for propane, and (b) prices for propane shall be based on the prices for propane in effect on May 15, 1973. The Adminis-

trator shall not allow costs attributable to changes in ownership and movement of propane gas where, in the opinion of the Administrator, such changes in ownership and movement occur primarily for the purpose of establishing a higher price; and

(12) perform such other functions as may be prescribed by law.

8. *H.R. Rep. No.* 748, 93d Cong., 2d Sess. (1974), *printed at* 1974 *U.S. Code Cong. & Adm. News* 2939, 2968.

9. *S. Conf. Rep. No.* 788, 93d Cong., 2d Sess. (1974), *printed at* 1974 *U.S. Code Cong. & Adm. News* 2972, 2974-75.

10. 15 U.S.C.A. §764(a) (Supp. 1975). Whether the word "specific" in the second limit is important is unclear. Portions of the DPA, a very unspecific Act, are delegated to the FEA, but have never been tested in court. It is unlikely that a court would void such a delegation.

11. Respectively, 15 U.S.C.A. §§766(c), 766(i) and 780, 774, 772, 766(i) (2), 781 (Supp. 1975).

12. 15 U.S.C.A. §765 (Supp. 1975).

13. 15 U.S.C. §751(a) (Supp. III, 1973).

14. *Contra* Union Oil Co. v. FEA, No. CV74-1943 (C.D. Cal., July 25, 1975), *printed at* 3 *CCH Energy Management* ¶26,007.

15. 15 U.S.C. §753(a) (Supp. III, 1973), *as amended* Pub. L. No. 94-163 §401(b) (1975).

16. 15 U.S.C. §753(a) (Supp. III, 1973), *as amended* Pub. L. No. 94-163 §451 (1975).

17. *E.g.,* OKC Corp. v. Oskey Gasoline & Oil Co., 381 F. Supp. 865 (N.D. Tex. 1974); *Union Oil, supra* note 14.

18. *H.R. Conf. Rep. No.* 628, 93d Cong., 1st Sess. at 1-2 (1973), *printed at* 1973 *U.S. Code Cong. & Adm. News* 2688-89 [hereinafter referred to as *EPAA Conference Report*].

19. *S. Conf. Rep. No.* 94-516, 94th Cong., 1st Sess., at 190 (1975). [hereinafter referred to as *Energy Policy Act Conference Report*].

20. Pub. L. No. 94-163 §457 (1975).

21. Pub. L. No. 94-163 §458 (1975).

22. Pub. L. No. 94-163 §3 (1975).

23. Pub. L. No. 94-163 §456 (1975).

24. 15 U.S.C. §753(b)(2)(A) (Supp. III, 1973), *as amended* Pub. L. No. 94-163 §402(a) (1975).

25. 15 U.S.C. §753(b)(2)(B) (Supp. III, 1973).

26. 15 U.S.C. §§753(b)(3), 753(c)(5) (Supp. III, 1973).

27. 15 U.S.C. §753(c)(1) (Supp. III, 1973).

28. *EPAA Conference Report, supra* note 18, 1973 *U.S. Code Cong. & Adm. News* 2706-07.

29. *EPAA Conference Report, supra* note 18, 1973 *U.S. Code Cong. & Adm. News* 2691.

30. Pub. L. No. 94-163 §402(c) (1975).

31. By way of brief description, the class of trade option might assume continued existence of the entitlements program for the protection of refiners. Below the refiner level, distributors and retailers would be divided into classes,

which could be extremely detailed or large, depending upon the needs of the time. Non-branded independents would compose one class. A base period would be selected and the total share of the market during that period for each class computed. Each refiner, or all, would be required to sell the same fraction of total product to "endangered" classes in times when supplies actually are short.

The class of trade option has never been adopted by the FEA, although it has been discussed as a possible step in de-regulation, rather than as an initial step toward regulation. It was considered because continued regulation was required and few persons liked the allocation regulations in times of surplus product.

32. Statement of Mr. Robert E. Montgomery, General Counsel to the FEA, Before the Subcommittee on Separation of Powers of the Senate Committee of the Judiciary, 94th Cong., 1st Sess. (June 3, 1975) [hereinafter cited as Montgomery].

33. The "banking" provision of the EPAA was intended to avoid unconstitutional taking problems, and to some extent the FEA considers more than the statutory limits in that area. Even so, officials do not see the Constitution as a major limit on flexibility.

The legislative history of some sections can also be important. For example, while Congress provided in section 6(c) that an FEA order or rule may be a defense to liability for breaches of some contracts, there is the admonition in the legislative history that contracts should be abrogated only where necessary. These types of limits are usually not strict requirements, but rather a suggestion that certain factors be considered. In a non-emergency situation, blatant disregard of such suggestions is likely to lead to political trouble, and perhaps also to court invalidation of agency actions.

34. 10 C.F.R. §211.51 (1975).

35. *Id.*

36. *Id.*

37. 10 C.F.R. §211.63 (1975). The freeze does not apply to several types of sales of crude oil: the first sale from a stripper well lease; mandatory sales under the buy/sell list; and sales of new and released oil only, where the freeze may be broken if a new purchaser outbids the present purchaser.

38. 10 C.F.R. §211.65 (1975); Zarb, *supra* note 6, at 49-51.

39. Zarb, *supra* note 6, at 52. There are 15 U.S. refiners which are not "small" or "independent" within the terms of the EPAA. With few exceptions, these are also the 15 largest integrated oil companies in the U.S. From February through May 1974, refiner-sellers were classified according to supply ratios, which caused some small, independent refiners to be required to sell. Since June 1, 1974, a regulatory change has made the 15 refiners mentioned above the only refiner-sellers.

More specifically, a refiner-buyer is allowed to purchase in each allocation quarter an amount equal to the difference between one-quarter of the crude oil it refined ("runs to stills" or "crude runs") during 1972 and that refined during the period from February through April 1974 (excluding buy/sell purchases or sales). This newer measure provides an incentive to obtain additional crude oil supplies, since new acquisitions do not decrease the amount which can be purchased through the buy/sell program. A refiner-seller must sell an amount corresponding to the ratio of its own capacity to the total refinery capacity of all 15 sellers as of January 1, 1973.

40. 10 C.F.R. § §212.94, 212.83(c) (1975).

41. Before the June 1974 change, the only incentives were the extra handling fees, yet the seller could still pass through extra costs for replacement imports. Now that his sales obligation is a fixed ratio, increased imports do not increase his sales obligation in the next period, although it did before June 1974.

42. 10 C.F.R. §211.67 (1975).

43. Pub. L. No. 94-163 §403 (1975). The cost entitlements exemption for small refiners may be modified or revoked if it is found to result in unfair competitive advantage *among small refiners*, subject to congressional review of the amending regulation.

44. Zarb, *supra* note 6, at 54-57. About 40 percent of the total national supply is price-controlled old oil.

45. 10 C.F.R. §211.9 (1975).

46. 10 C.F.R. § §211.9-.13 (1975); *see* Zarb, *supra* note 6, at 58-60.

47. 10 C.F.R. §211.12(b) (1975).

48. *Id.; e.g.,* propane and 10 C.F.R. §211.83(c) (1975); *see* Zarb, *supra* note 6, at 60-66.

49. 10 C.F.R. §211.103 (1975).

50. 15 U.S.C. §753(c)(1) (Supp. III, 1973); *see* notes 27, 28 *supra* and accompanying text.

51. This means that mutual assistance among companies is not totally pervasive below the refinery level of the industry. Even among refineries, those which obtained extra crude oil had higher fractions. Distributors who were assigned more new purchasers than others had lower fractions.

52. 10 C.F.R. §211.12(b)(1) (1975); *see* Zarb, *supra* note 6, at 62-66.

53. Alternatively, the FEA could have subjected all amounts to the fraction. This would have caused greater reductions to the service stations supplied by this distributor rather than a greater business volume for this distributor compared to others.

54. 10 C.F. R. §211.10(g) (1975). One effect of this rule is to create the potential for more mutual assistance among companies as soon as conditions begin to improve for some. There is probably no rationale for non-assistance during the peak of the shortage and switch with improvement, other than administrative ease, unless it forces companies to try harder to locate supplies during the worst of the shortage.

55. For a brief description, see Zarb, *supra* note 6, at 65-66.

56. 10 C.F.R. §211.17 (1975).

57. *See* Zarb, *supra* note 6, at 66-67; FEA, *Mandatory Petroleum Allocation Program: A Summary* 3-4 (1975) [hereinafter cited as *Summary*].

58. 10 C.F.R. §211.71 (1975).

59. The product was jet fuels, and the plan was dropped so soon after implementation that no one knows whether or not refineries complied.

60. 10 C.F.R. §212.31 (1975). The categories of wholesale purchaser-

reseller, wholesale purchaser-consumer, and end user are not used in the price regulations.

61. 10 C.F.R. §212.73 (1975).

62. 10 C.F.R. §§212.72–.74 (1975); 15 U.S.C. §753(e)(2) (Supp. III, 1973).

63. *See* Zarb, *supra* note 6, at 22–38. To prevent subsidiaries from merely increasing "transfer prices" on imported oil, which would be passed through to consumers and increase parent company profits, the FEA devised two major regulations for investigating and limiting transfer prices. First, companies are required to compute landed costs of imports "purchased" from affiliates with "customary accounting procedures generally accepted and consistently and historically applied by the firm concerned." Second, the FEA may investigate that accounting and disallow any costs for passthroughs. Standards for accounting and investigation may be found in 10 C.F.R. §212.83(f) (1975).

64. Pub. L. No. 94–163 §401(a) (1975).

65. *Energy Policy Act Conference Report, supra* note 19, at 121.

66. Pub. L. No. 94–163 §401(b) and §461 (1975).

67. Pub. L. No. 94–163 §401(a) (1975).

68. *Id.*

69. *Id.*

70. *Energy Policy Act Conference Report, supra* note 19, at 191.

71. *Id.* at 190.

72. Pub. L. No. 94–163 §401(a) (1975).

73. 10 C.F.R. §§212.81–.87; Zarb, *supra* note 6, at 28–29. A refiner will classify his purchasers for this purpose along the lines used historically. For example, all those who were charged the same price may be one class.

74. 10 C.F.R. §§212.31,–.82(c)–(d) (1975); Zarb, *supra* note 6, at 29. Because a firm can always place product costs in the bank, and pass through just non-product costs and product costs up to the profit margin, it is doubtful that this regulation is really a limit on profits.

75. 15 U.S.C. §753(b)(2)(A) (Supp. III, 1973), *as amended* Pub. L. No. 94–163 §402(a) (1975) (emphasis added).

76. 10 C.F.R. §212.83(e) (1975); Zarb, *supra* note 6, at 30. If product costs decrease, either banks must be reduced or prices lowered.

77. *Energy Policy Act Conference Report, supra* note 19, at 195. The reasons for such large banks are unclear, since a company presumably loses opportunity cost on that money. Competition is apparently one factor. Probably the desire to avoid actual refunds and price roll-backs is also a reason, since "banks" can often be used to compensate for reductions ordered by the FEA, in response to earlier price violations, or as a result of enactment of the Energy Policy Act's composite ceiling price requirement.

78. Pub. L. No. 94–163 §402 (1975).

79. Early regulations allowed the difference between the actual price charged and the maximum lawful price to be carried over as unrecouped costs. This made it possible to avoid the equal application rule if long-term fixed-price contracts existed for supplying a refiner's retail outlets, because the FEA would not allow those prices to increase. Consequently, for contracts entered into *after* September 1, 1974, the difference cannot be recouped. 10 C.F.R.

§212.83(e) (1975). Banks are limited in that the amount of increased product costs not recouped in the first month available for passthrough may be passed through in subsequent months in amounts limited to 10 percent of any subsequent month. This measure should avoid drastic price increases if shortages arise again. 10 C.F.R. §212.83(e)(3) (1975); *see* Zarb, *supra* note 6, at 33.

80. For example, if an integrated refinery wanted to pass on an additional 1 cent per gallon increased product cost to non-branded independent purchasers and not to its own outlets, 1 cent per gallon for all classes would be subtracted from the "bank." This tactic may close the price differential between outlets by 1 cent, but the refiner is credited with receiving revenue never collected. Thus, he pays a high price for the effort to increase his sales at the expense of independents.

81. 10 C.F.R. §212.83 (1975), especially subsection (c).

82. *See* Zarb, *supra* note 6, at 34–43.

83. Pub. L. No. 94–163 §402(a) (1975).

84. Pub. L. No. 94–163 §401 (1975). The passthrough of product cost decrease was previously required by regulation.

85. 10 C.F.R §212.93 (1975); Zarb, *supra* note 6, at 43–44.

86. 10 C.F.R. §§212.93,–.103; see also, *supra* notes 46–47.

87. No. CV74–1943 (C.D. Cal., July 25, 1974), *printed at 3 CCH Energy Management* ¶26,007.

88. *See* Marathon Oil Co. v. FEA, No. C75–36 (N.D. Ohio, Jan. 31, 1975), *printed at 3 CCH Energy Management* ¶26,015.

89. 381 F. Supp. 865 (N.D. Tex. 1974), *construing* 10 C.F.R. §210.62 (1975).

90. The supplier/purchaser freeze, as applied to producers and refiners, has since been upheld against an "arbitrary and capricious" attack in Condor Operating Co. v. Sawhill, 514 F.2d 351 (T.E.C.A. 1975). As far as the retail level is concerned, the legislative history shows that Congress intended the President to go as far as the Act would allow to prevent majors from terminating franchises for branded independents.

91. No. 74–921 (D.D.C., July 17, 1974), *printed at 3 CCH Energy Management* ¶26,013.

92. 502 F.2d 1154 (T.E.C.A. 1974).

93. EPAA Conference Report, *supra* note 18, 1973 *U.S. Code Cong. & Adm. News* 2690.

94. No. C75–36 (N.D. Ohio, Jan. 31, 1975).

95. FEA Monthly Litigation Status Report (C.D. Cal.).

96. *See* Marathon Oil Co. v. FEA., No. C75–36 (N.D. Ohio, Jan. 31, 1975); Gulf Oil Corp. v. FEA, 391 F. Supp. 856 (W.D. Pa. 1975).

97. 493 F.2d 1239 (T.E.C.A. 1974).

98. 507 F.2d 455 (T.E.C.A. 1974), *cert. denied,* 95 S. Ct. 1426 (1975); *construing* 10 C.F.R. §206.62(b) (1975).

99. *See, e.g.,* Consumers Union v. Sawhill, 393 F. Supp. 639 (D.D.C. 1975), *affirmed,* Nos. DC–32 and DC–33 (T.E.C.A., Sept. 19, 1975) on waiver of hearings on rulemaking. Interviews with FEA officials suggest they are very cognizant of this fact and have used it to their advantage.

100. Consumers Union v. Sawhill, 512 F.2d 1112, *reversed en banc,* No. DC-26 (T.E.C.A., July 7, 1975). *See Energy Management,* July 15, 1975, at 1-2. Previously it had been determined that the FEA is entitled to use the market price as a factor in deciding where to set prices. In late 1973, the Cost of Living Council allowed old prices to rise from $4.25 to $5.25 per barrel, as an attempt to increase supplies of oil and ease the shock of "forthcoming de-control." In Nader v. Sawhill, 514 F.2d 1064 (T.E.C.A. 1975), the court declared that those factors constituted a rational basis for the Council decision, but in that case, the regulated price was still well below that which would be set by the market.

101. 380 F. Supp. 560 (D.D.C. 1974).

102. EPAA Conference Report, *supra* note 18, 1973 *U.S. Code Cong. & Adm. News* 2701.

103. 382 F. Supp. 437 (D.D.C. 1974).

104. One minor area of interest is a challenge to FEA control of rental fees for retail stations and the prohibition against certain lease clauses. Shell Oil Co. v. FEA, No. 75-II-33 (S.D. Tex., August 7, 1975), *reprinted at* 3 *CCH Energy Management* ¶26,023, recently held FEA rent regulations invalid now that the Economic Stabilization Act has expired, because EPAA does not provide the authority, even if the purpose of rent control is to control prices. In another area, Mohawk Petroleum Company was granted permanent injunctive relief by a federal district court in California and then by TECA in its suit to require the Navy to comply with the supplier/purchaser freeze and continue sales of oil produced in the Elk Hills Naval Petroleum reserve, even though the initial contract had expired. Mohawk Petroleum Corp. v. Department of Navy, No. 9-27 (T.E.C.A., August 26, 1975), *reprinted at* 3 *CCH Energy Management* ¶26,026. In future legislation, applicability to the military should be specified to avoid litigation.

105. 15 U.S.C.A. §792 (Supp. 1975), *as amended* Pub. L. No. 94-163 §101 (1975).

106. 15 U.S.C.A. §792(a) (Supp. 1975), *as amended* Pub. L. No. 94-163 §101 (1975). Powerplants have a very low priority in the FPC natural gas curtailment policy, as do any of the major fuel-burning installations which may be ordered to convert.

107. *Id.* Based on very nearly the exact language of the Conference Report on ESECA, *H.R. Conf. Rep. No.* 1085, 93d Cong., 2d Sess. (1974), *printed at* 1974 *U.S. Code Cong. & Adm. News* 3302, 3305, the FEA has defined "capability and necessary plant equipment" to include, "but not be limited to, necessary coal handling facilities and appurtenances—internal and external; adequate facilities for the storage of coal; and other equipment such as a boiler, unloaders, conveyors, crushers, pulverizers, scales, burners, soot blowers, and special coal burning instrumentation and controls." 10 C.F.R. §305.3(b)(1) (1975).

108. 15 U.S.C.A. §792(b)(1)(A) (Supp. 1975); 10 C.F.R. §305.3(b)(2) (i)-(ii) (1975). It will also consider "the susceptibility of natural gas and petroleum products to volatile changes in price and to interruptions of supply." Probably the last element is a balancing factor, meaning that any facility sub-

ject to an FPC curtailment plan is a prime subject for conversion, if minimum conditions are met.

109. 15 U.S.C.A. §792(b)(1)(B) (Supp. 1975); 10 C.F.R. §305.3(b)(3) (1975).

110. 15 U.S.C.A. §792(b)(1)(C) (Supp. 1975); 10 C.F.R. §305.3(b)(4) (1975).

111. In issuing orders applicable to facilities for the period ending on June 30, 1975, the FEA had to consider the "likelihood that the power plant or installation will be permitted to burn coal after June 30, 1975." 15 U.S.C.A. §792(b)(2)(A)(iii) (Supp. 1975). Since no orders for that period were ever issued, the requirement is now irrelevant.

112. Section 3 of ESECA added section 119 to the Clean Air Act, 42 U.S.C. §§1857 *et seq.* (1970). Temporary suspensions of air quality standards were permitted through June 30, 1975, but the EPA could substitute other requirements, and in any case, the plant had to meet national primary standards. Because the FEA took no real action before that date, the only relevant environmental sections concern compliance date extensions. If a plant is issued such an extension, it may operate until January 1, 1979, even though in violation of air quality standards. *But,* an extension may only be issued by the EPA if the plant can: (a) meet national primary standards and the regional limits (specifically state implementation plans) and (b) submit a plant to the EPA showing how it will meet those requirements. This means that when the FEA issues a Prohibition Order and then goes to the EPA, three things can happen: (a) the plant may be able to meet all standards without needing a compliance date extension; (b) the plant may need and be eligible for an extension, in which case the Prohibition Order can be made effective immediately; and (c) the plant may need an extension, and be ineligible, in which case the EPA will ascertain when it could become eligible, so that a Prohibition Order can be made effective on that date.

113. 10 C.F.R. §§305.4(b)(1), 305.4(c) (1975). One hundred million Btu's can be produced from approximately 17 barrels of crude oil.

114. 15 U.S.C.A. §792(f) (Supp. 1975), *as amended* Pub. L. No. 94–163 §101 (1975).

115. By December 1975 the process had reached the EPA evaluation stage. The EPA must hold formal hearings before issuing a compliance date extension, consequently the whole process may take six months and not all who received a Prohibition Order will ultimately be required to convert. The FEA must also file an environmental impact statement which may necessitate further hearings before implementation. At this point, the FEA has not decided exactly how that will be done. The FEA projects savings of 64 million barrels of oil and 88 Tcf of natural gas if all the plants issued Prohibition Orders do in fact convert.

116. 10 C.F.R. §307.3(b) (1975).

117. *See Energy Management,* July 1, 1975.

118. 15 U.S.C.A. §792(c) (Supp. 1975).

119. 15 U.S.C.A. §792(d) (Supp. 1975).

120. 15 U.S.C.A. §792(e)(2) (Supp. 1975).

121. 15 U.S.C.A. §793(c)(2) (Supp. 1975).

122. 10 C.F.R. §§305.9, 307.9 (1975).

123. In December 1975, the DPA was extended for two years. 89 Stat. 15 (1975).

124. 50 U.S.C. App. §2071(a) (1970).

125. 50 U.S.C. App. §2071(b) (1970).

126. 50 U.S.C. App. §2154 (1970).

127. Pub. L. No. 94-163 §104 (1975).

128. *Hearings on Material Shortages Before the Permanent Subcommittee on Investigations of the Senate Committee on Government Operations,* 94th Cong., 1st Sess., at 75-76 (1975). Also in response to material shortages which could affect fuel supplies, as well as the entire economy, Congress amended the DPA by adding the National Commission on Supplies and Shortages Act of 1974, 50 U.S.C.A. App. §2169 (Supp. 1975), to recommend institutional adjustments for administering potential resource and commodity shortages.

129. 10 C.F.R. §§317.1, 317.5(b) (1975).

130. Space and time require us to omit from the discussion one major title of the Energy Policy Act which authorizes a variety of measures to improve the efficiency of energy use, including the prescription of average fuel economy standards for automobile manufacturers, energy efficiency labeling for consumer products other than automobiles, federal assistance to state energy conservation programs, industrial energy efficiency targets and energy conservation practices of federal agencies. Pub. L. No. 94-163 §§301-383 (1975). This range of subject matter is sufficiently important and complex to merit separate study.

131. Pub. L. No. 94-163 §3(8) (1975).

132. Pub. L. No. 94-163 §202 (1975).

133. Pub. L. No. 94-163 §203 (1975).

134. For text and related documents, see *Sen. Comm. on Interior and Insular Affairs, Agreement on an International Energy Program,* 93d Cong., 2d Sess. (Comm. print, 1974).

135. Pub. L. No. 94-163 §251 (1975).

136. Pub. L. No. 94-163 §§252-254 (1975).

137. Pub. L. No. 94-163 §106. MER is defined as "the maximum rate of production . . . which may be sustained without loss of ultimate recovery . . . under sound engineering and economic principles." TEPR is defined as "the maximum rate of production" above the MER "which may be sustained for a temporary period of less than 90 days without reservoir damage and without significant loss of ultimate recovery." Some fields may have no TEPR. The Secretary of the Interior is required to determine MERs and TEPRs for each field on federal lands which produces significant volumes of crude oil or natural gas. In determining such production rates, section 106 requires formal administrative rulemaking under the Administrative Procedure Act, 5 U.S.C. §551 *et seq.* (1970).

138. Pub. L. No. 94-163 §§151-166 (1975).

139. Pub. L. No. 94-163 §152(5) (1975).

140. Pub. L. No. 94-163 §154(c)(2) (1975).

141. It is noteworthy that the IEP contemplates initially that each participating country will develop the capacity to sustain consumption for at least 60

days with no net oil imports. Thereafter, upon decision by a special majority, the capability may be increased to 90 days. These undertakings are, of course, much more onerous for a country such as Japan or West Germany, where oil imports account for a very large fraction of energy consumption, than for the U.S., where imports, although very large in volume, still account for a relatively small fraction of total energy consumption.

142. Pub. L. No. 94-163 §161(d) (1975).
143. 15 U.S.C.A. §796 (Supp. 1975).
144. Pub. L. No. 94-163 §506 (1975).
145. Pub. L. No. 94-163 §503 (1975).
146. Pub. L. No. 94-163 §501 (1975).

Chapter Seven

Petroleum Allocation: Administrative Development and Implementation

The development and implementation of a plan for petroleum allocation is fully as important as the substantive content of the plan itself. Regulations which are too complex cannot be effective in emergency situations; overly simplistic regulations risk damage to the intricate structural arrangements of the petroleum industry.

This chapter considers how the EPAA allocation regulations were developed and the administrative procedures were used in implementing those regulations. The discussion is focused mainly on the EPAA because neither ESECA nor DPA has been fully developed and tested in practice. The procedures described are, however, applicable to ESECA, as well as EPAA, since the Federal Energy Administration Act requires these procedures for both statutes.

The Energy Policy and Conservation Act amendments leave the EPAA's administrative procedures basically intact, although, as described in Chapter Six, it adds numerous requirements for statutory findings and reports to the Congress as predicates for regulatory actions. In addition, the Energy Policy Act imposes specific congressional review procedures prior to a variety of major executive energy actions, including amendments to the petroleum allocation and pricing regulation to be promulgated under section 4(a) of the EPAA and contingency plans for energy conservation and rationing. These review procedures are discussed at the end of this chapter.

DEVELOPMENT OF REGULATION PURSUANT TO THE EPAA

Under the duress of the Arab oil embargo, the EPAA required almost immediate implementation after its enactment in late November 1973. The basic allocation regulations issued under the **EPAA** were published in the Federal Register on January 15, 1974.[1] It was possible to meet the statutory deadlines only because a contingency allocation program was already well developed within the Executive Branch. The program was not based on a careful evaluation of industry and economic data. Rather, it was largely the result of decisions based on what the policy makers considered *a priori* to be important priorities.[2]

In the summer of 1973, a small group of civil servants drawn from various government agencies and later known as the "reg writers," was established to draft allocation regulations. A group of interested officials met periodically with William Simon to develop general policy guidelines for the reg writers. Simon, John Sawhill, and several of their key staff members became the principal forces in designing the program. There were very few economists among the planners. Most of the reg writers were lawyers, engineers, or career civil servants. The Treasury Department, the Office of Emergency Preparedness (OEP), the Department of Interior's Office of Oil and Gas, and the Office of Management and Budget (OMB) all offered input.

During 1972 and 1973, independent companies at all levels of the petroleum industry had been complaining about pressure from the majors. By the summer of 1973, the independents had organized an extensive lobbying effort to ensure that shortages of crude oil were shared equally by all companies. In the fall of 1973, consumer groups joined the lobbying effort in favor of regulation.

As pressures mounted, import quotas were ended in April 1973 in order to allow increased supplies of crude oil to enter the country. A fee system replaced the quotas. Supplies had grown short enough to necessitate the implementation of a voluntary allocation program for crude oil in May 1973. Throughout this period, the Economic Stabilization Act was in effect, permitting (not mandating) price and allocation controls for petroleum and refined petroleum products.[3] The Cost of Living Council adopted a price freeze in June and fairly permanent petroleum price rules in August 1973. Despite the deepening shortages, Simon preferred to continue a program of voluntary cooperation with the major oil companies rather than to institute a mandatory allocation scheme.

By the fall of 1973, pressure for allocation was widespread. In response to the low inventories of propane and middle distillates, a mandatory allocation program was ordered effective on October 3 and November 1, 1973. The embargo began before these programs could ever be tested, however, and opposition to mandatory allocation was quieted. The Arab embargo was the catalyst which caused Congress to implement allocation to cope with a situation which had been worsening for months. Consequently, the EPAA was passed in November 1973.

The acute shortages of some petroleum products in December 1973, and January and February 1974, caused the program to be oriented initially toward avoiding regional inequity in supplies. The shortage hit hardest regions supplied heavily by independents. Soon, however, the primary objective of regulation seems to have become protection of the independent sector of the industry. Simon is said to have been a key supporter of that objective. Thus a severe petroleum shortage provided the immediate impetus for launching a massive regulatory program which quickly became justified in terms of much longer range policy concerns—namely, preservation of the petroleum industry structure.

When the petroleum allocation program was initially developed, there was no oil embargo and no really serious shortage of product. Moreover, there was no organizational consolidation of those within the government who had expertise in the petroleum industry. At the time, the White House was preoccupied with Watergate. In effect, what became the substantive allocation regulations were adopted in a policy and institutional vacuum. Many of the price and procedural regulations were taken directly from the Cost of Living Council regulations. Thus they were initially designed to fight inflation, a goal of only subsidiary importance to the FEO and later to the FEA.

The reg writers and policy planners did not use a significant staff study of options and alternative allocation strategies. The Cost of Living Council served as a somewhat theoretical, as well as practical, model for the design of a regulatory program. The planners decided that problem areas could be worked out after the regulations were in place. Consequently, there was no need for empirical data. Little or no substantive input came from Congress, the White House, or industry. The Executive Branch planners worked with Congress primarily to guarantee that the emergency legislation which was under consideration would permit the implementation of an already designed program.

Interviews suggest that the most important factors in the development of allocation regulations were: the personal opinions and ideas of those few high level executive officials who took an interest during 1973, particularly Simon, Sawhill, Roy Ash (from OMB), and other top staff; the internal power struggles among these individuals; and the conflicts between agencies as each bureaucratic unit tried to gain maximum control of decision-making.[4] While there were few alternatives for decision-making at the time, more informed decisions and a full examination of options would be desirable before petroleum allocation again becomes necessary.

Given the constraints on the reg writers, their only viable alternative for regulation development was a policy-oriented, rulemaking approach. They did not have the time and data available to be fact-specific in the original design, even though they began their work before the embargo. Moreover, a fact-specific regulatory design which was developed completely before the embargo might have been too oriented toward protection of independents rather than toward alleviation of overall shortages.

The major alternative to regulation by rulemaking is the use of individual adjudications and orders, similar to the FPC's procedures in the case of natural gas. An adjudicatory approach requires time for each hearing and an established administrative agency, neither of which was available to the reg writers. The large number of firms in the oil industry contrasts with the much smaller number in natural gas, particularly if only natural gas companies subject to FPC jurisdiction are considered. The more firms involved, the greater the likelihood that prompt and coordinated action is impossible under an adjudicative procedure. Adjudications may be best suited for fine-tuning within a rulemaking approach which allows prompt and coordinated action. The balance between rules and adjudications can be varied as need be in the course of developing and implementing regulatory programs. As we will see, both are critical elements of FEA regulation. Once the EPAA was enacted, the rulemaking approach was obligatory, and adjudications could be added at the agency's discretion.[5]

During this period, the FEA was different in several respects from many other more firmly entrenched government agencies. The General Counsel's Office made most of the decisions on how and what type of rules should be issued. The career bureaucrats were resentful of their limited role as suppliers of information. Presumably, high officials outside the General Counsel's Office had substantial input, but internal FEA memos indicate that below high-level policy decisions, the lawyers were in control.[6]

Within the Office of General Counsel, responsibility for drafting regulations was divided among pricing, allocation, ESECA, etc. Very few persons had a coordinated view of how the regulations interrelated. Interviews suggest that coordination was very informal, although the FEA has recently attempted to formalize the process. When a problem arose, draft regulations were proposed internally. There were, of course, policy constraints on the options for solving the problem, but the lawyers really began the rulemaking process, after the problem was brought to their attention.

Sometimes regulations were drafted and promulgated very rapidly; in other cases, the process lasted for over a year. In some areas, the FEA lawyers worked on the drafting of regulations for months without finding a solution, meeting frequently with industry and special interest representatives. Presumably, urgently needed regulations could be promulgated more rapidly, using subsequent revisions to avoid language difficulties.

As we have seen, authority for petroleum policy and regulation passed from the Office of Energy Policy to the Federal Energy Office, to the Federal Energy Administration.[7] Within the FEA, there are three basic organizational levels: the FEA national office, FEA regional offices, and FEA and state offices located in each state. The state level is subdivided into federal-state liaison offices and state energy offices.[8]

The FEA national office in Washington establishes all important policy, particularly that needed to resolve particular cases in regional offices (including compliance, application verification, and investigation). The national office also administers and issues allocation orders for the following programs: crude oil and refinery yield control, butane and natural gasoline, aviation fuels (only for civil air carriers and public aviation), residual fuel oil (for utilities), naphthas, and gas oils. The national office also handles coordination, regional redistribution, determination of allocation levels and state set-aside percentages, and review of appeals on nationally administered programs. All of these programs involve only a limited number of private sector participants, while regional offices handle programs involving many more participants.

Regional offices resolve cases, consider appeals from their own orders, and administer the following programs: middle distillates, motor gasoline, residual fuel oil (non-utility), aviation fuel (not controlled by the national office), and propane (except for multi-regional cases). A regional office has some coordination responsibility, but its primary purpose is to implement policies of the national office.

In each state there is a federal-state liaison office, which serves to coordinate federal-state relationships and monitor state activities. State energy offices allocate the state set-aside and gather information concerning local problems for the FEA. In some states, these offices are active in other areas not preempted by the FEA.

FEA ADMINISTRATIVE PROCEDURES

As we have seen, most of the administrative procedures of the FEA were taken directly from the Cost of Living Council regulations. The Council set out economywide regulations, and made modifications as necessary for particular industries. The FEO had only one industry to regulate, so it established industrywide regulations, and modified them as they were applied.[9] This type of regulation focuses on the adjustments necessary after initial implementation, rather then on preliminary development; it makes imperative a simple and expeditious administrative adjustment process. Before a specific discussion of how the FEA makes regulations, it is useful to consider the provisions of the Adminsitrative Procedure Act and how they relate to the FEA.

The Administrative Procedure Act (APA) and the FEA

At the outset, it should be noted that Congress is not obliged to make an agency abide by any of the APA procedures. The APA merely provides some general procedural features which may be made applicable to an agency.[10] The most common APA features are rules and orders. A rule tends to have general applicability and future effect, while an order is a final disposition other than a rulemaking. Orders are formulated by an agency adjudication.[11]

Rulemaking can follow an informal procedure, a formal procedure, or some blend of the two. Interpretive rules, procedural rules and policy statements are exempt from the APA requirements. The informal procedure requires the agency to publish notice of the proposed rule at least 30 days before its effective date. During that time, interested persons may submit comments on the proposal. After the comment period, the agency must include in the rule a "concise general statement of [its] basis and purpose."[12] A court may review this type of rule to determine whether it is arbitrary and capricious (lacking a rational basis), which is a very loose standard of review.[13] An agency may also exempt itself from these notice and comment requirements when it for "good cause" finds them to be "impractical, unnecessary, or contrary to the public interest."[14]

Formal rulemaking procedures must be followed when the statute authorizing agency action provides that rules are "to be made on the record after opportunity for an agency hearing."[15] In this case the agency must hold a formal hearing for the reception of oral or documentary evidence. Rebuttal evidence and cross examination are allowed, and decisions must be based solely on the evidence adduced at the hearing. All decisons of the agency must provide detailed findings and are subject to "substantial evidence" review in court.[16] Obviously, the formal procedure takes more time and effort for the agency than the informal notice and comment procedure. Adjudications require basically the same procedures as a formal rulemaking, except that somewhat stricter provisions apply to notice and decision-making.[17]

The FEA is exempt from the adjudicatory and formal rulemaking procedures of the APA.[18] Moreover, the informal rulemaking procedures of the FEA differ somewhat from the APA prescription, allowing a shorter comment period but making it more difficult to waive the notice requirement. With the exception of the rulemaking and petition for rulemaking regulations of the FEA, none of the administrative devices (adjustments, exceptions, assignments) are required by the APA.

The Federal Energy Administration Act (FEAA) requires the FEA to establish procedures for making such adjustments ". . . as may be necessary to prevent special hardship, inequity, or unfair distribution of burdens . . . ." Specifically mentioned in FEAA are interpretations, modifications, rescissions, exceptions, exemptions, and appeals.[19] The earlier Economic Stabilization Act imposed the same requirements on the FEO.[20] None of these procedures is required by the APA. In general, the FEA has statutory discretion as to whether a hearing should be provided.

FEA Rulemaking Procedures

The EPAA was designed with rulemaking in mind; rulemaking for allocation was mandatory. (This is in marked contrast to the FPC's procedural options under the Natural Gas Act discussed in Chapters Three and Four.) Before becoming effective, the initial EPAA regulations had to be submitted to the Attorney General and the Federal Trade Commission for comments on how the allocation regulations would affect competition.[21] According to judicial interpretation subsequent revisions of the regulations do not require this procedure.[22]

The EPAA does not mention how rulemaking authority is affected by the National Environmental Policy Act (NEPA) and the requirement of environmental impact statements. However, *Gulf Oil Corp. v. Simon*[23] held that Congress did not intend a NEPA impact statement to be necessary in view of the time required to prepare such a statement and the deadline within which the EPAA regulation was required to be promulgated. Since then, the FEA has not filed any environmental impact statement in association with regulation under the EPAA.

The EPAA incorporated by reference the administrative procedure and judicial review sections of the Economic Stabilization Act of 1970, as in effect on November 27, 1973. Section 207 of that Act exempts the FEA from the requirements of all but sections 552, 553, and 555(e) of the Administrative Procedure Act.[24] In other words, only notice and comment, or informal rulemaking procedure is required. Even the informal procedure is always subject to the "good cause" exemption described above. Consequently, the FEA used only informal rulemaking, and very often waived the notice and comment requirements. Once these requirements are waived, the agency is not obligated to grant hearings or a comment period after effectiveness, but on rare occasion the FEA did so.[25]

The FEAA, which became effective on July 1,1974, not only supplanted the FEO, which was within the Executive Office of the President, with the FEA, which is a full-fledged Executive Branch agency; but the FEAA also made several changes in petroleum allocation rulemaking. These were aimed at increasing public input.

1. The FEA was permitted to shorten the comment period to as little as 10 days.

2. The FEA must allow an oral presentation either before or after making any "rule, regulation or order . . . likely to have a substantial impact on the Nation's economy or large numbers of individuals or businesses."

3. The FEA can waive notice and comment only "where strict compliance is found to cause serious harm or injury to the public health, safety or welfare, and such finding is set out in detail in such rule, regulation, or order."[26]

Congress believed that subsequent comment would at least subject the FEA to some public scrutiny. If comments really are useful for obtaining information, an after-the-fact comment period may be fruitless. Yet there may be some benefit here in the area of public accountability. The tightening of waiver conditions was designed to prevent the FEA from continuing an old Cost of Living Council technique. The council, subject to the "good cause" exemption, had often waived the notice and comment requirements with boiler-plate language in promulgating regulations.[27]

Out of 61 FEO rulemakings before July 1, 1974, 47 were issued without an opportunity for prior comment; after July 1, 1974, only 25 of 71 FEA rulemakings were issued without prior comment. Of those 47 prior to July 1, only 4 provided for a comment period after the effective date, and 2 provided for hearings after effectiveness. After July 1, comments were received after effectiveness for 15 of the 25, and hearings were held in 11 proceedings. The number of notices providing for prior hearings increased from 2 before July 1, to 27 after FEAA became effective.

FEA officials explain the change on the ground that, in the early stages of regulation, time constraints were far more important than later, and there was a greater risk of major alterations in buying patterns in response to regulations which were announced before becoming effective. Nevertheless, stricter statutory notice and comment requirements had some limiting effect on waivers, even though the language of FEAA still allows the FEA to respond almost immediately in an emergency.

Court reaction to FEA procedures has been mixed, but in an emergency situation, it is again unlikely that an FEA rule would be invalidated. *Nader v. Sawhill*[28] involved the amendment of a Cost of Living Council regulation in 1973 which increased the price of old oil, without allowing notice and comment, by use of the "good cause" waiver. The plaintiffs alleged that the Council had not shown sufficient cause to satisfy the APA waiver requirements. The Temporary Emergency Court of Appeals found that, if prior notice had been given, companies might have withheld oil until the increase occurred, and that the FEA's failure to express that finding as a reason for its waiver of notice was only a technical flaw. Nevertheless, the FEA was admonished that circumstances with less potential for calamity would require stricter conformance with the APA.

California & Louisiana v. Simon[29] had earlier held that lack of technical compliance with the APA was permissible. In that case the FEA had provided less than a 30-day comment period before effectiveness.

However, *Consumers Union v. Sawhill*[30] held that the FEA lacked sufficient good cause for waiving notice when it adopted an interim rule on the price of unleaded gasoline. The court reasoned the FEA had enough time to permit a comment period if the agency had acted promptly after realizing that a rule was necessary. Since the interim rule was no longer in effect, and restitution was not ordered, the decision had little practical impact. It does mean that FEA delays may not justify actions not otherwise justifiable.

Section 553(e) of the APA requires that "[e]ach agency shall give an interested person the right to petition for the issuance, amendment, or repeal of a rule." Accordingly, the FEA has established the requisite procedures.[31] The petition as a device for public input to rulemaking is more a formality than a fruitful avenue. According to FEA officials, very few rulemaking proceedings have been the result of such petitions. Far more common than petitions, at least as effective, are telephone calls, letters, or informal and off-the-record meetings with FEA officials.

Whenever the FEA publishes notice of a proposed rule, it almost always includes the draft language, as well as a content analysis, in order to elicit comments. Notices often provoke a substantial number of comments, which are summarized. A lawyer in the General Counsel's Office reads each comment, as well as the summary. However, some FEA officials believe that formal comments are often not very useful; informal comments are regarded as generally more valuable. It is impossible to discern what changes FEA makes in response to comments, although many proposed regulations which are issued subject to comment are altered before being put into effect.

The Energy Policy Act now has mandated an FEA reevaluation of the entire petroleum allocation and pricing regulation promulgated under section 4(a) of the EPAA and as in effect in December 1975.[32] This reevaluation must begin by mid-February 1976, follow certain statutory procedures, and culminate in a report to the Congress in mid-April, 1976. A primary purpose of the reevaluation is to determine the continuing need for any provision of the current allocation and pricing regulation.

The administrative procedure specified for the conduct of the reevaluation requires public notice, an opportunity for interested persons to present "written and oral data, views and arguments," and taking a transcript of oral presentations. The subsequent report to the Congress may include regulatory amendments which are appropriate in light of the reevaluation and the elimination of any regulatory provisions which are no longer necessary. Any amendments resulting from the reevaluation procedure are, however, subject to prior congressional review.

The reevaluation requirement thus offers the FEA an initial opportunity for a comprehensive review and revision of its allocation and pricing regulation in light of current petroleum industry conditions and the Energy Policy Act amendments to the EPAA. The administrative procedures specifically mandated for the reevaluation, although short of formal rulemaking, seem to afford ample opportunity for an orderly and full consideration of the views of interested persons. Moreover, any party aggrieved will have a further opportunity to press his views before the Congress.

It is impossible to predict whether the outcome of the reevaluation will be simplification and partial deregulation or complication and enhanced protection of special interests, or some of both. Perhaps the need for continuity will result in minimal change.

FEA Adjudication and Administration of Regulations

This section is not a detailed explanation of the FEA adjudicatory procedures; rather, it is an illustration of the procedures required by the petroleum allocation scheme that FEA developed. The Code of Federal Regulations is very specific as to which office must be consulted for each type of request, time limits, extent of notice. etc.[33] In the following discussion we will first describe the main procedures which are common to all FEA adjudications. Thereafter, we will examine each major adjudicative device used by the FEA, including procedures FEA uses to explain actions short of regular adjudication.

Elements common to all adjudication. A petitioner for some form of relief from FEA's allocation regulations is generally required to notify "each person who is reasonably ascertainable by the applicant as a person who will be aggrieved by the FEA action sought." The FEA may relieve an applicant of this requirement if it determines such notice is "impractical."[34]

Applications for FEA action must provide "all relevant facts pertaining to the circumstances, act or transaction that is subject of the application." This may include names and addresses of parties, asserted business justifications, copies of contracts, and other business documents.[35]

The FEA may initiate an investigation to verify any information available to it for decision. Thus, an independent source of data is available. Petitions providing insufficient factual material on which to base a decision may be dismissed with or without prejudice.[36]

Varying limits are placed on the time the FEA may take for deliberation. Failure to decide within that time period may be considered a denial for the purposes of judicial review.[37] These limits are self-imposed, since they are not required by statute. They serve to keep some time pressure on those who must decide petitions, and allow a company to go to court if the agency refuses to decide or chooses to stall.

A petitioner is under a continuing obligation to inform the FEA of factual changes relevant to his application.[38] Those giving information may request confidential treatment, but the FEA makes the final decision as to confidentiality. This can be important because the FEA is subject to the Freedom of Information Act.[39] The FEA also has the authority to determine who may personally participate in public hearings and other agency proceedings.[40] Decisions, based upon the application and other relevant information, must be accompanied by a written statement of the factual and legal basis for the order.[41]

The regulations prescribe when conferences, hearings, and public hearings may be employed. Conferences are available "solely for the exchange of views," at either the request of the parties or the FEA. The decision on whether to grant a conference is discretionary with the agency. Conferences are not open to the public, and no formal report or finding is compiled.[42] Hearings are granted only in connection with exceptions or appeals, and only then if the FEA determines it would "materially advance the consideration of the issue," or the decision is "likely to have a substantial impact on the Nation's economy or large numbers of individuals or businesses. . . ." Notice of the issues to be involved in conferences or (private) hearings may be very general.[43]

Public hearings may be granted in connection with FEAA requirements for rulemaking or for such other proceedings as the FEA determines advisable. An agenda is prepared for all spokesmen allowed to participate, and notice is published in the *Federal Register*. The FEA makes a verbatim transcript of the hearing. However, the agency is not restricted to the hearing record and may use all relevant information in making a decision.[44] Public hearings need not provide opportunities for cross-examination of witness. Furthermore, the FEA is statutorily obligated to use a public hearing only if the order is "likely to have a substantial impact on the nation's economy or large numbers of individuals or businesses. . . ."[45]

Once a decision is reached, the FEA itself provides notice to those "aggrieved by the FEA action."[46]

Adjustments to base period volumes. Adjustments to base period volumes are necessary for the FEA to be able to maintain flexibility in the amount of product it allocates to various purchasers. A WPR may request an adjustment to his base period volume to compensate for unusual growth. The regulations define the conditions deemed sufficient to justify an FEA determination of unusual growth, but it consists basically of an increased sales volume. An end user or WPC who is entitled to 100 percent of current requirements may also petition for an adjustment to compensate for increased current requirements.[47] Prior to August 1, 1974, an adjustment could also be requested on the basis of changed circumstances. However, currently the FEA requires such applicants to petition for an exception instead.[48]

The applicant must request an adjustment from his supplier before invoking FEA assistance. The supplier must then certify the facts in the application to the appropriate FEA office. If the supplier refuses to certify, or cannot do so, the applicant must explain the lack of certification to the FEA in the adjustment petition.

An adjustment will be granted in accordance with the policy objectives of the EPAA, and only if an application, "fully supported" by detailed facts, figures, and relevant documentation, presents the agency a "compelling" situation requiring relief.[49] One temporary adjustment effective for a maximum of 90 days may be provided in special circumstances.[50] Appeal from an adjustment order may be taken to the appropriate Regional Office or the National Office of Exceptions and Appeals (OEA) within 30 days of service of the order.[51]

Assignments of suppliers. An assignment is "an action designating that an authorized purchaser be supplied at a specified entitlement level by a specified supplier."[52] Purchasers who do not have a base period supplier, including new end users and retailers, may petition the FEA to assign them to a supplier.

During surplus conditions, this is not necessary, except as insurance that a base period supplier who must continue sales will exist for a particular purchaser during a shortage. Assignments can also be used for equalizing allocation fractions among suppliers during a shortage. In this case, assignments are a form of mutual assistance. If a purchaser's base period supplier has an allocation fraction of .60, and another nearby supplier has one of 1.0, the purchaser would obviously like to be assigned to the latter.

Temporary assignments, either from the FEA or the state set-aside system, may be granted "only in dire circumstances" where an ordinary assignment may not be made consistent with usual regulatory requirements.[53] In such cases, the business information usually requested may be waived for good cause. A temporary assignment may be appealed by affected persons.[54] Assignments pursuant to these regulations do not affect fuels allocated under state set-aside systems.[55]

Exceptions. Exceptions are designed to waive or modify *specific* compliance with the FEA's allocation or price regulations. Exceptions may be contrasted with exemptions, which are designed for much broader relief and result in a broader waiver. Exceptions are a much more common route for petitioners, possibly because they are easier to justify than exemptions. Exceptions were intended to operate only as an alternative to adjustments, assignments, and interpretations (discussed below), but they have in fact become a critical way for the FEA to achieve flexibility in its regulation.[56]

An exception may be granted upon a clear showing of "serious hardship or gross inequity."[57] The gloss on that language is provided in agency decisions. Thus, it is necessary to show that one's obligations under the regulations are "so different in nature or extent from the obligations of others similarly situated as to result in a 'gross inequity,'" or that the regulations work "in such a unique or disproportionate manner as to contravene the realization of the policy objectives underlying" the EPAA.[58] "Gross inequity has been found to exist where, because of the unique business practices and other characteristics of a particular firm, the application of a general regulation to it results in financial consequences different from those intended by the regulations."[59] The FEA uniformly rejects statutory and constitutional challenges made through the exception procedure.[60]

Exceptions are filed with the Office of Exceptions and Appeals (OEA).[61] Each request is assigned to an Assistant Director and an analyst. The request is evaluated and then turned over to a committee within OEA for decision.

Officials in OEA recognize that the basis for exceptions must be consistent, so that each decision will have some value as a precedent. For that reason, all decisions on exceptions are published and indexed. At least in theory these decisions will be used subsequently as precedents by the OEA and other offices whose decisions are subject to OEA review.

The FEA believes that agency decisions on exceptions meet the goal of consistency, but many outside the FEA disagree. The critics contend that the agency decisions are arbitrary and inconsistent. The difference of opinion may very well be the result of facts known by those in OEA and not realized or known by those who follow the agency decisions.

In any case, OEA officials acknowledge that the precedents of its prior rulings on exceptions are often so unclear to petitioners that many do not realize which facts are critical to a decision until they appeal an initial OEA denial. Whatever the reason, the basis of agency decisions on exceptions does not seem to be well understood by the public, industry, or the Congress. In an extended program of allocation, an understanding of precedent may be essential in order for a firm to avoid serious consequences. Therefore, steps should be taken to ensure that affected persons will know in advance what constitutes grounds for an exception.

Exemptions. An exemption is a "release from the obligation to comply with any part or parts, or any subpart thereof," of the petroleum regulations.[62] An exemption application, if granted, results in a rulemaking proceeding, but the ordinary FEA rulemaking provisions do not apply.[63] An exemption application is intended to embrace a request for release which presents issues of national significance for policy or administration.[64] This administrative exemption process is distinct from the highly specific exception procedure, discussed above, and also is different from the partial deregulation process, which requires congressional acquiescence. The latter process is discussed further below.

Administrative exemptions are considered by the Office of Private Grievances and Redress.[65] The grant of an exemption is discretionary and rests on a finding that a rulemaking is appropriate with regard to such factors as economic justifications and the potential impact on the regulatory system. The petitioner must demonstrate the necessity of an exemption to meet his particular problem.[66] Exemptions have been granted: (a) in order to reconcile energy policy with other federal policies favoring employment or minority businesses;[67] and (b) where special geographic circumstances required a limited exemption for aviation fuel needs of certain air taxi flights to outlying towns.[68] Denials by the Office of Private Grievances and Redress of exemption requests are appealable to the OEA.[69]

As mentioned previously, the Energy Policy Act has added a new section 12 to the EPAA which provides authority and a special mechanism for exempting "a class of persons or class of transactions" from allocation and/or price regulation under section 4(a).[70] Domestically produced crude oil is not, however, eligible for exemption; all other petroleum product categories are.[71] An exemption may apply to only one product category, it may apply to allocation regulation or pricing, or to both, and it may provide for phased implementation.

An exemption from allocation regulation must be based on findings that the product category is no longer in short supply and that its exemption will not adversely affect the supply of any other petroleum product. An exemption from price control requires findings that market competition is adequate to protect consumers and that the exemption will not result in "inequitable prices" for any class of users of the exempted product.

Any amendment which effects such a partial or phased deregulation is subject to congressional review and acquiescence prior to becoming effective. Subsequent to an exemption, the President has continuing discretionary authority to reimpose regulation on the product concerned. The effect of an exemption under section 12 is thus to convert mandatory regulation to standby authority.

It is impossible to predict at this writing to what extent petroleum products will be exempted from allocation or pricing regulation under the EPAA in the near future. The supply of petroleum products should be adequate to satisfy demand, with the possible exception of propane, under current market conditions. However, allocation generally tends to protect the position of the small, independent firms in the petroleum industry. Accordingly, attempts to deregulate are likely to be politically controversial.

Interpretations and rulings.   An interpretation is supplied by either the General Counsel's Office or a Regional Counsel.[72] It is strictly limited to the single fact situation it describes, and only the parties involved may rely on it.[73] An interpretation may be modified or rescinded at any time through notifying the parties of the change. Nevertheless, a favorable interpretation provides a defense to a charge of violation of the regulations even if the interpretation is later declared invalid.[74] Interpretations may be appealed to the OEA.[75]

Rulings are issued by the General Counsel and are meant to deal more generally with recurring sets of circumstances and to assist the public in interpreting the regulation.[76] Like interpretations, a defense of reliance is permitted against agency sanctions. Unlike an interpretation, however, there is no administrative appeal of a general ruling.[77]

Both interpretations and rulings are intended to offer the equivalent of precedent to those who are regulated by the FEA. Rulings are obviously less fact specific than interpretations, and consequently are more oriented to general guidance. Both devices allow the FEA to flesh out initially unclear regulations without resort to the rulemaking process for amendments. In particular, the FEA can explain what the language of a rule is supposed to mean, before it has to be applied injuriously. In theory, it may seem preferable for a company to seek an interpretation before it risks violating a rule. In practice, however, the lack of severe penalties for violations probably makes the opposite course of action more attractive.

Guidelines.   Guidelines serve a purpose similar to that of rulings. They are issued in situations where the FEA deems it desirable to specify factors the agency will consider in making decisions. For example, there are guidelines for new motor gasoline retail sales outlets which describe the procedures and substantive criteria the FEA will use in assigning suppliers and volumes of a product. Such guidelines are general, and, in some respects, serve as precedent for agency decisions.[78] However, where interpretations and rulings commit the agency to some extent to a particular posture on a given question, guidelines give the agency far more room within which to make decisions.

FEA Compliance and Enforcement Actions

When the FEA began regulation, it lacked the staff necessary for extensive enforcement work. The early need for trained auditors caused the FEA to operate under a Memorandum of Understanding with the Internal Revenue Service (IRS). For the period from January 11, 1974, through June 30, 1974, the FEA transferred all compliance and enforcement responsibility for allocation and price regulation to the IRS. IRS assigned 300 investigators to this work, and began hiring and training additional energy investigators to be transferred to FEA on July 1, 1974. The FEA assumed control of enforcement activities in July with about 850 investigators. Understandably, the FEA has been reluctant to hire oil industry personnel to audit and analyze industry data, and has thus been limited in who it may hire for auditing.[79]

The FEA was also hampered in the early stages of regulation by the lack of consistent data. The FEA has very extensive statutory authority for gathering information. However, the accounting methods of large oil companies are so complex that verification of data is extremely time-consuming. Historically, the government relied largely on data compiled by the industry trade associations. Data gathered by the Bureau of Mines usually consisted of a compilation of figures submitted by the industry, largely without independent verification. Even now (perhaps due to definitional problems also), the FEA lacks a census of retail product outlets broken down into the categories created by the EPAA.

Both FEAA and ESECA grant to the FEA almost unlimited potential for information-gathering. The broadest grant is contained in the FEAA:[80]

> The Administrator may require, by general or special orders, any person engaged in any phase of energy supply or major energy consumption to file . . . reports or answers in writing . . . to enable the Administrator to carry out his functions under this chapter.

Pursuant to that authority, the FEA has required exhaustive monthly, weekly, and otherwise timely reports by consumers and suppliers of energy resources.

In addition, FEAA authorizes the FEA to conduct investigations, including physical inspections, sampling, and copying of records, for the purpose of verifying the submitted data.[81] If the FEA were unable to verify the accuracy of its information, it would soon find itself in an untenable position. In a crisis, confrontation, or disagreement, the agency would be dependent upon an industry which has clearly stated its opposition to regulation. The extent of oil company violations discovered by even a small investigatory effort indicates that independent verification of data is essential to effective regulation.

One of the easiest areas in which "cheating" might occur is in the transfer prices charged between affiliates of an integrated company. Investigation is also important for energy consumers, simply because of the stakes involved when some priority levels are low enough to cause substantial economic hardship. Nevertheless, one report suggested that FEA data acquisition and use are still usually inefficient and unverified.[81]

Because of all these problems, the importance of citizen complaints has been emphasized for bringing possible violations of regulations to the FEA's attention. A complaint must be directed to the appropriate regional office and it must include a description of both the transaction and the regulation allegedly violated.[83] The agency's response may be a Notice of Probable Violation (NOPV), a Remedial Order (RO), or a decision that no remedial action is appropriate.[84]

The typical consumer obviously lacks the sophistication required to uncover violations of complex regulations. Wholesale purchasers are more likely to be familiar with the regulations, particularly WPRs, but it is still fairly easy for a refiner to inflate his reported supply obligations or deflate his reported allocable supply.

In the event that the FEA declines to issue an NOPV or RO in response to a complaint, FEAA does not expressly provide for a citizen's enforcement action. To date, no one has attempted to bring such a suit, so the issue of whether FEAA created an implied action is still open.[85]

An NOPV initiates all enforcement proceedings, except under unusual circumstances in which a Remedial Order for Immediate Compliance may be issued.[86] The person notified by an NOPV has 10 days in which to respond with business information and legal justification for the transaction. "As utilized by the FEA, the NOPV is intended to solicit a response from the party under investigation."[87] The FEA may grant a conference whenever the agency determines that it will be useful for providing information or clarifying complex issues. Failure to respond to an NOPV is a concession. Although an RO may be appealed administratively, an NOPV may not.[88]

If a violation is found, a Remedial Order may be issued, to become effective immediately.[89] An RO for Immediate Compliance, waiving the procedures associated with the other two orders, may be issued on strong findings that a violation has probably occurred and that irreparable injury to the public interest is likely if the violation is not halted immediately.[90] The agency may refer a Remedial Order to the Department of Justice for further enforcement. Through that Department, the FEA may request injunctive relief when it finds that a violation is about to be committed.[91]

As amended by the Energy Policy Act, the EPAA now prescribes a stiff system of civil and criminal penalties for violations.[92] Whoever violates the section 4(a) allocation and pricing regulation is subject to a civil penalty, and whoever willfully violates the regulation is subject to a criminal penalty. The maximum penalties are graduated, depending on the level in the distribution chain. With respect to crude oil production, distribution and refining, the maximum civil penalty is $20,000 for each violation and the maximum criminal penalty is one year imprisonment and a $40,000 fine. At the retail level, the maximum civil penalty is $2,500 and the criminal maximum is one year imprisonment and a $10,000 fine. Penalties are cumulative, and each day of violation may be separately punished. Additionally, the FEA may order price rollbacks and refunds of overcharges running as high as the extent of the violation.[93]

Criminal (i.e., willful) violations are always referred to the Department of

Justice, although cases in which there is enough evidence to prove willfulness are rare. Even for collection of civil penalties, the FEA must go to court. However, the agency has a policy of compromising potential civil penalties and avoiding the expense and delay of formal court proceedings.[94]

The initial enforcement effort was directed primarily at the retail and small wholesaler level. When supplies were actually short, consumers were willing to pay "any" price, and the worst violations resulted in retail sales. Compliance officials in the FEA believe that, while future restitution is possible at other levels of the industry, nearly immediate remedial action is required in the case of retail sales to unspecified customers. In the early stages of the FEA's program, heavy political pressure was exerted to compel the FEA to rectify retail violations, yet insufficient staff was available to cover all areas.

The FEA later refocused its efforts upstream on the wholesaler, refiner, and producer levels. Special projects were created in areas where violations were thought to be more severe, such as wholesale sales of propane. Additional special projects are the Refinery Audit and Review Program, the Utilities Investigation, and the producer level audits.[95]

As of April 1975, the FEA had referred 114 cases for civil penalties and 12 cases for criminal prosecution to the Justice Department. Direct refunds or rollbacks had totalled $161 million; penalties, $898,000, and reductions in "banks," $418 million.[96]

Most recently, the enforcement effort has been criticized on three grounds: (a) the lack of guidance and coordination among regions, which has resulted in a wide difference in violations discovered in each region; (b) the assignment of personnel so that one or two auditors are responsible for the entire refinery operations of a major integrated company; and (c) a greater concentration of investigated violations among small independent refineries than majors.

Some critics believe the FEA has been more willing to investigate and pursue violations by small and independent refiners. Given the positive views of many FEA officials regarding the value of independent companies, the concentration of enforcement effort was probably not the result of any conscious discrimination. The FEA has felt that less complex operations were easier to audit, and hence has focused on them for some time. Moreover, some OEA officials suggest that the relatively large legal staffs of big companies have enabled such companies to do legally what smaller ones often could not do. Given the complexity of the FEA's regulations, this last suggestion should not be discounted entirely.

FEA compliance officials disagree with these criticisms, but high level officials acknowledge that more work is necessary to improve enforcement.[97] Probably no allocation program is feasible without substantial and widespread oil industry cooperation. Certainly the government lacks the expertise and management personnel to undertake detailed supervision. It must rely heavily on industry compliance with whatever directions are given. During the Arab embargo, many companies cooperated with considerable patriotism. They are likely to do so in future crises. Apart from the emergency situation, sufficient cooperation seems to require a credible threat of executive agency enforcement.

In enacting the Energy Policy Act, Congress also thrust itself powerfully, albeit indirectly, into the enforcement arena. Section 501 has endowed the General Accounting Office with sweeping powers to conduct "verification examinations" upon request of a congressional committee having legislative or oversight responsibilities with respect to energy matters.[98] The authorized targets of a GAO verification examination include: (a) any person required to submit energy information to the FEA, Interior Department of FPC; (b) any person engaged in the energy industry who has furnished (directly or indirectly, voluntarily or pursuant to a requirement) energy information to any federal agency, if the information is relied upon by the agency concerned; and (c) any vertically integrated oil company with respect to its financial information. In the conduct of a verification examination, the GAO may issue subpoenas, require answers to written interrogatories, enter business premises, inspect and sample stocks of energy resources, examine relevant documents, and have access to any energy information in the possession of any federal agency. The result of an examination is a report on the "accuracy, reliability, and adequacy" of the information subject to verification.

It is difficult to imagine how, in aid of its own oversight and legislative responsibilities, the Congress could have armed the GAO with broader investigatory powers regarding the energy industry. The conferees on the Energy Policy Act recognized that meeting its duties under the Act could potentially place a very large burden on the GAO, and cautioned in the Conference Report that GAO's responsibilities under the Energy Policy Act should be reasonably balanced against its other statutory duties.[99]

The congressional threat or use of verification examinations may have a salutary effect in upgrading the veracity of energy information, thus improving industry discipline and government regulation, or it may have a chilling effect upon voluntary cooperation by the energy industry with government regulators and policy makers. In any event, any person engaged in the petroleum industry should henceforth be vitally concerned about the character and quality of every bit of information he divulges to the government or the general public, as well as about the nature of the information he relies on himself in planning and conducting operations.

Review and Appeal of FEA Decisions

No agency can reasonably expect to make the correct decision in every adjudication after only one level of decision. Congress accepted this view of the administrative process, and in the FEAA made provision for administrative appeals, including modifications and rescissions, and judicial review.[100] Stays are self-imposed by the agency, rather than required by statute.

Stays. A stay of administrative action will only be considered incident to an appeal from an FEA order, an exception, or pending judicial review.[101] Criteria considered in ruling on a petition for a stay are: (a) whether irreparable injury will occur if the stay is denied; (b) the relative hardships of the petitioner and the other affected parties; (c) public policy; and (d) the impossibility of fulfilling the original order.[102] The FEA may stay an order on its own initiative, but its decision on a request for a stay is not administratively reviewable.[103]

Because of the far-reaching effects of FEA decisions, a procedure for delaying implementation of orders is essential. Without such a procedure, orders would be able to effect major changes in the industry which subsequent reversal of the orders could not undo. This is not to suggest that stays should frequently be granted. Nevertheless, they are necessary for administrative flexibility, especially in view of the number of FEA orders reversed on administrative appeal.

Administrative appeals. Appeal from agency orders or rulings is generally required by both the FEAA and FEA regulation in order to exhaust administrative remedies before obtaining judicial review.[104] A petition for appeal must state the grounds for the relief sought and notify the FEA as to whether the questions raised by the appeal are being considered by any other agency or court.[105] Appeal of a Remedial Order must be filed within 10 days of service of the order on the appellant. The agency will not consider issues raised at a prior hearing whose decision the Remedial Order is meant to enforce.[106] The simple promulgation of regulations, without any agency action taken thereon, is not subject to agency appeal.[107]

The Office of Exceptions and Appeals (OEA), within the FEA national office, is responsible for all applications for exception, modification, or rescission, and appeals of all orders and interpretations issued by the FEA national office.[108] Regional office orders may generally be appealed to the regional OEA.[109]

Internally within OEA, an appeal petition that is received is assigned to an assistant director and an analyst, as is an exception request. If the initial decision was made in the OEA, the appeal is never assigned to the same persons who handled the case previously. Appeals, like all adjudications by the FEA, are exempt from the adjudicatory requirements of the APA. Consequently, the final decision can be made by the same committee that handles all requests. Conferences may be granted if OEA believes they would be helpful. Officials in OEA believe that, given the time delays involved, hearings contribute so slightly to improving decisions that they should be used only rarely.

The Office of Private Grievances and Redress (OPGR) is required by the FEAA to provide "special redress, relief, or other extraordinary assistance, apart from, or in addition to" that specifically required of the FEA (e.g., exceptions).[110] The OPGR handles such problems as: (a) complaints that the FEA or a state Energy Office is not complying with the proper statutory or regulatory requirements; (b) appeals of state Energy office orders; (c) exemptions; and (d) special questions arising under the EPAA regulations.[111] The OPGR may grant special relief from the application of regulations which "will frustrate the achievement of the policies and objectives set forth in [the EPAA and the FEAA]."[112]

Petitions to the OPGR for special redress are not intended as an alternative course of action subsequent to an initial appeal to OEA. Special redress relief is also to be distinguished from the exemption procedure, although both are handled by the OPGR and involve only a small number of petitions. Special redress petitions are designed as a catch-all appeal for avoiding onerous burdens; exemptions, which have a general purpose, are oriented toward freeing the petitioner from a particular regulatory program. Decisions of the OPGR may be appealed directly to the courts.[113]

A modification or rescission of any order or interpretation may be sought from the original issuing office. These options *are* "post-appellate" in nature; that is, the one seeking modification must have already received an appeal order or exhausted the time normally allowed for the appeals process.[114] The petitioner must show a significant change of circumstances or newly discovered facts or legal authority, and the burden is on the petitioner to justify the lack of submission at the original proceeding. There is no administrative appeal of a denial of a request for modification or rescission. If no action is taken within 90 days of filing, a petitioner may seek judicial review.[115] Again, there are relatively few petitions for modification or rescission.

Administratively, OPGR has three separate units: the Office of Special Redress Relief (directly controlled by the director of OPGR), the OEA, and the Oil Import Appeals Board. The latter two are administratively controlled by the director of OPGR, and to December 1975, the same person heads OPGR and OEA.

By way of illustration, in the period from October 1 to December 31, 1974, OEA resolved 193 cases by full Decisions and Orders, and dismissed another 146. The Oil Import Appeals Board decided 22 cases concerning whether to grant license fee-exempt import authority for established amounts of crude and unfinished oils. The Office of Special Redress Relief did not decide any cases during that period.[116]

As with most FEA adjudications, the decisons are published in the Commerce Clearing House Energy Management Reporter. The main purpose of publication is to provide some course of precedent. The precedential value of these decisions has been seriously challenged by some officials outside the FEA.

One indication of the value these decisions hold as precedent may be the number of initial FEA decisions reversed on appeal. Between one-fourth and one-third of all OEA appeals decisions are reversals of initial FEA orders. Some OEA officials suggest that this is the result of the fact that parties often do not know what the FEA considers valuable data and important arguments when they draft petitions and provide information. After an initial rejection and a decision which explains what is important to the FEA and what is irrelevant, the arguments for relief in an administrative appeal can be more persuasively presented. Correspondingly, the large number of reversals also mean that the provisions for exhaustion of administrative remedies actually are beneficial; petitioners *are* satisfied without judicial review.

If our analysis is correct, the FEA's published decisions have little value as precedent. Alternatively, it is possible that petitioners do not use the precedent wisely or that the number of reversals would be even higher without the precedent.

Judicial Review of FEA actions. Both the Economic Stabilization Act and the EPAA were designed in response to short-term emergencies. Congress incorporated into the EPAA from the Economic Stabilization Act provisions which allow relatively rapid judicial review of actions taken by the FEA under the EPAA. The Stabilization Act provisions are still applicable, even though the Act itself has expired.[117]

Local United States district courts have original jurisdiction over all cases and controversies arising under EPAA regulations and orders. The district courts have the authority to declare a regulation arbitrary and capricious or otherwise unlawful, to declare an order invalid because it exceeds FEA authority or is not supported by substantial evidence, and to issue preliminary injunctions. However, the district courts may enjoin the enforcement of any regulation or order only as it applies to persons who are parties to the litigation before it. Moreover, the district courts lack jurisdiction to decide any constitutional question arising under the EPAA.[118]

Appellate jurisdiction of cases arising under the EPAA is vested exclusively in the Temporary Emergency Court of Appeals (TECA).[119] In addition to hearing appeals, TECA has jurisdiction to decide constitutional questions certified to it by the district courts. It may also permanently enjoin the enforcement of any regulation or order issued under the EPAA as to those not parties to the litigation. Only "substantial" constitutional questions, those not plainly without merit or foreclosed by Supreme Court decisions, can and must be certified to TECA. If it chooses, TECA may decide any pendent nonconstitutional questions.[120] TECA decisions may be taken to the U.S. Supreme Court, although so far, the Supreme Court has consistently denied certiorari in such cases.

Because of a peculiarity in the wording of the judicial review sections of the EPAA, an interlocutory order, such as a preliminary injunction, issued by the district court can be appealed to TECA only if the district court certifies it and if TECA also decides to permit the appeal.[121] There is no appeal of right from an interlocutory order. Although this may appear to be a mere technicality, the FEA expressed its misgivings about the peculiar restriction on appeals in a case it recently won, *Exxon Corp. v. FEA, Marathon Oil Co. v. FEA.*[122]

The FEA is concerned that it may be enjoined preliminarily in a future case, and then have to wait a year before being able to apply its regulations to the plaintiff. In the past, a district court often granted *or* denied a request for a preliminary injunction and immediately an appeal was taken to TECA. Because a full decision was not reached in the district court, a timely decision was assured on the validity of the FEA regulations at issue. The statutory omission of appeals as of right from certain interlocutory orders endangers the continuation of that method. So long as a district court is willing to certify the issue to TECA, nothing is changed. However, the case above itself shows that courts do not always certify.

Obtaining a preliminary injunction against the FEA requires a showing of irreparable injury if the injunction were denied, likelihood of success on the merits of the case, that the public interest favors granting an injunction, and that the harm to the petitioner outweighs the harm to third parties caused by the injunction.[123] Efforts to enjoin the enforcement of FEA regulations have generally been unsuccessful, although a court will be more likely to enjoin the FEA when, in the judge's view, a supply "emergency" or shortage does not exist.

For reasons not made clear in the legislative history, the FEAA prescribes procedures for judicial review of actions taken under it which are different from those for review of actions taken under the EPAA, as previously discussed.[124] Since the petroleum allocation regulations are promulgated under EPAA, the district court to TECA route is the one most often followed. Once orders made pursuant to ESECA are made final, however, the judicial review provisions of FEAA will apply to them.

FEAA provides for judicial review of rulemaking and controversies as follows:[125]

> Judicial review of administrative rulemaking of general and national applicability done under this Act, *except that done pursuant to the Emergency Petroleum Allocation Act of 1973,* may be obtained only by filing a a petition for review in the United States Court of Appeals for the District of Columbia within thirty days from the date of promulgation of any such rule, regulation, or order, and judicial review of administrative rulemaking of general, but less than national, applicability done under this Act, *except that done pursuant to the Emergency Petroleum Act of 1973,* may be obtained only by filing a petition for review in the United States Court of Appeals for the appropriate circuit within thirty days from the date of promulgation of any such rule, regulation, or order, the appropriate circuit being defined as the circuit which contains the area or the greater part of the area within which the rule, regulations, or order is to have effect.

Thus, the district courts are by-passed in reviewing FEA actions which are not based upon the EPAA.

Opinions differ on which procedure for judicial review is superior. The average time for disposition of a case in a circuit court of appeals is about eight months, TECA requires only 100 days.[126] The FEA favors the EPAA provisions for several reasons.

1. Use of the district courts allows compilation of a factual record, which most often gives substantive support to an FEA rule.

2. TECA is faster and has developed some degree of expertise in petroleum regulation.

3. A single court of appeals precludes forum shopping and secures a single controlling precedent below the Supreme Court level.

4. Use of district courts and the flexibility of TECA has meant that the courts are made more convenient to plaintiffs than the D.C. Circuit could be.[127]

Some critics support the use of TECA, but claim that the district courts serve no purpose which is not better filled by TECA: the assumption is that the district courts are unnecessary for compiling a formal record.[128] The use of the review-or-preliminary-injunction technique suggests that TECA would not have great difficulty in obtaining the facts it needs. Other critics have noted a theoretical difficulty, since the Economic Stabilization Act provides for "substantial evidence" review, which typically requires evaluation of a formal record compiled in an agency hearing.[129] FEA attorneys suggest that use of district courts and thorough briefs avoids the problem.

Since the FEA is an Executive Branch agency, it must rely upon Justice Department attorneys for all litigation. Practically, this means that Justice attorneys must approve legal briefs submitted by the FEA and deliver all oral arguments. The doubling up on staff may very well be wasteful. Furthermore, those with a thorough understanding of the oil industry and FEA regulations should be in positions where they can control litigation. The existing arrangement has been blamed for the initial FEA loss before TECA in *Consumers Union v. Sawhill*,[130] concerning two-tier pricing, and other poorly written opinions which left the FEA with little judicial guidance.

CONGRESSIONAL REVIEW

The Energy Policy Act requires the Executive Branch, principally the FEA, to promulgate and administer a variety of important new regulations. The Act also requires that the main energy regulations promulgated be submitted to the Congress for review and acquiescence prior to their becoming effective. Henceforth, the Congress may become deeply and almost continuously immersed in the details of massive energy regulation, including petroleum allocation and pricing.

The regulatory actions under the EPAA which require prior congressional review include the more important amendments to the oil allocation and pricing regulation under section 4(a), such as: an amendment providing a production incentive adjustment or a combined production incentive and inflation adjustment in excess of the statutory limits; an amendment exempting North Slope

Alaskan oil from computation of the composite ceiling price; an amendment exercising the authority granted in section 12(a) to exempt a class of persons or class of transactions from allocation or pricing regulation; an amendment restricting the statutory exemption of small refiners from requirements to make payments under the entitlements program; and an amendment exercising the authority granted in section 13(a) to make the United States government an importer of crude oil and petroleum products for resale.

Section 551 of the Energy Policy Act sets forth the procedure to be followed by the Congress in circumstances where prior review is required for one of the proposed energy actions enumerated above.[131] Basically, the proposed regulation may become effective after 15 calendar days of continuous session of Congress have elapsed following transmittal, unless within that period either House passes a resolution of disapproval. In order to assure timely review, section 551 requires immediate referral of the proposed executive action to a committee, consideration of a motion to discharge if the committee fails to report the matter within five days, and a debate in each House limited to 10 hours.

It is noteworthy that the only action the Congress can take under this review procedure is to approve or disapprove in its entirety the action proposed by the executive. Nevertheless, the necessity for congressional review and the risk of disapproval will place the appropriate congressional committees and leaders in a strong position to bargain with the Executive Branch over the details of any major regulatory change that is contemplated.

Energy conservation and motor fuel rationing contingency plans, which are developed pursuant to section 201 of the Energy Policy Act, follow a congressional review procedure that differs from the procedure applicable to amendments to EPAA allocation and pricing regulations in two major respects: first, the period within which Congress must act is lengthened to 60 days; and, second, each House must affirmatively approve the proposed plan within the prescribed time.[132]

Furthermore, in the case of motor fuel rationing, a previously approved plan may not be actually put into effect unless the President finds that a severe energy supply interruption exists and he transmits a request to the Congress to implement the rationing plan. The rationing plan is then subject to congressional review and acquiescence in accordance with section 551. In other words, in the case of motor fuel rationing, the contingency plan must first be affirmatively approved by the Congress, and use of an approved plan must thereafter be reviewed and not disapproved by the Congress. Quite obviously, the development and implementation of a gasoline rationing plan is a matter of highest political importance in an automobile dependent society.

CONCLUSIONS

The FEA's petroleum allocation program was implemented initially under the stress of an actual oil supply emergency, the 1973-74 Arab oil embargo. The program was developed with certain policy preconceptions and a largely abstract, generalized picture of the petroleum industry uppermost in the minds of the administrators.

The design of a workable allocation program required, first, detailed knowledge of the industry's structure and operations and, second, an understanding of the industry's reaction to the kind of massive government regulation that allocation entails. In both respects, the FEA was deficient, not only because it was a new agency, but also because, through the FEA, the government was attempting to regulate intensively and intrusively a complicated, dynamic and hitherto unregulated private industry.

In light of FEA's experience so far, an improved allocation program for use in a possible future oil supply emergency can be developed on a contingency basis and publicly discussed in advance of implementation. In any event, an allocation program must continue as long as price controls are maintained on crude oil and/or petroleum products. The Energy Policy Act and the EPAA, as amended, now provide a comprehensive, although complex, legal framework for the administration of petroleum prices and of any future petroleum shortage due to the possible interruption of oil supplies from foreign sources.

Both rapid action and flexibility, are required to administer a shortage in an emergency, such as an Arab oil embargo. However, public and industry scrutiny of FEA policy formation and participation in agency rulemaking are necessary in order to develop fair allocation programs in advance of a supply emergency. While formal agency rulemaking, including a hearing on the record, would be too cumbersome for this purpose, informal rulemaking with nothing more than notice and comment would be insufficient to establish widespread confidence in government plans. The hybrid rulemaking procedures contained in the FEAA and the Energy Policy Act might be used in the future to increase the government's accountability to the public and industry.

FEA adjudicatory procedures are necessary to fine-tune the rules and to apply them to specific companies and cases. The petroleum industry is too complex for allocation or price regulation to work without adjustment mechanisms, and individual enforcement orders require adjudication.

A two-tier adjudicatory process might be developed. The FEA would retain summary practices for use in actual oil supply emergencies. However, the agency would use conferences and, to the extent practicable, provide adjudicatory hearings for specific cases during non-emergency situations.

Finally, an effective petroleum allocation program requires a high degree of compliance. This in turn necessitates effective enforcement which can only be brought about by sufficient legal authority, agency staff and information. FEA enforcement has been deficient in the past, especially in regard to adequate staff and information. As a result, smaller companies who are easier targets have borne the brunt of FEA enforcement activity.

Existing problems in this area may be difficult to correct on a contingency basis when adequate petroleum supplies are available. Nevertheless, FEA enforcement efforts can and should be improved, in view of the possibilities for financial gain through abuse of the allocation and pricing regulations during a prolonged period of price controls, as well as the need to assure compliance during a supply emergency. Here again, the Congress has, in the Energy Policy Act, created a potentially large supporting role for itself.

NOTES TO CHAPTER SEVEN

1. *Petroleum Allocation and Price Regulations* 39 Fed. Reg. 1425 (1974).

2. Much of the information for this chapter was obtained through interviews. A brief history of some of the events leading up to the EPAA is contained in the Statement of Frank G. Zarb, Administrator of the FEA, Before the Senate Committee on Interior and Insular Affairs, 94th Cong., 1st Sess. at 8–14 (May 19, 1975).

3. Economic Stabilization Act of 1970, Pub. L. No. 91–379, 84 Stat. 799, set out as a note under 12 U.S.C. §1904 (Supp. III, 1973).

4. Apparently one major conflict was between Roy Ash, Chief of OMB, and William Simon. OMB had some hard data on the industry and a small expert staff, but Simon and Ash would often oppose each other's suggestions, regardless of content.

5. Specifically, 15 U.S.C. §753(a) (Supp. III 1973).

6. *See* Memorandum from Gorman Smith to John Hill, March 4, 1975, at 2–3.

7. *See* Chapter Six *supra. See also* Zarb, *supra* note 2, at 19–20; Federal Policy Agencies, 1 *CCH Energy Management* ¶¶2501–2601, at 2503–2601.

8. Much of this organizational breakdown is taken from FEA *Mandatory Petroleum Allocation Program: A Summary* 9–14 (1975) [hereinafter cited as *Summary*].

9. For a discussion of administrative procedures of the CLC, see Note, *Phase IV: The Cost of Living Council Reconsidered,* 62 *Geo. L.J.* 1663 (1974).

10. For a more extensive discussion of the APA, see K. Davis, *Administrative Law Text* (1972).

11. 5 U.S.C. §551 (1970).

12. 5 U.S.C. §553 (1970).

13. 5 U.S.C. §706 (1970).

14. 5 U.S.C. §553(b)(B) (1970).

15. 5 U.S.C. §553(c) (1970).

16. 5 U.S.C. §§556, 557 (1970).

17. 5 U.S.C. § 554 (1970).

18. Section 207 of the Economic Stabilization Act exempts those actions taken under the EPAA. Actions taken under ESECA and FEAA are subject to stricter requirements. 15 U.S.C.A. §766(i)(1)(A) (Supp. 1975). Only informal rulemaking procedures are required, in a modified form. Any order having the effect of a rule as defined by the APA is subject to the APA requirements. However, subsequent subsections make it clear that hearings are not required for most adjudications.

19. 15 U.S.C.A. §766(i)(1)(D) (Supp. 1975). The term "adjustments" is not used in the same sense here as it is in the FEA regulations.

20. Section 207 of the Economic Stabilization Act.

21. 15 U.S.C. §755(c)(3) (Supp. III, 1973).

22. *See* Reeves v. Simon, 507 F.2d 455 (T.E.C.A. 1974), *cert. denied,* __ U.S. __, 95 S. Ct. 1426 (1975).

23. 502 F.2d 1154 (T.E.C.A. 1974).

24. 15 U.S.C. §754(a)(1) (Supp. III, 1973).

25. The FEA has compiled tables which list all agency rulemakings and the administrative procedures afforded at each. Much of this information is taken from those tables.

26. 15 U.S.C.A. §766(i)(1)(B) (Supp. 1975).

27. *See* Note, *Phase IV: The Cost of Living Council Reconsidered,* 62 Geo. *L.J.* 1663 (1974).

28. 514 F.2d 1064 (T.E.C.A. 1975).

29. 504 F.2d 430 (T.E.C.A. 1974).

30. 393 F. Supp. 639 (D.D.C. 1975).

31. 5 U.S.C. §553(e) (1970); 10 C.F.R. §205.161(b) (1975).

32. Pub. L. No. 94–163 §454 (1975).

33. FEA Administrative Procedures and Sanctions are set at 10 C.F.R. §§205.1–205.237 (1975).

34. 10 C.F.R. §§205.53(a)–(b), –.104(a), –.133(a), –234(a)–(b) (1975).

35. 10 C.F.R. §§205.24, –.34, –.54, –.74, –.83, –.94, –.124, –.134, –.183, –.235 (1975).

36. 10 C.F.R. §§205.25(a), –.35(a), –.55(a), –.84(a), –.106(a), –.125(a), –.135(a) (1975).

37. 10 C.F.R. §§205.27, –.28, –.37 –.38, –.57, –.58, –.77, –.78, –.86, –.96, –.97, –.109, –.137 (1975).

38. 10 C.F.R. §205.9(d) (1975).

39. 10 C.F.R. §205.9(f) (1975).

40. 10 C.F.R. §205.3 (1975).

41. 10 C.F.R. §§ 205.26, –.36, –.56, –.76, –.95, –.107, –.126, –.136, –.237 (1975).

42. 10 C.F.R. §205.171 (1975).

43. 10 C.F.R. §205.172 (1975).

44. 10 C.F.R. §205.173 (1975).

45. 15 U.S.C.A. §766(i)(1)(C) (Supp. 1975).

46. 10 C.F.R. §§205.23, –.33, –.53(c), –.104(c), –.123, –.173, –.234(c) (1975).

47. 10 C.F.R. §§205.22, 211.13(b)–(d) (1975).

48. *Summary, supra* note 8, at 3.

49. 10 C.F.R. §§205.22, 205.25(6), 211.12(h)(4) (1975). *See also,* Pacific Gas and Electric Co., 3 *CCH Energy Management* ¶20,242 (FEA, 1974).

50. 10 C.F.R. §205.29 (1975). The circumstances are basically when notice under 10 C.F.R. §205.23 (1975) is not feasible.

51. 10 C.F.R. §205.28 (1975). Appeals are discussed in 10 C.F.R. §§205.100–.109 (Subpart H) (1975).

52. 10 C.F.R. §205.2 (1975).

53. 10 C.F.R. §205.39 (1975). The FEA may make such assignments under 10 C.F.R. §211.12(h) (1975); and states pursuant to 10 C.F.R. §211.17 (1975).

54. 10 C.F.R. §205.34 (1975).

55. 10 C.F.R. §205.30 (1975).

56. 10 C.F.R. §205.55 (1975). *See* Gulf Oil Corp., 3 *CCH Energy Management* ¶20,197 (FEA, 1974); Gulf Energy and Development Corp., 3 *CCH Energy Management* ¶20,232 (FEA, 1975).

57. 10 C.F.R. §§205.50, -.55(b)(2) (1975); Exxon Co., 3 *CCH Energy Management* ¶20,123 (FEA, 1974).

58. Getty Oil (Eastern Operations) Inc., 3 *CCH Energy Management* ¶20,140, at 20,210 (FEA, 1974); Texaco, Inc., 3 *CCH Energy Management* ¶20,231, at 20,475 (FEA, 1975).

59. Western Propane, Inc., 3 *CCH Energy Management* ¶20,205, at 20,395–96 (FEA, 1974).

60. Cities Service Oil Co., 3 *CCH Energy Management* ¶20,143 (FEA, 1974); Texaco, Inc. (Giant Industries, Inc.), 3 *CCH Energy Management* ¶20,184 (FEA, 1974).

61. 10 C.F.R. §205.52 (1975).

62. 10 C.F.R. §205.2, -.70 to -.78 (1975).

63. 10 C.F.R. §205.71 (1975). Specifically, 10 C.F.R. §205.160-.162 (1975) does not apply.

64. 10 C.F.R. §205.75(b)(2) (1975).

65. 15 U.S.C.A. §780 (Supp. 1975); 10 C.F.R. §205.73 (1975).

66. 10 C.F.R. §205.74 (1975).

67. Small Business Administration, 3 *CCH Energy Management* ¶21,102 (FEA, 1974).

68. Attorney General of Alaska, 3 *CCH Energy Management* ¶21,103 (FEA, 1974).

69. 10 C.F.R. §205.78 (1975).

70. Pub. L. No. 94–163 §455 (1975). The Energy Policy Act also deleted §4(g) of the EPAA, 15 U.S.C. §753(g) (Supp. III, 1973), which provided that after making certain findings, the President could deregulate crude oil and refined products, but only if neither House of Congress disapproved. With the EPAA, this procedure produced only a deadlock between Congress and the President and was not a satisfactory method of deregulation.

71. The Energy Policy Act amendments to the EPAA provide special treatment for asphalt. As originally enacted, the EPAA did not cover asphalt. As amended by Pub. L. No. 94–163 §460 (1976), section 17, which is added to the EPAA, provides discretionary authority for allocation and price regulation of asphalt.

72. 10 C.F.R. §205.80 (1975).

73. 10 C.F.R. §205.84(a)(2) (1975).

74. 10 C.F.R. §205.85(c)–(d) (1975); *see also* Greenbelt Consumer Services Inc., 3 *CCH Energy Management* ¶20,211 (FEA, 1974).

75. 10 C.F.R. ¶205.86 (1975).

76. 10 C.F.R. §§205.150–.151 (1975).

77. 10 C.F.R. §§205.152(b), –.154 (1975). It should be noted however that exceptions to Rulings may be granted. As of June 3, 1975, 35 Rulings had been issued. Statement of Robert E. Montgomery, Jr., General Counsel to the FEA, Before the Subcommittee on Separation of Powers of the Senate Committee on the Judiciary, 94th Cong., 1st Sess. at 24 (June 3, 1975) [hereinafter cited as Montgomery].

78. Montgomery, *supra* note 77, at 17–18.

79. GAO, *Problems in the Federal Energy Administration's Compliance and Enforcement Effort* at 4–5 (1974) [hereinafter cited as *GAO Report*].

80. 15 U.S.C.A. §772(c) (Supp. 1975). The ESECA provision is 15 U.S.C.A. §796 (Supp. 1975).

81. 15 U.S.C.A. §772(d) (Supp. 1975).

82. *GAO Report, supra* note 79.

83. 10 C.F.R. §§ 205.13, –.180, –.183 (1975).

84. 10 C.F.R. §205.185 (1975).

85. See the language of 15 U.S.C.A. §766(i)(2)(B) (Supp. 1975). "[A]ll other controversies" is not defined, and some could argue that the section grants jurisdiction for an implied cause of action based upon the regulations.

86. 10 C.F.R. §§205.190(b), –.191(a) (1975).

87. 10 C.F.R. §§205.191(c)–(d) (1975). *See* Air Transport Association, 3 *CCH Energy Management* ¶20,218 (FEA, 1975).

88. 10 C.F.R. §205.195(a) (1975).

89. 10 C.F.R. §§205.192(a)–(c) (1975).

90. 10 C.F.R. §205.193 (1975).

91. 10 C.F.R. §§205.192(c), –.203 (1975).

92. Pub. L. No. 94–163 §452 (1975).

93. 10 C.F.R. §§205.194, –.200(a), –.202(a) (1975).

94. *See* FEA, *Fact Sheet on FEA Compliance Activities* at 1 (1975). FEA policy with respect to pricing violations is to seek price rollbacks or refunds where it can be shown that the violations resulted in prices higher than the legal ceiling. To the extent that a company had sufficient "banks" at the time of violation to have passed the cost through anyway, the FEA *cannot* show the occurrence of overpricing. In those cases, the "banks" are simply adjusted downward. Where possible, the FEA prefers to require refunds, rather than rollbacks. Refunds are possible only where the overcharged customers are identifiable, such as with heating oils. For products like motor gasoline, rollbacks are ordered until the overcharge amount is returned to customers. When a rollback is ordered, the FEA freezes the company's "bank" and requires a reduction in current actual prices, rather than the maximum lawful prices.

95. *Id.* at 2–3.

96. *Id.* at 1–3.

97. Memorandum from Gorman Smith to John Hill, March 4, 1975.

98. Pub. L. No. 94–163 §§501, 502 (1975).

99. *S. Conf. Rep. No.* 94–516, 94th Cong., 1st Sess. at 211 (1975).

100. 15 U.S.C.A. 766(i)(1)(D) (Supp. 1975).

101. 10 C.F.R. §205.120 (1975).

102. 10 C.F.R. §205.125.

103. 10 C.F.R. §§205.126(d)–(e) (1975); *e.g.,* Pakistan International Air-

lines, 3 *CCH Energy Management* ¶21,672 (FEA, 1975); Mobil Oil Corp., 3 *CCH Energy Management* ¶21,667 (FEA, 1974).

104. 15 U.S.C.A. §766(i)(1)(D) (Supp. 1975); 10 C.F.R. §205.100 (1975). Appeals may be taken from orders regarding adjustments, assignments, exceptions, exemptions, interpretations, remedial orders, and other proceedings. Provisions for appeals of state office orders are in 10 C.F.R. §205.230 (1975), which deals with the Office of Private Grievances and Redress.

105. 10 C.F.R. §205.105 (1975).

106. 10 C.F.R. §§205.108(a)–(b) (1975).

107. Associated Gas Distributors, 3 *CCH Energy Management* ¶20,214 (FEA, 1974).

108. 10 C.F.R. §205.52, -.103, -.132 (1975).

109. 10 C.F.R. §205.103(b) (1975).

110. 15 U.S.C.A. §§780(a)–(b) (Supp. 1975).

111. 10 C.F.R. §§205.230(b), -.231 (1975).

112. *E.g.,* Greater Richmond (Va.) Transit Co., 3 *CCH Energy Management* ¶21,302, at 21,302 (FEA, 1974), which cited §4(b)(1)(A) of the EPAA and several sections of the FEAA supporting mass transit systems.

113. 10 C.F.R. §205.237(b) (1975).

114. 10 C.F.R. §§205.130, -.132, -.135 (1975).

115. 10 C.F.R. §205.137 (1975).

116. *FEA Quarterly Report on Private Grievances and Redress, October 1, 1974 to December 31, 1974* (1975). Of those petitions OEA dismissed, primary reasons for dismissal included: applicant stated that relief was no longer necessary (78), applicant failed to respond to requests for more information (42), applicant failed to correct filing deficiencies (16), and applicant filed with the national OEA when it should have gone to a regional office (11). Some cases were dismissed for multiple reasons.

117. 15 U.S.C. §754(a)(1) (Supp. III, 1975).

118. Section 211 of the Economic Stabilization Act; Montgomery, *supra* note 74, at 28–29.

119. TECA was newly created for the Economic Stabilization Program and was continued under the EPAA. TECA is comprised of judges designated by the Chief Justice of the United States, from judges sitting on the United States district courts, and United States circuit courts of appeals.

120. Section 211 of the Economic Stabilization Act; Montgomery, *supra* note 77, at 28–30.

121. The peculiarity consists of incorporating into EPAA section 1292(b) of title 28, U.S.C., but not section 1292(a). Section 1292(a) provides a right of appeal from certain interlocutory orders, including injunctions, whereas section 1292(b) requires certification from the district court and permission from the court of appeals. If the omission was intentional, Congress failed to show that in the legislative history, and only recently has the issue arisen. Since then, the General Counsel of the FEA has urged a statutory revision to incorporate section 1292(a).

122. 516 F.2d 1397 (T.E.C.A. 1975).

123. Union Oil Co. v. FEA, No. CV74-1943 (C.D. Cal., July 25, 1975), *printed at 3 CCH Energy Management* ¶26,007.

124. 15 U.S.C.A. §766(i)(2)(A) (Supp. 1975).

125. 15 U.S.C.A. §766(i)(2)(A) (Supp. 1975) (emphasis added).

126. (remarks of Senator Mathias). 121 *Cong. Rec.* 3938 (daily edition March 13, 1975).

127. Montgomery, *supra* note 77, at 30–32.

128. Statement of Warren Belmar, on behalf of the American Bar Association, Before the Subcommittee on Separation of Powers of the Senate Committee on the Judiciary, 94th Cong., 1st Sess. (June 3, 1975).

129. *Id.*

130. 512 F.2d 1112 (T.E.C.A.), *reversed en banc,* __ F.2d __ (T.E.C.A. 1975).

131. Pub. L. No. 94–163 §551 (1975).

132. Pub. L. No. 94–163 §552 (1975).

✳ *Chapter Eight*

Administration of Energy Shortages: Generic Issues and Options

Having analyzed the federal government's recent experience in administering natural gas and petroleum shortages, we turn to the generic issues and options raised. How may government action dealing with an energy shortage be initiated and terminated? What are the policy and procedural options available to administer government controls over available supplies? And, finally, what are the alternatives for government organization? These questions are, of course, deeply interwoven, although they must be separated for purposes of discussion.

We consider issues and options primarily in relation to the kind of energy shortages that are reasonable to anticipate in the late 1970s. During the period, it seems prudent for the U.S. government to plan for two major kinds of energy shortages: increased natural gas shortages and increased vulnerability to an interruption of oil imports. These two weaknesses in the U.S. energy posture are likely to grow concurrently during the late 1970s, despite a large number of steps the government and industry may take to increase and conserve available energy supplies in the long run. It also seems reasonable to plan for cold winters and slow-to-moderate economic recovery, both of which would increase pressures on available supplies. The possibility of an Arab oil embargo during a cold winter, in conjunction with economic expansion, is a risk that cannot safely be ignored. The simultaneous occurrence of these contingencies would cause a major breakdown in the U.S. energy supply system. Without adequate preparations in advance, this might result in disastrous consequences for the national economy.

The ensuing discussion is organized, to a large extent, around the three general criteria outlined in Chapter One—fairness, practicality, and consistency with other public policies. The analysis is unavoidably incomplete in some areas and merely a sketch in many others. In particular, the criterion of consistency or minimum interference with other important public policies is extremely difficult to apply, and we have limited ourselves to stating what appear to be the most obvious problems of conflict. Nevertheless, organizing the discussion this way serves to shed light on the enormous difficulties inherent in any government attempt to administer energy shortages "fairly."

This chapter does not attempt to provide a "rational" basis for making choices between alternatives. An adequate basis for decision-making of this type would require large-scale, empirical studies. Although the results of such studies would tend to be inconclusive, they would be useful in narrowing the uncertainties and widening understanding of the possible consequences of various alternatives. Actual decisions will inevitably be made on the basis of argument that is informed by more or less fragmentary information.

Here we must recall that in administering an energy shortage, jobs, profits, lifestyles, and votes are at stake. The administrative process may be flooded with empirical data in support of every conceivable position and the debate preceding decison may be framed by careful argument connecting each bit of information to a lofty social, economic or philosophical principle. Yet the outcome is likely to be determined largely by the political weights of the competing interests at stake and by the relative effectiveness of each interest in bringing its weight to bear.

INITIATION AND TERMINATION

A government decision to intervene in the energy market in order to control the distribution of available supplies is a momentous step. If the decision is made too early, it may result in unnecessary disruption to the energy industry and inconvenience to millions of consumers. But if the decision is too late, the amount of the ensuing shortage will tend to be magnified and be much more difficult to manage.[1] Therefore, as an integral part of the machinery to administer an energy shortage, it is important to have some means to ensure that initiation of government control over distribution is well timed.

A mechanism to trigger government action may be designed to work quite automatically, or it may be simply a delegation of broad discretionary authority to the administrator. An automatic trigger would prescribe in advance the events that would cause an administrative program to be implemented. A stepped trigger, which would initiate different actions depending upon the severity of the shortage, is also possible. A discretionary trigger would give the President, or a particular agency, the authority to intitiate action on the basis of a judgment about the total situation. Depending on the character of the agency given discretion, and whether it is part of the Executive Branch or an independent agency, a wide variation in outcomes may be expected.

In any event, the decision to initiate direct government controls over the distribution of available energy supplies is highly political. The choice between an automatic and a discretionary triggering mechanism will depend partly on whether the designer of the trigger has confidence in the person whose finger will be on it. If, for example, in enacting standby authority to allocate petroleum products, the Congress has confidence that the President or the FEA will act wisely in a shortage, the decision as to when to initiate allocation may be left largely to the President's or the FEA's discretion. If, on the other hand, Congress fears either procrastination or premature action by the Executive Branch, then statutory authorization for allocation may include a quite precise definition of circumstances in which the allocation authority is to be used, or an opportunity for congressional review and disapproval as in the case of contingency plans under the Energy Policy Act. In any event, a discretionary trigger would, depending on the decison-maker, provide capability for either a quicker or slower response to a shortage than an automatic activating mechanism.

An automatic trigger may use "dead" or "live" indicators, or a combination of both. An illustration of a dead indicator is the amount by which supply has fallen or is projected to fall below demand. This type of indicator has been adopted in the International Energy Agreement as a means of activating the Agreement's emergency oil sharing scheme.[2] Live indicators reflect the effects of shortages, such as the amount of unemployment caused or the number of businesses closed.

The design of an automatic trigger would involve finding acceptable solutions to a number of difficult problems including inaccuracy of data, the time of delay in data collection and processing, and the overall costs.[3] To develop a comprehensive picture, an automatic trigger may have to consist of an index of a dozen or more variables.[4] However, the greater its complexity, the more difficult and costly the trigger would be to administer.

In actual operation, the distinctions between automatic and discretionary trigger mechanisms are likely to be blurred. In the exercise of a grant of broad discretion, an administrator may try to inform himself with the best available data. Alternatively, in using the simplest kind of automatic trigger, the administrator will be interpreting somewhat ambiguous data, and therefore he is likely to find considerable room for discretion. As a practical matter, it seems unlikely that any statute or regulation would include a trigger device that could not somehow be overridden by discretionary authority.

The necessity for a trigger in order to administer an energy shortage effectively depends partly on the abruptness of the anticipated occurrence. The natural gas shortage surfaced gradually in the early 1970s amid prolonged debate about whether the shortage was real or manufactured by the industry in order to raise wellhead prices. The FPC action was in response to reports from certain interstate pipelines of their inability to fulfill all their contract commitments. The Natural Gas Act itself contains no trigger.[5]

The petroleum shortage in 1973-74 occurred quite abruptly, though working inventories and crude oil already in transit provided a cushion against the effects of the Arab embargo. Congress itself triggered the mandatory allocation program by the enactment of the EPAA. However, in passing the EPAA, Congress effectively ordered the Executive Branch to implement allocation programs that were already largely developed and on the shelf. The decision to initiate government action was thus a joint affair.[6]

A major issue in choosing between an automatic and a discretionary trigger is whether advance notice is desirable. An automatic trigger in standby legislation for an energy supply emergency may communicate a clear signal to foreign governments that the U.S. government will not vacillate in a crisis. An automatic trigger will also give the energy industry and American consumers advance notice which would be lacking if the initiation of government action were discretionary.

Advance knowledge would seem advantageous since each person could follow the indicators and make his own preparations to avoid or minimize the adverse consequences of the government allocation or curtailment scheme. Moreover, voluntary conservation efforts might be encouraged if the public were generally aware of how close the situation was to one requiring mandatory control. However, advance knowledge coupled with an automatic trigger might also lead to last-minute hoarding by purchasers, refusals to sell by suppliers, or subversion of the pending government distribution plan by overconsumption in order to show a high base period volume.[7]

The preferred solution to the problem of initiating government controls over energy supplies may well be a trigger mechanism that contains both automatic and discretionary elements. The automatic element might be relatively simple, such as a specified percentage shortfall in projected supplies. A statute or regulation may specify objective circumstances in which government action is mandatory, unless the administrator makes a finding to the contrary.[8]

Finally, there is the problem of terminating government controls over the distribution of energy supplies. The issues that arise in the course of designing a trigger to decontrol will be quite similar to those involved in the design of a trigger to initiate controls.

It may be tempting to ignore the deactivation problem on the theory that once an acute scarcity no longer exists, controls will quickly disappear. However, just as the energy industry and consumers are required to make more or less costly changes in behavior when government controls are applied, so also will they incur costs in adjusting to the termination of controls. Moreover, certain firms are likely to have specially benefited by the control program. The independent oil companies were protected by the petroleum allocation program under the EPAA, and a high priority may guarantee 100 percent of current requirements to residential users of natural gas. Consequently, there is a risk that a government-administered energy distribution program will take on a life of its own as interests become vested on the basis of the regulatory framework imposed to deal with a shortage.[9]

The risk seems greater when the government intervenes to allocate supplies in a more or less competitive energy market, such as the petroleum market, than when the government undertakes to administer a shortage in an industry that is already heavily regulated, such as the natural gas industry. If their aggregate political weight is sufficient, the economic security of marginal firms in a competitive industry seems likely to be improved by government allocation regulation. As discussed in Chapter Six, the Energy Policy Act has amended the EPAA to provide a mechanism for conversion of mandatory controls to standby authority.[10]

ADMINISTRATIVE OPTIONS

The primary substantive options for the administration of an energy shortage include utilization of: (a) existing contractual arrangements, (b) pro rata reductions, (c) end-use priorities, and (d) negotiated settlements. It is unlikely that any single option would provide an acceptable administrative solution to an energy shortage. Instead, administering a shortage is likely to involve the use of a combination of some or all of the generic approaches enumerated above. It is also important to note that the appropriate approach is likely to vary with the level in the distribution system. For example, a pro rata approach may be applied to wholesale purchasers for resale while end-use priorities are applied to purchasers for consumption.

Contract

Government action to direct or control the distribution of energy supplies in response to a shortage is bound to disturb existing private contractual relationships and historical supplier-purchaser relationships. An agency decision to administer an energy shortage by contract may be, in effect, a decision to refrain from intervention and to let the burden of the shortage fall where it may. Alternatively, the responsible government agency may decide to use existing contractual relationships as one of the bases for an active administrative program.

In the case of natural gas, the industry developed historically on the basis of very long-term supply contracts between interstate pipelines and distribution companies. Transportation was the key. In addition to the opportunity to earn an appropriate rate of return on capital invested, contract certainly was necessary in order to attract the enormous amounts of private capital required to construct long-distance pipelines needed to transport gas from the prolific producing fields in the Southwest to the large markets located along the Atlantic and Pacific Coasts, and in the Middle West.

It is remarkable, given the importance of contract stability to the growth of the U.S. natural gas industry, that the FPC was so emphatic in its original rejection of existing contracts as a basis for curtailments in the face of the emerging shortage. The contract approach was deemed, in principle, unacceptable "simply because contracts do not necessarily serve the public interest requirement of efficient allocation of this wasting resource."[11] Nevertheless, the FPC did not discard the contract approach entirely, and the preferred end-use curtailment policy retains the firm-interruptible contract distinction. On balance, the FPC's approach tends to allow the contractual distinction between firm and interruptible service to determine relative priority within its prescribed end-use categories.

In contrast to the natural gas industry, the petroleum industry developed through integration. At the outset, a few large companies controlled the distribution system and retail markets. Control over crude oil reserves became the key to profits. Thus, the companies with large retail markets integrated upstream into crude oil exploration and production, and companies controlling large crude reserves integrated downstream. Smaller, independent companies were eventually able to enter every phase of the market, and some became more or less integrated themselves. But most independents depended on the spare capacity of the large integrated companies for crude oil, and particularly, refined petroleum products. In this sense, "independent" is a misnomer, since the survival of these firms in competition with integrated firms depended on the existence of surplus supplies that could be purchased on a spot market, and excess production capacity that could be contracted for in the short term.[12]

When faced with a shortage, the FEA froze current supplier-purchaser relationships. Unlike the FPC, the FEA used existing distributional relationships—relationships that in many cases were short-term or even fleeting—as a basis for its allocation program.[13] Over time, of course, more and more of these relationships became outmoded, and administrative adjustments were required.

Thus, although the natural gas distribution system is inherently rigid, the FPC adopted an administrative curtailment option that assumed flexibility rather than a policy based on underlying contracts. In contrast, even though the petroleum distribution system is inherently quite flexible, the FEA adopted an allocation option that attempted to make the system much more rigid. These ironies may be explained largely by the constituency which was apparently uppermost in the minds of agency policy makers—millions of small residential and commercial consumers in the FPC's case, and tens of thousands of small businessmen in the petroleum distribution chain in the FEA's case.[14]

Fairness. In favor of existing contracts, it may be argued that it is only fair to give the parties what they bargained for. Natural gas customers with interruptible contracts bargained for and received lower rates and less secure supplies than customers with firm contracts. Similarly, some independent oil refiners, marketers, and large-volume purchasers chose to rely on spot purchases and short-term contracts for their supplies. They benefited from lower prices than refiners or marketers with long-term supply contracts, as long as a buyer's market continued.

It is fair, the argument runs, to let these arrangements stand when a shortage occurs or when a buyers' turns into a sellers' market. Indeed, it would be extremely unfair in time of shortage to deprive prudent purchasers of precisely what they bargained for: a more secure supply at higher prices.

There is also a fairness argument opposed to maintaining existing contracts in a shortage. It begins with the assertion that the new energy situation was unforeseen. Firm supply contracts, which may run as long as 20 years in the case of natural gas, were based on shared assumptions that have turned out to be grossly erroneous. Moreover, some interruptible contracts were forced upon gas purchasers by state laws, administrative regulations or distribution company policies.[15] In the case of oil, the Arab embargo largely strengthened the bargaining power of the vertically integrated majors in relation to the independents. In such circumstances it would be arbitrary to let contract rights determine who gets scarce energy supplies, thereby driving independents from the market.

As to fairness, the argument on both sides may be sharpened if we ask: fairness to whom? If the primary concern is with the energy industry, then leaving purchasers and sellers to their contract rights, or freezing relationships as they existed before the shortage, may come close to meeting the fairness criterion in many cases.[16] Some within the industry were more cautious or expert than others, and at least the main dimensions of the new energy situation were foreseeable and were in fact foreseen by those with specialized knowledge. On the other hand, it may be argued that it is unfair to permit the large oil companies with long-term supply contracts or integrated operations to squeeze out the small independent companies in temporary shortage situations.[17]

If, however, the basic concern is with fairness to the energy consumer and economic activity dependent on energy consumption, then intra-industry contractual arrangements may have to give way in order to bring about an equitable distribution of the shortage. Many energy consumers are in no position to determine the adequacy and security of their suppliers' energy position.

The contract approach also raises difficult issues of fairness as between geographic regions. Gas consumers generally have no choice as to either the interstate pipeline company or local distribution company serving them, although they may choose where to locate initially.[18] Consumers do have some choice as between suppliers of petroleum products, although there are pronounced regional variations in the respective market shares of the various companies—major companies as well as independents.[19] A difficult issue is the extent to which consumers in different regions should be treated differently in time of shortage because of contractual arrangements elsewhere in the energy distribution system and to which they were not parties.

Practicality. It may be argued that administrative non-interference, or maximum use of existing contract rights, is the most practical approach to an energy shortage. It would avoid or minimize entry into an area that is immensely complicated to administer and for which the government has little expertise.

It may appear at first glance that chaos would result if government stayed out of the energy market as a serious shortage developed. However, if everyone were convinced the government would do nothing either to help or hurt, existing contract rights might be assigned or renegotiated for a price in response to the changed market conditions. The outcome might be a redistribution of energy supplies that would be at least as economically efficient as any scheme the government might devise and impose.

In opposition to the contract approach, it may be argued that the government has no practical alternative to intervention during a serious energy shortage. A free market may theoretically offer a solution in that every contract can be changed for a price.[20] In practice, however, the market is very imperfect. Many contracts are quite inflexible, and the transaction costs of renegotiation would be very high. Some suppliers are likely to find themselves in a position to price gouge their customers or to squeeze out their competitors. If government simply left suppliers and consumers to their own devices in an energy shortage, an irrational struggle for survival might quickly replace rational economic behavior in a competitive market.

Even if an administrative agency uses contract rights as merely a subsidiary basis for administering an energy shortage, serious difficulties may arise. Natural gas supply contracts afford a useful example. The difference between "firm" and "interruptible" service contracts is frequently unclear when actual contract provisions are considered.[21] Consequently, administrative definitions are required. Despite continuing confusion concerning the meaning of its definitions, the FPC has declined to issue a clarifying order on the ground that no single definition could be drafted to cover every conceivable agreement.[22] Thus, to the extent that the firm-interruptible distinction is ambiguous and must be clarified in such individual proceedings, a principal advantage of using the contract approach—administrative simplicity—may be lost.

Finally, as a practical matter, the role of the courts needs to be considered. If an administrative agency failed to intervene, an energy shortage would be thrown piecemeal into various courts. A good deal of litigation seems unavoidable in order to settle disputes about whatever is left of contract rights.[23] Furthermore, court review of some key administrative decisions seems inevitable. Nevertheless scattered court decisions are not adapted to distributing, in the first instance, the damage of an energy shortage across society.

Consistency with other policies. It may be argued that a contract approach to an energy shortage is consistent with economic and energy policy considerations and with the basic principles of a free enterprise system. Government nonintervention would maintain private incentives to seek additional energy supplies. Without the government to fall back on, every energy supplier would have a large profit incentive to find and develop new sources of supply, and every energy purchaser would have large incentives to cut back on energy use, to develop relationships with new suppliers, and to become as self-reliant as possible. Furthermore, the principle of stability of private contracts would be preserved as a planning factor for future private investment in the energy industry. Administration of energy shortages in this way would reinforce the position that, in the long run, the best solution to America's energy problem is a free market solution, not a government-determined solution.

On the other hand, it may be argued that present energy shortages or threatened shortages are manifestations of a major shift in the long-run energy outlook. The shortages signal a discontinuity and need for an abrupt transition between the present and a very different future situation. Existing contracts and historical supplier-purchaser arrangements are major obstacles to rapid adaptation to the new situation.[24] Therefore, government action should be taken in the transition period that will free the market of obsolete and counter-productive relationships.

Pro Rata Reductions or End-Use Priorities?

Assuming that government action is necessary to control the distribution of energy supplies in time of shortage, the main choice in principle is between pro rata reductions and end-use priorities. The outcome in practice, however, will inevitably be some blend of both principles. On the one hand, a departure from a strictly pro rata approach results from assigning different allocation fractions to different customer classes or from granting exemptions or prohibitions. On the other hand, the administration of end-use priorities may involve pro rata reductions within a customer class that is only partly curtailed. The degree to which one principle is emphasized over another may, however, vary widely between different schemes.

One major factor influencing the choice between pro rata reductions and end-use priorities will be the severity of the shortage. In general, a pro rata approach may be useful in managing a relatively slight shortage. Almost every energy consumer can cut back a small fraction of his current use. The more severe an energy shortage becomes, however, the more necessary it will be to develop and implement priorities. This aspect of planning for shortages may be crucial in determining the success or failure of the administrative program.[25]

The FPC has adopted a natural gas curtailment policy that emphasizes end-use priorities. The Commission made its decision as a matter of discretion, with virtually no statutory guidance, and over the vigorous objections of many within the natural gas industry. Moreover, the FPC lacks authority to carry out its declared policy preference due to the limits of its jurisdiction. In short, the FPC policy aims at, but cannot effectively reach most energy users.

In contrast, the FEA adopted a mixed policy in petroleum allocations: pro rata reductions for resellers; and end-use priorities for large consumers purchasing from distributors above the retail level.[26] The basic option of pro rata reductions for resellers was mandated by the Congress in the EPAA. If left to its own discretion, the FEA might have placed more stress on end-use controls than it did. Unlike the FPC, the FEA approach was built on a broad jurisdictional base which in theory allowed the FEA to implement its policies. FEA implementation was thus hampered less by the legal obstacles than by the lack of adequate resources for effective enforcement.

Pro Rata Reductions

Fairness. A plan based on pro rata reductions may rest on an overall judgment that the fairest way to distribute an energy shortage is for everyone to reduce his energy consumption by the same proportionate amount. This judgment, in turn, appears to rest on one of two alternative assumptions: (a) a fair distribution of energy exists at the time the shortage arises; or (b) the existing distribution of energy may or may not be fair, but a shortage should not be used as a redistribution mechanism.[27]

Many people will perceive proportionate cutbacks as a fairer way of distributing a shortage than end-use priorities. A pro rata approach avoids controversial judgments about the social utility and efficiency of each energy use. Furthermore, a pro rata plan may appear fair because it achieves participation from the maximum number of consumers. In terms of eliciting the cooperation from energy users which is essential for a successful program, such appearances may be as important as the actual facts.

A would-be high priority user, however, will not see pro rata reductions as fair to him. Moreover, the failure to make value judgments, and the refusal to apply economic logic to distinguish more efficient energy uses from the less efficient, are tantamount to an abdication of government responsibility in an emergency.

All other things being equal, pro rata reductions may seem unfair to energy-efficient users and to energy-intensive industries, activities, and lifestyles. It is possible that energy-intensive industries, such as metals and petrochemicals, actually waste proportionately less energy than other users. This is because the cost of energy is a major factor determining total product cost, justifying more effort to avoid waste.

Under a pro rata scheme, moreover, consumers who wasted energy in the past are given a painful but reasonable level of supply. Those who earlier complied with voluntary conservation programs and have already eliminated wasteful uses may be unable to continue operations if further mandatory pro rata reductions are imposed. Such an impact on conserving consumers is most unfair, precisely because these are the consumers who were attempting to solve the problem somewhere short of regulation. Commuting workers would obviously be affected more seriously by pro rata reductions in motor gasoline than those who work closer to home. Yet commuters chose where to live before the advent of the energy shortage.

As to fairness in geographical distribution, uniform pro rata reductions applied nationwide would be superimposed on a country in which large regional differences exist with respect to energy supplies and consumption patterns. If use of any particular fuel were to be reduced pro rata throughout the country, the impact of the reduction would vary widely between various regions and localities.[28]

Finally, the fairness of pro rata reductions depends in large part on minimizing the number of exceptions which inevitably will be granted (e.g., to the military for motor gasoline and aviation fuel). Each exception will create pressure for further exceptions from users who perceive themselves as "absolutely essential." Of course, every exception that is allowed dilutes the initial claim to equity of the pro rata approach.

Practicality. Turning to administrative practicality, one advantage of a pro rata plan is that it is conceptually easy to understand. This theoretical advantage is real, however, only if it can be translated into ease of administration. In general, the administrative simplicity of pro rata reductions depends on the number of suppliers or purchasers subject to the plan.

In the case of natural gas curtailments, the pipeline-distributor level should be distinguished from the distributor-consumer level in the administration of pro rata reductions. At the pipeline-distributor level it would be a rather simple task to find out how much gas a given interstate pipeline expects to be able to deliver, and how far that volume falls short of anticipated demand. The amount of the shortfall would then be spread equally among all the distributors and direct sales customers, each receiving the same percentage of its base period volume. The relatively small number of parties involved makes possible negotiations to resolve differences that may arise over the choice of base periods or other technical aspects of administration. Compliance may be assured by the use of stiff overtake penalties.

Simplicity of administration of a pro rata plan would not generally apply to the distributor-consumer level. As discussed in Chapter Two, it is not possible to apply percentage curtailment by reducing the volume of gas supplied through the pipeline. Instead, the customer must measure his gas take and be sure not to exceed the agreed-upon allocation. Therefore, pro rata reductions may be practical for larger volume industrial customers, but impractical for small-volume commercial and residential consumers. The use of surcharges as an enforcement device against millions of small-volume users may also raise more problems than it solves.[29]

In the case of petroleum, pro rata reductions cannot be implemented for some products and markets. The larger number of purchasers makes application to wholesale purchaser resellers more difficult than with natural gas, but still reasonably practical. However, sales to customers with more than one supplier will complicate computation of reductions, unless a supplier-purchaser freeze is initiated.

Practical difficulties become more serious at the retail level, particularly with some products. Pro rata reductions cannot feasibly be applied by retail gasoline stations in their sales to unidentified motorists who are free to shop around. A variation of a pro rata plan applied to retail gasoline sales is to limit sales to a specified maximum, e.g., 10 gallons. The approach results in discrimination against purchasers without free time, inconvenience to purchasers who return more frequently to retail outlets, and "topping off" practices that burden station workers.

Hence, coupon rationing seems to be the only practical way to administer a serious gasoline shortage.[30] Coupons cannot be issued on a pro rata basis because individual consumption levels are unknown and certainly unverifiable.

With other refined petroleum products, pro rata reductions are easier to compute because suppliers often keep records. The only problem is the large numbers involved. The government could avoid that difficulty by requiring suppliers to calculate the reductions.

In addition to problems due to the number of suppliers or customers involved and the level in the distribution system to which pro rata reductions apply, there are a number of other administrative problems related to pro rata reductions which we should consider.

Base Periods. If energy supply is to be reduced by some fraction, the choice of the time period from which the fraction is to be determined is very important. A base period may be fixed ("frozen") or rolling ("ambulatory").

A fixed base period is some period which is to be retained for the duration of the shortage for the purpose of computing fractions to be reduced.[31] A rolling base period is one that is changed over time. For example, with natural gas we might choose the preceding 12-month period. Each year the base volume data would reflect the changes in demand patterns that occurred in the preceding year. In this way such factors as seasonal fluctuations and annual variations are reflected in the updated information.

If a fixed base period is used, the period should be removed in time from the occurrence of the shortage. Otherwise, the base period's reduction fractions would reflect distortions in demand patterns that were due to the emerging shortage condition.[32] For example, when faced with an imminent shortage, some consumers may build up reserve stocks, while others may forego consumption in response to pleas for voluntary conservation. If the base period is too close in time to the shortage, it may benefit those who hoard or splurge at the last minute, while penalizing those who attempt to conserve—a result which would invert justice.

A rolling base period is likely to be much more complicated to administer than a fixed period. In a sense, the rolling period raises many of the questions of priorities involved in an end-use priorities scheme, but without achieving the larger advantages of distribution based on end use.[33] Nevertheless, we should recognize that the longer an energy shortage continues, the greater would be the distorting effects of a fixed base period. Thus, any fixed period will require an adjustment process.

Base volumes. In addition to a time period, if energy supply is to be fractionally reduced, the volume against which the reduction fraction is applied must be determined. Historical demand, contract entitlement, or estimated future demand are three alternatives.[34]

With historical demand, the volume against which a reduction fraction is to be applied would be the volume actually distributed or consumed during the base period. With contract entitlement, the volume would be that to which the purchaser was entitled during the base period, whether or not that amount was actually taken. A future estimate as a base volume would be analogous to a rolling base period in attempting to factor a dynamic situation into the reduction scheme.

Annual, seasonal, monthly, or daily reductions. The period of time over which reductions are spread also presents difficulties. Some means must be found to deal with the fact that consumers will not use uniformly over time the amount of energy they are entitled to.

A volumetric limitation computed only annually may not provide sufficient control over the volumes actually taken during the year. However, a daily limitation may not provide sufficient flexibility for customers to meet variations in their requirements.[35] A monthly or seasonal limitation would allow a customer to exceed the volumetric limit on a given day or series of days, as long as the total taken during the longer period did not exceed the limit imposed.

New customers. A final issue which compromises the basic simplicity of a pro rata approach is whether a distributor should be permitted to take on additional customers. For example, a natural gas distributor may wish to build up his load factor by adding additional summer seasonal customers. Adding on summer load may not worsen winter curtailments, if available storage capacity is already filled. Moreover, fixed charges can be spread over more customers, thereby lowering individual rates. However, allowing distributors to add non-premium users may be unwise in the face of an indefinite decline in total available supplies. The same "valley gas" supplied for industrial use during the summer might be made available for increased storage injection, thereby ameliorating the winter supply situation.

At this point, coordination of petroleum and natural gas regulation becomes imperative. Although policy may suggest that new customers should be denied access to either, or to any, fuel, the agency given that denial power becomes authorized to shape economic and technological growth for years to come.[36]

Consistency with other policies. A pro rata approach tends to maintain existing structural relationships within the energy industry and to have a minimum impact on the composition of energy demand. By spreading an energy shortage as thinly as possible across demand, a pro rata approach may tend to minimize adverse economic consequences, but only if the shortage is relatively mild. In a more severe shortage, the same percentage reduction applied to various users may require one to shut down, another to switch to an alternate fuel, and permit a third to continue to operate relatively unimpaired at a reduced level.[37] Pro rata reductions do not take these differences into account. Therefore, as an energy shortage becomes more severe, the burden of a pro rata reduction plan will become more and more asymmetrical in its impact across society.

As with the contract approach, pro rata reductions may clash with national goals premised on assumptions that some users are superior to others in terms of economic contribution, national defense, physical efficiency, and the like. The importance to be placed on these goals, as opposed to others, is, of course, a political decision.

Finally, in relation to energy policy, pro rata reductions are consistent with the view that an energy shortage should not be an excuse for instituting far-reaching changes. Long-term policy is designed to eliminate energy shortages as a phenomenon. When and if shortages occur, however, the administrative approach should be to get through them as quickly as possible, without permanent change in industry structure or consumption patterns.

End-Use Priorities

End-use priorities may be developed to be immediately responsive to the particular needs and political weight of various interest groups. Alternatively, priorities for energy distribution during a shortage may be established to assist in the achievement of long-term energy policy objectives, by forcing the phase-out of a particular fuel in one or more specific uses. The end-use priorities in the FEA's petroleum allocation program seem to have been partially developed with the needs of particular interest groups in mind. On the other hand, the priorities in the FPC's natural gas curtailment policy seem aimed at shifting long-run consumption patterns.[38] Thus, there is an inherent tension between short- and long-run considerations in the designation and ranking of particular end uses of energy.

Established priorities may be little more than a reflection of the preconceptions held by the top administrators, more or less guided by statutory authority. Alternatively, priorities may result from complex empirical studies of the energy system and the role of energy in the national economy.[39]

Regardless of the administrator's preconceptions and the results of empirical studies, however, political factors are likely to weigh heavily at some stage in the development of a specific end-use priorities scheme. Unlike pro rata reductions, end-use priorities are based on a premise that government knows best or is the only entity capable of knowing at all.

Fairness. An end-use priorities approach is inevitably the result of a judgment that some energy uses are either more important or less costly to convert to alternate fuels than others. Fairness, therefore, means that the burden of a shortage in a particular fuel should fall most heavily on those uses that the government deems least important or easiest to switch to alternate fueld. End-use priorities assume it is possible for government to make the necessary discriminations.

The concept of "premium" and "inferior" uses of natural gas deserves special attention since it is the basis of the FPC's curtailment policy and has been hotly contested. The main argument is that the use of gas to fire industrial boilers for running factories, thereby providing jobs, products, and profits, is not necessarily inferior to the use of gas to heat homes. The strength of the argument is its recognition of the economic importance of gas even in so-called inferior uses. The weakness of the position is two-fold.

First, it takes a short-term view of the problem. If natural gas supplies are inadequate for a given heating season, fueling jobs may indeed be more important than heating homes to normal temperatures. But if curtailments are expected to continue, those uses of gas where low cost is the main attraction, as in industrial boilers, should be distinguished from uses in which the form or unique chemical qualities of the gas are a primary reason for consumer preferences. An end-use plan (or a hybrid plan with some end-use aspects) can make these necessary distinctions.

Second, the argument against assigning a low priority to gas use as industrial boiler fuel is only valid if alternate fuels are not available. The issue of alternate fuels is more complicated than determining, however, that ample supplies of petroleum are likely to be available to replace natural gas in the short run. The cost of conversion must be considered, including capital costs and increased fuel costs. This may be difficult to do except on a plant-by-plant basis. Moreover, the full cost of conversion must be weighed in the balance, not just costs at plant sites. Thus the economic and environmental impacts of switching must be analyzed and compared throughout both fuel cycles. Finally, long-run considerations must be fully assessed. In an industrial boiler presently burning natural gas, it would make little sense to install an alternate capability to burn residual fuel oil if two years from now the plant will be required to convert to coal.

The priorities established for petroleum allocation pursuant to the EPAA did not completely eliminate any uses. The dichotomy of "premium" and "inferior" uses was not as clear as in the case of natural gas. Regulation under ESECA will prevent some uses of petroleum products, but on an individual adjudicatory basis. Each decision must consider all of the factors listed above, although general policy guidelines are likely to be followed.

Since the thrust of an end-use plan is to discriminate among various uses and hence among users of energy, it may be argued that particular priority schemes create objectionable inequities of various kinds. An end-use plan may result in: (a) competitive inequalities between companies producing similar products for the same market but using different processes or fuels; and (b) local and regional inequalities due to the asymmetrical impact that a uniform system of priorities is bound to have on diverse energy distribution and consumption patterns.[40]

In view of these inequities, it may be argued that any *nationwide* system of end-use priorities is inherently unfair. This problem might be handled by allocating supplies among regions on a pro rata basis, and permitting each region to develop its own end-use priorities. Another way to mitigate the inequities which could result from an end-use type plan is to provide for some form of compensation arrangement under which those users who receive more than their pro rata share would be obligated to compensate those users who receive less.[41]

There is generally a trade-off between fairness and practicality which is illustrated by the compensation issue. The more detail and refinement that is introduced in order to treat all energy consumers fairly, the more complex and less workable the process becomes. In any event, the development and administration of a compensation plan would be easier if the priorities were developed and applied on a regional basis, as noted above.

Finally, there is the problem of fairness as between present and future consumers under an end-use priorities scheme. Total consumption in each established priority may be frozen for purposes of computing entitlements during a shortage, or growth may be permitted and taken into account. Growth in the higher priorities would, of course, occur at the expense of the lower priorities in time of shortage. Those placed in a low priority may argue that permitting growth to continue in the higher priority categories, despite continuing and perhaps worsening shortages, is unfair because it compounds the original inequity of the priorities scheme. On the other hand, consumers in a higher priority may reply that upgrading the pattern of energy consumption is the only fair way to deal with future consumers.[42]

Practicality. The administration of an energy shortage according to end-use priorities involves many of the same problems that arise in administering a pro rata plan, including base periods and volumetric limits. In addition to these problems, however, end-use priorities involve a unique range of problems regarding data. These are outlined below, while the problems common to pro rata reductions are not discussed further.

An end-use priorities plan rests on an assumption that adequate data are available as to how much energy is being used for the various purposes around which the priorities are established. Data are required only from energy suppliers in order to administer a pro rata plan. However, large amounts of information may be required from consumers in order to administer an end-use plan.[43] Consequently, end-use data problems are numerous, and some are very difficult to solve at reasonable cost.

For an end-use plan to be effective and reasonably equitable, the data base must be recent, consistent, and complete. Such end-use data are often not available, however. Data that are available have often been compiled by inconsistent methods, using varying assumptions and interpretations of key terms. Precise information concerning end-uses of energy may be considered proprietary information in some industries. Furthermore, every end user initially, and every reseller in the distribution chain, has an incentive to classify as much as possible of his consumption or supply in the highest possible priority.[44]

Natural gas poses special problems. The line between commercial and industrial use is not always clear, even though commercial end users are classified by the FPC in either priority 1 or 2, and industrial use can range from priorities 2 through 9, depending on type of contract, end-use, and volumes required.

Some distributors have classified their customers under the Standard Industrial Classification Code. Others have applied the classification used in their existing rate schedules, calling small industrial customers "commercial" because they are served under a commercial rate schedule. Still other distributors have classified by predominant use, a practice which can be very misleading when one customer uses gas for many purposes having different priorities.[45]

Similar difficulties arise in attempting to distinguish true "process" uses of natural gas (where the unique qualities of natural gas are utilized) from other process uses (where alternate fuels could be substituted without substantial difficulty, although at some cost penalty). The incentive and opportunity for each consumer or distributor to resolve borderline cases in favor of the higher priority use is inherent in any end-use priorities scheme, regardless of how clearly the definitions may be drafted.

Finally, there is the problem of data collection and verification.[46] The FPC has neither the authority to compel each end user to submit information, nor the staff to verify such information in case the authority were obtained. Instead, the Commission relies on the pipelines and distribution companies to gather the information as well as to verify it.[47] The FEA has far-reaching authority to gather data on all forms of energy use, although the ability of even the FEA to reach the final consumer may be limited. Cooperation between the FPC and the FEA has occurred in regard to natural gas data.[48] But the FEA, like the FPC, has limited resources to devote to the problem.[49]

Consistency with other policies. In theory, a principal advantage of end-use priorities over pro rata reductions is that the priorities can be designed specifically to fit with other important public policies. Adverse effects of the shortage on national goals may be minimized, and a shortage may be managed in a way that is oriented toward long-term energy policy objectives. In practice, there are two main obstacles to designing an end-use priorities plan that will be as consistent as possible with other policies.

The first problem is technical. Many important effects of implementing a priorities scheme will not be foreseen, either because of inadequacies in the data base and analytic methods used to develop the plan, or because the effects are simply unpredictable. These problems can be dealt with through adjustments in light of experience, as they were by the FEA under the EPAA.

The second obstacle is political. Any set of priorities to manage an energy shortage is bound to impair some political objectives more than others. No policy-maker is likely to volunteer his particular program or interest for a low priority; indeed, each policy-maker will do his best to protect his interests in the design of priorities. Thus, if the problem of consistency is squarely and openly faced, it is likely to result in an intense political struggle at the policy-making level.

The sharpest conflict may emerge between the short- and long-term perspectives. The short-run perspective would seek to design priorities to minimize impact on jobs, profits, and lifestyles for the expected duration of the immediate shortage at hand—the following winter, for example. The long-run perspective would develop priorities to ensure over time that energy shortages gradually disappear as equilibrium between supply and demand is restored and maintained.[50]

Negotiated Settlements

From the preceding discussion, it is apparent that no particular approach—contract, pro rata reductions, or end-use priorities—is likely to be applied in pure form. Each approach has advantages and drawbacks in particular circumstances and from various points of view. Given the complexities and uncertainties inherent in any serious energy shortage, government administration will necessarily involve some more-or-less arbitrary actions.

It is also apparent from the preceding discussion that the effectiveness of any administrative program for managing an energy shortage will depend largely on cooperation from those affected. It is extremely difficult to enforce compliance by industry or consumers if there is widespread defiance.

In administering a shortage in some circumstances, the government may have an alternative to imposing its own solution on industry and consumers. This option is to facilitate a series of ad hoc negotiated settlements within functionally or geographically related groupings. A negotiated approach would still require the government to determine how much energy each group or area is to receive. Beyond that decision, however, the distribution problem would be solved by negotiation among the parties concerned, rather than by government administrators. The shortage would be dealt with by agreement, rather than by dictate. If used where practicable, a negotiated approach may substantially reduce the risks of arbitrary government action, on the one hand, and public rejection and defiance, on the other. As we will see below, negotiation may be more practical in the case of natural gas than petroleum.

In administering an energy shortage through negotiated settlements, three broad problems would be encountered. The first is ascertaining appropriate negotiating groups; the second is determining the amount of energy to which each group is entitled; and the third is the conduct of negotiations within each group. Considerations of fairness and practicality are involved in each of these problems.

A group might be composed along functional lines within the energy system or along geographical lines. An example of a functional grouping would be wholesale-purchaser-resellers in the case of petroleum, or interstate pipelines in the case of natural gas. The group might include just one, or several levels in the distribution chain. Only distributors might be included, or only consumers, or one group might include both distributors and consumers. A geographical grouping might embrace only one distributor's service area, one state with several distributors, or an entire region with many distributors and many millions of consumers.

In composing appropriate groups, fairness would seem to require that no single interest within the group should dominate the outcome. In other words, the bargaining strength of the interested parties should be reasonably balanced. Fairness would also require that certain competitors should not be included in the negotiations,[51] while others are excluded.

It would seem that negotiating groups should be consumer-oriented, if possible. The burden of the shortage must ultimately be distributed across the spectrum of energy consumption. Distributors as a whole have less at stake in the outcome than consumers. It is noteworthy in this regard, that for practical reasons both FPC natural gas curtailment proceedings and some FEA petroleum allocation programs directly involve only very large consumers.[52]

Assuming that the energy supply allocated to the group is fair, and that the group is structured in a balanced way, the outcome of the negotiation should be perceived as fair. The distribution should be tailored to the particular requirements and objectives of the group involved. Considerable diversity would be expected between plans developed by different negotiating groups. If all interests are appropriately balanced, a negotiated plan is likely to be considered fairer by the group as a whole than a plan designed by the government.

The main practical problem in composing an appropriate group would be to reduce the parties to a manageable number that is still representative of the group as a whole. This could be done through forming subgroups and ensuring effective representation of each subgroup.

Determining the amount of energy to be allocated to a group for purposes of negotiation would probably require the development of an overarching government administrative plan based on some blend of contracts, pro rata reductions, and end-use priorities. The alternative would be to provide a scheme for inter-group bargaining. A workable scheme of this sort seems very difficult, if not impossible, to develop.

Having taken the first step by developing an overarching government allocation plan, it may be asked why it is not preferable for the government to follow through and develop a complete plan to administer the shortage. One answer is that at a high level, it may be relatively easy to agree upon a very general allocation based on historical consumption and geographical equity. Such an allocation is likely to be accepted as fair as far as it goes. The hard choices are encountered at lower levels, and these choices may possibly be made more equitably by negotiation among those affected than by government administrators. Ensuring consistency with national goals may remain a problem, however.

The conduct of negotiations within the group would have to be subject to administrative supervision in order to ensure that the group actually reached a decision as to how its energy supply should be distributed. A government administrator might also play a mediating role, thereby facilitating negotiations. In addition, on appeal by one or more of the parties, the negotiated settlement might be subject to administrative review as to its fairness, practicality and consistency with the public interest. The negotiating process is likely to be complicated and time-consuming. But the administrative process involved in dealing with an energy shortage is certainly no less cumbersome.

The opportunities for administering an energy shortage through negotiated settlements appear especially interesting in the case of natural gas. The number of distributors are relatively few, and the service areas of the various distribution companies are geographically defined. The fact that the natural gas distribution system is a series of interlocking regulated monopolies means that competitive relations among distributors is not an important consideration in the design of a plan to distribute an energy shortage.

In the case of natural gas, therefore, the various consumer interests within a service area of regional grouping of service areas may negotiate more or less directly among themselves over how to distribute the burden of the particular shortage they all face. The various consumer interests may be quite clearly differentiated, starting from the existing schedule of tariffs with some refinements. Appropriate representation for each interest may then be arranged. Finally, in view of the diversity of interests and multiple roles (as residential users and also as workers), there would seem to be ample room for trade-offs in an overall settlement.[53]

Application of the negotiated settlement approach to petroleum would be substantially more difficult. Different groups must be selected for each refined product, particularly from the consumer side. Those products which are sold by relatively few suppliers to only a few purchasers (e.g., jet fuel, petro-chemicals, residual fuel oil), would not be so complicated as those products which are sold to a large number of purchasers, (e.g., motor gasoline, middle distillates).

Balancing the negotiating groups between majors and independents would require a decision as to how much voting weight each group would have. An equitable formula would be difficult to devise. With each fuel, the effect of that decision might be different, and consequently the negotiated settlements could be extremely favorable to one of the factions.

Determining the amount of energy to which each group is entitled involves more than geographical allocation, since refinery yields of each product vary during the year and can be adjusted to emphasize one product only at the expense of others. Thus, many of the decisions which this approach attempts to leave to negotiation must in actuality be made by the government.

Finally, the negotiated settlement approach is the least tried of any we have discussed. It offers the potential of a new method but lacks the history valuable for both evaluation and design. The lack of experience may be responsible for delay in implementation at a time when delay can be very costly.

ADMINISTRATIVE ORGANIZATION

In organizing an administrative capacity to deal with energy shortages, one issue is allocating authority between the federal government and the several states, a second is locating authority at the federal level, and a third is selecting administrative procedures. The federal-state relations problem is primarily an issue of federal preemption of areas traditionally left to the states, while at the federal level the locational choice is between an executive and an independent agency. Of course, interagency or intergovernmental "coordination" is a device that may be used to blur distinctions and make choices appear less clear-cut. Finally, after authority to regulate is assigned, the methods by which that authority will be exercised must be chosen Some combination of generic rulemaking and adjudicatory procedures is likely, but there is considerable room for differences in emphasis.

in discussing organizational issues it is important to have in mind the current distribution of administrative capacity. Powerful economic and political interests are vested on that basis. It is equally important to consider the underlying structure of the shortage to be administered. If this is ignored, the administrative organization will be doomed to ineffectiveness.

Existing Administrative Structure

As to natural gas, most of the power to deal with the recurrent shortage is currently vested in the several states, not in the federal government. Controls on natural gas production, retail distribution, and consumption are applied at the state level.

The several governments of gas-producing states may control production for conservation purposes. They may also set higher prices on gas distributed intrastate than the FPC-approved interstate price, thereby creating incentives to sell gas locally rather than for export.

The governments of gas-importing states may control retail prices and distribution. In the event of shortages, they may establish and enforce curtailment plans for the retail markets. These plans regulate primarily the local distributor-consumer relationship.

The federal role in administering the natural gas shortage is narrowly limited, not by the U.S. Constitution (see Chapter Nine) but by the Natural Gas Act of 1938. As we have seen previously, the Gas Act left unimpaired state power over production and local distribution. Consequently, the Gas Act limited FPC jurisdiction over the natural gas industry to interstate transportation and wholesale sales transactions. The FPC's curtailment authority thus focuses on the interstate pipeline and the interface between the pipeline and the local distributor. Moreover, the FPC cannot accomplish by indirect control what it cannot do directly. The Commission cannot require federal end-use priorities, which may be used to compute curtailments by a pipeline to its distributor customers, to be carried through to determine curtailments to end users.[54]

Finally, federal authority to administer the natural gas shortage is concentrated in the FPC, an independent economic regulatory agency. In principle, the FPC is intended to be somewhat distant and aloof from, if not entirely immune to, the political pressures that are brought to bear in executive agency policymaking.[55] In practice, however, the pressures are often felt to some degree. The Commission, both under its statute and because of its primary function of approving wholesale rates, is heavily oriented toward adjudicatory procedures.

As to petroleum, the EPAA preempts state power to deal with the shortage, and federal authority is vested almost completely in the FEA. To the extent that states have a role, it is determined initially at the federal agency level.

Moreover, the FEA is an executive agency,[56] responsive to the wishes of the President and fully exposed to the interagency bureaucratic and political pressures that are normal within the Executive Branch.[57] The FEA is oriented primarily toward administrative rulemaking.

Thus, the existing administrative structures and procedures to manage natural gas and petroleum shortages are worlds apart. While efforts to coordinate between the FPC and FEA are possible, it is doubtful whether coordination can accomplish much in view of the fundamental disparity in the two administrative structures and procedural capacities.

Underlying Problem Structure

An energy shortage is an emergency condition. Supply is inadequate to meet demand at established prices and government action is deemed necessary to effect an appropriate distribution. The emergency may be short-lived, as with the 1973–74 Arab oil embargo, or recurring, as with the natural gas shortage.

In view of the emergency character of the problem, action to deal with it must be both timely and flexible. And, since an energy supply is essential to sustain almost every activity, the exercise of government power over energy distribution in a shortage becomes a highly charged political act.

Finally, we must note that the recurrent natural gas shortage and the potential petroleum shortage in the U.S. are extensively and massively interrelated. Whatever action—emergency or long-term—is taken to deal with one fuel will deeply affect the other.

Organizational Alternatives

It is clear that there is no existing administrative capacity to manage the kind of energy shortages that are generally anticipated in the late 1970s. The FPC lacks both jurisdictional and procedural capacity to administer a national natural gas shortage. Obviously, the several states cannot be left to manage the shortage for themselves, especially when the interstate sales price is federally controlled. The FEA had nearly adequate jurisdiction to administer petroleum shortages under the EPAA.

The need to deal with energy shortages is simply not reflected in the current structure of regulation. Yet there are few who would argue that the risks of energy shortages can be safely ignored.

Natural gas. With regard to organizational alternatives for the natural gas shortage, the threshold issue is how much of the problem the federal government should take over. Since the FPC's existing curtailment authority is limited to interstate transportation, additional federal authority might be considered at both ends of the natural gas supply system.

At the producer end, it would be possible for federal authority to require interconnections between pipelines and to order transfers of gas between pipelines in a shortage situation. Federal interconnection authority might be limited to interstate pipelines, or it could be extended to intrastate pipelines as well. Beyond the pipeline, federal authority might be applied to the gas fields and to include regulation of gaswell production. The ability of the government to coerce production during peacetime may, however, be constitutionally limited. (This issue is discussed in Chapter Nine.)

On balance, federal production controls are likely to be counterproductive. Such controls would be an important encroachment on an area traditionally under state control, an area over which the producer states have historically exercised extensive authority during the decades of surplus that preceded the shortage of the 1970s. Moreover, federal production controls are likely to create disincentives for private activity aimed at expanding natural gas supplies.

As to interconnection and transfers between pipelines, however, federal authority probably needs to be extended as far as is politically feasible. Authority to order interconnections and to transfer gas from the intrastate to the interstate market during a shortage need not mean that gas taken by federal action from the intrastate pipelines must be subject to FPC price regulation. In fact, the opposite result would seem fairer and more politically feasible. Likewise, it would be important in devising a system for mutual assistance among interstate pipelines in time of shortage to preserve incentives for each pipeline to continue to seek additional supplies. Special incentives might be provided by the price or payback provisions applicable to emergency transfers.

At the retail distribution end of the natural gas supply system, federal authority might be enlarged to include allocations made by local distributors, and even to end-use controls applied directly at the burner tip. Both types of federal authority would supplant state authority. The application of federal controls directly to consumers would be feasible in the case of large-volume consumers, but not small commercial and residential customers.

Federal controls applied directly to the burner tip might be limited to large industrial boilers. Moreover, federal authority need not oust the states from a role in natural gas redistribution. Instead, the federal agency could formulate guidelines that the state utility commissions would then administer.[58]

In locating authority at the federal level itself, the most serious organizational issue is whether Congress should give the FPC expanded authority by amending the Natural Gas Act, or whether it should transfer some of the FPC's current natural gas curtailment authority to an executive agency with even more extensive powers. The executive agency would presumably be the FEA, or any successor agency that would also be given standby authority to administer possible petroleum and other energy shortages. Supportive of an expansion of the FPC's authority are the Commission's technical expertise and bureaucratic momentum. In favor of the FEA are the emergency and political characteristics of the problem, and the interlock between natural gas and petroleum.

If the FPC's jurisdiction is to be expanded, its statutory procedures applicable to natural gas would also need to be revamped. Moreover, the FPC curtailment policy should probably be subject to some type of formal Executive Branch scrutiny to determine its consistency with other public policies.[59] However, if the FEA receives primary authority to administer the natural gas shortage, one alternative is to focus that authority on the development of federal guidelines to be applied and enforced by the FPC and the appropriate state governmental bodies, according to the existing allocation of their jurisdictions.

The FPC seems to have nearly exhausted its own administrative remedies, especially regarding the end-use curtailment option. There may be no expansion or reallocation of relevant authority at the federal level. Without a legislative assist, the FPC might consider reducing its emphasis on Order 467-B priorities, and focus more attention on pro rata reductions among the various states served by particular pipelines and on the possibilities for negotiated settlements. Alternatively, the FPC might attempt to focus simply on a "fair" allocation among the several states leaving each state to distribute the shortage across the local economy or various service areas involved. These approaches would seem more nearly within the FPC's current jurisdictional and administrative capacities than a continued effort to implement Order 467-B end-use priorities.

Petroleum. For the foreseeable future, the Energy Policy Act, discussed in Chapter Six, seems to have satisfactorily resolved the major organizational issues regarding the administration of petroleum shortages. There is a clear need to retain the FEA or to create a similar agency. Within the federal government's complicated and gigantic energy bureaucracy, some executive agency must expedite energy policy implementation and have authority to act in emergency situations. Having weathered one oil embargo and obtained massive amounts of previously undisclosed information about the petroleum industry in particular, it would seem wasteful to permit the FEA to expire.

Procedural Alternatives

Once administrative options for government intervention in the energy markets are selected, the procedures used by the agency in applying and enforcing its decisions are critical to effectiveness and acceptance. Agency procedures may be imposed statutorily or adopted voluntarily, with the former far more common.

Two polar procedural models are rulemaking and individual adjudications. The methods chosen in the future will probably include elements of each model, seeking both the flexibility inherent in rulemaking and the fairness involved in adjudication.

The FPC began with a primarily adjudicative approach to natural gas curtailments, later moving to include some rulemaking aspects as best it could (see the second part of Chapter Four). In designing regulatory authority to deal with energy shortages, it may be desirable to include the power to proceed by rulemaking. For example, it may be easier administratively to allocate natural gas under a pro rata approach by using a primarily rulemaking approach.

The FEA began regulation by adopting broad rules, largely in order to act quickly. In the short term at least, the FEA sacrificed some of the fairness involved in an adjudicative approach. (See the third section of Chapter Seven.) thereafter, the FEA used adjudications to mitigate the harsher effects of such broad rules, but even then adjudication procedures were quite informal.

After selecting a rulemaking or adjudicative model, consideration should be given to the specific procedures for reaching decisions. Rulemaking may follow formal or informal APA requirements, or even some hybrid form (see the second section of Chapter Seven). Adjudication procedures may also include varying degrees of formality.

Finally, procedures for investigations, enforcement, administrative appeals, and judicial review should be chosen. Investigations rarely require detailed provisions, but it may be desirable to specify by statute the amount of data to be available through the Freedom of Information Act. Enforcement proceedings may be very formal, emphasizing fairness over speed, or such proceedings may be informal, relying upon judicial review to guarantee due process. The same choice holds for administrative appeals. Judicial review may be varied in terms of the scope of review allowed to the courts by statute, exhaustion requirements, the type and location of the court initially reviewing the decision (a federal district court or a circuit court of appeals), and the court for appellate review. Ultimately, it may be preferable to adopt two tiers of procedures, the application of each depending upon the necessity of quick decisions.

NOTES TO CHAPTER EIGHT

1. This is especially true of crude oil and refined petroleum products. The working inventories maintained by suppliers decrease the need for government involvement in shortages of minor quantities and/or short duration. Where the shortage is more severe, and government action is not timely, inventories and flexibility may be seriously diminished, supply lines disrupted, and consumers permanently affected.

2. Articles 12–24 of the Agreement provide activation measures in time of an oil supply emergency. Under Article 13, activation occurs "whenever the group sustains or can be expected to sustain a reduction in the daily rate of its oil supplies at least equal to 7 percent of the average daily rate of its final consumption during the base period." Article 17 contains a comparable trigger for activating certain measures in the event any single participating country sustains a 7 percent shortfall. The text of the International Energy Agreement is reprinted in *Hearing on U.S. International Energy Policy Before the Subcomm. on International Food, Resources and Energy, House Comm. on International Relations,* 94th Cong., 1st Sess. at 81 (1975).

3. The FEA never demonstrated that it could overcome these problems, because it was not forced to deal with them. Before creating an automatic trigger, planners should have some assurance that the problems are surmountable. The problems will arise with respect to current data on supplies. If regulation is likely to be triggered, it would be to the advantage of the companies owning most of the supplies to manipulate and delay data collection. "Live" figures have never been gathered by the FEA, and are generally harder to obtain within a short time.

4. Some FEA officials suggest that the inability to quantify these variables will necessitate use of a discretionary trigger. The projected length of a shortage must be considered, yet it cannot be predicted accurately. The location of the shortage within the United States may vary with the contingencies considered here. More easily included "dead" figures are the season of the year, the particular refined products affected, and the companies which have shortages. "Live" figures may be included in the index, since it may not be wise to trigger regulation if unemployment, business closings, and non-energy product shortages are not occurring, regardless of the depth of shortage. Ultimately, with a dozen parameters, each with three potential values, the total number of values for the index would exceed three to the tenth exponential power—a clearly impractical result.

5. The proposed Natural Gas Emergency Act of 1975 (H.R. 9464) assumes the existence of a supply emergency period.

6. As discussed in Chapter Seven, section 203 of the Economic Stabilization Act of 1970 contained a discretionary trigger:

(a) The President is authorized to issue such orders and regulations as he deems appropriate, accompanied by a statement of reasons for such orders and regulations, to— . . . .

(3) provide after public hearing, conducted with such notice, under such regulations and subject to such review as the exigencies of the case may, in his judgment, make appropriate for the establishment of priorities of use and for systematic allocation of supplies of petroleum products including crude oil in order to meet the essential needs of various sections of the Nation and to prevent anticompetitive effects resulting from shortages of such products.

In this case, the discretion was invoked just before Congress automatically triggered a different, previously developed program.

7. In the petroleum context, an appropriately designed statute can correct for these particular adverse consequences. Specifically, by providing that the regulatory agency may order sales of hoarded supplies once the program is triggered, the economic advantage may be eliminated. Refusals to sell for that purpose may result in orders to sell larger quantities after regulation begins. Finally, the use of a pre-set base period volume, e.g., each month of 1972, diminishes the incentive to overconsume. In short, proper statutory design can make the advantages of voluntary control and cooperation very real.

8. This combination reduces the data and design problems of an automatic trigger. Part of the rationale for an elaborate index is the need to consider all important factors. A discretionary override eliminates that necessity and allows for judgment in decisions about the data. This may work only one way, however, allowing discretionary action to stop the implementation of regulation, but not to initiate it if the automatic trigger indicates otherwise.

The discretionary element of this combination may take a variety of forms. Basically it would allow the President or the administrator to make a finding that implementation is inappropriate. For political purposes, the authorizing statute may require some type of congressional acceptance of the discretionary finding. This acceptance could be either a requirement of approval or a provision that the finding may be rejected by Congress. The difference is in the presumption given to the agency finding.

9. The categorization of benefited groups is, of course, overgeneralized, but the political consequences are not. The FEA is unusual in pressing for deregulation, which is contrary to the employment interests of many workers. The involvement of Congress is more important than agency sensitivity to pressure for deregulation. If Congress has a discretionary override on this trigger, too, the concepts of consumer protection and votes become directly involved in deactivation decisions.

10. Pub. L. No. 94–163 §455 (1975).

11. FPC Order 467, 49 FPC 85, 38 Fed. Reg. 1503, 1504, issued Jan. 8, 1973.

12. This is not to imply that the relationship has always been parasitic. For many years, the most profitable segment of the industry has been crude oil pro-

duction, and sales to independents allowed the majors to increase volume at their most profitable level. Similarly, as discussed in Chapter Five, the "spot market" sales of refined products facilitated refinery expansion and optimal use of facilities. When shortages appear, however, the relationship tends to benefit only the independents.

13. Unlike the natural gas industry, the heavy investment required by the oil industry does not make supplier-purchaser relationships rigid or necessitate long-term contracts. The extensive vertical integration minimizes risks with regard to sales at all levels except retail. Moreover, most small amounts of product are transported by trucks, which are not bound to any particular route. The large transcontinental petroleum pipelines are regulated by the ICC as common carriers and are virtually assured of usage. Consequently, long-term contracts were often not desirable in the petroleum industry, and were the exception more than the rule in times of price escalation or shortages.

14. In the case of the FEA, the supplier/purchaser freeze may also be explained by the need for rapid action when the emergency arose. The temporal relationships among suppliers and purchasers made non-contractual administrative options and monitoring virtually impossible. This decision was, however, largely a function of the goals of policy makers. (See Chapter Seven.)

15. For example, California administrative regulations require all industrial gas users over a certain size to contract on an interruptible basis. In other cases the local gas distributor may not offer firm service. Dayton Power and Light adopted such a policy in 1970 with regard to large-volume customers even though identical type customers attached prior to that date had been able to choose firm service. Finally, with respect to both oil and gas, many public facilities in all parts of the country (schools, minicipal offices, etc.) are served under interruptible contracts due to statutorily mandated bidding procedures that require such users to accept the lowest bid for various services.

16. At least this is true for the majors. Independents denied the right to purchase by long-term contract do not consider this option fair at all.

17. This argument is complicated by the allegations of anticompetitive practices by the majors. If the majors did, in fact, prevent the independents from expanding or refused to enter into long-term supply arrangements, it seems particularly inequitable to allow the majors to benefit from the independents' difficulties.

18. As pointed out earlier, contracting patterns vary in different regions of the country. (See Chapter Two.)

19. As discussed in Chapter Five, in regions heavily dependent upon independents for supplies, consumers may be unable to obtain fuel unless the majors are allowed to purchase the independent outlets. Another facet of the unfairness argument is that given some refinery product yield flexibility, e.g., between motor gasoline and middle distillates, an integrated refiner would favor production of fuels which are most often sold through integrated channels and by long-term contract. This decision might disadvantage consumers of less favored products, such as middle distillates.

20. Sales made without contract to unidentified purchasers are obviously not susceptible to the contract approach. This includes retail sales of motor gasoline

and diesel fuel oil. Other sales made to identified purchasers, though not by contract, can be distributed by a supplier-purchaser freeze, without a pre-set contract or an obligation to sell. This includes retail sales of heating oils and propane. Although natural gas distributors frequently do not serve residential or small commercial users under written contracts, the consumer still is identifiable. Only with respect to wholesalers can the contract approach be fashioned to exclude government involvement.

21. Provisions allowing interruptions in service may range from what are essentially *force majeure* provisions, in case of war, acts of God, etc., through what are termed "weather curtailment" provisions, where the customer anticipates interruption on perhaps three or four very cold winter days. The elasticity in the concepts is illustrated by the 1975 Columbia Gas negotiations where the dominant view was that contracts providing for anticipated interruptions of no more than 10 days per year (later extended to 30 days) should be classified as firm "seasonal" or "off-peak" contracts.

22. *See* FPC Order 493, 50 FPC 831, 38 Fed. Reg. 27531, and FPC Order 493–A, 50 FPC 1316, 38 Fed. Reg. 36432. The definitional difficulties are discussed in Chapter Four.

23. See, for example, the confusion regarding the question of the gas pipelines' liability for breach of contract discussed in Chapters Three and Four.

24. Thus, long-term gas supply contracts for boiler fuel use allow the continued waste of irreplaceable natural gas in the face of an emerging national policy goal of conserving energy resources.

25. Each industrial or commercial energy user has a minimum level of consumption below which the business will shut down. For some, the minimum level will be close to 100 percent of current requirements. Even a small pro rata reduction may force a shutdown. For most users, however, the necessary minimum will be substantially below current requirements. Thus, as a pro rata shortage deepens, the number of businesses cut back below their minimum will begin to increase far more rapidly.

Moreover, where a pro rata reduction forces two or more firms to shut down where there is sufficient energy to fuel at least one, it becomes important to establish priorities. Otherwise, the administrative program will succeed only in exacerbating the impact of the shortage.

26. End-use priorities were also used for identifiable retail purchasers of refined products.

27. If current wealth distribution were deemed acceptable, it would be more efficient economically to transfer the dollar equivalent of the appropriate amount of energy, rather than to transfer actual energy supplies. Consumers who received the money could decide whether to spend it for more energy or for some other goods or services, or even to save or invest it.

On the other hand, it may be argued that the American political process rarely responds except in crisis situations. In that case, those who favor redistributional goals may argue that the shortage is a particularly good occasion for this type of action.

28. Whether geographic discrimination is heightened or relieved by a pro rata plan (as compared to end use) depends on whether the focus is on the economic

impact on a region, or on the treatment of different consumers of the same product in two geographic regions. If economic impact is the key, then the geographic variations are decreased by a pro rata approach. For example, industrial use in North Carolina is treated the same as residential use in Ohio. Both customer classes would be required to reduce consumption by the same proportion. But if the focus is on consumers of the same product in different regions, geographic inequality will be least with a priority system which treats similarly situated consumers equally. Thus home owners in different parts of the country would be treated most equally if an identical priority were assigned to both consumers for the same product, e.g., No. 2 fuel oil.

The problem is further complicated by variations in weather. The fairness argument rests in large part on equal sharing of the suffering, not merely sharing of the percentage shortfall. Thus a strict pro rata allocation which fails to adjust for geographic variations in weather will not be fair even though identical allocations are seemingly made.

29. Significant technical difficulties facing the use of consumer surcharges include computation of base period and volume (which may vary enormously from one period to another depending on changes in family size, income, weather, and energy use habits), and assignment of base data for new customers and new homes. Washington Gas Light, for example, estimates that annual turnover among its customers is approximately 25 percent.

Perhaps more important, however, are the political problems associated with surcharges. During the oil embargo winter 1973–74, both the State of North Carolina and the City of Los Angeles attempted to use surcharges to enforce reduction in electric energy demand. Yet in neither case was a single penny of surcharge ever collected. In the Los Angeles case, some 10 percent of residential customers—representing tens of thousands of individual complaints—appealed for an adjustment in their allowance. Had the penalties actually been applied, appeals would probably have been even more numerous. Within two weeks of the announcement of the North Carolina order, a flood of public criticism rolled in, capped by a motion by the State Attorney General underlining the unresolved practical difficulties and harsh inequities of the plan, and asking for a revision. The penalty provisions were quickly dispensed with. For a technical study of the Los Angeles experience, see Acton and Mowill, *Conserving Energy by Ordinance: A Statistical Study,* R-1650 FEA, Feb. 1975 (a Rand report). The actions of the North Carolina Utilities Commission are detailed in the orders issued in Docket No. 6–100 Sub. 18 (1973).

30. The distinction between identifiable and non-identifiable purchasers is basic to any kind of regulation reaching end users; only rationing makes them all identifiable.

31. Base periods used in gas curtailment plans typically cover a 12-month period. In contrast, the base period used by the petroleum allocation regulations was usually the corresponding month or quarter of a preceding year.

32. Changes in the weather during the base period may also have a substantial impact in calculating allocations. Transco, for example, has chosen the 12-month period April 1972–March 1973, a time of warmer-than-normal weather. Since the plan utilizes actual takes during the base period, some distributors feel it understates their real requirements.

33. Planning for supplemental and non-historic gas supplies may be frustrated if the base period is subject to modification. Thus, a distributor who has not sought new supplies or placed limits on the addition of new customers may be able to get a free ride on the supplemental supplies of another distributor. This possibility may in turn discourage distributors from undertaking the extensive planning and investment required for SNG, LNG supplies, or natural gas storage facilities.

34. The FPC has left the choice among these alternatives largely to the pipelines. The FEA, however, chose historical demand as the basis in most instances. For high priority users, however, the FEA used estimated current requirements.

35. At the same time, many customers may not be able to control their consumption on a daily basis and may be forced to cut sales back well below the curtailment level in order to avoid overtake penalties. The effect is to reduce unnecessarily the total volume available to consumers.

For petroleum in general, and especially for small end users, the period for reduction should be the same as the base period; it seems illogical to establish a figure for a monthly supply allowance and then require daily compliance. The latter approach eliminates all flexibility for the consumer, and is impossible to administer in the case of petroleum products. The effort applied to enforcing daily reductions is useful only to ensure that the reduction from the base period is made. For that purpose, better devices are available.

36. The FEA regulations required prior approval before acceptance of some type of purchasers. A different policy may be desirable for reselling purchasers and consumers, or for large purchasers and small. It may be more difficult politically to deny access to new small end users. Congress apparently considered this in the EPAA by virtually requiring that LPG be allocated to users whose natural gas supplies were curtailed (see Chapter Four).

37. Firms will react differently in the short and long term to reductions in their marginal revenues. In the long term, more firms will close and liquidate their investment, even though their marginal revenue is sufficient to justify continued short-term operation. Consequently, expectations of long or recurring shortages are very important in determining whether to close immediately or sustain temporary losses through continued operation.

38. While interest groups played some part in the FEA selection of regulations to protect independents and a few consumers, many of the allocation decisions were made in a political vacuum prior to the passage of the EPAA (see Chapter Seven) on the basis of individual judgments of the essentiality of fuel supplies. Little effort was made at that time to force conversions to other fuels. Subsequently, Congress attempted through ESECA to redirect some long-run consumption patterns.

39. The FEA has recently received several studies of the economic effects of various allocation levels and plans. See Resource Planning Associates, Inc., *Further Revision of the Petroleum Allocation Regulations Priority Classification System* (Report prepared for FEA Office of Regulatory Programs, 1975).

40. A salient example is found in the high concentration of large utility-type boilers using gas which is found in the gas-producing areas. Major differences are also found between nearby cities. For example, under the Order 467–B priorities, Baltimore Gas and Electric would have been curtailed over 25 percent dur-

ing the 1974–75 winter, while nearby Washington Gas Light, serving a much less industrial area, would have absorbed a mere 6.3 percent cutback. *See Hearings on Federal Power Commission Oversight—Natural Gas Curtailment Priorities Before the Senate Comm. on Commerce,* 93d Cong., 2d Sess., pt. 2, at 139 (1974).

41. The FPC has rejected compensation provisions in curtailment plans in the past as not in the public interest. The New York State Public Service Commission, however, has implemented a compensatory pooling plan proposed by Niagara Mohawk Power Corporation. See Renshaw, *How to Ration Dwindling Gas Supplies,* Public Utilities Fortnightly, May 8, 1975, at 27.

The FEA has been more receptive to the idea of sharing the shortage, as shown by the buy/sell program which helped insure that no wholesale purchaser would be cut off entirely.

42. This problem is particularly pronounced with respect to gas distributors "upgrading" load, that is, increasing the portion of their sales to high priority users, without exceeding overall volumetric limitations. The FPC contends that it lacks authority to deal with this practice, which in fact appears to be beyond its jurisdiction. The Commission has, however, attempted to place the risk of upgrading on the distributor by using fixed base periods. With the base period frozen, the distributor does not have an opportunity to have his end-use data reflect the increase in high priority customers. Thus, if curtailments deepen, the distributor runs the risk that he will be unable to obtain increased allocations to cover the new customers.

43. Both the FPC and the FEA shifted this data-gathering duty to the suppliers. The approach imposes substantial burdens on industry and by no means assures that the information so obtained will be accurate.

44. A graphic demonstration of this incentive was given in a recent curtailment proceeding where the data as to firm or interruptible service were gathered from the parties before they were aware of the implications of Order 467–B. After impact statements were sent out informing each distributor how much it would be curtailed, unilateral revisions were submitted by a large number of parties: over 50 MmcF were reclassified from "interruptible" to "firm."

45. Under this view, a manufacturer using 49 percent of his gas for industrial process use can be classified "commercial" if the remaining 51 percent of his consumption is for space heating. The result, obviously, is to effectively convert "industrial" to "commercial" use.

46. The primary technique developed by the FPC to check the data submitted is the use of "Data Verification Committees," composed of representatives of all (or almost all) the pipeline's customers, the Commission staff, and the pipeline itself. The Committees try to reach agreement on difficult points of interpretation and methodology used in developing the end-use data. Although helpful, such a procedure is no substitute for computing and preparing the figures in some uniform manner in the first instance.

47. In many cases, where the fuel is used for more than one end use by the same customer, it may be simply impractical to obtain accurate data for each distinct use. This creates further opportunities to "upgrade" use into higher priorities, as noted above.

48. Form 69, promulgated by FPC Order 531, 53 FPC __, 40 Fed. Reg. 27645 (June 25, 1975) was developed in conferences between the two agencies. The FEA, with its much broader authority, was to gather identical information from gas suppliers beyond the reach of the FPC.

49. In this respect, under FPC Form 69, the responding pipelines are only required to certify the accuracy of the information (obtained from the distributing companies) to the best of the pipeline's knowledge. Order 531 makes clear that the pipelines are only responsible for using reasonable care in assuring the accuracy of the information. An independent investigation by the pipeline is not required. See Order 531, 53 FPC __, 40 Fed. Reg. 27645 (June 25, 1975).

50. However, in many instances long-term and short-term goals are reasonably compatible. For example, reductions in driving and home heating fuel demand may be desirable from both perspectives.

51. Thus, composition of bargaining groups for petroleum products must consider not only the balance between suppliers and purchasers, but also that between majors and independents within supplier and purchaser groups, respectively.

52. The FEA petroleum allocation programs, since they were developed by rulemaking instead of adjudication, did not directly involve purchasers or consumers, except as they requested adjustments. The regulations affected all consumers of some fuels, but only the large ones for products such as motor gasoline.

While consumers obviously have a great deal at stake, in the petroleum industry, the same is true of many of the distributors (wholesale-purchaser-resellers). In contrast to natural gas distributors, there is still some competition and the potential for business failure in the petroleum industry, especially among the less stable independents. To the extent that the current structure of that industry is to be retained during a shortage, petroleum distributors, as well as consumers, must be represented.

53. In the past, however, the FPC has not been particularly receptive to negotiated settlements where an Order 467–B-type plan was not adopted. The Commission rejected a negotiated settlement proposed by Transco in 1974, leading Transco to submit a 467–B plan, stating that it had "no choice other than to make this filing." For a discussion of the facts relating to the Commission's action, see Consolidated Edison Co. v. FPC, 511 F.2d 372 (1974). In the 1975 proceeding on the Columbia Gas Transmission plan, the Commission also rejected a negotiated plan and called for full briefs on the 467-type plan. The D.C. Circuit has remarked in dicta that the FPC must at least consider a submitted settlement plan and state its reasons for choosing to reject it. See Consolidated Edison Co. v. FPC, 518 F.2d 448, 449 (1975).

54. Despite the indirect pressure which has been applied, only a handful of states have chosen to follow the FPC lead and adopt the 467–B priorities. See Chapters Three and Four as to the reach and effect of Commission curtailment orders.

55. For example, the Commission's staff operates under so-called ex parte

rules, which require timely reports of all communications received from one side of an issue where a representative of opposing interests is not present.

56. There are two types of Executive Branch agencies: those actually within the Executive Office of the President, such as the Energy Policy Office and the Federal Energy Office (which were predecessors of FEA), and those outside the Office which have their own statute, yet are still subject to Presidential control. The former type are generally created by Executive Orders and are thought to be more closely controllable by the President. The distinction, while not critical, may be important in a decision about the necessity of creating an agency by statute, as well as separation from political pressure.

57. Other considerations in the choice between an independent and Executive Branch agency include the applicability of ex parte rules only to independent agencies, and the reliance of executive agencies upon the Department of Justice during litigation.

58. The guidelines approach may help to reduce political tension in the federal-state relationship and encourage state-sponsored conservation plans or other actions to meet the shortage. In its 1973 order requiring a 15 percent reduction in gas use, the North Carolina Utilities Commission pointedly observed,

> If this reduction is achieved, up to 15% more gas will be available for use to prevent or limit plant closings. . . . The Commission places all parties on notice that its action . . . should result in more gas becoming available. . . . for the North Carolina interruptible use, and that the State of North Carolina does and will continue to claim this gas for the benefit of the people of the state of North Carolina. (Interim Order Establishing Emergency Procedures for Allocation of Natural Gas, in Dkt. No. G–100, Sub 18, issued December 5, 1973, at 6.)

59. An Executive Branch review for policy consistency may, however, be difficult to reconcile with the independent status of the Commission. One way to avoid this difficulty would be to transfer the responsibility for formulating curtailment policy to an executive agency with implementation left to the Commission.

Chapter Nine

Constitutional Authority for Government Administration of Energy Shortages

Many aspects of the energy industry are currently regulated, and the constitutionality of much of that regulation has already been tested. This chapter reviews existing authority to determine whether any current regulation by the Federal Power Commission (FPC) or the Federal Energy Administration (FEA), or any alternatives for future regulation may be unconstitutional.

Because natural gas and petroleum are so closely related in terms of their impact on the economy and nation, they will be treated together. Any authority upholding regulation of natural gas is probably equally applicable to petroleum.

The first section considers federal and state authority to regulate and allocate energy supply, and to control energy use. The next section discusses the constitutional limits on state and federal regulation, and the federal-state relationship.

POWER TO REGULATE

Federal authority to regulate energy is drawn mainly from two constitutional bases: the Commerce Clause and the war power, both found in Article I, section 8. State regulation, where it is not prohibited, is based on the state's police power.

"Rationing," "curtailment," "allocation," and "regulation" have different technical meanings, but for constitutional analysis, the terms can be used interchangeably.

Federal Commerce Clause

The Commerce Clause grants to Congress the power "to regulate Commerce with foreign nations, and among the several states, and with the Indian Tribes."

Since the late 1930s, federal authority to regulate based on this power has grown considerably.

National Labor Relations Board v. Jones & Laughlin Steel Corp.[1] upheld the Labor Relations Act and its provisions for collective bargaining in all industries affecting interstate commerce on the ground that labor strife in one factory could affect the cost and supply of goods in other states. *United States v. Darby*[2] upheld the Fair Labor Standards Act (which set minimum wages applicable to all goods shipped in interstate commerce) as applied to an employer who produced goods, some of which were later shipped in interstate commerce. Shipment of goods produced with labor paid less than the minimum wage would conceivably endanger commerce. The Agricultural Adjustment Act, which set quotas for wheat production, was upheld in *Wickard v. Filburn*[3] as applied to a farmer who claimed not even to sell the wheat he grew in excess of the quota. The additive effect that such small excesses might have on a farmer's demand for wheat, and the potential effect on supply if the excesses were sold, justified regulation for the protection of interstate commerce.

Together, these three cases provide for an additive effect test which can reach almost any aspect of an industry. They provide authority for the pretextual use of the Commerce Clause where the real purpose is different from regulation of commerce, and for the complete prohibition of "illegal" goods in interstate commerce. As applied to the energy industry, these precedents show that regulation of energy resource producers, even those selling in what the FPC has defined as the intrastate market with respect to natural gas, is authorized by the Commerce Clause. The fact that some sales in that market can affect the interstate market allows regulation of all sales. Similarly, all consumers have an effect on the whole industry and consequently are subject to regulation. Regardless of the real motivation for regulation, a court would look no further than to say that interstate commerce is affected.

The Natural Gas Act[4] relies on the commerce power, as section 717(a) would suggest. Two major cases have upheld this reliance. Shortly after the Gas Act went into effect, the Illinois Public Service Commission ordered a company to extend its gas lines to an area already served by another company. In *Illinois Natural Gas Co. v. Central Illinois Public Service Co.*[5] it was first determined that the FPC had jurisdiction over the company, and then that the Gas Act required a certificate before the company could expand its service area. Most importantly, the Court held that extensions were so related to commerce, because the volume of gas moving into the state and the distribution among the states would be affected, that the Gas Act's requirement of certification was valid exercise of the commerce power. Since the FPC had jurisdiction, the state order was denied effect.

Later that same year, the rate-setting sections of the Natural Gas Act were upheld in *Federal Power Commission v. Natural Gas Pipeline Co.*[6] In that case, the FPC had found that the company's rates previously in effect were too high and ordered a reduction. Citing *Illinois Natural Gas,* the Court applied the effect test and found regulation justified by the commerce power.[7] Since that time, courts have assumed that all of the Gas Act is soundly based on the Commerce Clause, and the issue of constitutional authorization has either not been raised or not seriously considered.

Thus, the authority of the FPC to require curtailment plans and prohibit some end uses has only been considered within the narrow statutory framework of the Act, rather than in constitutional terms.[8] This does not mean that the federal government lacks constitutional authority in the area. General precedents on the Commerce Clause suggests that no problem exists.

The Emergency Petroleum Allocation Act (EPAA) of 1973[9] is also based on the congressional power to regulate commerce. Section 751 states that the purpose of the Act is "to grant to the President . . . specific temporary authority to deal with shortages . . . or dislocations in their national distribution systems." The authority is to "be exercised for the purpose of minimizing the adverse impacts of such shortages or dislocations on the American people and the domestic economy." Finally, Congress found that "such dislocations jeopardize the normal flow of commerce" and are "a threat to the public health, safety, and welfare. . . ."

The Energy Supply and Environmental Coordination Act (ESECA) of 1974[10] does not indicate in its declaration of purpose that it is based on the commerce power. The sections of the Act relevant to mandatory conversion (to coal from oil or natural gas) and construction orders could probably be based on the Commerce Clause, since the use of fuel by an industry affects interstate commerce.

Neither the EPAA nor ESECA have been challenged as to constitutional authorization, even though they allow the FEA to control the use of all petroleum, not just that which is shipped across state lines. The EPAA also permits FEA regulation at the producer level, both to control prices and allocate supplies. This is much broader than FPC authority. The exemptions under the Gas Act for intrastate gas at not constitutionally necessary, given the authority of *Wickard* and *Darby,* and constitutional challenges to the EPAA and ESECA would seem to be fruitless.[11]

Since the turn of the century, Congress has used the Commerce Clause as a pretext or substitute for a federal police power. Although courts sometimes mention such a federal police power, no congressional legislation appears to have been based wholly or in part upon it. Most federal safety regulation is based on the Commerce Clause.[12] No case authority exists upholding a federal statute based on a police power, and courts have gone to great lengths to find alternative justifications in order to avoid the issue.[13]

Federal War Power

Article I, section 8 of the Constitution gives to Congress the power to declare war, and, through the "necessary and proper clause," the power to enact comprehensive legislation controlling the economy for the purpose of national defense. During World War II, the Emergency Price Control Act of 1942 was upheld as applied to beef price regulation in *Yakus v. United States*[14] and as applied to rent controls in *Bowles v. Willingham.*[15] Bowles pointed out that "[t]he controls adopted by Congress were thought necessary in the interest of the national defense and security" and for "the effective prosecution of the present war."

After the fighting was over, Congress enacted the Housing and Rent Act of 1947, which continued rent controls, and it was upheld as a valid exercise of the war power in *Woods v. Miller Co.*[16] Even though hostilities were ended, the war power authorized legislation to correct a situation caused by the war. The Act itself did not purport to be based on the war power, but the Court went into the legislative history of the purpose to determine that it was valid.

The Defense Production Act (DPA) of 1950,[17] which authorizes the President to allocate resources, including oil and perhaps natural gas, is also based on the war power. Section 2062 declares that

[i]n view of the present international situation and in order to provide for the national defense and national security, our mobilization effort continues to require some diversion of certain materials and facilities from civilian use to military and related purposes. It also requires the development of preparedness programs and the expansion of productive capacity and supply beyond the levels needed to meet the civilian demand, in order to reduce the time required for full mobilization in the event of an attack on the United States.

Although the language is somewhat dated, Congress has recently extended the Act again.

The first major case regarding the DPA upheld the sections authorizing price ceilings. These sections were almost identical to those of the Emergency Price Control Act of 1942. In *United States v. Excel Packing Co.,*[18] the Act was challenged on the ground that, at the time of its enactment, no state of war or general emergency existed. The Tenth Circuit responded that even though the fighting against Germany and Japan was over, the war was not officially ended until 1952, after the DPA was enacted. But regardless of the state of declared war, the court said:[19]

The power and duty of Congress under its war powers to legislate for the national security and welfare exists from the date of recognition of the existence of war emergency and ceases only when it can reasonably be said that the national emergency has come to an end.

Although little case authority exists,[20] this language suggests that oil and natural gas regulation at all levels could be based on the war power of Congress, even in times of relative peace. An oil embargo or an extremely cold winter could have sufficient impact on the economy to endanger national defense.

The closest recent application of the war power to energy allocation came in *Mandel v. Simon.*[21] Governor Mandel had obtained a writ of mandamus in district court ordering the delivery of 16 million gallons of gasoline to Maryland, and the mandamus was reversed on appeal. The court assumed that the Federal Energy Office allocation program was valid under the war power and discussed it as such. The Oil Import Program, which began in 1959 and limited imports of crude oil, was also held to be validly based upon the war power.[22]

The exercise of legislative power is often prompted by what may be called an "emergency." No cases have directly considered whether a *federal* emergency power exists. Two cases concerning state regulation, while upholding the statutes involved, have denied the existence of any independent emergency power at either level of government.[23] Federal emergency legislation can be based on the war power instead.

In conclusion, ample constitutional bases for federal energy rationing are provided by the commerce and war powers. Either power could probably justify almost any form of regulation which is not prohibited by other provisions of the Constitution. However, the case law in areas such as end-use curtailment plans and intrastate energy production and sales gives few direct answers.

State Police Power

State regulation which is not a violation of the Fourteenth Amendment, the Supremacy Clause of the Constitution, an undue burden on commerce, or a violation of the state's own constitution, would be authorized by the reserved police power of the states. As we will see below, the limits on state regulation are quite substantial and may preclude concurrent regulation with the federal government. Nevertheless, many states do regulate the production or consumption of oil and gas where the federal government has not acted.

For example, the New York Public Service Commission has the power to regulate the "manufacture, conveying, transportation, and furnishing of gas . . . and the generation, furnishing and transmission of electricity. . . ."[24] Section 66-a of the New York Public Service Law provides for conservation of gas, preference for domestic use, and discontinuation of supply to industrial consumers when shortages occur. In Texas, the Railroad Commission has comprehensive powers to control the production of gas and oil, including methods to obtain maximum recovery and set prices.[25] Regulation by the Texas Railroad Commission is a prime example of the type of producer state regulation which has been permitted to continue despite the broad scope of the federal power.

Congress has not yet legislated with respect to production or intrastate consumption and transportation of natural gas, although the Federal Power Commission has been found to have some authority under the Natural Gas Act to affect those areas.[26] In addition, section 1 of the Gas Act provides that exempt matters are declared to be "matters primarily of local concern and subject to regulation by the several states."

Before the Gas Act was enacted, *Pennsylvania Gas Co. v. Public Service*

Commission of New York[27] held that New York could set rates on direct sales by pipelines to New York consumers of interstate gas. The Court noted that Congress could preempt the state regulation, but that it had not yet done so. Previously, *Public Utilities Commission v. Landon*[28] had held that rates charged by a distributor to the public were regulatable by the states because that gas was in intrastate commerce.[29] When Congress first enacted the Natural Gas Act, it intended mainly to fill the gap in regulation created by Supreme Court decisions limiting the state's power. Prior decisions had held that the states could regulate interstate gas only after pressure was reduced and it entered the local distribution system.[30]

The various exceptions contained in section 1 of the Gas Act[31] are not contained in the Emergency Petroleum Allocation Act. The omission does not mean that the states have less inherent regulatory power in the absence of federal regulation, but it does increase the likelihood that state regulation will be held preempted or will be found to burden unduly interstate commerce. Absent those limits, a state could regulate any aspect of production, refining, or marketing within its borders.

The states have no more of an independent emergency power than Congress does, but the state police power can justify very extensive regulation during an emergency. *Home Building & Loan Association v. Blaisdell*[32] considered a state law extending the redemption time on mortgages in order to prevent foreclosures. Though the alleged "emergency" was the Depression, the Court upheld the statute on the basis of the state's police power and said with respect to the "emergency":[33]

> Emergency does not create power. Emergency does not increase granted power or remove or diminish the restrictions imposed upon power granted or reserved. . . . While emergency does not create power, emergency may furnish the occasion for the exercise of power.

The Court analogized to the war power of Congress, pointing out that emergency federal legislation could be based upon it. The language of *Blaisdell* concerning "the occasion for the exercise of power" may have been important in the past. However, the relatively light scrutiny the courts have given to economic regulation in recent years makes the phrase much less important now.[34] Consequently, any state regulation of oil and gas will have to be based on the police power.

LIMITS ON THE POWER TO REGULATE

Whatever the constitutional authority of Congress or the states to regulate energy supply, the Constitution also places limits on how far regulation may intrude on private rights. For the sake of continuity, the limits unique to state regulation will be discussed first.

Undue Burden on Commerce

Any state regulation which creates an undue burden on interstate commerce is unconstitutional. To be valid, a state regulation must analytically meet three criteria: (a) it must safeguard an obvious and legitimate state interest; (b) it must not discriminate against interstate commerce; and (c) the state interest in regulation must outweigh any national interest precluding state regulation.[35]

Almost any state regulation of energy supply could be considered protective of a legitimate state interest. Although no case law exists for relating this doctrine to petroleum, several regulations of natural gas have been considered. *Cities Service Gas Co. v. Peerless Oil & Gas Co.*[36] concerned Oklahoma regulations setting minimum wellhead prices for natural gas and requiring ratable takings from wells in various fields. Even though most of the gas was eventually sold in interstate commerce, the regulation met the three criteria and was not considered an undue burden. Importantly, the preemption issue was not present in the case.

Some other aspects of local gas regulation have not been as permissible. Prior to passage of the Natural Gas Act, a West Virginia law required priority for all in-state users of natural gas before it could be "exported" to other states. *Pennsylvania v. West Virginia*[37] held that this law was an unconstitutional burden on interstate commerce and an invalid means to protect the state interest in conserving natural resources. This case is probably still good authority. Therefore, any state rationing scheme favoring in-state users is likely to be considered unconstitutional.

State regulation of gas which does not discriminate against out-of-state consumers has often been permitted under the Commerce Clause. *Panhandle Eastern Pipe Line Co. v. Michigan Public Service Commission*[38] allowed Michigan to require a certificate of public convenience before interstate gas could be sold directly by a pipeline company to in-state consumers. The Court decided that even though the requirement limited interstate gas (commerce), the sale was really local. A further factor in finding that the burden was not unconstitutional was that the FPC could not regulate those sales under the Natural Gas Act.

Prior to passage of the Gas Act, state regulation of rates on sales by distributors to consumers was permitted because only intrastate commerce was affected.[39] Rate-setting on direct sales of interstate gas to consumers had also been upheld as a reasonable burden on interstate commerce.[40] Several years after the Gas Act was passed, the issue on direct sales was raised again in *Panhandle Eastern Pipe Line Co. v. Public Service Commission of Indiana.*[41] The Court reviewed the history of the Natural Gas Act and agreed that the state was attempting to regulate interstate commerce. It suggested that the Commerce Clause probably was not violated, but found an easier basis for a decision. The exemptions in section 1 of the Act were held to authorize this state regulation, even if it burdened interstate commerce.[42]

Limits on state rate regulation solidified some time ago. The question

252 Administration of Energy Shortages

remains, however, as to whether there are constitutional limits on what states may do to control energy supplies, as long as there is no discrimination against out-of-state users. The answer will depend on the third factor mentioned above: the balancing of the national and state interests. Discussion of interest balancing must resort to general precedents because of the small amount of relevant oil and gas case law. The Supreme Court has never struck down an allocation or curtailment plan established by a state regulatory commission on the ground it was an unconstitutional burden on interstate commerce, even though the priorities established by the states are sometimes different from those favored by the FPC. A number of factors are relevant in balancing state and national interests.

From the state viewpoint, if a state must create exceptions in its scheme of regulation for companies which supply interstate markets, the effectiveness of regulation may be destroyed.[43] State regulation of commerce passing through the state may also be valid. *South Carolina State Highway Dept. v. Barnwell Brothers, Inc.*[44] upheld a law restricting the size and weight of all carrier trucks driven in the state. The effect of the regulation was to prevent 80 percent of all trucks currently used from continuing in commerce, a substantial hindrance to interstate commerce. In a very deferential opinion, the Court said that reasonable state highway standards were valid in the absence of any national legislation.

Conservation of natural resources and prevention of environmental destruction are often upheld as legitimate state interests. *Parker v. Brown*[45] considered a California law restricting competition in the raisin business, where 95 percent of the raisins eventually moved into interstate commerce. It was agreed that interstate commerce was affected, but the regulation had effect while the raisins were still in the state. Thus, in the absence of a conflicting national interest, the law was a valid means to "conserve the agricultural wealth of the state." Regulations limiting pollution from ships have been upheld largely because the national interest supports the state interest.[46]

From the national viewpoint, there is a national interest in uniformity of regulation of interstate commerce. This broad interest may sometimes override otherwise legitimate state interests. *Southern Pacific Co. v. Arizona*[47] closely examined and found invalid a state law restricting the length of trains. Under unusually close scrutiny, which provoked dissents, the Court found that the state law in question did not really protect the interest it was intended to guard. The law did force railroads to restrict train lengths in other states, however, causing a great deal of expense and lost time. The national interest in uniformity to avoid the burden on commerce, was overriding. The Court in *Southern Pacific* distinguished *Barnwell* on the tenuous basis that highways are traditionally areas of greater state concern than railroads.

An Illinois law requiring mudguards on trucks was held to be an unconstitutional burden on commerce in *Bibb v. Navajo Freight Lines.*[48] The mudguards Illinois required were different from those permitted in 45 states and were prohibited in 1 other state. The rationale of the decision was the predominant national interest in uniformity and in maintaining free trade. In this case, the earlier *Barnwell* decision was distinguished on the ground that the state law in *Barnwell* did not require equipment that was illegal in other states.

The import of these general precedents for state energy allocation regulation is unclear. At the producer level, a state may set limits on the manner and amount of oil or gas which may be produced, and hence exported. However, a state cannot prohibit sales that cause energy resources to leave the state. At the consumer level, a state may regulate distribution of gas within its borders, even to the point of using a different priority scheme than the FPC's, without unduly burdening interstate commerce.

Federal Preemption

Preemption occurs when the federal government legislates in a field, and the Supremacy Clause of the Constitution precludes state regulation in the same field. Not all federal statutes result in preemption. Even when a statute does preempt, the scope of preemption remains to be ascertained.

Clearly, Congress can enact legislation which preempts virtually all state energy regulation. The only real question is how much state action is preempted by existing federal legislation, based upon a court's understanding of congressional intent. The relevant factors in this regard are the legislative history of federal statutes, the pervasiveness of the federal scheme of regulation, the need for uniformity of regulation, and whether the objectives of federal and state regulation conflict.[49]

Section 6(b) of the EPAA expressly preempts any state or local program for the allocation of petroleum products if it conflicts with the scheme administered by the FEA. The Natural Gas Act does not have an express preemption clause. However, courts have implied preemption in some areas where the FPC is empowered to regulate.

Generally, wherever the FPC is statutorily required to act, preemption exists. The question that arises with FPC curtailment policy is whether that policy, by implication, preempts state policy which is conflicting.

An attempt by Ohio to set rates which an interstate gas pipeline company could charge to a local distributor was held to be preempted by the Natural Gas Act in *Public Utilities Commission of Ohio v. United Fuel Gas Co.*[50] The FPC was held to have exclusive authority over the interstate pipeline's rates.[51] Even though unable to set rates, the state could, however, compel the pipeline company to submit data and records concerning its costs.

Another case in the line of preemption decisions under the Natural Gas Act is *Northern Natural Gas Co. v. State Corp. Commission of Kansas.*[52] Kansas had ordered Northern to take ratably from the wells connected to its pipeline. This was contrary to Northern's contractual obligations and probably to the tariff system it had filed with the FPC. The Court held that Northern was a purchaser, not a producer, and therefore subject to FPC regulation. Thus, the FPC's jurisdiction preempted state regulation. State conservation measures applicable to producers, which are permissible, were distinguished from state regulation of takes by pipeline purchasers from producers.

The cases under the Gas Act have followed a pattern of analysis whereby the court first determines whether the FPC can directly regulate the area. If it can, state statutes are preempted. State authority over a field which the FPC cannot regulate directly is not barred. This means that while concurrent regulation is not allowed, complementary regulation covering areas not reached or exempted by the Gas Act is probably permissible. Thus, the cases support the Congress' intent, in enacting the Natural Gas Act, to fill the gap that state regulation could not reach.[53]

Some state natural gas curtailment plans clearly conflict with FPC established policy. The inability of the FPC, within the existing jurisdictional limits of the Gas Act, to reach local distribution directly, as discussed in Chapter Three, prevents the Commission from being able to rely on the preemption doctrine in order to force state commissions to follow FPC curtailment policy.[54]

State pollution laws may also conflict with petroleum or natural gas allocation regulations. If a federal statute, and the regulations promulgated under it, require a company to take action which would violate state pollution laws, the federal law would presumably prevail. However, almost all case authority on the preemption doctrine concerns situations where a state and Congress have acted in the same specific area for similar purposes.

Impairment of Contracts

The Contract Clause of the Constitution, Article I, section 10, provides that a *state* may not impair the obligations of contracts. Although rarely put in so many words, the Contract Clause does not apply of itself to the federal government.[55] Notwithstanding the absolute language of the Contract Clause, contract rights are subject to the valid exercise of state police power.

One of the leading cases relating the Contract Clause to utility regulation is *Union Dry Goods Co. v. Georgia Public Service Corp.*[56] The utility had contracted to sell Union electricity, but the State of Georgia legislated an increase in rates. Union claimed the Contract Clause prevented the state commission from establishing a higher rate than the contract price. However, the Court responded:

> That private contract rights must yield to the public welfare, where the latter is appropriately declared and defined and the two conflict, has been often decided by this Court.

Where state action under the police power has been necessary, the prohibition against impairment of contracts has not been a serious obstacle. In *Home Build-*

ing & Loan Association v. Blaisdell[57] private contract rights were temporarily suspended, and in *Veix v. Sixth Ward Building & Loan Association*[58] the contract rights were permanently impaired, yet the state statutes were still upheld as valid because of the paramount authority of the state police power. In both cases, the impairment occurred after the parties had contracted.[59]

A state can make compliance with state regulations a condition both of contracts and of doing business in the state. Most states experiencing natural gas shortages have adopted curtailment programs requiring the impairment of contracts. The Contract Clause probably does not preclude such state action. Under the police power, the states can lawfully impair some contracts and preserve others in the event of a shortage.

Taking Property Without Compensation

Thus far, we have considered constitutional limits on state power to act in an energy shortage. We turn now to limitations on the exercise of both federal and state power.

Both the federal and state governments are prohibited by the Fifth and Fourteenth Amendments from taking private property for public use without just compensation.[60] This prohibition has been understood as directed only to direct appropriations, and not to consequential injuries.[61] *Knox v. Lee*[62] said of the Fifth Amendment:

That provision has always been understood as referring only to a direct appropriation, and not to consequential injuries resulting from the exercise of lawful power.

The taking argument has two separate facets which may arise in the context of redistributing energy supplies in a shortage: property may not be taken by the government for *private* use even with compensation; and property may not be taken for *public* use without compensation. The most relevant and extensive general precedent for allocation regulations is *United States v. Central Eureka Mining Co.*[63] That case upheld a 1942 order of the War Production Board closing all nonessential gold mines in an effort to force the reallocation of scarce industrial mining capabilities. The Court noted that regulation can so diminish value as to constitute a taking, but held that deprivation of the most profitable use of property is not necessarily enough to require compensation. *Eureka Mining* is broad case authority to ration or allocate scarce materials, provided that the value of the property involved is not too drastically reduced.[64]

The first major case to address the taking question with respect to the Gas Act was *FPC v. Hope Natural Gas Co.*[65] The FPC had ordered Hope to lower its rates, and the Court found that the requirements of the Constitution concerning taking were not more demanding than the standards of the Natural Gas Act. Since the FPC's rate reduction order was reasonable within the meaning of the Gas Act, it was constitutional. Since *Hope,* challenges to rate orders have usually been on statutory rather than constitutional grounds.

In a case more relevant to rationing, *J.M. Huber Corp. v. FPC*[66] held that FPC refusal to allow abandonment of service by a company was not a taking, as long as the rates set by the FPC were not too low so as to be confiscatory. In other words, as long as rates are reasonable, the FPC can constitutionally require service for any customer.[67]

Federal regulation of oil has also been sustained against taking challenges. *Texas American Asphalt Corp. v. Walker*[68] considered the oil import quota program as applied to a company denied import tickets. Even though the plaintiff would be forced out of business by the denial, the court found the plan legitimately based on national security needs and not a taking. It pointed out that everyone is subject to the risk of injury from the exercise of government authority. Several years later, *Gulf Oil Corp. v. Hickel*[69] also upheld the import program against a similar argument, noting simply that some have to suffer for the sake of national security.

Condor Operating Co. v. Sawhill[70] upheld the buy-sell program established by the FEA under the Emergency Petroleum Allocation Act (EPAA). Condor, which had previously sold its oil to Phillips, sought to terminate its option contract and make a greater profit, but the FEA refused to allow the termination. The Temporary Emergency Court of Appeals found that even though this regulation required an affirmative act (whereas most cases in the past dealt with negative limits), no taking for *private* use had occurred as long as there was adequate compensation.

The issue in *Condor* was what the FEA could order the company to do once the oil was produced. This is to be distinguished from actually ordering an oil company to produce crude oil or requiring a refinery to remain in operation. Apparently, the federal government has not previously chosen to undertake the latter type of regulation and the Supreme Court has not directly considered the issue.

The Energy Policy Act, however, now authorizes the President to order crude oil and natural gas to be produced at specified rates in certain circumstances.[71] It would seem that ordering a reservoir to be produced at the maximum efficient rate, as statutorily defined, would not involve a taking since, by definition, there would be no loss in ultimate recovery from the reservoir, and, of course, the owner would be fully compensated for the oil or gas produced. Although ordering a reservoir to be produced at the temporary emergency production rate may result in some loss in ultimate recovery, according to the definition, the amount would not be "significant." It may be argued that any taking would be de minimis and highly speculative in amount and, consequently, that the affected property owner would still not be entitled to compensation under the Constitution.

The FEA regulations forcing sales to independents at reduced prices were at issue in *Union Oil Co. v. FEA.*[72] The court first held that given Congress' intent to protect independents, the power to allocate and set prices under the EPAA did not end when the scarcity was over. Then it refused to grant a temporary restraining order because there was very little likelihood of success for the plaintiff's taking argument.

Similarly, the FEA's entitlements program, under which well-supplied companies have to pay for the right to process part of their "old" oil, did not present a substantial enough constitutional taking question to justify certification to TECA.[73] The Court recognized that the entitlement purchase price could be passed on to the consumer. Although the refiner might still incur some loss, it was not enough to be a taking.

The question arises whether the Fifth Amendment applies any more stringently to legislation enacted under the Commerce Clause than under the war power. *United States v. Central Eureka Mining Co.*[74] pointed out in dictum that in time of war, courts are especially reluctant to find that a taking has occurred. *Omnia Commercial Co. v. United States*[75] held that wartime regulation of steel production, which impaired contract rights, was not a taking necessitating compensation. The Court acknowledged that some rights had been taken, but during wartime so many contracts had to be disrupted that on policy grounds the government could not afford to provide compensation. These cases do not specify whether the war power merits lower constitutional restraints, or whether the risk of war balances more heavily against constitutional rights than the federal needs usually invoked for regulation under the Commerce Clause. If the former is really true, rationing under the Defense Production Act may be less restrained than under the EPAA.[76] Regardless of the reason, federal regulatory action taken in an emergency is not likely to be struck down for constitutional reasons. The FEA has carefully taken advantage of this flexibility.

Because the Contract Clause does not apply to the federal government, courts have sometimes been willing to use the Fifth Amendment to protect contract rights, particularly if the United States itself is one party to the contract instead of an "impartial" regulator. In *Lynch v. United States,*[77] a federal statute, which repealed all federal laws granting yearly renewable insurance, was held violative of the Fifth Amendment. Without compensation, it deprived owners of insurance policies of contractual rights acquired from the federal government.

Valid contracts are property, whether the obligor be a private individual, a municipality, a state, or the United States. Rights against the United States arising out of a contract with it are protected by the Fifth Amendment. . . . As Congress had the power to authorize the Bureau of War Risk Insurance to issue them, the due process clause prohibits the United States from annulling them, unless, indeed, the action falls within the federal police power or some other paramount power. . . .[78]

Situations where the federal government is not a party to the contract generally yield a different outcome in court. In *Gajewski v. United States*[79] a farmer, who was prosecuted for a violation of the Agricultural Adjustment Act, unsuccessfully claimed that federal limits on land he purchased without restrictions were an unconstitutional impairment of contract. The court referred to the right of Congress to enact laws in the public interest, and declined to even seriously consider the contract argument. Similarly, *Block v. Hirsh*[80] upheld an act of Congress which greatly restricted a landlord's right to evict a tenant who continued to pay rent, against a claim that the law was an unconstitutional restriction on the right to contract. In both of these cases, a taking argument also failed to protect the contract.

Should the Congress specifically restrict contracts for oil and gas, such regulation would be valid. In *Mississippi River Fuel Corp. v. FPC*[81] the Natural Gas Act was upheld as a constitutional regulation of an industry subject to control for the public good, even though it impaired contracts made prior to the effective date of the Act. The court relied largely on *Union Dry Goods Co. v. Georgia Public Service Corp.*[82] discussed above, to reach its conclusion.

Even though Congress can constitutionally impair many contracts for oil and natural gas, the legislative histories of the Gas Act and the EPAA make it clear that this regulatory approach is to be followed only to the extent necessary. Courts generally try to avoid constitutional questions, and in this case Congress has tried to help. Avoidance of the contract problem may in the future result in strained interpretations of regulatory acts.[83] Another input for consideration is whether gas and oil companies need the government to impair their contractual obligations in order to protect themselves from liability in suits for damages reaching into the billions of dollars.[84]

In general, as long as any federal regulation of oil or natural gas allows a reasonable amount of compensation, the taking without compensation argument will fail, whether the regulation forces sales, denies the right to produce, or sets prices. State regulation meeting those same criteria would also be valid.

Undue Discrimination

Almost any plan for allocating energy will treat some purchasers more favorably than others, and will also favor some sellers, i.e., independents and small refiners. Yet if there is any rational basis, the different treatment will not constitute unconstitutional discrimination.[85]

Under the Sugar Act of 1948, the Secretary of Agriculture was authorized to set quotas on sugar sales from various regions and to allocate production among refineries. The Secretary went so far as to allocate production among refineries only for Puerto Rico. Yet *Secretary of Agriculture v. Central Roig Refining Co.*[86] held that the distinction was not arbitrary and capricious, and therefore not unduly discriminatory.

With respect to the natural gas industry, differences in FPC treatment based upon the mandates of the Gas Act have been upheld. *Superior Oil Co. v. FPC*[87] upheld the different treatment afforded pipeline companies and producers under the FPC's rules. It was held that the Gas Act contemplated classification and authorized the FPC distinctions. Similarly, as to the petroleum industry, *Union Oil Co. v. FEA*[88] held that granting greater benefits to large independent refiners was not an arbitrary and capricious distinction, given the intent of Congress expressed in the EPAA.

Procedural Due Process

A regulatory agency will be forced to make many decisions affecting the energy industry and the national economy once it intervenes in order to direct the distribution of available supplies. Theoretically, all such decisions are subject to the constitutional requirements of procedural due process. Practically, however, the balancing of factors involved in particular situations will impose stricter due process limits on some decisions than on others.

Internal policy decisions cannot be challenged until they are manifested in a decision that affects someone directly. However, some agency actions which are not normally thought of as decisions are nevertheless subject to certain limitations. Particular functions which we will discuss here include investigations, rulemaking, adjudication, and judicial review.

Before any elements of due process are required by the Constitution, it must be found that the government action affects an interest in "life, liberty, or property." The administration of an energy shortage is most likely to affect individual property rights. Such rights were discussed in *Board of Regents v. Roth:*[89]

> . . . the property interests protected by procedural due process extend well beyond actual ownership of real estate, chattels, or money. . . . To have a property interest in a benefit, a person must . . . have a legitimate claim of entitlement to it. . . . Property interests . . . are created and their dimensions are defined by existing rules or understandings that stem from an independent source, such as state law—rules or understandings that secure certain benefits and that support claims of entitlement to those benefits.[90]

Decisions as to whether a sufficient property interest exists to merit due process protection are somewhat result-oriented and thus not entirely predictable. It is clear that resource owners and probably also contract purchasers, whose ability to purchase may be impaired, have sufficient property interests. The more difficult question concerns non-contractual purchasers such as individual motorists. Perhaps a showing of the effect energy allocation, such as motor gasoline rationing, would have on other property and liberty interests would be enough to require procedural due process in decisions affecting them.

With any government rationing scheme, at least some individuals or companies will have a sufficient property interest to reach at least the balancing stage of procedural due process. Analytically, three factors will be considered in deciding whether a party is entitled to any particular element of procedure: (a) the interest of the party challenging the current procedure and the extent to which that interest is affected; (b) the interest of the government agency in not having to grant the aspect of procedure; and (c) the contribution the particular element is likely to make toward reaching a fair and just decision on the merits.[91] These factors may require some elements of procedure, e.g., notice or hearing, and not others, e.g., administrative appeal or judicial review, depending entirely upon the facts of a given case.

Investigations. An agency may use investigations for several purposes. They can be used to discover information, publicize illegal activities as an enforcement device, pressure industry, and educate the public. Sometimes investigations are completely internal and without hearings. On other occasions, hearings may be held. The FPC and FEA generally do not hold investigatory hearings. The FEA's primary investigatory devices are audits and Notices of Probable Violation. The FEA does not provide any of the procedures commonly associated with due process for either device.

To the extent that the FPC or FEA seek only to hold hearings for the purpose of investigation, as opposed to adjudication, few elements of judicial procedure are required. For example, *Hannah v. Larche*[92] found that investigations by the Commission on Civil Rights of allegation of racial discrimination did not deprive anyone of due process rights. Therefore, the Commission was not required to inform a witness of the specific charges against him, to allow a witness to confront his accusor, or to permit a witness to cross-examine other witnesses. In general, cases are rare where courts have required some particular procedures for investigatory hearings.

Rulemaking. For FPC or FEA rulemaking, few procedures are constitutionally compelled. Those that are required are mandated either in the applicable statutes or the APA.

A leading case on price controls, *Bowles v. Willingham,*[93] held that public hearings were not required before regulations imposing price controls went into effect. The Court said that Congress need not give notice and a hearing before it acts; and, therefore, those procedures are not required if the task is delegated to an administrative agency under its rulemaking authority. *Bi-Metalic Investment Co. v. State Board,*[94] an earlier decision which developed the legislative/adjudicative fact distinction, was cited as authority for the proposition that it was simply impractical to give notice to all landlords during wartime. Subsequently, *Bowles* has been cited for the general statement: "[n]or is there any constitutional requirement under the Due Process Clause of the Fifth Amendment, or otherwise, for public evidentiary hearings in connection with such rulemaking."[95]

Another important case of more recent vintage on procedural due process is *United States v. Lieb,*[96] in which a landlord was enjoined from increasing his rent. The landlord claimed he was denied due process since he was unable to get an administrative hearing on his claim that the economic stabilization regulations exceeded the statutory authority granted to the Cost of Living Council. The Temporary Emergency Court of Appeals noted that an administrative hearing was available on other claims, and held that the full hearing the landlord received in District Court was all that was necessary for due process. The FEA has also occasionally used this substitution of judicial review for administrative hearings.

Other cases involving wage-price controls relied on the emergency nature of the situation in reaching decisions that the government interest in avoiding a hearing before the promulgation of rules outweighed any individual's need. For example, the plaintiffs in *California Teachers Association v. Newport Mesa Unified School District*[97] attempted to enjoin application of the freeze to their salary increase. The teachers lost when the court held that ". . . one may be deprived of property by summary Federal Administrative action taken without a hearing when such action is essntial to protect a vital governmental interest."

Pacific Coast Meat Cutters Association, Inc. v. Cost of Living Council[93] held that the 1973 freeze on beef prices did not require formal hearings because of the emergency situation, but the constitutional issues were not reached until *Western State Meat Packers Association v. Dunlop.*[99] Citing *Bowles* and *Lieb,* the court there said that a requirement of notice and hearing would frustrate the entire scheme, so they were not required by the Fifth Amendment. These cases suggest that in the event of an embargo or very cold winter, the federal government would not be under constitutional compulsion to grant hearings before adopting temporary or short-term allocation rules.

In fact, the FEA frequently did not provide a hearing before rulemaking, and the procedural due process argument was never seriously considered as a limit on the agency's ability to act in an emergency. In a non-emergency situation, the issue may become more serious. However, the applicable requirements of FEAA, the Gas Act, and the APA are probably stricter than the Constitution requires. It should be noted that the decided cases assume subsequent judicial review was available to provide hearings without reducing the agency's ability to act quickly in an emergency. Therefore, a long-term allocation plan may require hearings after a temporary plan is implemented.

Superior Oil Co. v. FPC[100] upheld such an FPC rulemaking practice against a procedural due process challenge. The court there, perhaps overbroadly, said that "[i]n legislation, or rule-making, there is no constitutional right to any hearing whatsoever." Subsequent cases have held that when the FPC establishes rates by rulemaking, the Gas Act requires various procedural elements.[101]

262 Administration of Energy Shortages

However, the Constitution alone requires few procedural elements for rule-making regarding federal energy rationing.

Adjudication and administrative appeal. Adjudication in the sense used here includes orders issued to companies and consumers which are not rules. The FEA uses a wide array of adjudicatory devices for adjusting, enforcing, and appealing agency decisions and policies. Congress exempted the FEA from the adjudicatory requirements of the APA. Consequently, the agency does not provide a hearing, the right to have counsel, an impartial decision-maker, or any other typical judicial procedure; it usually allows submission of evidence, but not always. The FEA has never lost in the courts on due process as applied to its administrative procedures, but judicial review has always been available to those affected. What would be constitutionally required in the absence of judicial review is unclear, but it would probably not be extensive.

The courts have also been flexible toward the FPC's adjudicatory procedures where they have not been prescribed by the Gas Act or the APA. *Sun Oil Co. v. FPC*[102] held that notice of adjudication was not required to a co-owner of gas who did not sign the contracts or operate the wells when only issues of law were to be considered. *Interstate Power Co. v. FPC*[103] allowed the FPC to reject suggestions made during hearings for zone definitions for uniform rates and select new ones without holding a new hearing. The fact that the FPC is considered an "expert agency" led the court to conclude that there was no violation of due process.

Judicial review. Courts are somewhat more reluctant to preclude judicial review of agency decisions, although it is constitutionally permissible. "[O]nly a showing of clear and convincing evidence of legislative intent will justify a court in precluding access to judicial review."[104]

In appropriate circumstances, however, courts have held administrative action non-reviewable. *Schilling v. Rogers*[105] held non-reviewable decisions of the Director of the Office of Alien Property concerning eligibility to recover property seized under the Trading with the Enemy Act. In this case, judicial review was precluded by the finding that the matter was "committed to agency discretion," within the meaning of section 10 of the APA, and that Congress had specifically precluded review in the Trading with the Enemy Act. *Chernock v. Gardner*[106] decided that attorney's fees set by the hearing examiners in Social Security Act hearings were not judicially reviewable, no matter how arbitrary the hearing examiner's decision may have been.

> It is within the power of Congress to provide the conditions under which an administrative proceeding may be reviewed in the Courts and to determine their jurisdiction.[107]

* * *

In conclusion, the Constitution imposes very few significant limits on federal action during an emergency. The limits on state action are more substantial, but most often state limits are the result of prior federal action.[108] As far as the capacity of the federal government to administer an energy shortage is concerned, there is no significant constitutional limitation. The most important possible limitation would be on the supply side, and that would be concerned with the government's ability to compel production of oil or gas from lands that are privately owned. Even here, the outcome would probably depend on the exigencies of the case.

NOTES TO CHAPTER NINE

1. 301 U.S. 1 (1937).
2. 312 U.S. 100 (1941).
3. 317 U.S. 111 (1942).
4. 15 U.S.C. §§717 *et seq.* (1970).
5. 314 U.S. 498 (1942).
6. 315 U.S. 575, 582 (1942).
7. The Court also interpreted the Natural Gas Act provisions for "just and reasonable" rates as permitting any rates which were not so low as to be confiscatory and hence a violation of the Fifth Amendment of the U.S. Constitution.
8. In FPC v. Transcontinental Gas Pipe Line Corp., 365 U.S. 1 (1960), an FPC refusal to certify transportation of gas into a state where it would be used as boiler fuel was upheld. The Court mentioned preemption of pipeline space and effects on the price level of gas, so it was probably valid under the Commerce Clause, but the issue was not directly addressed. Again in FPC v. Louisiana Power & Light, 406 U.S. 621 (1972), in which a curtailment plan affecting direct sales was upheld as within FPC jurisdiction, the constitutional issues of FPC authority under the Commerce Clause and taking without compensation were not raised.
9. 15 U.S.C. §§751 *et seq.* (Supp. III, 1973).
10. 15 U.S.C.A. §§791 *et seq.* (Supp. 1975).
11. The Sugar Act of 1948, which set quotas for sugar sales by producers within areas of the United States and authorized allocation among refineries for production, was upheld in Secretary of Agriculture v. Central Roig Refining Co., 338 U.S. 604, 614 (1950). Regulation of *all* sales (including intrastate) was validly based on the Commerce Clause, since without allocation the competitive nature of the sugar industry might be destroyed, thereby impairing interstate commerce. This rationale is analogous to one purpose of the EPAA, namely, that of protecting independents and small refiners and distributors.
12. *E.g.,* Northern States Power Co. v. Minnesota, 447 F.2d 1143 (8th Cir. 1971), *aff'd mem.,* 405 U.S. 1035 (1972), regarding regulation of radioactive effluent releases from nuclear power plants by the U.S. Atomic Energy Commission (now Nuclear Regulatory Commssion).

13. An example of how courts have avoided relying on a federal police power is shown by the interpretation of the Labor Management Relations Act, 29 U.S.C. § § 151 *et. seq.* (1970) in United Steelworkers of American v. United States, 361 U.S. 39 (1959). The Act provides in §178 for enjoining strikes where they would affect an industry in interstate commerce *and* "imperil the national health or safety" if continued. Rather than uphold the Act on national welfare grounds, the Court found that the existing steel strike could endanger national defense, and upheld the injunction and the Act on that basis. This Act also was designed to cope with an emergency, but the Court ignored that as a constitutional justification.

14. 321 U.S. 414 (1944).

15. 321 U.S. 503 (1944).

16. 333 U.S. 138 (1948).

17. 50 U.S.C. App. § § 2061 *et seq.* (1970).

18. 210 F.2d 596 (10th Cir.), *cert. denied,* 348 U.S. 817 (1954).

19. *Id.* at 598.

20. Other lower courts also upheld DPA regulations of prices, *e.g.,* United States v. K. & F. Packing & Food Corp., 102 F. Supp. 26 (W.D.N.Y. 1951); United States v. Ericson, 102 F. Supp. 376 (D. Minn. 1951), *appeal dismissed,* 205 F.2d 420 (8th Cir. 1953).

21. 493 F.2d 1239 (T.E.C.A. 1974).

22. *E.g.,* Texas American Asphalt Corp. v. Walker, 177 F. Supp. 315 (S.D. Tex. 1959).

23. Veix v. Sixth Ward Building & Loan Association, 310 U.S. 32 (1940); Home Building & Loan Association v. Blaisdell, 290 U.S. 398 (1934).

24. N.Y. Pub. Serv. Law §64 (McKinney 1955).

25. Texas Rev. Civ. Stat. art. 6008 (1925).

26. FPC v. Louisiana Power & Light Co., 406 U.S. 671 (1972).

27. 252 U.S. 23 (1920).

28. 249 U.S. 238 (1919).

29. Note that these two cases were decided before the Natural Gas Act was passed, and that subsequent holdings on preemption have modified the extent of state authority. The discussion here is meant only to show what action is permitted by the police power.

30. *See generally,* FPC v. East Ohio Gas Co., 338 U.S. 464, 472 (1950).

31. 15 U.S.C. §717 (1970).

32. 290 U.S. 398 (1934).

33. *Id.* at 425–26.

34. Veix v. Sixth Ward Building & Loan Association, 310 U.S. 32 (1940), considered a state statute which permanently impaired the obligations of a contract. Again, the statute was upheld as based on the police power, but not any emergency power. The important aspect of the holding was that the emergency which gave rise to the legislation did not limit or constrain its continuation after the emergency conditions ended.

35. This description of the criteria was taken from Cities Service Gas Co. v. Peerless Oil & Gas Co., 340 U.S. 179, 186 (1950). Many decisions and commentators use different descriptions, but analytically the criteria are the same.

36. *Id.*

37. 262 U.S. 544 (1922).

38. 341 U.S. 329 (1951).

39. Public Utilities Commission v. Landon, 249 U.S. 236 (1919).

40. Pennsylvania Gas Co. v. Public Service Commission, 253 U.S. 23 (1920).

41. 332 U.S. 507 (1947). The major issue in that case was whether the Natural Gas Act preempted the state regulation which had previously been allowed.

42. The Court relied heavily for authority upon Prudential Ins. Co. v. Benjamin, 328 U.S. 408 (1946), which allowed discrimination against out-of-state insurance companies based on a "delegation" by Congress. This case is the major source of precedent in the area of congressional "consent" to undue burdens on commerce.

43. *See, e.g.,* Milk Control Board v. Eisenberg Farm Products, 306 U.S. 346 (1939). In that case, Pennsylvania sought to prosecute the defendant for violation of a state statute requiring licenses, minimum prices, and filed bonds for all milk dealers. Most milk production went into intrastate sales, and Eisenberg claimed that its interstate sales exempted it. The Supreme Court found that the defendant could be regulated, since there was no discrimination and Congress had not displayed a national interest in the field.

44. 303 U.S. 177 (1938).

45. 317 U.S. 341 (1943).

46. Huron Portland Cement Co. v. Detroit, 362 U.S. 440 (1960).

47. 325 U.S. 761 (1945).

48. 359 U.S. 520 (1959).

49. A good framework for analysis in the complex area of nuclear power plant regulation is provided in Northern States Power Co., v. Minnesota, 447 F.2d 1143 (8th Cir. 1971), *aff'd mem.,* 405 U.S. 1035 (1972).

50. 317 U.S. 456 (1943).

51. This situation should be distinguished from state regulaton of rates charged by distributors to consumers, which is expressly not preempted.

52. 372 U.S. 84 (1963).

53. Almost any time a field is regulated by Congress for national defense or foreign affairs reasons, supplementary state regulation is preempted. Hines v. Davidowitz, 312 U.S. 52 (1941), struck down the Pennsylvania alien registration scheme, citing national supremacy in foreign affairs and the need for uniformity (even though no conflict existed). Pennsylvania v. Nelson, 350 U.S. 497 (1956), invalidated a state law punishing sedition against the United States. The federal interest in punishing sedition for national defense was so dominant that all state laws on the subject were impliedly preempted. The deference paid to national defense legislation may mean that state energy rationing schemes would be more likely preempted if future federal legislation were based on the war power than if it were based on the commerce power.

54. At this point, some of the particular fact situations where litigation could arise should be noted. Currently the FPC does not enforce a curtailment plan at the distributor level, and only determines the amount to be sold to each distributor by the pipeline. The result of the priority plan is that distributors

within a state may be supplied at widely varying levels in relation to current requirements. This may cause a state to be unable to implement its own priorities without moving gas from one distributor to another. The only physical interconnection existing will be the pipeline, and to effect the redistribution, a state may deny one distributor the right to purchase above a set level, hoping to force the pipeline and the FPC into allowing sales to other distributors.

Another question concerns direct sales which have been curtailed by the pipeline. If the FPC required a distributor to supply that purchaser, it would divert supplies from higher FPC priorities. The differences between what the state agencies and the FPC can directly order and de facto require will enormously complicate litigation and make resort to statutory interpretation and legislative history very difficult.

55. In some cases, private contract rights are protected against federal action through the Fifth Amendment prohibition against taking for public use without compensation. *See* United States v. One 1962 Ford Thunderbird, 232 F. Supp. 1019 (N.D. Ill. 1964).

56. 248 U.S. 372 (1919).

57. 290 U.S. 398 (1934).

58. 310 U.S. 32 (1940).

59. In a more recent case, City of El Paso v. Simmons, 379 U.S. 497 (1965), a state law limiting the time for redemption to avoid forfeiture of public land sales contracts was upheld, citing *Blaisdell* as authority that the Contract Clause is subject to the state police power.

60. Probably the two amendments pose identical limits on the states and Congress; at least, no distinction is apparent. Most of the case law considers the Fifth Amendment and federal statutes. State courts still tend to scrutinize legislative decisions more closely than federal courts, thus a state statute *practically* may be more difficult to sustain, especially given state constitutional provisions and their interpretation.

61. In any case, only rights protected by law require compensation when taken for public use. United States v. Willow River Power Co., 324 U.S. 499, 510 (1945), found that the government navigation work which indirectly raised the level of a navigable stream and thereby decreased the plaintiff's ability to generate electricity was not a taking. The Court pointed out that not all economic interests are property rights, and this one was not.

62. 79 U.S. (12 Wall.) 457, 551 (1870).

63. 357 U.S. 155, 166, 168 (1958).

64. Most precedents concern price or rent regulations rather than allocation-type situations. One major case concerning the elimination of a landlord's previously held rights is Fleming v. Rhodes, 331 U.S. 100, 107 (1947). The Court upheld provisions of the Emergency Price Control Act of 1942 which prevented landlords from evicting tenants, even though the rights were previously acquired. In general, federal regulation of future action based on previously acquired rights is not an unconstitutional taking.

65. 320 U.S. 591, 607 (1944).

66. 232 F.2d 550 (3d Cir. 1956), *cert. denied,* 352 U.S. 971 (1957).

67. Subsequent cases in lower courts have upheld other aspects of FPC regulation against taking claims. Gas Service Co. v. FPC, 282 F.2d 496 (D.C.

Cir. 1960), *cert. dismissed,* 366 U.S. 927 (1961), considered the inability of the FPC to suspend industrial rate increases or require bonds from the gas company, and easily decided that purchasers were not deprived of property.

68. 177 F. Supp. 315 (S.D. Tex. 1959).

69. 435 F.2d 440 (D.C. Cir. 1970).

70. 514 F.2d 351 (T.E.C.A. 1975).

71. Pub. L. No. 94–163 §106 (1975). Litigation officials in the FEA, however, believe this is a serious constitutional issue. Much of the problem with such a statute or regulation affirmatively ordering production is psychological acceptance, because the government has never before taken such an extreme step in regulation. In terms of profitability, the industry is not affected differently, but in some senses it has become government-operated for the public benefit.

The Thirteenth Amendment and its prohibition of involuntary servitude has also been mentioned in this context. The Supreme Court has rarely considered that prohibition, and even more rarely in the regulation of business. Marcus Brown Holding Co. v. Feldman, 256 U.S. 170 (1921), upheld a New York law which made it a misdemeanor for a lessor not to provide some specified services if required by the lease. Without any discussion of precedent, the Court stated that the acts were not strictly personal services, but rather ones analogous to services which under the old common law were attached to the land. More recently, and equally tersely, Heart of Atlanta Motel, Inc. v. United States, 379 U.S. 24 (1964), upheld the sections of the Civil Rights Act of 1964 requiring operators to serve blacks. No case has considered the harder question behind these cases: could the landlord be prevented from withdrawing his property from the market and the hotel stopped from refusing to serve *all* customers in defiance of anti-discrimination provisions?

72. No. CV74–1943 (C.D. Cal., July 25, 1974), *printed at* 3 *CCH Energy Management* ¶ 26,007.

73. Gulf Oil Corp. v. FEA, 391 F. Supp. 856 (W.D.Pa. 1975).

74. 357 U.S. 155 (1958).

75. 251 U.S. 502 (1923).

76. Yet the war power is limited by individual constitutional rights and the Fifth Amendment. Aptheker v. Secretary of State, 378 U.S. 500 (1964), held that even though protection of national security justified the Subversive Activities Control Act of 1950, as applied to some people, the powers of government must be exercised in achieving that end in a manner not unduly infringing constitutionally protected freedoms. United States v. 15.3 Acres of Land in the City of Scranton, Pa., 154 F. Supp. 770 (M.D. Pa., 1957), *reversed on other grounds,* 264 F.2d 112 (3d Cir. 1959), held that even if the war power is used, the government cannot take land without paying.

77. 292 U.S. 571 (1934).

78. *Id.* at 578.

79. 327 F.2d 239 (8th Cir. 1964).

80. 256 U.S. 134, 156 (1921).

81. 121 F.2d 159 (8th Cir. 1941).

82. 248 U.S. 372 (1919), discussed note 56 supra.

83. In Amoco Production Co. v. FPC, 491 F.2d 916, 922 (10th Cir. 1973), the court said that the Gas Act was not intended to abrogate private contract

rates and the FPC could change negotiated contract rates only if they were so low or so high as to affect the public interest. At issue was an FPC regulation limiting a maximum price-supply cost difference for a company shipping interstate gas. Rather than adjust the contract price which created a greater profit for the company, the regulation was interpreted to avoid the conflict.

84. It is by no means clear that such use of the federal government's privileges can protect companies from liability. Logically, performance of the contracts was impossible absent government action, and most impossibility of performance cases (along these lines) arise because the government itself created the impossibility. It is arguable that the risk of inability to obtain supplies should fall on the pipelines, but a court will be uneasy about subjecting a pipeline company to damages of a billion dollars when such a result would greatly aggravate an existing curtailment in service. *See* International Paper Co. v. FPC, 476 F.2d 121, 125 (5th Cir. 1973), discussed in Chapter Three.

85. The Equal Protection clause of the Fourteenth Amendment is not included in the Fifth Amendment. In order to apply the same standards to both levels of government, however, courts have used an analysis whereby federal due process includes equal protection.

86. 338 U.S. 604 (1950).

87. 322 F.2d 601 (9th Cir. 1963), *cert. denied,* 377 U.S. 922 (1964).

88. No. CV74-1943 (C.D. Cal., July 25, 1974), *printed at 3 CCH Energy Management* ¶ 26,007.

89. 408 U.S. 564, 570 (1972).

90. *Id.* at 571-72, 577.

91. Bell v. Burson, 402 U.S. 535 (1971), concerning revocation of driver's licenses after accidents, held that the interest in being able to drive is sufficient to require a hearing. Fitzgerald v. Hampton, 467 F.2d 755 (D.C. Cir. 1972), found that the right to hold specific private employment and follow a chosen profession free from unreasonable government interference comes within the liberty and property interests of the Fifth Amendment. *See also* Goldberg v. Kelley, 397 U.S. 254 (1970). A good general description of the factors involved and their application is found in Hahn v. Gottlieb, 430 F.2d 1243 (1st Cir. 1970). This analysis is almost universally accepted, with only minor modifications.

92. 363 U.S. 420 (1960).

93. 321 U.S. 502, 519 (1944).

94. 239 U.S. 441 (1915).

95. California Citizens Band Association, Inc. v. United States, 275 F.2d 43 (9th Cir.) *cert. denied,* 389 U.S. 844 (1967).

96. 462 F.2d 1161 (T.E.C.A. 1972).

97. 333 F. Supp. 436 (C.D. Cal. 1971).

98. 481 F.2d 1388 (T.E.C.A. 1973).

99. 482 F.2d 1401 (T.E.C.A. 1973).

100. 322 F.2d 601 (9th Cir. 1963), *cert. denied,* 377 U.S. 922 (1964).

101. *See, e.g.,* American Public Gas Association v. FPC, 498 F.2d 718 (D.C. Cir. 1974).

102. 256 F.2d 233 (5th Cir.), *cert. denied,* 358 U.S. 872 (1958).

103. 236 F.2d 372 (8th Cir. 1956), *cert. denied,* 352 U.S. 967 (1957).

104. New Jersey Chapter, Inc. of A.P.T.A., Inc. v. Prudential Life Ins. Co., 502 F.2d 500 (D.C. Cir. 1974).

105. 363 U.S. 666 (1960).

106. 360 F.2d 257 (3d Cir. 1966).

107. *Id.* at 259.

108. This discussion would not be complete without mention of the non-delegation doctrine. Put simply, "no responsible delegation is likely to be held unconstitutional. The non-delegation doctrine does not prevent the delegation of legislative power. It does not prevent delegation of power to make law and to exercise discretion in individual cases. And it does not even assure meaningful legislative standards." K. Davis, *Administrative Law Text* §2.01 (1972).

A few cases have briefly considered the non-delegation doctrine as applied to the Defense Production Act and the Emergency Petroleum Allocation Act. United States v. K. & F. Packing & Food Corp., 102 F. Supp. 26 (W.D.N.Y. 1951), held that Presidential allocations under the DPA were not unconstitutional delegations. FEA regulations were upheld as lawful delegation in Condor Operating Co. v. Sawhill, 514 F.2d 351 (T.E.C.A. 1975).

Rationing under existing federal legislation will not be struck down as an unconstitutional delegation of legislative authority. Any future legislation which included purposes of the Act, and probably even if it did not, would be valid. Some states still adhere to remnants of the non-delegation doctrine, e.g., State v. Traffic Tel. Workers' Federation of N.J., 2 N.J. 335, 66 A.2d 616 (1949), but it is not likely to be a major barrier to a rational state rationing plan. K. Davis, *supra* at §2.06.

❋   *Chapter Ten*

Administration of Natural Gas and Petroleum Shortages

This chapter summarizes the problem of administering the kind of petroleum and natural gas shortages that may be expected in the United States in the late 1970s, and sets forth our conclusions and recommendations. As this book goes to press, the Energy Policy and Conservation Act of 1975, which substantially affects the administration of petroleum shortages as well as the pricing of petroleum products, is still a relatively fresh piece of legislation. The Act remains to be developed administratively. Moreover, the Senate and House have each passed bills which would deregulate natural gas prices, but in radically different ways. Meanwhile, an emergency bill specifically designed to deal with the natural gas shortage has been shunted aside in the House. The political atmosphere surrounding the natural gas pricing issue is thus highly charged as the 1976 election year begins. The various forces at work may neutralize each other in the short run, and thereby further postpone major new natural gas legislation.

The question whether or by how much an increase in U.S. energy prices will bring about an expansion of domestic reserves of petroleum and gas remains unanswered. Any attempt to provide an answer will be necessarily speculative and surely controversial.

Our study has not addressed the merits of government deregulation of energy prices. However, it does reveal over and over again the difficulties, distortions, and inefficiencies that arise from government intervention in the energy market in order to direct the distribution of supplies. In this sense, our study may be read as an indirect or implied justification for primary reliance on the price mechanism as a better allocator of energy supplies in the long run than any practical method of government administration in a society with democratic political institutions.

271

Nevertheless, in view of the deepening natural gas and potential petroleum shortages that appear likely in the late 1970s and early 1980s, the U.S. government would be derelict in its duty and the American people might be gravely and unnecessarily injured unless an administrative capacity is developed and used to manage energy shortages effectively and fairly. It is sometimes argued that any step to make government administration of energy shortages more effective and equitable should be avoided because it would reduce political pressure for deregulation of energy prices. This argument is not persuasive in view of the increased damage to the nation that would result from ineffective government administration of a shortage.

Whatever government does to administer an energy shortage will cause hardship for large numbers of persons. But the damage will be much greater if nothing is done.

THE PROBLEM SUMMARIZED

Energy is a pervasive necessity in an advanced industrial society such as the United States.

Currently, natural gas provides about 30 percent of total U.S. energy consumption. Natural gas provides more than 50 percent of the energy used directly in the household and commercial sectors, almost 50 percent of the energy used directly in the industrial sector, and about 20 percent of the primary energy used to generate electricity which is then distributed to the other sectors.

Petroleum provides about 45 percent of total U.S. energy consumption. It accounts for 45 percent of the household and commercial sectors, more than 25 percent of the industrial sector, about 95 percent of the transportation sector, and almost 20 percent of the energy required for electricity generation.

The U.S. economy and American society in general are likely to become increasingly vulnerable to energy shortages in the future.

It is generally accepted that in the late 1970s the severity of the natural gas shortage will increase substantially. It is difficult to estimate the shortfall between available supply and demand because of the existence of alternate fuel capabilities in the industrial and electric utility sectors and because of the uncertain future of federal price regulation or deregulation at the wellhead.

In the interstate market, natural gas curtailments were forecasted to reach 15 percent of total demand in 1975. However, an abnormally warm winter, a slack economy, and increased switches to fuel oil by industrial concerns fearing substantial curtailments, reduced actual demands for natural gas so that the curtailment problem was quite manageable. A cold winter in 1976–77 could increase whatever shortfall then is forecasted by 5–10 percent. Moreover, economic recovery would increase demands for natural gas in both interstate and intrastate markets, reducing any surplus in the intrastate market that would be available for emergency interstate sales at unregulated prices. Therefore, beyond the 1975-76 winter the natural gas supply outlook is likely to worsen, at least until the 1980s and perhaps indefinitely.

It is difficult to measure accurately the U.S. vulnerability to an interruption in its oil supplies from foreign sources because of numerous uncertainties, including the following: the particular policies of the various Arab countries in event of a future embargo; the effectiveness of Arab management of a future embargo and possible countermeasures taken by oil importing countries; the future availability to the U.S. of non-Arab sources of foreign oil; and actual demand for refined petroleum products at the time of interruption.

In 1975 about 35 percent of U.S. petroleum requirements were met by imports, and the level will probably reach 50 percent in the late 1970s. Currently, more than 15 percent of U.S. oil imports come from Middle East sources, and this fraction is likely to increase to 50 percent in the near future. Hence, U.S. vulnerability to an oil supply interruption is very likely to increase substantially in the late 1970s.

The deepening natural gas shortage and the growing petroleum supply vulnerability are interrelated.

As natural gas supplies dwindle some large industrial and electric utility users may switch to coal. However, in many cases oil is likely to be preferred to coal on environmental grounds. Moreover, oil is the only alternate fuel capability many industrial and commercial firms have. Because domestic petroleum production is likely to continue to decline at least throughout the remainder of the 1970s, the natural gas shortage will increase the U.S. vulnerability to an oil supply interruption.

The natural gas shortage and petroleum supply vulnerability are nationwide in scope simply because the natural gas industry is nationwide and the U.S. petroleum industry is worldwide.

A few states in the Southwest—principally Texas and Louisiana—account for the vast bulk of the natural gas and crude oil currently produced in the United States. California is also a large oil producer, though not an exporter. Alaska will become a large exporter of oil and gas to the lower 48 states beginning in the late 1970s.

While only a few states are large producers (also consumers) and exporters of natural gas and petroleum, the rest of the states are importers and consumers. In view of the different distances from production centers and availabilities of alternate fuels such as coal, hydro, and nuclear, there is substantial diversity among states and regions within the U.S. in their consumption patterns for natural gas and petroleum products. There are also large regional variations in the degree of dependence on foreign oil imports.

Viewed as a whole the natural gas and petroleum industries each include nationwide distribution systems. However, it is essential to bear in mind that, downstream from resource development and production, the natural gas and petroleum distribution systems are radically different in their technical and economic characteristics. Government administration of shortages of these two primary fuels must take the differences fully into account. In particular, it is important to recall the long history of pervasive state and federal government regulation of natural gas transmission and distribution companies as public utilities. This background is in stark contrast to the basically unregulated character of petroleum refining and marketing until the advent of price controls in the early 1970s.

The deepening natural gas shortage and the petroleum vulnerability in the U.S. during the late 1970s raise serious risks to the welfare, safety, and security of the American people.

A major task of the U.S. government will be to deal effectively with these reasonably foreseeable risks:

One risk is welcome. A recovery from the 1974–75 economic slump may cause a resumption of near historical growth rates in demand for natural gas and petroleum as the economy moves closer to its full productive capacity. Ineffective government administration of an energy shortage during an economic recovery might endanger the recovery process.

A second risk is in the lap of the gods. Demand for natural gas and petroleum varies with the seasons. A cold winter may cause a large increase in requirements for natural gas and fuel oils. The increase in oil demand during a cold winter would be compounded by the increased shortfall in natural gas. Ineffective government administration during a cold winter might endanger public health and safety, as well as the national economy.

A third risk is in the hands of the governments of the countries bordering on the Persian Gulf. Despite recent progress on the Israeli-Egyptian front, the Middle East seems likely to remain a powder keg indefinitely. The risk of an interruption of U.S. oil imports at any given time will depend on the state of the Middle East political environment at that time. The risk of damage to the U.S. in the event of an oil supply interruption will, however, increase with the size of U.S. oil imports from Arab sources. Ineffective domestic administration of the petroleum shortage that would follow a future Arab oil embargo might jeopardize U.S. capabilities to fulfill its oil-sharing commitments to other OECD countries participating in the International Energy Program, complicate U.S. diplomatic efforts aimed at achieving an early end of the embargo, and substantially increase the damage from the embargo to the U.S. economy.

A fourth risk is to American government. The consequences of a serious energy shortage would be acute and yet pervasive. A serious energy shortage will affect jobs, profits, lifestyles, and votes. Ineffective government administration might lead to serious social conflict, as well as widespread economic disruption. Increased public cynicism about government and mistrust of private industry would probably follow.

The U.S. natural gas shortage and petroleum supply vulnerability are in-

escapable and must be administered effectively, no matter what long-term national energy policies are ultimately developed and implemented.

Policies may be designed to restore and maintain a balance between U.S. energy supply and demand in the long run. Mismanagement of energy shortages would, however, make long-term national energy policies more difficult to achieve.

Most measures implemented now in order to expand domestic energy supplies will not yield substantial results until the 1980s. Similarly, many actions taken to increase the efficiency of energy-consuming buildings, machines, appliances, and processes will not realize large conservation savings for several years. Whether energy prices are decontrolled gradually or intensive regulation continues, shortages will persist in the near future. (Even abrupt and complete deregulation may not bring supply and demand into immediate balance if demand proves to be very price inelastic in the short run.)

The problem of administering an energy shortage is largely political; yet a shortage is especially difficult to deal with politically in a federal democracy during peacetime.

The problem is political because it involves government action to control and distribute energy supplies by non-price methods. Democratic institutions, with their supporting administrative mechanisms, have proven to be reasonably capable of determining who gets how much of an expanding pie. An energy shortage, however, requires the government to intervene in the market in order to determine who gets how much of a shrinking pie.

Faced with a shortage, every important group in society, whether functionally or territorially based, can be expected to react strongly in order to minimize the damage to its essential interests. In administering an energy shortage, the government must deal fairly, and appear to deal fairly, with the manifold interests competing for a shrinking supply of a vital necessity.

CONCLUSIONS

1. *Government authority over the natural gas shortage is fragmented in a way that makes effective administration impossible. The Federal Power Commission (FPC) does not have sufficient jurisdiction to cope with the problem at the federal level.*

At the federal level, governmental authority to administer the shortage is vested by the Natural Gas Act of 1938 in the FPC, which is an independent economic regulatory agency. The FPC's curtailment jurisdiction is limited mainly to the interstate transportation of natural gas via pipeline. The FPC has *no* authority: (a) to allocate among the various interstate pipelines natural gas that is produced and sold in the interstate wholesale market; (b) to allocate gas that is sold and delivered by distributors in retail markets; (c) to allocate gas that is produced and consumed in the same state. Therefore, the FPC's authority to administer the nation's natural gas shortage is narrowly focused on the interface between the interstate pipeline and the local distributor or direct sales customer.

Primary governmental power to administer the nationwide natural gas shortage is divided among the several states. State power includes authority: (a) to control natural gas production; (b) to regulate retail distribution; and (c) to determine retail prices and allocate supplies among end users. In most states, this authority is vested in the public utilities commissions or analogous state agencies. The thrust of state regulatory authority varies to reflect the fact that only a few states are large natural gas producers (and consumers) while the rest are primarily consumers.

2. *Faced with a natural gas shortage with nationwide dimensions, the FPC has developed a national curtailment policy based on end-use priorities. The Commission cannot effectively implement such a policy.*

Because it lacks authority to order interconnections between pipelines, the FPC has been forced to administer curtailments, including its end-use policy, pipeline-by-pipeline. The amount of shortage varies widely among the interstate pipelines. Consequently, use of natural gas as industrial boiler fuel continues in some states served by relatively well-supplied interstate pipelines subject to FPC jurisdiction, while at the same time suppliers for even residential and small commercial users are threatened in other states.

The FPC's curtailment proceedings are adjudicative, and its end-use policy is not binding on the parties to particular proceedings. In some cases the interstate pipelines, their local distributors, and their direct sales customers have advocated plans emphasizing different concepts, such as contract entitlements or pro rata reductions. In other cases the parties have advocated end-use priorities different from the FPC's. In any event, the FPC's end-use policy as applied in curtailment proceedings before the Commission itself has persuasive, not mandatory effect.

While the FPC is attempting to implement its end-use policy pipeline-by-pipeline, that policy is often being frustrated at the state level. The several state utility commissions have primary authority to allocate available natural gas supplies among various end uses within their respective states. The FPC's end-use priorities may determine the amount of gas imported into a state, but the state utility commission's priorities will largely decide who in fact gets how much of the imported gas. In practice, some states have cooperated with, some have modified, and some have quite ignored the FPC's curtailment policy.

3. *The FPC's administrative process may break down under the stress of a deepening natural shortage. The FPC is not equipped with procedural devices required to manage an emergency shortage effectively.*

The Natural Gas Act of 1938 not only limits the FPC's curtailment jurisdiction, but also requires the use of procedures that are not suitable for the administration of a natural gas shortage. The procedural alternatives available in the Natural Gas Act were intended for ratemaking proceedings, not curtailment. The Act requires a primarily adjudicatory type of proceeding that is inherently too slow to permit a timely and flexible response to emergency conditions.

The FPC has attempted to speed up the administrative process by permitting proposed curtailment plans to become effective almost immediately on a temporary basis. While the use of interim plans has enabled the FPC and the pipelines to have an approved curtailment plan in effect during winter peak curtailments, the temporary nature of the relief and the recurring and deepening character of the shortage mean that permanent curtailment plans may never be finally approved in many cases. Curtailment proceedings for a pipeline might, therefore, be endless.

The FPC has also attempted to make the administrative process flexible through emergency and extraordinary relief procedures. A severe shortage, however, may overload the Commission with petitions for extraordinary relief at the worst possible moment from the standpoint of crisis management. This is a critical unresolved problem of administrative procedure.

The FPC does not have the authority to require the natural gas industry and consumers to provide much of the data it needs in order to implement an end-use policy efficiently and fairly. If the FPC could obtain the data, it is doubtful that it would have adequate resources to process and use them effectively. This is another critical unresolved administrative problem.

4. *The natural gas shortage cannot be effectively administered by the several states, and, therefore, federal legislation is necessary.*

As noted above, governmental power to control the distribution of available natural gas supplies, aside from interstate transportation, is divided among the several states. Given their diverse resources and interests, there is no way for the states to distribute the burden of the natural gas shortage equitably among themselves and throughout the nation.

Federal legislation is, therefore, necessary to expand the jurisdiction of the federal government. The states have an important role to play in administering curtailment policy, but that policy should be fashioned at the federal level and be mandatory for the states to follow.

5. *The Federal Energy Administration (FEA) possesses adequate statutory authority to deal with potential petroleum shortages.*

Petroleum allocation authority was vested in the FEA under the Emergency Petroleum Allocation Act of 1973 (EPAA). That Act has been substantially strengthened and extended by the Energy Policy and Conservation Act of 1975, which also provides for the gradual decontrol of domestic oil prices over a 40-month period.

The FEA's jurisdiction covers the entire distribution system for petroleum products throughout the nation, preempting state authority (except as delegated by the FEA under the state set-aside program). The FEA is empowered to control the distribution of petroleum products throughout the system after crude oil production through retail sales for final consumption.

Conclusions 6 through 8 are based upon our analysis of the FEA's petroleum allocation experience under the EPAA prior to enactment of the Energy Policy Act.

6. *The most important policy decisions involved in administration of petroleum shortages were explicitly, though generally, mandated in the EPAA itself: minimum interference with existing supplier-purchaser relationships; protection of small independent oil companies; and dollar-for-dollar passthrough of cost increases.*

These policy decisions had been made within the Executive Branch on a contingency basis while the Administration continued generally to oppose mandatory allocations. The Congress more or less agreed with these policies and embodied them in the EPAA.

In general, the EPAA sanctioned what the Executive Branch was predisposed to do. The explicitness of the legislation provided several anchors that helped to stabilize the development of a massive regulatory program in a very short time under tense conditions (the 1973-74 Arab oil embargo).

7. *Given the exigencies of the embargo in early 1974, the FEA had little room for choice in the procedures it used to implement a petroleum allocation program. These procedures were summary for the most part.*

The FEA proceeded largely through informal rulemaking. Much of the allocation program became effective immediately upon publication with no notice or period for public comment. Formal rulemaking accompanied by public hearings would have been impossible to complete in time, and, if attempted, the results might have contributed more heat than light to many of the intricate allocation problems involved.

The FEA also created adjustment, exception, and exemption procedures that were highly informal, given the adjudicatory nature of the decisions being made. Such procedures may be justified in an actual supply emergency, but should not be continued in use after the emergency has ended.

The FEA began the petroleum allocation program armed with extensive investigatory and data-gathering authority under the Federal Energy Administration Act. However, within the agency, there were few persons who were knowledgeable about the inner workings of the petroleum industry. As a result of implementing the allocation program, there is now a cadre of knowledgeable persons in the FEA and an enormous amount of data has been gathered, though much of it remains to be digested.

8. *In hindsight, the FEA's administration of the petroleum shortage resulting in 1974 from the Arab oil embargo may be judged to have worked reasonably well, given the short term nature of the emergency. Nevertheless, some were unfairly or unnecessarily harmed or inconvenienced, while others were unduly advantaged.*

The 1974 Arab oil embargo illustrates the serious risks involved in, and the difficulty of administering, an energy shortage. The embargo was imposed at a time when U.S. imports from the Arab countries were lower than at present. It was only half-heartedly enforced by some of the Arab governments. Moreover, the embargo was lifted just as it was becoming fully effective.

In order to administer the resulting shortage, sweeping governmental powers were exercised with little concern for the procedural rights of private persons. The damage the embargo caused to the U.S. economy reached tens of billions of dollars.

Once the embargo was lifted, the FEA's administration of the shortage of price-controlled domestic crude oil became necessary. The extension of the FEA's allocation program into a period when there was a surplus of most petroleum products is evidence of the difficulty of dismantling a regulatory program even after it has outlived at least one of its major original purposes.

9. *Federal legislation, necessary to give the FEA comprehensive authority to administer petroleum shortages, has been enacted in the Energy Policy and Conservation Act.*

Government allocation of price-controlled products will be necessary as long as price controls exist. Moreover, standby authority to administer possible sudden and severe petroleum shortages will be necessary as long as the U.S. remains vulnerable to large interruptions in its foreign supplies.

The Energy Policy Act has amended the EPAA in several important respects regarding the FEA's petroleum allocation authority. Under the EPAA, as amended, the FEA has specific discretionary authority to control refinery operations and to control inventories throughout the distribution system. The President has discretionary authority to constitute the government as exclusive purchaser of crude oil and petroleum products from foreign sources for import into the United States. Moreover, legal doubts concerning the FEA's authority to allocate propane and other liquids derived from natural gas have been removed. Finally, the EPAA, as amended, provides a detailed oil pricing policy based on a composite ceiling price for the first sale of domestically produced crude oil, and the Act now requires the continuation and gradual phasing-out of price controls through mid-1979.

In addition to strengthening and extending the EPAA, the Energy Policy Act also contains major new duties and authorities relevant to the administration of potential petroleum shortages. These include a requirement to develop standby contingency plans for energy conservation and motor fuel rationing, and requirements to develop an early storage petroleum reserve of 150,000,000 barrels within three years and to plan for a larger strategic reserve to be implemented subsequently. However, the strategic reserve is likely to be inadequate unless it is substantially enlarged because the required amount of the reserve is determined by reference to an historical base period which does not take account of probable future increases in oil import levels.

Furthermore, authority is provided for the U.S., and U.S. based multinational oil companies, to participate fully in international emergency oil sharing arrangements under the Agreement on an International Energy Program concluded within the OECD framework for industrial country cooperation. Finally, the Energy Policy Act contains far-reaching authority for the government to obtain and verify energy information as necessary for policy making and administration.

10. *The administrative and congressional review procedures mandated in the Energy Policy Act provide interested persons with ample opportunities to participate in the administrative policy-making process for petroleum allocation.*

The Energy Policy Act requires a comprehensive reevaluation of the basic petroleum allocation and pricing regulation under the EPAA. In addition to the general notice and comment requirements for informal rulemaking, the procedural requirements prescribed by statute for this reevaluation specifically include an opportunity for interested persons to make written and oral presentations, and a transcript of oral presentations. Similar procedural requirements must be followed in developing contingency plans for energy conservation and rationing which could directly affect the entire population if they were put into effect. These hybrid procedures, which are short of formal administrative rulemaking, should nevertheless provide adequate opportunities for industry and citizen inputs into the future development of petroleum allocation regulation.

The Energy Policy Act also requires prior congressional review of proposed modifications in the petroleum allocation and pricing regulation, and proposed conservation and rationing contingency plans. The revised allocation and pricing regulation, and subsequent significant amendments, are subject to congressional review and disapproval by a majority vote of either House. Proposals to lift by regulation certain statutory limitations and proposals for exemption from regulation of classes of persons or transactions are subject to the same review. Contingency plans for energy conservation and rationing require affirmative approval of both Houses. These review procedures provide the Congress with a substantial measure of continuing control over executive action related to petroleum allocation.

As of this writing (December 1975), the extent and effectiveness of industry and citizen participation in the administrative process and of congressional review regarding petroleum allocation regulation remain to be seen.

RECOMMENDATIONS

The following recommendations are focused on the future administration of the nation's natural gas shortage, since we have concluded that existing legal authority and administrative capacity are deficient in this respect.

The Congress should enact legislation for the specific purpose of administer-

ing the natural gas shortage on nationwide basis. The legislation, which should be considered in addition to or as part of legislation on natural gas prices at the wellhead, might contain the following elements:

—The purpose would be to achieve an equitable distribution of the costs and burdens of the natural gas shortage throughout the country, taking into account: the price and availability of alternate fuels; the cost of switching to alternate fuels; the impact of curtailment on employment and the local economy; and the impact of curtailment on the public health and safety.

—The FPC would be granted primary authority to administer the natural gas shortage nationwide. This authority would be exercised in close coordination with the FEA and in consultation with state public utilities commissions.

—The FPC would have comprehensive emergency authority to allocate natural gas supplies at all levels in the distribution system after production through retail distribution, in both interstate and intrastate markets. The extent of the FPC's jurisdiction to administer natural gas shortages would thus be roughly comparable to the FEA's authority to administer petroleum shortages.

—The FPC would have authority to order physical interconnections among pipelines and, in case of supply emergencies, to order transfers of gas between pipelines, including transfers from intrastate to interstate pipelines in certain circumstances (outlined below).

—The FPC, in coordination with the FEA, would be directed to develop federal guidelines for administration of the national natural gas shortage. In connection with developing such guidelines, the FPC and the FEA would review and, as appropriate, modify existing FPC curtailment policy. Factors to be considered in developing priorities would include economic and technical efficiency, the diverse roles of natural gas in the economies of various regions, environmental impacts, and an equitable geographical distribution of the shortage.

—In developing proposed guidelines, the FPC would be authorized to proceed by administrative rulemaking. Rulemaking procedures for this purpose would provide notice and opportunity for interested persons to make written and oral presentations, and, to the extent practicable, an opportunity for rebuttal. A transcript of oral presentations would be required.

—The FPC would be specially directed to consult with the governors and state utility commissions of the several states. Proposed guidelines would be presented to Congress and become effective as regulations unless disapproved by a majority vote of either House.

—The FPC would be empowered to delegate authority to the several states to administer natural gas shortages at the retail sales level. State administration would be pursuant to plans developed by the state concerned in accordance with the federal guidelines and approved by the FPC. Federal guidelines for the retail level would be sufficiently flexible to permit the states to take appropriate account of local circumstances in determining final allocations to end users. The FPC would continue to administer the shortage at the interstate pipeline level.

—Distressed interstate pipelines, unable to meet predicted requirements of their customers for essential uses, would be authorized to purchase new natural gas, not previously dedicated or prospectively available to the interstate market, at prices comparable to prevailing prices in the relevant intrastate markets. Existing FPC orders authorizing emergency direct purchases of gas from intrastate markets by certain interstate pipeline customers would be given express statutory sanction.

—Transferors under an FPC emergency transfer order would receive the same price for transferred gas as they were entitled to receive from their contract purchasers. If the transfer price were less than the prevailing price for natural gas in the relevant intrastate market, the recipient distressed interstate pipeline would be required to reimburse customers of the transferor for increased fuel costs incurred as a result of being deprived of natural gas. A transfer order could not be issued unless the FPC found that a supply emergency existed for the distressed interstate pipeline, and that the pipeline had attempted unsuccessfully to purchase new natural gas.

The preceding legislative recommendations are largely a blend of certain ideas drawn from the Energy Policy Act and various proposals for natural gas emergency legislation, especially the proposed Natural Gas Emergency Act of 1975 (H.R. 9464 as originally reported by the Committee on Interstate and Foreign Commerce to the House of Representatives on December 15, 1975). However, our suggestions go considerably beyond the proposed Emergency Act in an attempt to develop a governmental capacity adequate to administer natural gas shortages for the duration.

In developing the preceding recommendations, we have found one organizational issue to be especially troublesome: whether the FPC or the FEA should be the lead agency in coping with the natural gas shortage. This issue is perhaps more theoretical than practical, but it merits exposure and brief discussion.

As a matter of principle, the administration of a serious or prolonged energy shortage, or shortage of any other essential commodity, seems to be more properly a function of the Executive Branch of government than of an independent economic regulatory agency. In order to be fair, the administrative process must be politically responsive. In order to be effective, it must be swift and flexible. An appropriate executive agency, such as the FEA, would come closer than the FPC to these attributes.

Furthermore, the natural gas shortage will impact increasingly on alternate fuel supplies. It seems preferable for one agency to have responsibility for administration of all energy shortages at the federal level. Specifically, whatever agency administers the natural gas shortage should also be responsible for administering a potential petroleum shortage. Of all the agencies within the federal energy bureaucracy, the FEA should have the most comprehensive overview of the energy situation, and it is armed with broad investigatory and data gathering authority regarding the energy industry as a whole.

Finally, the administration of a natural gas shortage should be as consistent as possible with other national energy, economic and environmental policies. Specifically, gas curtailment priorities should be developed with the full range of these other policies in mind. The necessary policy perspective may not be achieved by the FPC, whose primary responsibility is to regulate wholesale prices of natural gas and electricity.

Yet there are weighty arguments in favor of preserving the present government organization. These are primary grounded in considerations of practicality and expediency.

One argument is that the FPC's valuable experience and bureaucratic momentum in administering natural gas curtailments would be lost if primary policy responsibility were transferred to the FEA. However, the FPC's actual experience has been jurisdictionally and procedurally confined. The Commission's expertise could be utilized in a continuing administrative role with respect to interstate pipeline curtailments, even if the FEA were given the lead in policy making.

In addition, natural gas curtailment and pricing policies interact deeply and subtly. Keeping these two interwoven strands of natural gas policy administratively together seems more important than dealing with petroleum and natural gas shortages within one executive agency. This argument in favor of maintaining the existing organizational framework seems to us most persuasive.

Finally, it may be politically expedient for both the Executive Branch and the Congress to keep the natural gas curtailment problem within the FPC. Because of the FPC's status as an independent agency, the President and his policy makers and the members of Congress might thereby minimize the direct impact of a no-win problem on their respective political fortunes.

It is understandable that politicians would seek to avoid direct responsibility for a clearly unpopular government administrative program. Yet effective and fair administration of an energy shortage will be necessarily grounded on political considerations. Both political branches of government should therefore share direct responsibility for making basic policy in this area.

On balance, we have opted for organizational stability, recommending a continuation and substantial expansion of the FPC's leading role in coping with the nation's natural gas shortage. However, under our recommendations that role would be played in much closer cooperation with the FEA and with more detailed scrutiny by the Congress than in the past. Coordination between the FPC and FEA in developing basic administrative policy would, in our view, entail a good deal of FEA initiative and perhaps even explicit concurrence in the outcome. It should be recognized, however, that the close coordination necessary for effective administration may erode the FPC's independence from the Executive Branch.

* * *

In an industrial democracy such as the United States, an energy shortage constitutes a serious threat of economic disruption and social disorder. Hence, an energy shortage poses a grave challenge to government.

Even now after the shocking energy price increases of the early 1970s, most Americans continue to expect an abundance of energy in the future. Yet in the later 1970s, U.S. vulnerability to an oil supply interruption will grow to ominous dimensions, and the American people will have to endure the hardship of increasing natural gas shortages.

In view of these dangerous prospects, there is a clear and urgent need for government to strengthen its capacity to administer energy shortages fairly and effectively. This task must be an integral part of any national energy policy for America.

Index

Abzug, B., 141
adjudication, 100, 182; defined, 262; and OEA, 197; and petroleum allocation, 187; provisions, 184
Administration Procedure Act, 84, 85; provisions, 183
Air Transport Association v. FEO, 158
Alaska, 13
Algeria: LNG, 14
Algonquin Gas Transmission Co., 18
allocation: adjustment, 189; authority, 213; aviation fuel and embargo, 126; end-use, 84; enforcement, 195; EPAA, 146; formulas, 165; legal decisions, 252; and Natural Gas Co., 51; petroleum, 139; pipeline, 48; refined product, 148
American Public Gas Association v. FPC, 63
American Smelting and Refining Co. v. FPC, 48
Arkansas, 28; *–Louisiana Gas Co.*, 85
Ash, Roy, 181
Atlantic Refining Co. v. Public Service Commission, 49
Atlantic Seaboard Corporation, 22

Belmar, Warren, 209
Bibb v. Navajo Freight Lines, 252
Bi-Metalic Investment Co. v. State Board, 260
Block v. Hirsh, 258
Board of Regents v. Roth, 259
Bowles v. Willingham, 248, 260
Brennan, Justice, 45

California, 28; *–and Louisiana v. Simon*, 186; *–Teachers Association v. Newport Mesa Unified School District*, 261
Canada: natural gas, 14; oil imports, 110
Chernock v. Gardner, 262
Cities Service Gas Co. v. Peerless Oil and Gas Co., 251
Congress: and discretionary overrides, 237; enforcement and Energy Policy Act, 196; EPAA, 142; judicial review of FEA, 199; needed legislation, 280; program implementation, 214; role in Energy Policy Act, 201
consumers: differentiated interests, 230; groups on regulation, 180; and Notice of Probable Violation, 194; and overpricing, 207; range of and end-use plan, 227; stake, 240–243; *–Union v. Sawhill*, 186
consumption: and curtailment, 32; and partial curtailment, 32
Columbia Gas Transmission Corp., 13
Condor Operating Co. v. Sawhill, 256
conservation: voluntary, 214
Consolidated Edison of New York v. FPC, 92
Cost of Living Council, 180
crisis: confidence and authority, 213; FEA and due process, 261; limits on government behavior, 255–260; pro rata approach, 220–224; regulation structure, 233; shortages and policy, 6; and state authority, 250
curtailment: and adjudication strategy, 89;

administrative efforts, 77; and American Smelting, 50; commercial users, 26; guidelines, 82; hearings, 101; mechanics, 31; *Michigan Power*, 55; and Monsanto, 57; natural gas, 219; Order 467-C, 93; Pacific Gas and Electric, 66; *Panhandle*, 45; policy development, 80; and rate-setting, 49; state authority, 254; and *State of Louisiana*, 53; tariff schedule, 52

decisionmaking: embargo and options, 181; and OEA, 190; Office of General Counsel, 182; strategy, 212
Defense Production Act, 140, 161
demand: natural gas, 24; and refined products, 119
deregulation: FEA, 237; and price, 67
distribution: administrative options for energy shortage, 215; allocation, 34; and direct sales, 26; emergency sales, 78; natural gas, 15; negotiated settlement, 228; oil, 111, 115; and Order 467, 91; and partial curtailment, 32, 33; and pro rata plan, 220, 221; regional discrimination, 28; storage, 19; technology, 23

Economic Stabilization Act of 1970, 139, 180, 201; discretionary trigger, 236
Eisenhower, D.D.: on natural gas deregulation, 3
electricity: generation, 27
El Paso Natural Gas Co., 50
embargo: background, 4; and cargo market, 116; contingency plans, 164; defense strategy, 180; and FEA actions, 278; as impulse behind allocation, 203; motor gasoline, 120; refining, 113; risks and contingencies, 211
Emergency Petroleum Allocation Act, 111, 140–143; adjustments, 189; authority and regulation, 145; constitutional basis, 247; crude oil price controls, 151; exemptions, 191; price computation, 154; and rule-making approach, 182; on violations, 194
energy: agency crisis administration, 282; 283; allocation, 96; allocation regulation, 147; boiler fuel, 30; consumer/supply information, 193; contract rights, 217; curtailment, 12; distribution, 8; group interests, 229; industry and information, 196; Order 493-A, 98; ownership pattern, 23; policy and conservation act, 163; policy options, 211; retail oil market, 16, 117

Energy Policy and Conservation Act, 140, 179, 271; contingency plan, 213; and FEA authority, 279
Energy Policy Act: role for Congress, 202
Energy Supply and Environmental Coordination Act (ESECA), 140, 158; authorization, 247; guidelines, 225
entitlement: concept of, 147; and reduction strategy, 223; and TECA, 257
entry: energy production, 16
environment: impact statement, rulemaking and EPAA, 184; pollution control, 85; pollution and land use, 7; residential fuel oil, 123; restrictions and natural gas use, 4
Exxon Corporation v. FEA, 199; *−v. FEO*, 156

Federal Energy Act (FEA) 116; adjudication procedures, 187, 235; and administrative rulemaking, 232; and APA relationship, 184; authority, 227; comments, 186; constituency, 216; curtailment, 12; decisionmaking, 182; and end-use priorities, 224; energy administration, 139; enforcement effort, 195; interpretation and rulings, 192; judicial review, 197, 262; judicial review procedures, 199; mixed policy for petroleum allocations, 219; on pricing violations, 207; recommendations, 281; statutory authority, 277
Federal Energy Administration Act (FEAA) 141, 184; judicial review, 200
Federal Energy Office (FEO), 140
Federal Power Commission (FPC); adjudication strategy, 89; Atlantic Refining Co., 50; authority, 227; constituency, 216; contract approach, 218; court decisions, 50–55; curtailment authority, 232; curtailment and compensation, 242; curtailment procedures, 77; *−v. East Ohio Gas Co.*, 45; emergency relief, 93; *−v. Hope Natural Gas*, 41, 255; jurisdiction, 44; jurisdiction, lack of, 59, 275; jurisdiction and natural gas, 234; liability, 58; *−v. Louisiana Power and Light Co.*, 45, 81; natural gas curtailment policy, 219; *−Power Commission v. Natural Gas Pipeline Co.*, 246; natural gas shortage, 12; Order 431, 80; Order 467, 83; Order 493-A, 97; Permian Basin, 61; rate-setting, 64; recommendations, 281; rulemaking, 99; structural limitations, 276; *−v. Transcontinental Gas Pipe Line Co.*, 47, 54
fertilizer, 31
Florida, 28

Freedom of Information Act, 188
Federal Trade Commission (FTC): and
  price-setting, 42

Gajewski v. United States, 258
General Accounting Office: jurisdiction,
  196
government: adjudication and FEA, 188;
  administrative organization, 231; agency
  control, 179; APA and FEA, 183; authority and natural gas, 233; controls
  and deactivation, 214; energy redistribution, 8; enforcement staff, 195; and
  FEAA and administration, 185; negotiated shortage settlements, 228; redistribution of risks/benefits, 8; role in
  allocation, 203; and role in shortages,
  217; shortage administration, 274; shortage experience, 211; source of authority,
  245
Granite City Steel Co. v. FPC., 48
Gulf Oil Corp. v. Hickel, 256; *–Oil Corp.
  v. Simon*, 156, 184

Hannah v. Larche, 260
Hinshaw Amendment, 24, 58
*Home Building and Loan Association v.
  Blaisdell*, 250, 255
House Commerce Committee Subcommit-
  tee on Energy, 79
Huber, J.M. Corp. v. FPC., 256

Illinois, 24; *–Natural Gas Co. v. Central
  Illinois Public Service Co.*, 246
imports: risk, 274; and Oil Import Appeals
  Board, 198
Indiana, 24
Indonesia, 110
Internal Revenue Service: and FEA en-
  forcement, 192
International Energy Agreement, 163, 213
International Paper Co. v. FPC, 57
Interstate Power Co. v. FPC, 262
intervention: and contract renegotiation,
  218; FEA, 182; initiation and termina-
  tion, 212; and Notice of Probable Viola-
  tion, 194, "reg writers," 180
Iowa, 24
Iran, 110

jurisdiction: and contract rights, 218, 219;
  and FEAA audits, 193; federal controls
  and natural gas, 234; and FPC, 58, 59;
  Natural Gas Act, 43

Kansas, 24, 28

Knox v. Lee, 255

legislation, 67; and FEAA, 184; and imple-
  mentation, 181; need for, 277
LNG (liquified natural gas), 14
load balancing, 19
Lone Star Gas Co., 18
Louisiana, 28; *–v. FPC*, 58
LPG (liquified petroleum gases), 15, 123;
  products, 117
Lynch v. United States, 257

Mandel v. Simon, 157, 249
Marathon Oil Co. v. FEA, 157, 199
market economy: allocation, 30; and price
  regulation, 154; and refined products,
  127; retail marketing, 16, 116; wholesale
  oil, 114; and wholesale purchaser con-
  sumers, 146
Michigan, 24; *–Consolidated Gas Co. v.
  Panhandle Eastern Pipe Line Co.*, 58;
  –Power Co. v. FPC., 55
Minnesota, 24
Mississippi, 28; *–River Fuel Corp. v. FPC*,
  258
Missouri, 24
Mobil Oil v. FPC., 62
Mohawk Petroleum Corp. v. FEA, 157
Monsanto Co. v. FPC., 57
Moss, Rep., 141

Nader v. Sawhill, 186
Nassikas, John N., 47
National Environmental Policy Act, 60
*National Labor Relations Board v. Jones
  and Laughlin Steel Corp.*, 246
national security: Defense Production Act,
  162; and government authority, 248;
  and public interest, 184; risks of shortage,
  7; shortages and embargos, 5; shortage
  vulnerability, 274
Natural Gas Act, 17, 232; analysis, 61; and
  FPC, 46, 47; history of, 42
Natural Gas Emergency Act, 67
natural gas: administrative options, 215;
  consumption, 3, 27; and crisis distribution, 230; imports, 14; need for legislation, 281; Order 493-A, 98; ownership
  pattern, 23; residential use, 29; shortage,
  5, 11
Nebraska, 24
National Environmental Protection Agency
  (NEPA): and curtailment plans, and rulemaking, 184
New York: state authority, 249
Nigeria, 110

Nixon, R.M., 139
North Carolina, 13
North Dakota, 24
Northern Natural Gas Co. v. State Corp. Commission of Kansas, 253

Omnia Commercial Co. v. United States, 257
OPEC: role in embargo, 4
Office of Exceptions and Appeals (OEA), 190, 197
Office of Private Grievance and Redress, 197, 198
Ohio, 24
oil: crude allocation, 147; exploration, 111; middle distillates, 122; residential fuels, 118; retail markets, 116, 117; transportation, 112. See petroleum.
OKC Corp. v. Oskey Gasoline and Oil Co., 156
Oklahoma, 28, 251

Pacific Coast Meat Cutters Association Inc. v. Cost of Living Council, 261
Pacific Gas and Electric Co. v. FPC., 60, 66, 91
Panhandle Eastern Pipe Line Co. v. Michigan Public Service Commission, 251; *–v. Public Service Commission*, 45
Parker v. Brown, 252
Pennsylvania Gas Co. v. Public Service Commission of New York, 250
Permian Basin Area Rate Cases, 61
petrochemicals, 126
petroleum: FEAA and rulemaking, 185; and FEO strategy, 182; industry integration, 216; industry structure and allocation, 203; industry structure, 167; inventory, 236; negotiated settlement, 228; overview, 109; refined product price controls, 153; shortages, 5
Pennsylvania v. West Virginia, 251
Phillips Petroleum Co. v. FPC, 3, 17, 62; *–v. Wisconsin*, 44
pipeline, 18; load factor, 24; Natural Gas Emergency Act, 69; oil, 112; Order 431, 80; Order 467, 87; Order 467-C, 93, 94; pro rata plan, 221; tariff schedule, 52
policy: embargo and gas, 120; and Energy Policy Act provisions, 280; energy redistribution, 8; EPAA mandate, 278; FPC, 60, 65; FPC and Order 467, 85; and hearing availability, 188; interpretation and rulings, 192; legal decisions, 250–252; nature of, 60; oil imports, 110; options, 211; Order 431, 80; Order 467, 86; Presidential authority, 153; and pro

rata strategy, 224; "reg writers," 181; shortage administration, 9; strategy for energy shortage, 215; TECA and judicial review, 201
politics: FEA and Office of General Counsel, 182; and natural gas pricing, 271; and priorities scheme, 228
pollution: air quality standards, 13
price mechanisms: *Consumers Union v. Sawhill*, 201; controls, 6; deregulation, 67; exceptions and exemptions. 191; FEA review, 187; regulation, 151, 179
priorities: criteria, 8; curtailment, 83; emergency sales, 78; end-use, 34, 219; end-use defined, 224, 225; end-use and limitations, 276; establishing of, 8; and Presidential authority, 165
process gas, 30
production: aviation fuel, 125; incentive and price system, 152; natural gas, 11–14; Natural Gas Emergency Act, 68; petroleum, 110; refined products, 131; refinery, 112; vertical integration, 17
public interest: contract stability, 215
Public Utilities Commission v. Landon, 250; *–of Ohio v. United Fuel Gas Co.*, 253

rate-setting: authority, 52; design, 22; and Phillipps Petroleum, 62; and rulemaking, 66; and Supreme Court, 44; contingency plans, 202
Reeves v. Simon, 157
regulation: constitutional authority, 245; and consumer groups, 180; Cost of Living Council, 186; and diversity, 100; and end-use priorities, 225; enforcement, 195; and EPAA, 143, 144, 179; interstate pipelines, 3; judicial review procedures of FEA, 199; Natural Gas Act, 17; ownership pattern, 23; petroleum allocation, 139; and price mechanism, 2; pro rata reduction, 220
rollbacks, 207
rulemaking: administrative organization, 232; guidelines, 192; judicial review, 200; legal precedants, 260; procedure, 184

Sawhill, John, 180
Schilling v. Rogers, 262
Secretary of Agriculture v. Central Roig Refining Co., 258
Shell Oil Co. v. FPC, 65
shortage: administration criteria, 9; administrative options, 215; embargo, 4; energy defined, 2; and FPC, 47, 55; natural gas, 12; government strategy, 211; Natural

Gas Act, 43; and OEA, 190; and pro rata reductions, 220; and public policy, 9; rationing, 222; vulnerability, 272
shrinkage: defined, 15
Simon, William, 180
South Carolina, 13; *—State Highway Dept. v. Barnwell Bros. Inc.,* 252
South Dakota, 24
Southern Pacific Co. v. Arizona, 252
state: authority, 249; and impairment of contracts, 254; role of in natural gas shortage, 231
State of Louisiana v. FPC, 53
State of Missouri v. Kansas Natural Gas Co., 42
storage: oil, 115; Order, 467, 88
Sun Oil Co. v. FPC, 262
Superior Oil Co. v. FPC., 259, 261
supply: adjustment to base period volumes, 189; allocation and interruption, 163; concentration, 273; curtailment, 12; end-use priorities and fairness, 226
Supreme Court: FPC authority in Permian Basin, 61; *FPC v. Hope Natural Gas,* 41; Louisiana Power and Light, 45; Phillips, 17, 44; *State of Missouri v. Kansas Natural Gas,* 42; state police power, 250

Temporary Emergency Court of Appeals (TECA), 199; composition, 208; expertise, 201
Texas, 28; *—American Asphalt Corp. v.*

Walker, 256; —Eastern Transmission Corp., 89; state authority, 249
Transcontinental Gas Pipeline Corp., 13
transmission: natural gas, 17
transportation: and distribution, 215
Trans World Airlines v. FEO, 157

Union Dry Goods v. Georgia Public Service Corp., 254
Union Oil Co. v. FEA, 156, 257
United Gas Pipe Line Co., 22, 56, 86
United States v. Central Eureka Mining Co., 255, 257
United States v. Darby, 246
United States v. Excel Packing Co., 248
United States v. Lieb, 261

Veix v. Sixth Ward Building and Loan Association, 255
Venezuela, 110
Virginia, 13

Western State Meat Packers Association v. Dunlop, 261
Wickard v. Filburn, 246
Wisconsin, 24
Woods v. Miller Co., 248

Yakus v. United States, 248

Zarb, Frank G., 204

Biographical Notes

THE AUTHOR

Mason Willrich is a professor of law at the University of Virginia. He was Assistant General Counsel of the U.S. Arms Control Agency from 1962 to 1965. Prior to 1962 he was in private law practice in San Francisco. Mr. Willrich has served as consultant to the Ford Foundation, the RAND Corporation, the U.S. Arms Control and Disarmament Agency, the Administrative Conference of the United States and various private companies.

Mr. Willrich's previous books include *Energy and World Politics; Nuclear Theft: Risks and Safeguards* (co-authored with Theodore B. Taylor); *SALT: The Moscow Agreements and Beyond;* and *Global Politics of Nuclear Energy.* He is also the author of numerous articles concerning energy matters and national security issues. Mr. Willrich was awarded a Guggenheim Memorial Fellowship in 1973. He graduated from Yale University in 1954 and received his law degree from the University of California, Berkeley, in 1960.

THE CONTRIBUTORS

Philip M. Marston is a third-year law student at the University of Virginia. Following graduation in June 1976, he will enter private practice in Washington, D.C. He graduated from Dickinson College in 1971.
David G. Norrell is a second-year law student at the University of Virginia and a member of the *Virginia Law Review.* He graduated from Florida State University in 1974.
Jane K. Wilcox is a second-year law student at the University of Virginia and a member of the *Virginia Law Review.* She graduated from Vanderbilt University in 1974.